HISTORY
OF
TRAVANCORE

HISTORY
OF
TRAVANCORE

FROM THE EARLIEST TIMES

P. SHUNGOONNY MENON

With Many Illustrations

Full many a gem of purest ray serene,
The dark unfathomed caves of ocean bear;
Full many a flower is born to blush unseen,
And waste its sweetness on the desert air
Gray

GYAN

Published by

Gyan Publishing House
5, Ansari Road
Daryaganj, New Delhi-110002
Phone: 011-47034999, 9811692060
E-mail: books@gyanbooks.com

Distribution Network
gyanbooks.com
India, USA, Canada, UK, Australia, France

ISBN : 978-81-212-4525-8 (HB)
First Published, 1878

2nd Impression 2020

Printed at: Gyan Press, Delhi.

History of Travancore
Author: P. Shungoonny Menon

DEDICATED

BY PERMISSION

TO

His Most Gracious Highness

SREE PADMANABHA DASA VANJI PALA RAMA VURMAH

KULASEKHARA KIREETAPATHI MUNNAY SULTAN

MAHARAJ RAJAH RAMARAJAH BAHADUR SHAMSHEERJUNG

MAHARAJAH OF TRAVANCORE,

KNIGHT GRAND COMMANDER OF THE MOST EXALTED

ORDER OF THE STAR OF INDIA,

BY

HIS VERY HUMBLE, LOYAL AND GRATEFUL SERVANT,

THE AUTHOR.

PUBLISHED BY MESSRS HIGGINBOTHAM & CO. — LITH. MADRAS.

PADMANABHA PURAM PALACE.

PREFACE.

TRAVANCORE, the southernmost State in India, was well known in early times. Nevertheless, its early history, extent of its territory, and other particulars are mostly buried in obscurity, owing to the non-existence of a correct and detailed history of the kingdom. The existence of the king dom going back to pre-historic times, no historical facts are found recorded illustrating its antiquity.

There is scarcely a kingdom on the face of the earth, whose dynasty continued to exist in an unbroken line of succession, from the time of its foundation to the present day.

The mother-country of Travancore was the Mandala kingdom Chera, which once covered the best portion of Southern India, and which underwent various changes during the four Yugas according to the Puranic accounts. In the present age, Kali Yuga, it was gradually reduced to the present Travancore with its area of 6653¼ square miles, situated between the 8th and 10th degree of north latitude. In this reduced state, Travancore became more strongly protected by natural boundaries, the south and the west being bounded by the Indian Ocean, the east, by the range of the high ghauts, and the northern parts being mostly covered with back-waters, rivers, lakes, &c. Thus the situation of Travancore being unfavourable for the march of horses and elephants that formed the best portion of an army in those days, saved it from the incursions of foreign invaders.

When maritime powers began to rise, Travancore finding itself too weak to resist them, made alliance with them and pursued its original policy of commerce, thus avoiding quarrels.

Travancore is perhaps the only kingdom in India which preserves its original caste, religion, customs, manners, institutions, &c., &c., and the compiler of the Travancore records is perfectly right in saying that "Travancore is one of the "very few remaining specimens of a pure Hindu Government, "the institutions of which have never been affected by the "Mahomedan conquest."

The peculiar class of Numboory Brahmans whom Parasu Rama newly organized, retain without any change whatever, all their Brahmanical observances even to the present day. The four castes introduced by Parasu Rama, and subsequently multiplied to seventy-two by Sankara Acharyar, as shown in the Kerala Ulppathy, are still flourishing in Travancore, as will be seen from the Travancore Census Report, recently published.

The Chera characters, the Tamil and Grandha, are the national letters in Travancore, and the former is still the character in which the Government records are written. From its original state, as Chera Mandalam, the largest of the three Mandala kingdoms, covering the best portion of Southern India, it was reduced to a small province, bounded by Canara, Coimbatore, Tinnevelly and the Indian Ocean. Subsequently we find that it flourished under its present name Travancore, and continued tributary to the Rayers of Vijayanaggur, when Viswanatha Naicker assumed the Government of Madura. Under the Rayer dynasty, Travancore was still reduced and humiliated by being degraded to the low position of a feudatory chief. The Rev. W. Taylor, in his translation of Historical manuscripts, page 161, observes that during the sway of Thirumali Naicker of Madura, the Malayalam, Nanjenaud Rajah (King of Travancore) was included among "the seventy-two Palliyams (feudal chiefs) appointed to guard the bastions of the Pandian capital."

From the position of a feudatory State, Travancore rose again, slowly but surely, and recovered many of its lost possessions, both in the east and in the north.

An important feature in the history of Travancore, is, that even after being reduced to a feudatory State, its sovereigns were able to extend their dominions to its present extent, solely at the point of the sword, through the bravery of Travancore's sons alone, unaided by any external agencies, till the beginning of the present century, thus showing that the natives of Travancore are quite competent for the administration of the country, in its Revenue, Civil, and Military branches. This history will shew how the sovereigns and the Statesmen of Travancore distinguished themselves in the government of the kingdom, when western enlightenment and civilization were unknown in India.

This remarkable native State, being situated at the southernmost extremity of the Indian empire, had not been brought forward prominently before the public in early times, nay, not till the assumption of the Government of India by the British Crown; and consequently, it is not surprising that its original history remained in obscurity. In the absence of a correct and detailed history of the country in print, it is impossible for the public to possess any real and true knowledge of the past and present political affairs connected with this kingdom. Hence, we find, the character of the former administration of the country and of its sovereigns spoken of from erroneous data, and writers indulging themselves in advancing comparatively false views of persons and things.

There are some short accounts of Military operations and other political events concerning this country, embodied in modern works published at various times, but nothing in the form of a full and true history has hitherto appeared in the English language.

In the Malabar year 1043, a small work in the shape of a Malayalam pamphlet compiled by one Pachu Moothathu of Vycome, a Sanscrit scholar and a Native Practitioner, attached to the palace of His Highness the Maha Rajah of Travancore, appeared at Trevandrum. This work, however, short and abridged and based upon erroneous data on certain important points, contains many trustworthy and real accounts connected with the progress of the kingdom, under the present dynasty and the good and memorable administration of the sovereigns as well as the meritorious labours of many of the able Ministers of the State. Great credit is due to the author of that pamphlet, as he was the first person who made such a praiseworthy attempt. I have been in a measure benefited by reference to this work, in writing this, in which my spare time has been spent for many years.

I would have, long ago, brought this work before the public; but when I had finished the first five chapters in 1870, I learnt that the then Dewan of Travancore, Sir T. Madava Row, K.C.S.I., had commenced writing a History of Travancore, and, therefore, I naturally dropped my pen, as my work, if completed, would not compete with that of this eminent Statesman.

In the year 1873, a Malayalam translation of Sir Madava Row's History of Travancore appeared in print, but it consisted only an account of the history of two reigns. As a complete history of the country from his able pen cannot be expected at present, I resumed my work. For want of sufficient and trustworthy materials, the progress was very slow for some time, but His Most Gracious Highness the present Maha Rajah, very kindly gave directions to the Palace Officials, to furnish me with all necessary information from the palace archives, and also to render me every assistance towards the completion of my labours. Backed by such indulgences, I proceeded on with my work, and have now brought it to a close.

Almost all the illustrations, this work contains, were obtained from the Palace Gallery with the exception of a few, which were drawn according to traditional accounts by Kilimanoor Revi Vurmah Koil Thumpuran, the artist who gained medals in the Madras and Calcutta Fine Arts Exhibitions. To this able and ingenious artist my most sincere thanks are specially due.

It would be necessarily difficult to offer my thanks individually to every one who has rendered assistance in this useful undertaking, and so, I acknowledge generally my obligation to all, from whom any aid had been obtained towards the completion of this work, which I hope will prove useful and acceptable to the public.

The best available hands in Madras were procured for the Lithographs, yet I cannot say that the work has been satisfactorily accomplished. The great amount of time taken by the Lithographers has caused the delay in the appearance of the book.

The heading of Chapter II has been printed "Reign of Dasa Vanji Pala Marthanda Vurmah Kulasekhara Perumal" through an oversight, it ought to be properly "Reign of Sri Padmanabha Dasa Vanji Pala Marthanda Vurmah Kulasekhara Perumal."

SHARETALAY IN TRAVANCORE,
November 1878.

CONTENTS.

CHAPTER I.

Page.

Ancient names of the province—Titles of its Sovereigns explained—Early mention of Travancore in the Puranas—The Puranas as historic records—Brief description of the 18 Puranas—The Ramayana, Bharatha and Harivamsa—The Madura Temple—The 56 kingdoms of Bharatha—Boundaries of ancient Chera—Early emperors—Ancestral line of the Chera dynasty—Kerala or Malayalam recovered from the sea—The exploits of Parasu Rama—The Kerala Mahatmyam—Udaya Vurmah, the head of the Cola Royal family—List of kings in the Kali Yugam—Kulasekhara Perumal, the great Vaishnava devotee and poet—The era of Vicramadithya—Konga kings—Caste of the Konga and Chera kings—Chera incorporated with Travancore—Old inscriptions—A copper sasanum—Kerala Ulppathy—Pachu Moothathu's account of Travancore—Cheraman Perumal—Sanscrit scholars in Keralam—Further proof of the antiquity of the Travancore dynasty—Astronomical calculations—The Travancore and Cochin Royal families—Difference between Samantha and Samanther—False notions about Hirannya Garbham—Brief account of the ceremonies Thulapurusha danam and Hirannya Garbha danam—The Numboory community—The renowned Vedanthist Sankara Acharyar—Rules for protecting female chastity—The Devaswams—The Military system adopted by Travancore kings—Travancore coins—The end of the Perumal Viceroyalty—Origin of the Cochin Rajah and the Zamorin of Calicut—The five Swaroopams—A new era introduced by king Udaya Marthanda Vurmah—The Panthalam Rajah—The Cochin Rajah extends his sovereignty—Mahomedan invasion—Short notices of some Travancore kings—Ecclesiastical system organised—Conspiracy against king Adithiya Vurmah—A Mahomedan Sirdar forces, Mahomedan customs—Battle between Kerala Vurmah and the Sirdar—Victory of the former who is subsequently assassinated—Adoption of a member into the Royal family—Prince Marthanda Vurmah and his exploits—Treaty with the Madura Government—Intercourse with Europeans in early times........ 1

CHAPTER II.

King Ramah Vurmah's successor—State of the kingdom—His efforts to improve it—Difficulties with the Pandyan Government—Raising of a Maraver army—Withdrawal of the Trichinopoly

Page.

contingent—A confederacy—Disputes about the throne—Rebuilding of the Trevandrum Pagoda by the Rajah—Works of public utility undertaken—Papu Thamby plots against the Rajah—Destruction of Papu Thamby and his party—War with Kayemkulam whose Rajah sues for peace—Annexation of Territory—Disputes between Travancore and Dutch East India Company—A Dutch detachment defeated by the Travancore army—Dutch reinforced from Ceylon—Travancore treats with the Government of Pondicherry—Battle of Colachel—Treatment of Dutch Prisoners—Eustatious D'Lanoy and Donadi—The siege of Kilimanoor—Fall of Cottayam—A diary of the Rajah's warlike movements—Confederacy of Petty Chiefs—Treaty with the Dutch—The Ambalapulay Rajah defeated and taken prisoner—Capture of Chunganacherry—Renewed struggle with Cochin—Some of the Malabar Princes rebel—Travancore comes in contact with Hyder Ali—The Nabob's Viceroy at Trichinopoly, declares his independence—Mahomed Ali and the English alliance with him—Capture of Kalacaud fort—Defeat of the Zamorin of Calicut—D'Lanoy appointed Commander-in-Chief of the Travancore army—Measures taken to protect Travancore—The reform of its Administration and the promotion of the welfare of its people—An important council held—Celebration of the first Murajapom—An act of Religious Devotion—Useful Public Works carried out—The death of Rama Iyen Dalawah—The last instructions of the Maha Rajah—Providential interpositions—Review of the Maha Rajah's career........ 114

CHAPTER III.

Rama Vurmah—Travancore divided—The Zamorin of Calicut—Construction of Fortifications—War with Maphuz Khan Sahib—Yusuff Khan rebels—The Madras Government interferes—Kasava Pillay—Treaty between Hyder Ali and the Madras Government—Ambassador sent to Mysore—Survey of Travancore—War with Hyder Ali—Death of D'Lanoy—Pilgrimage to Ramaswaram—Intercourse with Europeans—Prosperous state of Travancore—Kasava Pillay—Tippoo invades Malabar—English officers and Sir Archibald Campbell—Negotiation with the Dutch—The Madras Government remonstrates—War with Tippoo—Madras Government declare war with Tippoo—Contributions to the war—The Malabar Princes—Improvement of Alleppey—Forest Conservancy—Public Works—Revised Treaty with British Government—Death of the Maha Rajah—His acts........ 186

CHAPTER IV.

Bala Rama Vurmah—The favorites of His Highness—Death of Dewan Rye Kasava Dass—Jayanthen Sankaren Numboory raised to power—Extortion—Valu Thamby and his party rebel—New Dewan appointed—Palace intrigues—Murder of two high officials—Valu Thamby appointed Dewan—The system of administration improved—Major Macauly appointed Resident—Valu Thamby Dalawah's administration—Revolt against him—Lord Wellesley's letter on the same—The new Treaty of 1805—Embarrassed state of Travancore finances—Disputes about payment of troops—Death of Suba Iyen—Conspiracy and attempt on Colonel Macauly's

Page.

life—Murder of British Soldiers—Report of the Resident—Proclamation of the Dewan—Its effect—Proclamation of the British Government—British Force sent against Travancore—Reward offered for the apprehension of the Dewan—His death—Leaders of the insurrection punished—Narrative of proceedings of British troops—Measures of the new Dewan—Differences between him and the Maharajah—The Eliah Rajah—Colonel Munro appointed Resident—Death of the Maha Rajah—Review of his reign.......... 288

CHAPTER V.

Her Highness Lekshmi Bhye—Her character—Colonel Munro acts as Dewan—Reforms—Financial improvements—Death of Her Highness—Her prosperous reign—The Satta Wariola—Review of the Ranee's reign.................. 363

CHAPTER VI.

Prince Rama Vurmah—The Regent Gouree Parwathi Ranee—Selection of a Dewan—His dismissal—Ramen Menon appointed—His high character—European Commercial Agent at Alleppey—Colonel McDowall appointed Resident—Description of the Marriage ceremonies of Princess Rugmini Bhye—Colonel McDowall died 1820—Colonel Newall appointed—Palace intrigues—Administration of Peishcar Vencatta Row—The studies of the two Princes—Liberal treatment of Missionaries by the Ranee—Opening of Syrian College at Cottayam—The Ranee's Regency closes... 383

CHAPTER VII.

The real king of Travancore—His scholastic attainments—Suba Row's administration—Mr. Lushington, Governor of Madras, visits Travancore—Improvements—Code of Regulations—English school opened at Trevandrum—The Observatory—Irrigation and Maramuth department—The Maha Rajah's Court—General Cullen appointed Resident—Misunderstandings—Religious acts of the Maha Rajah—Financial embarrassments—The last hours and death of the Maha Rajah.................. 402

CHAPTER VIII.

His Highness Marthanda Vurmah, Maha Rajah—His Highness' character and attainments—His Highness' devotion to medical science—The Maha Rajah's visit to H. M.'s Frigate *Jupiter*—European style of living—Lord Elphinstone and the Maha Rajah—Dewan Krishna Row's reforms—Newspaper criticisms on the Travancore Government—Education of the young Princes—Inspection of an English Steamer—Patronage of Literature and Science—Press and Calendar—Revenue from Pepper—Travancore contributions to London Exhibition 1851—Receipt of a letter from H. M. the Queen—Excessive Rainfall—Questions about Native Converts—Abolition of Slavery—Opening of a new Bridge—Census of Travancore—Appointment of Sir Madava Row as Dewan—Lord Harris' visit—Some incidents of the Maha Rajah's reign.................. 443

LIST OF ILLUSTRATIONS.

A Panaroma of Travancore—Frontispiece.

	Page.
Sree Bhagavathi	2
Emperor Yayathi	4
Parasu Rama	19
Installation of Bhanu Vicrama as King of Kerala.	24
Kulasekhara Alwar	28
Veera Kerala Vurmah	52
Representation of Golden Tub for Padma Garbham ceremony	57
Coins struck for the Tulabhanam	72
Cheraman Perumal	85
Veera Marthanda *alias* Chera Udaya Marthanda	94
Marthanda Vurmah Maha Rajah...	114
An Ettu Veetil Pillay	125
Rama Iyen Dalawah	131
General D'Lanoy's Military Sepoys	137
Padmanabhapuram Fort and Magazine	164
Pagoda Tower, Trevandrum	167
Trevandrum Sewalipuray	167
Padmanabhapuram Palace	168
Marthanda Vurmah Maha Rajah performing Thulapurusha Danum	169
Marthanda Vurmah Maha Rajah entering into the Tub ...	170
Marthanda Vurmah Maha Rajah making over the Kingdom to Padmanabha Swamy...	171
Rama Vurmah Maha Rajah	186
The Rajah of Cochin	189
Iyeppen Marthanda Pillay Dalawah	193
Granite Paddy store at Manacudy	208
Tippoo Sultan	211
Nair and Sikh Sepoy and Rocket-bearer	226
Clock Tower, Trevandrum	249
Kulasekhara Mundapom	250
Rye Kasava Dass Dewan	255
Aswati Thirunal, Elia Rajah	257
Bala Rama Vurmah Maha Rajah	288
Valu Thamby Dalawah	300
The Maharajah and his attendants	333
Dewan Umminy Thamby	348
Colonel Munro, British Resident	358

	Page.
Her Highness Lekshmi Bhye	363
Rajah Rajah Vurmah Koil Thampuran...	364
Her Highness Gouree Parwathi Bhye	383
Princess Rugmini Bbye	389
Cochu Koil Thampuran...	392
Dewan Vencatta Row	395
Rama Vurmah Maha Rajah...	402
Dewan Subba Row	408
General Cullen, British Resident	423
Marthanda Vurmah Maha Rajah	443
Dewan Krishna Row	454
His Highness the Third Prince	476
His Highness the First Prince	482
The Prince Atthum Thirunal	484
Her Highness Lekshmi Ranee	487
The Prince Moolum Thirunal...	488
Dewan Madava Row	492

ADDENDA.

Page 32, line 15, *for* 7th century, *read* 11th century.
„ 39, „ 8, „ Rakshapumshen, *read* Rakshapurushan.
„ 53, „ 32, „ Systerna Brahminacum, *read* Systema Brahmanicam.
„ 82, „ 12, „ and in the possession, *read* and are in the possession.
„ 126, „ 36, „ assisting the Quilon Rajah restoring, &c., *read* assisting the Quilon Rajah in restoring, &c.
„ 128, „ 1, „ of the Kayemkulam, omit *the*.
„ 140, „ 35, „ 21st Makaram, *read* 20th Makaram.
„ 260, „ 6, „ Kariakar, *read* Harikar.
„ 270, „ 6, „ Madacava, *read* Nadacava.
„ 302, „ 38-39, „ Valu Thamby the Dalawah's mother, *read* Valu Thamby Dalawah's mother.
„ 368, second line from the end, omit *both*.
„ 370, line 9, omit *both*.
„ 448, „ 16, *for* described, *read* descried.
„ 496, „ 26, „ returned from, *read* return from.
„ 500, „ 25, „ to see beautiful steamer, *read* to see the beautiful steamer.
„ 513, „ 28, „ but, *read* and.

HISTORY OF TRAVANCORE.

CHAPTER I.

EARLY HISTORY OF TRAVANCORE.

THE present Dynasty of Travancore is one of the most ancient in India, the period assigned to its origin being the beginning of the world. The original designation of Travancore was Chera, or, as we find it spelt by some authors, Sera or Cera.

Chera, the first of the three Southern Mandala kingdoms, has, according to the Tamil Nighandu (Dictionary), numerous appellations, but with the exception of a few, they appear to have become now obsolete.

Subsequent to the dismemberment of the main part of the Chera kingdom, and the embodying of the rest with its Southern and Kerala possessions, the designations were, first, Sreevalumcode or "Tiruvarumcode,"[1] abode of prosperity, which name was vulgarised into Thiruvancode, from which Travancore, the name used by the English is derived; second Vanavanaud, abridged into Venaud; third, Keralam; fourth, Vanji Desam; and fifth, Thiru Adi Desam.

All the ancient designations of Cheren are found in the Tamil language and the Nighandu has such desig-

1. Then shall Travancore indeed be what she is now fancifully denominated by her people, Tiru-varung-kodu, the sacred, prosperous kingdom, Vanji Bhumi, the Treasure Land, Dharma Bhumi, the land of Piety, Charity and Truth. Revd. Mateer's Land of Charity, page 370.

CHAP. I. nations arranged in it, of which a few may be quoted here as specimens :—

Cheren, Cheralen, (Keralen) Kollykavelen, Kodacon, Pothintharaven, Porunayattan, Vanjiventhen, Kothayar, Vanavarempen, Malayaman, &c.

All these names have special meanings which will be found in the Tamil Akarathi.

Chera monarchs had the titles Chakravarthy, Kulasekhara Perumal, and Thiru Adikel. The meaning of the first title both in Sanscrit and Tamil is Emperor; the second is a mixed word, a compound of Sanscrit and Tamil, Kula, Sekhara, Perumal, signifying Head of the race of Kings, Kulam being race, Sekhara, Head, and Perumal, King; the third, Thiru Adikel in Tamil, signifies "Sacred or prosperous feet."

The title, Veera Kerala, is the same as that of Cheren, for, the western boundary of the kingdom of Chera extended beyond the Suhhyen mountains (the Western Ghauts) to the Arabian Sea, and the coast between the sea and the Ghauts was called Malayalam or Keralam (so called the first, from its situation at the foot of the hills, and the second from the fact of the land abounding with cocoanut, which in Sanscrit is called Keram, the owner of this land Cheren being as a matter of course styled Keralen.*)

The Sanscrit word *Sree* (CERES) is pronounced in Tamil, Thiru. The following are examples :—Thiruvancode instead of Sreevalumcode, Thiru Adikel for

* 1. Land of Perumals, page 38.

2. Cochin Administration Report for 1875-76.

3. "But, though what the Kerala Mahatmyam relates might be accepted, seeing that the Copper Plate Document, No. I, proves that Veera Kerala was the first Prince of Kerala; yet, on the other hand, there may be no harm in surmising, that this name of Veera Kerala may have had reference to the said country of Kerala which he governed." Madras Journal of Literature and Science, Vol. 5, No. 9, New series.

4. Dr. Caldwell in his "Comparative Grammar of Dravidian Languages," says that the word *Kerala* was known under various forms, such as *Keralam, Cheralam, Cheram, Keram, Seram,* &c. He supposes *Kera* to be "the earliest form of the word."

SREE BHAGAVATHI.

PUBLISHED BY MESS.RS HIGGINBOTHAM & CO. C. PASZKOWSKY LITH: MADRAS

Sree Adikel, Thiru Vanjicolam for Thiru Vanji Kovilakam, &c. CHAP. I.

The Chera dominions which include the best portion of the Dravida country had Tamil as its vernacular from the earliest time, and the Grandha and other characters originated in this kingdom. Dr. Burnell testifies to this fact in his Paleography wherein he says that, "The Grandha, modern Tamil, Malayalam "and Telugu alphabets all have their origin in the "Cera character, a variety of the Cave character, "which was used in the Cera kingdom during the "early centuries A.D. From the third to the seventh "century appears to have been the most flourishing "period in the modern history of this kingdom; it then "extended over the present Mysore, Coimbatore, Salem, "Tondainadu, South Malabar and Cochin. It was, "however, one of the three great old Dravidian king- "doms and existed already in the third century B.C."

The Puranas and other ancient Sanscrit and Tamil historical writings connected with, and bearing upon, the Puranas, describe the origin, in the Kritha Yugam (the first age), of three contemporary kings in Southern India called Cheren, Cholen and Pandyan, who ruled over three countries called after their names Chera Mandalam, Chola Mandalam and Pandya Mandalam. These three kings were brothers and were Soma Vamsa Kshatrias.

The Kshatrias are of two classes, namely, the Soorya Vamsa and Soma Vamsa, an account of whose origin will be interesting.

The Hindu chronology divides the age of the world into four Yugams, viz.: Kritha Yugam 4,800 years, Thretha Yugam 3,600 years, Dwapara Yugam 2,400 years, and Kali Yugam 1,200 years; the whole being equivalent to 12,000 years of the immortals.

In the Kritha Yugam two races of Kshatrias were begotten; one from the sun and the other from the moon, on whom the administration of the whole earth originally devolved.

CHAP. I.

Brahma, the Creator, begot a son Kásyapen. His son was Sooryan. His son Vaivaswatha Manu. His son was Sudyumnen alias Ilen, who, by a peculiar adventure, (which it is not to our present purpose to detail here) became a female; Ila, and by her the Emperor Purooravass was born to Budhen. His son was Ayush, his son Nahushen, his son Yayathi; he had two wives Devayani and Sarmishtta, the former was the Brahman Rishi Sukren's daughter, who had two sons named Yedu and Durvasu, and to the latter Prince the Emperor Yayathi assigned sovereignty over the Southern part of India. The posterity of Durvasu are the three kings of Chera, Chola and Pandya. Of these three, Cheren was the head of the present Travancore Dynasty, which is also called Keralen.

The celebrated and popular work called Harivamsa,[1] has in its 32nd Chapter a detailed narrative of the origin of the abovementioned Dynasties, the substance of a few verses of which may be given below.

Durvasu's son was Vahni, his son Gourbhanu, his son Thraisanu, his son Karendhamen, his son Maruthen, who had no male issue but only a daughter by name Sammatha, whom the king gave as *Kanniaka Danam* to *Jupiter's* brother, Samvarthen, a Brahman endowed with great wisdom and learning. Maruthen adopted Dushenthen from Pooruvumsam, and they thus became united with the renowned Pooruvamsa. Dushenthen's son was King Guryamen or Karendhamen; he had four sons called Pandyan, Keralen, Solen and Kolen. The kingdom was divided among the sons by their father, who called the divisions after their names Pandya, Sola, Kerala and Kola.

1. When those observations passed through the Press we had not met with a passage in the Harivamsa, adduced by Col. Wilford, which confirms the statement of our manuscripts by assigning the South country to Duruvsu, and adding that in the tenth generation after him four brothers divided the Peninsula among them; they being respectively named Pandya, Cerala, Cola and Chola, of whom Cola had the most Northern portion. W. Taylor's Preface, p. 11 and 12, Historical Manuscripts Translation, Vol. 1.

THE EMPEROR YAYATHI.

PUBLISHED BY MESS.RS HIGGINBOTHAM & CO. C. PACZENRY LITH: MADRAS

Other Authors[1] make allusion to only three Dynasties, *i.e.*, Chera, Chola and Pandya, of which Chera was subsequently styled Kerala, in which Kola appears to have been embodied. The Puranas are the chief authorities for the above accounts.

For such information as is pre-historical, we are obliged to depend upon the Puranas alone, though many are of opinion that these are not trustworthy. Indeed, the descriptions of things and deeds narrated in the Puranas are certainly open to such criticism, but as we do not hesitate to place credence on the Bible, the Koran and such writings, conveying to us religious instructions and Divine commands, we may generally place our belief in the Puranic accounts, rejecting the exaggerations and such fictitious descriptions as the authors of the Puranas may have added to embellish their works.

Even some of the best European authors have taken the view that the Hindu Puranas are acceptable authorities in such matters. In page 86 of "A Historical Sketch of Sanscrit Literature," the author says, "The Puranas hold an eminent rank in the religion "and literature of the Hindus. Possessing like the "Vedas the credit of divine origin and scarcely inferior "to them in sanctity, they exercise a more extensive "and practical influence upon Hindu society. They "regulate their ritual, direct their faith and supply in "popular legendary tales materials for their credulity. "To European scholars, they recommend themselves "on other accounts; and they have been considered to "contain not only the picturesque and mythological "part of Indian superstition, but as the treasury of "extensive and valuable historical remains whose data "reach back at least nearly to the deluge. The "Puranas include ancient traditions respecting the "Gods, religions, doctrines and rites, the creation,

1. Tradition and native records represent the Southern portion of the Indian Peninsula as being anciently divided into three contemporary kingdoms; 1, The Pandya; 2, Chola or Sora; 3, Chera Sera or Konga. Professor Dowson's Journal Royal Asiatic Society, Vol. 8.

"the ages of the world, cosmography, and the genea-"logy and history of the ancient kings as well as the "deeds of their successors."

We think that the fabulous narratives recorded in the Puranic writings might be easily and well sifted out and authentic and credible facts collected from them.

The following are the names of the eighteen Puranas, with brief notes of their substances:

I.—*The Brahma Purana* contains an account of the creation and of the Manwantharas, the history of the solar and lunar races to the time of Krishna, a description of the Universe, a life of Krishna and a treatise on the mode in which Yoga is to be performed. It treats also of the Supreme power of the Omnipotent and Omnipresent Being, the importance of the Vedas and the works assigned to Brahmans and other classes. It describes the sanctity of various holy places including Ananthásayanam (Trevandrum).

II.—The *Padma Purana* is divided into five parts; (1), Srishti Khanda; (2), Bhoomi Khanda; (3), Swarga Khanda; (4), Pathala Khanda; (5), Uttara Khanda. These contain treatises on the creation after the deluge, the origin of Brahma, the Vedas, the Manus, &c., &c.

III.—The *Vishnu Purana* is that in which Parasara, beginning with the events of the Varaha Kalpa, expounds all duties. This Purana introduces the substance of almost all the other Puranas.

IV.—The *Vayu Purana.* The Purana in which Vayu has declared the laws of duty in connection with the Sweta Kalpa and which comprises the Mahatmyam of the Rudra. This is narrated by Sootha to the Rishies of Naimisarannya. It is divided into four Padas termed severally Prakriya, Upodghata, Anushanga and Upasamhara. The first treats of the creation. The next contains the subject of the creation and describes the various Kalpas. The genealogies of the Patriarchs, the description of the Universe, and the incidents of the first six Manwantharas are all treated in this part. It contains also praises of Siva. A long account of the Pithrus and the stories of some of the celebrated Rishies are also to be found. The third part commences with an account of the seven Rishies and their descendants and describes the origin of the several classes of created beings. Then comes a long and full account of the Solar and Lunar Kshatria Dynasties. The last portion describes briefly the future Manwantharas, the measures of space and time, the end of the world, the efficacy of Yoga and the glories of Sivapura.

V.—The *Sree Bhagavatha* consists of twelve Skundhas or Chapters. The first nine Chapters contain treatises on various subjects, such as the origin of the Purana, the creation, renovation and the end of the world, a descriptive account of Kali Yugam, the various stages of human life and a comparison of the human system and its functions to a Fort with nine gates, a description of good and evil deeds, and the reward and punishment for such acts, a view of Heaven, Paradise, and Hell, an account of the incarnation of Vishnu, description of the world both terrestrial and celestial, the churning of the oceans, an account of the king of Pandya being cursed by Agusthyar, the origin of the two races of Kshatrias, &c., &c.; the tenth dwells exclusively on the birth and life of Krishna; the eleventh on Vedic discourse and metaphysics, concluding with Krishnen's deification; and the twelfth contains a history of the kings of Kali Yugam, the work closing with numerous instructive lectures and Vedic discourses.

Some persons are of opinion that the Purana called Devee Bhagavatha is the one to be reckoned amongst the eighteen Puranas and not the one which is generally denominated Sree Bhagavatha, but we are of opinion that the latter is the proper Purana to be included among the eighteen.

VI.—The *Naradeeya Purana*. In this, Narada

CHAP. I. describes the duties which were observed in the Brehat Kalpa. It contains praises of Vishnu, the birth of Markandeya, the destruction of Sagara's sons and the Vamana Avathara. It contains also a geographical treatise on Bharatha Khandam (India), in which the existence of the Dynasties of Chera (Kerala or Travancore) is mentioned.

VII.—The *Markandeya Purana* like most other Puranas dwells much on the creation, condition and destruction of the world by a deluge. It also treats of the birth of the Manus, the mode of prayers to Durga, the victory of the Goddess Bhavani over the Asuras, giants, and the story of the birds that were acquainted with right and wrong as related by Markandeya and the holy sages. It lays down rules for the observance of various classes and makes mention of the sanctity of the shrine of Benares and other holy places.

VIII.—The *Agni Purana* describes the Isanu Kalpa. It contains a description of the Avatharas, instructions for the performance of religious rites, duties of kings, a distribution and arrangement of the Vedas and Puranas, and a chapter on Gifts. It further contains an account of medicine and some instructions on the worship of Siva and Devee. The work concludes with a treatise on Rhetoric, Prosody and Grammar, according to the Sutras of Panini. In addition to this, rules for the due observance of the ceremonies on the occasion of a widow burning with the corpse of her husband are laid down.

IX.—The *Bhavishyat Purana* is that in which Brahma, having described the greatness of the sun, explained to Manu the existence of the world and the characters of all created things in the course of the Aghora Kalpa. It chiefly treats of matters to come, Bhavishyat meaning prophetic, such as the events of a future age, all that will come to pass up to the end of the world being predicted. It prophesies the end of the Government of the Kshatria kings of both races, with the exception of the Soma Vamsa King of Kerala

(Travancore and Cola), the Cola conquest of the Veeralas (Belalas or Holsalas) and the rule of Kerala by this Kshatria King of Travancore and his relative Cola, the possession of Hindustan by Mletchas (Mahomedans), and then by the Hoonas (Europeans), to whom the King of Kerala (Travancore) will be tributary. The incarnation of Vishnu, as Kalkee, towards the end of the world, is also prophesied. In this Purana a description of Southern India with copious accounts of Chera, Chola and Pandya is given in detail.

X.—The *Brahmavaivartha Purana* contains an account of the greatness of God and of Krishna, and the events of the Rathalva Kalpa. It is divided into four parts called Brahma, Devee, Ganesa and Krishna. In this, the rules of Yoga Abhyasam (a certain devotional service performed by meditating on God while the body is in a certain fixed posture with a mind undistracted. The power and sanctity of various manthrams (devotional spells) are also described.)

XI.—The *Linga Purana*. In this, Maheswara, present in the Agni Linga, explains virtue, wealth, pleasure and final liberation at the end of the Agni Kalpa. Accounts of the creation, praises of Siva and Vishnu and a description of the universe are also given.

XII.—The *Varaha Purana* is that in which the glory of the great Varaha is predominant. It describes like other Puranas the creation of the world, and the deluge, and the advantages derivable from sacrifices and other divine offerings. It contains some allusions to the consecration of an image of Varaha Moorthi at Ananthasayanam (Trevandrum).

XIII.—The *Skanda Purana* is that Purana in which Skanda relates the events of the Thadpurusha Kalpa. It dwells upon the greatness and sanctity of Siva, the birth of Skanda or Subrahmanya, and the origin of Madura in the Pandyan country. It contains various prayers and hymns. It has also several branches such as Halassya Mahatmyam, &c.

CHAP. I.

XIV.—The *Vamana Purana* is that in which is recorded how the four-faced Brahma taught the three objects of existence as conducive to the account of the greatness of Thrivikrama. It contains an account of the Siva Kulpa and of the dwarf incarnation of Vishnu. A detailed account of the Emperor Maha Bali and his righteous administration and an excellent lecture on charity, together with an account of the sanctity and holiness of the river Ganges, are also given in it.

XV.—The *Koorma Purana* is that in which Janardana in the form of a tortoise in regions under the earth, explained the objects of life, duty, wealth, pleasure and liberation, in connection with Indradyumna and the Rishies in the proximity of Sakra which refers to the Lakshimi Kalpa.

XVI.—The *Matsya Purana* is that in which for the purpose of promulgating the Vedas, Vishnu, in the beginning of a Kalpa, related to Manu, the story of Narasimha and the events of the seven Kalpas. It contains a copious description of the oceans, seas and their courses.

XVII.—The *Garuda Purana* is that in which Vishnu recites instructions in Garuda Kalpa, and dwells chiefly on the birth of Garuda. It treats of the doctrine of transmigration of the soul. A description of hell and the treatment of sinners in it, and of the eternal enjoyment in Paradise by the souls of those men who reverenced and observed the commandments of God is given. It also lays down rules for the observance of funerals and ceremonies connected with them.

XVIII.—The *Brahmanda Purana* is that which relates the origin or evolution of the world in the shape of an egg. It contains an account of the creation of the elements and every thing appertaining to the Universe as also the birth and life of Parasu Rama.

Independent of the above eighteen Puranas, there are eighteen more, denominated Upa Puranas; 1, *Sanalkumara Purana*; 2, *Narasimha*; 3, *Naradeya*;

4, *Siva*; 5, *Durvassa*; 6, *Kapila*; 7, *Manava*; 8, *Ausanasa*; 9, *Varuna*; 10, *Kalika*; 11, *Samba*; 12, *Nandi*; 13, *Saura*; 14, *Parasara*; 15, *Adithya*; 16, *Maheswara*; 17, *Bhargava*; 18, *Vasishta*.

Besides these there are three other Puranas equally sacred and more popular. These are the *Ramayana*, *Bharatha* and *Harivamsa*, composed by Rishies, the first by Valmiki, and the other two by Vyasa. These three Puranas are more generally read among modern Hindoos. The contents of these may be briefly sketched.

1st.—The *Ramayana* commences with a treatise on the cause of the incarnation of Vishnu as Sree Rama and that of his three brothers, Rama's progress in life, his going to the wilderness as an illustration of parental respect and obedience, the abduction of Seetha by Ravana, his erecting Sethu (Adam's Bridge), his victory over Ravana in Lunka (Ceylon), his crowning of Vibheeshana (Ravana's younger brother) as king of Lunka, his recovery of Seetha and his return to Ayodhya (Oude); his ruling over India as Chakravarthy for several thousand years with justice and wisdom and the existence of the kingdom of Keralam are also recorded in this Purana.

2nd.—The *Bharatha* opens with a general history of all the kingdoms and kings of the Solar and Lunar races in Bharatha Khandam. It contains an account of the birth and life of all the Rishies, the Couravas and the Pandavas; Arjuna's pilgrimage and his visit to Madura, Cape Comorin and Keralam (Malabar); the pilgrimage of Bela Rama (Krishna's brothers), to all the holy shrines; Sree Krishna's embassy to the court of Duryodhana; Vidura's instructive lecture to the old king Dhritarashtra; the commencement of the great war between the Couravas and the Pandavas; the conclusion of the war; installation of Dhurmaputhra as Chakravarthy (Emperor) after being victorious and levying tribute from all the kings of Bharata Khandam, including the king of Keralam (Travancore); the performance of the great sacrifice Aswamedham,

CHAP. I. his reigning over India with justice for a period of thirty-six years; Sree Krishna's deification, the end of the Dhurmaputhra's reign, and his translation to Heaven. This is one of the largest Puranas and contains most of the Hindu canons and laws, the duties of kings and the government of kingdoms. In this are laid down the highly renowned Hindu doctrines called Bhagavat Geeta and several others equally instructive. It contains narrations up to the end of the Dwapara Yugam and the commencement of the present age Kali Yugam. That the king of Keralam (Travancore) fought in the Bharata Yudhům on the side of the Pandavas and was killed in battle is also mentioned in it.

3rd.—The *Harivamsa* describes the origin of the world and the creation. It contains some treatises on religion, gives a full and detailed genealogy of Kshatria kings both of the races of Soorya and Soma from their very origin to the early part of the present age Kali Yugam, and describes the origin of the Chera, Chola and Pandya dynasties as already stated.

There are various other works branching out from the Puranas and Upa Puranas. Almost every place of note has a work of its own, denominated Sthala Mahatmyam, which narrates particular events connected with the city or town about which it treats, with historical notes in some cases. But such writings chiefly dwell upon the sanctity or virtue of a shrine or a river in its neighbourhood. These being almost all exaggerated appear fabulous at the very first blush. Nevertheless, valuable and reliable accounts will be found in them. For instance, the Sthalapuranam of Madura contains a description, in highly exaggerated terms, of the Madura Temple and its surrounding buildings, with an account of the then ruling Pandyan dynasty. Though the accounts and descriptions are exaggerated, yet no one can deny the magnificence and grandeur of the Temple as well as the existence of the ancient dynasty of the Pandya kingdom.

The Sthala Mahatmyam of Thiru Avanasi, Peroor, Chera Maha Devi, Mannar Kovil, and other places, contains exaggerated accounts of the existence of Chera, while that of Conjepuram contains historical remarks on the dynasty of Chola.

There are two special works called Kerala Mahatmyam and Kerala Ulppathy; the one in Sanscrit and the other in Malayalam, which narrate the origin of Keralam. Both of these works contain reliable accounts concerning Keralam (Travancore).

The Hindu geography which corresponds with that of the European, particularly in regard to the shape of the earth, divides the world into nine divisions, of which Asia is denominated Jemboo Dwipu, in which is included Bharata Khandam (India).

This land of Bharatha is divided into 56 kingdoms, viz.: Casmeerah, Nappala, Kosala, Camboja, Paunchala, Simhala, Aunga, Kalinga, Kamaroopa, Saovira, Kuroo, Bhoja, Vithaiha, Valmeeka, Kekaya, Vunga, Sourashtra, Punnadaga, Parpara, Kuluntha, Soorasena, Dangana, Martha, Saindhava, Purashara, Pandhara, Saliva, Kudaka, Neisheedha, Thoorka, Durga, Marda, Poundra, Magatha, Chethiya, Maharashttra, Gundhra, Carnadaka, Dravida, Kukkada, Lada, Mahrva, Magara, Desarna, Ottiya, Bachu, Yavana, Baguvane, Konkana, Kashyva, Dungana, Latcha, Chola, Pandya, Chera and Kerala.

Of these, the last two kingdoms, Chera and Kerala, were owned by one and the same king, viz., that of Travancore.

The kingdom of Chera was the most southern and largest among the three States already alluded to.

The boundaries of the kingdom of Chera which are variously defined by ancient Tamil authors, were according to one, the Pulney Hills in the north, the town of Peroor in the east, the sea about Cape Comorin in the south, and the range of the great mountains on the west, extending about 80 cathams (800 miles).

Another Tamil author extends the northern boundary to the Coorg Hills and the western to Calicut.

But Dr. A. C. Burnell, who is a more reliable authority than many others, says in his Paleography already referred to, that the Chera kingdom existed in the early centuries A.D., that it then extended over Mysore, Coimbatore, Salem, Tondainadu, South Malabar and Cochin, and that it was one of the three great Dravidian kingdoms and was divided into the eastern and western Chera, the former extending up to Madras.

The Chera Dominions bordered on the Pandyan and Chola countries, the principal towns being Salem, Avanasi or Thiru Avanasi in Coimbatore, Trichencode near Trichinopoly, Thenkasi, Valliyoor, Thrikanankudy and Chera Maha Devi, all south-east of Avanasi in the District of Tinnevelly.

On the Malabar coast or in Keralam, the capitals were Thiru Vanjicolam[1] (Sree Vanji Kovilakam, the residence of the prosperous Vanji dynasty), Colicode (Calicut), and Kollum (Quilon).

In India (Bharatha Khandam), the mode of Government followed from the earliest times as narrated in the Puranas, was that any king on becoming more powerful than all the others conquered them and declared himself Chakravarthy (Emperor).

A few of the most renowned emperors who governed as Chakravarthies in each Yugam from Kritha to Dwapara and almost all the Chakravarthies in Kali Yugam (the present age) according to the Puranas are the following:—

In Kritha Yugam (the first age), Harrischundren, Muchukunden, Pariyawathen, Hirannyakshen, Banen, Maha Bali and others.

1. Sera metropolis, we conjecture to be no other than Tiruvanche, the capital of the Sera Desam, according to our Manuscripts.—Rev. W. Taylor, page 13. Preface.

In Thretha Yugam, Sagaren, Karthaveeryen, Reghu, Desarethen, Sree Ramen and others.

In Dwapara Yugam, Budhen, Pariasathen, Nalen, Pandu, Dhurmaputhra and others.

In the Kali Yugam (the present age which has now come to the 4979th year), Pareekshithu (Abhimanyu's son), Jenamejeyen, Sathaneekan, Prakrethirethen, Jehganu, Chithrarathen, Chithrasenan, Thrisanku, Pariplavan, Sunayan, Madhavee, Robhunjeyan, Thikunan, Shathaneekan, Thendapani, Nimi, Autchanakan and twenty-six other kings, who reigned up to the year 656 in the early part of this Yugam.

Subsequent to the above period, the system of Chakravarthy or imperial Government by the northern Kshatria kings appears to have been at an end, and each of the various rulers of India irrespective of caste, became supreme in his own kingdom. Some of the most powerful sovereigns contrived to bring the neighbouring potentates to subjection by war and declared themselves petty Chakravarthies over a few other kings. Of such Emperors, we have accounts written both in the Puranas, as also in modern histories. The authors of the Puranas, we find, record the history and the heroic exploits of the Chakravarthies up to the early part of Kali Yugam, and the subsequent history of the emperors and kings and their kingdoms in India is narrated by modern historians.

We have instances of the above kind in the Dynasties of Nanda, Mourya, Kala Bhoorya, Yadava, Kola, Vicramadithya, Salivahana, Bhoja, the Yavanas, the Mohamedans of Delhi, the Rayer of Anagoondy (Vijayanuggar) the Mahrattas and the English.

So also there have been instances of the Southern kingdoms of Pandya, Chola and Chera being ruled alternately by one among themselves as Chakravarthy, and at other times each governing his own kingdom. Narratives, however imperfect and brief, could be found regarding these kings and their kingdoms in various works.

CHAP. I.

The origin of the ancestral line of the Chera dynasty (Travancore), in the first age of the world, Kritha Yugam, has been already shown and we will now endeavour to trace out and follow this dynasty down to the present time in an unbroken line.

In describing the Pandyan dynasty through all its revolutions, Mr. Taylor shows the existence of the Chera dynasty as co-existing[1] with the Pandyan, up to the time of the dissolution of its original house.

The Purana called Halassya Mahatmyam already alluded to makes mention of sixty-four Leelas (amusements), and the king of Chera is mentioned in the 12th, 14th, 42nd, 49th, and 62nd Leelas, which Mr. Taylor in his Historical Manuscript Translation calls "Thiruvilaudel."

In Thretha Yugam, Kerala or Malayalam is said to have been recovered from the sea by Parasu Rama, the sixth incarnation of Vishnu. Several Puranas relate the story though the versions vary. One account says that with the permission of Varunen (the God of the sea), Parasu Rama flung his weapon from Cape Comorin and it fell at Gokurnam, whereupon the sea receded from those two points to the present extent of the Malabar Coast and he called it Keralam; that in the reclaimed part of the land Parasu Rama established cities, towns, villages, &c., and invited people from various countries and peopled the land throughout; while another account states that the weapon was flung from Gokurnam and it fell at Cape Comorin. A third account states that the holy temple at Gokurnam having been buried under the sea in the first age (Kritha Yugam), and in the next age (Thretha Yugam), Parasu Rama, at the request of the people, asked the lord of the sea to recede, and from Gokurnam flung his wooden spoon (used for sacrificial pur-

1. The Sora-desam, Sera-desam and Pandya-desam, are most frequently alone enumerated as co-existing; and our manuscript authorities in the first volume allude to no other, in the remote period of antiquity.

poses) which fell at Cape Comorin and the sea receded. Of the fabulous accounts of the Puranas we have already said enough, and so we shall now try to sift out the probable facts. CHAP. I.

The western part of the range of hills called Sahhyen (between Canara and Quilon) must have been a tract of land at the creation of the earth but had been submerged in the sea. Subsequently, the sea receded and a large portion of the land between Quilon and Mangalore remained uncultivated during the reign of the Chera King Keralen, when the Brahman warrior Parasu Rama visited this land of Keralam, established himself there, organised a Brahman community, introduced a new system of Government, lived there for a considerable period of time and then retired.[1] A writer in the Cottayam College Quarterly Magazine, in its issue of July 1866, has the following observations in regard to the origin of Keralam.

"Can there be a doubt that this legend chronicles "in the style of the Poets, the effects of volcanic agency "on this coast centuries ago; first that there was "once a subsidence, probably sudden, at Gokurnam, "and secondly, that there was afterwards a perceptible "uprising, most probably in this case gradual, of at "least some portion, if not of nearly all the coast "between Gokurnam and the Cape."

"The whole appearance of the coast of Kerala, "wherever at least we find the low-lands and back-"waters, would appear to indicate, that it has thus "been raised, certainly during the present era; and "if, as our legend would seem to tell, this has happened "under the eye of man, it becomes the more deeply "interesting. Nor can we forget that even now there "are decided evidences of unstable "equilibrium"

1. Kookel Keloo Nair the District Munsiff of Malabar and afterwards Sub-Judge of Calicut, gives a similar opinion in a Memorandum on the Syrian and Jewish Copper Plates, published in Vol. 5, No. 9. New Series of the Madras Journal of Literature and Science. Keloo Nair's opinion on the land of Keralam alone is accepted here, and not his opinion on the Copper Plates.

CHAP. I

"along the coast line. The sea at Alleppie is considerably further from the town than it was but a "few years ago, which shows that the shore is rising; "the same is the case at Cochin to an extent that we "think can scarcely be accounted for by accumulating "sand; while to the north of Cochin the sea is as "evidently encroaching, and in some parts has for "years past caused great destruction of property. "Moreover we are not altogether strangers in Kerala "to the shocks of earthquakes; in 1856, especially, "repeated shocks were felt; in 1823, 1841, and 1845, "shocks have also been recorded at Trevandrum. In "several cases the shocks seem to have been propagated from the north-west; and on September 1st, "1856, a ball of a pendulum in the Trevandrum Observatory 17 feet long, is recorded to have been moved "about 4 inches in the direction north-west by north "and south-east by south which is about the direction of the coast line."

"All these facts would appear to favour the conclusion that the low-lands of the Malabar coast have "been raised from beneath the sea-level by subterranean forces, and that this has happened, in all "probability in comparatively modern times."

The fact of the land between Gokurnam and Kunnya Cumari having been submerged in the ocean at one time is testified to by the Brahmanda Purana in which it is said that the holy pagoda of Gokurnam had been under water for a long time; that certain Rishies and others interested in the pagoda went to Parasu Rama and begged him to take steps for its recovery; that Parasu Rama proceeded to Gokurnam and prevailed upon Varuna, the Neptune of the Hindus, to recede to a certain distance between Gokurnam and Cape Comorin; and that the land of Keralam was thus reclaimed.

As Parasu Rama is generally represented to have been the sole creator of the land of Keralam, it would not be uninteresting to give here a brief account of his life.

PARASU RAMA.

PUBLISHED BY MESSRS HIGGINBOTHAM & CO.
S. PACZESSKY LITH. MADRAS

According to the Brahmanda Purana, this celebrated Brahman was a descendant of the renowned Rishi Bhrigu and is believed to have been the sixth incarnation of Vishnu. He is said to have been born in the second age of Thretha Yugam in a hermitage on the banks of the river Nurbuda. His father was a sacred devotee named Jamadagni. His mother's name was Renuka. Jamadagni had five sons of whom Rama was the youngest. While the whole family was living comfortably in the hermitage during Rama's minority, a sad event disturbed their quiet and peaceful life.

One day Jamadagni left his hermitage to procure things for his devotional services, while Renuka left it to bring water from the neighbouring river Nurbuda. Jamadagni returned, but did not find his wife as usual. He grew angry at her absence. After a while, Renuka returned, and on being questioned, she confessed that she was detained at the bank of the river Nurbuda by seeing the reflection in the water of a Gandharvan (Genii) called Chithrangaden, passing through the air. The shape of the spirit was so beautiful that she was tempted to have a moment's look at the shadow and thus a little time was lost. At this declaration of his wife's weakness, the enraged Rishi was so vexed that he resolved on her immediate death and calling his sons one by one before him, ordered them to kill their mother, but four of them refused on the plea that the Law prohibits the killing of a female and further that in this case the female was their mother. But Rama, on being ordered, declared that nothing would prevent him from obeying his father. So saying he cut off Renuka's head at once. When Renuka fell on the ground, Jamadagni was exceedingly pleased with the prompt obedience shown by his youngest son and said to Rama that he might ask for anything which he liked and that he would have it immediately. Rama said that he wished to see his mother restored to life without loss of time. Jamadagni, being a Rishi who had gained the blessings of God by his devotions, prayed to the All-powerful Being for the resuscitation

CHAP. I. of Renuka and God vouchsafed life to her at once. Rama was delighted and they all lived comfortably for some time more.

Subsequently, Rama was sent by his parents to the hermitage of his great-grandfather Bhrigu, to be educated in the Vedas and other literature. Here he spent some time to complete his education and afterwards, acting upon the advice of that venerable sage, Rama proceeded to the Himalayas to meditate on the deity Siva. Here he spent many years in meditation and penance. These devotional exercises pleased Siva, who appeared to Rama in person, conferred on him all sorts of blessings and directed him to visit all the holy places on the face of the earth which Rama did and returned to the Himalayas where he resumed his devotional meditations. While Rama was thus engaged, a war broke out between the Devas and the Asuras. The former, being defeated and driven out of Swarga, went to Siva and represented their grievances. Whereupon, Rama was sent for and Siva asked him to assist the Devas giving him all necessary instructions as to the mode of conducting the war and the use of various weapons. Siva presented him with a battle-axe called Parasu and from this day Rama was called Parasu Rama. He proceeded to the war, with great energy fought against the Asuras and gained a decisive victory. The Devas, as well as Siva were extremely pleased with Parasu Rama and conferred upon him the choicest blessings. Parasu Rama again repaired to the Himalaya mountains and recommenced his devotional penance. A considerable time afterwards, Siva, having been exceedingly pleased with Parasu Rama, paid a visit to him and presented him with a supernatural chariot and an arrow which were to appear before him whenever he wanted them. Parasu Rama entrusted these to Siva's own attendants, Kundodaren and Mahodren. Thus, having obtained all his wishes, and his wants being supplied, Parasu Rama left the Himalayas and came to his great-grandfather Bhrigu. There he spent some time, and then returned to his parents on the banks of the Nurbuda, where the family were living together comfortably. Now, Karthaveerarjuna, the king of Hehaya came to the neighbouring forests on a hunting excursion and being fatigued entered the hermitage for a little refreshment. Jamadagni, Parasu Rama's father, entertained the party, and on the departure of the king on the next morning, he took a fancy to the Rishi's cow called Kamadhenu. This the king informed his minister, who resolved to get the animal at any risk. He sent a messenger to ask Jamadagni to sell the cow to the king. On his refusing to part with it, a party of soldiers was despatched to the hermitage and they took the cow by force. Thereupon a severe struggle ensued between Jamadagni and the king's men, in which the Rishi was killed. Parasu Rama was absent from the hermitage at the time. On his return he had the mortification of seeing his father's body mutilated and lifeless and his mother and brothers weeping. When the mother saw Parasu Rama, she beat her breast with her hand twenty-one times. Bhrigu divining the state of affairs in his relatives' family, immediately repaired to the scene and on carefully examining the body of Jamadagni, he found that life was not extinct and by the aid of certain medicines Jamadagni was restored to life. Parasu Rama afterwards proceeded to Karthaveerarjuna's capital, and standing at the Palace gate, with his Parasu, bow and arrow, sent a message to the effect that the king should give an explanation of his cruel conduct in ill-using a Brahman and forcibly taking away his property. At the same time he asked him to restore the cow and seek the pardon of the venerable Brahman for the outrage he had committed and in case of his refusing to do so to meet Parasu Rama in single combat.

The king, when he heard of this proposal, sneered at such a ridiculous menace and ordered his guards to drive away the Brahman. The guards were, however, killed by Parasu Rama, whereat the king grew angry and equipped himself to meet Parasu Rama. A severe

CHAP. I. and sanguinary battle ensued and Arjuna was defeated and slain.

Afterwards, five of Arjuna's sons, who survived him met Rama in battle. When they were about to fall victims to Rama's Parasu, they, under divine inspiration, put down their weapons and besought Parasu Rama's pardon, promising to give up the cow and make full reparation for the wrongs done by their father.

Parasu Rama after restoring the cow to his parents, retired to the Himalayas and resumed his penitential exercises. In his absence, the then reigning king, one of the sons of the late king Karthaveera of Hehaya, happened to pass by the Nurbuda, and casting his eyes on the hermitage of Jamadagni, enquired whose property it was, and he was told that it belonged to Jamadagni. On hearing the name, the king entered the hermitage sword in hand and meeting Jamadagni severed his head from his body at one blow, and on the funeral pile of Jamadagni perished Renuka, Parasu Rama's mother.

Some time afterwards, Parasu Rama returned from the Himalayas and learning the fate of his parents set out for the country of the Hehayas, and in order to fulfil his vow, proceeded with his bloody axe to continue the work of destroying the Kshatria kings. After going one round and finishing his work of destruction, he retired to do penance again. He repeated these deeds twenty-one times.

It is also said that on the last occasion he collected all the Kshatria kings at a place called Kurukshetram and having beheaded the whole of them he performed certain ceremonies with their blood for the salvation of the souls of his parents!

After this, Parasu Rama retired to the Mahendra Mountains, and performed penance for some time. He then went round the earth three times and returned to the hill of Mahendra, where he performed the Aswamedha sacrifice and many other religious ceremonies.

While at Mahendra, Kasyapa and other Rishies visited him and he consulted them as to the best means of expiation for the sin of killing his own mother and the Kshatria race. Acting upon their advice, he gave up the whole of the conquered lands to the Brahmans. Parasu Rama then continued his religious penance in a grotto of the Mahendra hills, and there passed many ages.

During the interval, certain peculiar circumstances occurred which caused a sudden rise of the ocean, and the sacred shrine of Gokurnam, together with several other remarkable shrines on this coast were submerged in the ocean, as has been already mentioned. The Rishies interested in these sacred places repaired to Parasu Rama and besought his help in recovering the sacred buildings. Rama came to Gokurnam, and after making arrangements with Varuna, flung his wooden sacrificial spoon, thus causing the sea to recede from Gokurnam up to Cape Comorin.

Parasu Rama then invited the Brahmans, who having received grants of lands were located in sixty-four gramams. He invited other castes also from foreign countries to occupy his new land, restored the sovereignty of the original Chera, and after living on the coast for a long time, retired to his grotto on the Mahendra hills, where he is supposed to be still living.

The time occupied in the establishment of Keralam as well as the exact period of Parasu Rama's abode in this land are not exactly ascertainable from any accounts in the Purana. The period mentioned in the Kerala Ulppathy is fifty thousand years.

The labors of Parasu Rama, in re-establishing Keralam and peopling the country between Cape Comorin and Gokurnam, and his other occupations are described in detail in a work called Kerala Mahatmyam.

This work, which consists of one hundred and five Chapters, is an interesting one, but the narratives recorded are like those in the Puranas, intermingled with exaggerations and romances, so that it requires

CHAP. I.

no small amount of discriminative power to strip it of its poetical embellishments.

This work corroborates the above facts. In it we find it stated that Parasu Rama, after founding Keralam, invited Brahmans from the north to settle in the country which he divided into sixty-four gramams; that he ordained several grades of Brahmanical heads; consecrated numerous shrines between Gokurnam and Cape Comorin; and that the superintendence of each pagoda was entrusted to a Samuntha (Soma Kshatria called "Kovil Adhikarikal," *i. e.*, manager of pagoda). After finishing almost all his works, and consecrating the Temple at Sreevardhanapuram (Padmanabhapuram), Parasu Rama invited a Soma Kshatria (certainly a member of the family of the king of Chera since there were no other Soma Kshatria kings then close at hand) named Bhanu Vicrama and three of his brothers, the last being named Kulasekharen, and assembling the Brahmans of the sixty-four gramams, declared to them that the capital of his newly reclaimed country, between Cape Comorin and Gokurnam, shall be Sreevurdhanapuram (Padmanabhapuram) near Sreevalumcode (Thiroovithancode and Veera Keralapuram); that Bhanu Vicrama shall be the king over his land of Keralam, and that he was then placed on a throne of gold set with gems and had holy water and pearls poured over his head. Parasu Rama then giving him his own sword, together with many royal privileges, styled him king of the land between Cape Comorin and Gokurnam. A gold coin, called Rasi, was then minted and made over to the king for circulation as the currency throughout his dominions. One of the three brothers of this king was stationed at Gokurnam. This was the king of Kolathnaud who ruled South Canara under the designation of Cola. It is also stated that a long time afterwards, Parasu Rama personally crowned Bhanu Vicrama's nephew, Adithya Vicrama, at Sree Vurdhanapuram, presenting him with a sword as bright as the sun, and nominating eight ministers under him.

INSTALLATION OF BHANU VICRAMA AS KING OF KERALA.

It is likewise stated that latterly, Parasu Rama took a great interest in Udaya Vurmah, the head of the Cola Royal family, who was called the Northern Perumal, and made him the king of North Kerala, that a relative of Udaya Vurmah, who was in charge of a separate portion of the Cola country, became a Bhuddist, and built several temples and lived apart from the Royal family; that the Bhuddist king proceeded to Mecca and died there; that his funeral rites having been accidentally performed by one of the females of his house the Brahmans excommunicated the whole family with which King Udaya Vurmah was connected, whereupon Parasu Rama, consulting the great sage Narada, instructed Udaya Vurmah to perform the great ceremony called Hirannya Garbham, by constructing a golden cow and a silver bull, each weighing hundred thousand fanams (about ninety lbs.), to perform certain ceremonies, and to distribute gold and silver among the Brahmans; that Parasu Rama instituted a national ceremony called Mahamakham[1] and performed it with great splendour at Thirunawaye on the banks of the Bharathapulay (a river running to the south-west of Shoranore): that when the Brahmans of the sixty-four gramams and the chiefs and petty rajahs of the country between Cape Comorin and Gokurnam were assembled at that place, the first seat in the assembly was assigned to Kulasekhara Perumal, king of Travancore, and the next to Udaya Vurmah of Kolathnaud, to the latter being assigned the duty of the future performance of this ceremony every twelfth year. We find also that the art of war was introduced by Parasu Rama and that the kings were taught the use of various weapons; that Parasu Rama then retired from Keralam, promising the Brahmans that on an emergency, he would appear at Trichoor, should the Brahmans of the sixty-four gramams meet together, and meditate on him; that the Brahmans wanted to make a trial and Parasu Rama

1. Madras Journal of Science and Literature, No. 30, page 124.

4

CHAP. I. appeared, but having learnt that there was no particular occasion for his being summoned, pronounced an imprecation on the Brahmans of the sixty-four gramams saying that they would never in future be able to meet there together.

This Mahatmyam is said to be an Upa Purana, deriving its origin from Bhoogola Purana, and is in the form of a discourse between Yudhishtira and the sage Gurgga.

In "Valmiki Ramayana" we find that the emissaries of Rama were ordered to search for Seetha in Keralam also. We have now got through the second age, Thretha Yugam.

In the third age, Dwapara Yugam, the king of Kerala is often mentioned in the renowned work "Maha Bharata." The king of Kerala was as already mentioned one of the tributaries of the Emperor Yudhishtira, and during the great war, the Kerala king fought on the side of the Pandavas and died in the war. It is also said that the Pandavas, during their secret wanderings, visited Trevandrum and made several vows to the Deity Padmanabha Swamy.

During his pilgrimage, Arjuna visited Madura, where he married the daughter of the Pandyan king, and by her he had a son named Bebhruvahanen. On his way to Dwaraka, Arjuna visited Cape Comorin and Trevandrum and is generally believed to have consecrated a temple dedicated to the Goddess Durga on the banks of a tank, which is still called Phalgunan Kulam (Arjuna's Tank). He is said to have visited several places in Keralam before he returned to his capital.*

In a certain Tamil poem, the author says that Bela Rama, Sree Krishna's brother, visited the Chera kingdom, and attended the coronation of the then king, crowning him with his own hand.

* W. Taylor's Historical Manuscript Translation, vol. I, p. 226.

Now we enter into the present age (Kali Yugam). In the early part of this age Bharatha Khandam (India) was under the rule of the Emperor Yudhishtira, and the king of Kerala, as heretofore, was tributary to him. After the close of Yudhishtira's reign, which is said to have ended in the 36th year of Kali, the subordinate relation to the succeeding emperors continued as a matter of course. CHAP. I.

Up to the tenth century of the Kali Yugam, 48 kings reigned over the Chera kingdom. A list of their names has been preserved by one Kodumudi Ramalingam Kavirayer (Poet), now residing in the Erode Talook, most likely belonging to an ancient family of poets formerly attached to the Chera king's court.

This list shows that these kings reigned 905 years in the Kali Yugam. The 8th, 17th, 26th and 48th names in the list being unintelligible, are omitted, and the rest are the following :—

1, Yadukula Cheren; 2, Vamsothunga Cheren; 3, Manumurainatatha Cheren; 4, Veeraprathapa Cheren; 5, Vikramaheswara Cheren; 6, Ripukulaksheya Cheren; 7, Samasardoola Cheren; 8—9, Pulikotiparitha Cheren; 10, Ellaikarakanda Cheren; 11, Rajagambheera Cheren; 12, Rajamarthanda Cheren; 13, Raja Rajeswara Cheren; 14, Rajaprathapa Cheren; 15, Munril Maniyitta Cheren; 16, Mummurthi Cheren; 17— 18, Ananthaguna Cheren; 19, Vamsa Paripala Cheren; 20, Mangalakara Cheren; 21, Dhana Vishthara Cheren; 22, Varagunotpala Cheren; 23, Asramanilayitta Cheren; 24, Anubhuthi Cheren; 25, Ava Cheren; 26— 27, Sivapada Sikhara Cheren; 28, Tiruneetu Cheren; 29, Eludisa Cheren; 30, Maiporul; 31, Banarku Nidhi Thantha Cheren; 32, Bhaskara Bhanu Cheren; 33, Aksheya Pathra Cheren; 34, Siva Dharmottama Raja Cheren; 35, Sivanesa Cheren; 36, Sivotpala Cheren; 37, Daivakunjara Cheren; 38, Sindhuvarunya Cheren; 39, Thrikedara Cheren; 40, Thridesaranga Cheren; 41, Athulaprathapa Cheren; 42, Aganithakeerthiprathapa Cheren; 43,

CHAP. I. Veera Rajendra Cheren; 44, Bheemeswara Cheren; 45, Nirmala Cheren; 46, Panchakshara Cheren; 47, Kantabharana Cheren; 48.

The above sound more like regal titles than the real names of kings.

In the 28th Prabhava year *i.e.*, 1860 of the Kali Yugam there was born at Thiruvanjicolam, in the month of Masi, Thursday, Punar Poosham Asterism, one of the most celebrated of the Chera kings, Kulasekhara Perumal, of the royal family of Chera. His father was Kshatria Dhrida Vrita, Maha Rajah. Kulasekhara was installed when he passed his minority and became Kulasekhara Perumal. He is also known by the titles of "Kolly Kavalan," "Chalpi Kon," and "Kukuda Puradheesen."

Kulasekhara Perumal unlike his predecessors evinced a very extraordinary attachment to his religion. After ruling the kingdom for some years he abdicated in favour of his heir, and became a Vaishnava devotee, and added Alwar to his name, a common epithet of Vishnu, as shown above. He was from that time known as Kulasekhara Alwar and Kulasekhara Thiru Adikel.

He set out on a pilgrimage to all the renowned Vishnu shrines, especially Thripathi and Sreerangam, where he commenced preaching the Vaishava religion. He was known as a great Vaishava devotee and had numerous followers. He was also a poet and composed numerous hymns in praise of Vishnu at various Vishnu Temples, especially at Thripathi, Sreerangam, Thirumala, Alwar Kovil, Ayodhya, Thiruvithoocode, Van Purushothaman, Thrikkannapuram, Thillai and Thrichithrakoodam.

Kulasekhara Perumal Alwar lived to the age of 57, and was deified at his residence in the Brahmadesam Talook of the Tinnevelly district. His body was interred inside the Mannar Kovil Pagoda and the Vishnuites consider him to be a saint. His image is cut in granite and is placed in the Pagoda close to the

KULASEKHARA ALWAR.

Published by Messrs. Higginbotham & Co. G. Paczensky Lith. Madras.

image of Vishnu where poojas and other religious rites are performed along with those to the deity to the present day. His image has also been consecrated and placed for public worship in several other Vishnu Pagodas. This saint was highly respected by the kings of Pandya and Chola. Several inscriptions, containing the terms of grants allotted for poojas and other ceremonies to this saint, are to be found on the walls of the Mannar Kovil Temple. There are also copper sasanams in the possession of persons attached to that temple.

Though many of the works composed by Kulasekhara Alwar are now extinct, still there is a sacred hymn called Thiruvamoli in existence which is printed and published in Tamil and which the Vaishnavas reverence as Christians do the Holy Bible.

The correct name of the successor of this venerable sovereign as well as of many others of his line cannot be found but that the monarchy continued to rule its Chera possessions is a fact supported by traditions and several works.

In continuing our researches, we find that the rule of Vicramadithya is said to have ended in the three thousand one hundred and seventy-ninth year of the Kali Yugam. In the Bhavishyat Purana, the ninth in the list of Puranas, it was predicted in the eleventh chapter, that Vicramadithya will be born one thousand years after the commencement of the Kali Yugam, and will live to rule, by the divine blessing, for 2000 years; that Dheera Kerala Vurmah, king of Keralam, will be a contemporary of Vicramadithya and that that king will rule Keralam with great vigour and success.

Now from this prediction, we may conclude that Vicramadithya was born in the Kali year 1179, and that there were kings of Chera during that great monarch's reign.

It will be seen from the Revd. W. Taylor's manuscript translation already alluded to that some of the Pandyan kings who ruled Madura hundreds of years

CHAP. I. subsequent to the reign of Vicramadithya, Salivahana and Bhoja, had jurisdiction over the Chera and Chola kings and that "Veera Vurmah Pandyan inherited the Pandyan kingdom and reigned forty years. He conquered the Malayalam (or Sera) country and other places, and derived tribute from them." Thus we have now come down to above 4000 years in the Kali Yugam, in our narrative relating to the Chera dynasty, which, in a great measure, is buried in obscurity, both in regard to chronology as well as to its successive rulers, and in their attempts to throw light on what is obscure many writers have been baffled. Our endeavours, however, have not been totally abortive.

The policy of the Chera kings would appear to have been peace at any price and their policy and avocations were decidedly more of a commercial than of a warlike nature.

Though there were continual feuds between Chola and Chera, and occasional misunderstandings and quarrels with Pandya, Chera appears to have been of a peaceable disposition and during any great struggle, retired to his Kerala possessions, which always afforded him an asylum from its peculiar situation, it being a well known fact that south Kerala is the only province in India which has escaped foreign invasion.

It is seen that the Malayalam country afforded an asylum to the Pandyan king whenever his kingdom was invaded by his enemies. And it is perhaps in consequence of this, and their friendly relations, that Chera is confounded with Pandya by some persons, and the one taken for the other. These are the two kingdoms known to the earliest European travellers.

Ptolomey the author of *Periplus*, *Marco Polo*, *Strabo*, and other early writers, allude to these two kingdoms as existing in the Peninsula of India.

The Chera dynasty continued in power, though constantly engaged in warfare with its neighbours Pandya and Chola, till central Chera was overrun by the Konga Rajahs; the original dynasty of Chera then finally retired to its southern possessions, and joined the family residing in the south (Travancore). Many seem to suppose that Konga is identical with Chera, but in our opinion it is not. For these two dynasties, Konga and Chera, are separate families. The Kongas having invaded and ruled over a part of Chera, came to be considered as the kings of Chera itself; but several local and circumstantial facts prove the absurdity of this supposition.

The very word Konga will show that that dynasty had its origin in the north about Concan.

The names of the kings of the Konga dynasty greatly differ from those of the Chera. The names and titles of the kings of the former dynasty are so unlike those of the Cheras, that it is impossible to suppose that Malla Deva, Trivicrama Deva, Kumara Deva, Givuda Deva, &c., men with titles mostly of Canarese origin were kings of Chera.

It is also noteworthy that the name Kongani Vurmah is often applied to the Konga kings, and not even once to the Cheras. The word Kongani, we find, is used in naming the inhabitants of Concan; for instance, the whole community who emigrated from Canara to Malabar and settled at Cochin, Alleppy, &c., &c., is called Kongani.

All the great deeds, sasanams, as well as stone inscriptions of this early period given by Chera kings, begin with Sree Veera *Kerala* Chakravarthy, or Chera Marven Thribhuvana Chakravarthy, while all the Konga deeds of grants, &c., begin with Sree Veera *Raya* Chakravarthy.

The word Raya, which appears along with the names of all Konga kings and which does not even in a single instance appear with the names of either the Kerala or Chera kings, is an additional proof of the former being Canarese. The word also often occurs in the names of the people of the north Canarese and Telugu countries. The king of Chera has for his title

CHAP. I.

Kulasekhara Perumal, which is a title borne by the Mandala kings as already said, but such an appellation could scarcely be found in other countries or in that part of the Chera country which was assumed by the Konga Rajakal.

It is also to be observed that in the southern part of Chera, no Konga inscriptions are to be found in any of the temples or other places, while there are many inscriptions connected with the Chera grants. That Chera and Konga are not one, has been maintained by the Revd. Mr. Taylor in his addendum to the translation of the Konga Desa Rajakal.*

This conclusion is supported by the statement of Cumper, a Tamil Poet, attached to the court of Chola, who flourished in the 7th century and who is the author of the popular Tamil work called Cumper Ramayana. This Poet defines the boundaries of the Chera and Konga possessions separately in his poem, and states that Chera is the kingdom which lies between Pulney, Thencasi, Calicut, and the sea extending over an area of eight hundred miles, while Konga, he points out to be a smaller one, extending to 120 miles and situated within the limits of Thalamalah, Vygavoor, Vallikunnu and Kulithalay.

These two dynasties had their separate capitals; Chera having Salem, Thiruavanasi, Chera Maha Devi, Valliyoor Kalacaud, &c., in the south Sreevalumcode (Travancore) and Thiruvananthapuram (Trevandrum) Kolicode (Calicut) &c., in the west. The Konga had Scandapuram or Talicaud or Dalavapuram for its capitals. The Revd. W. Taylor observes in his criticism of Mr. Dowson, "that the boundaries given "by Professor Wilson and quoted from Dowson (Des. "Cata. Int., p. 62) may be allowed to pass as a general "approximation, only supposing that Chera and Konganaud, have been at some period one. It begs "however the question, because it proceeds on the

* Madras Journal of Literature and Science, Vol. 7.

" assumption, in the catalogue, that the Konga Desa " Rajakal is a history of the Chera Rajahs; which "I submit it is not; but only of a few rulers of " Konganaud before the latter was conquered by " the Chola kings. I cannot submit to Dr. Francis " Buchanan's authority, unless I were assured that he " too has not confounded Konganaud and Chera Desa " together." CHAP. I.

A further proof is the caste of the two dynasties. The Konga Rajahs belong to the Reddy caste, while the Chera kings are Kshatrias; a fact to be borne in mind, as we shall have to speak of it hereafter.

Konga, we see, was conquered by the Cholas, Oissallas, Hari Hara Raya dynasty and Veeranarasinga Raya dynasty. And in the thirteenth and fourteenth centuries A.D., we find that the Konga kings Narasinga II., (1237—1278) and Hari Hara Raya, (1367—1391) exacted tribute from the Chera or Kerala kings. This proves that the Chera dynasty had not become extinct, but that it existed in its southern possessions of Kerala (Travancore) in the 13th and 14th centuries, and retained the name Chera. The list of sovereigns in the Travancore calendar also bears testimony to this fact.

The remnant of the Chera kingdom appears to be then extended to the Mysore Frontier on the north, the District of Salem on the east, the Travancore coast up to Calicut on the north-west, as described by Mr. Dowson in his account of Chera. This was the latter kingdom of Chera called Travancore, in our opinion.

It must have been at this period that the old Chera was finally incorporated with Travancore and its original name Chera forgotten.

Now Chera is generally recognized as Kerala or Travancore. Many eminent, ancient and modern authors indiscriminately use the one for the other. In his manuscript translation Mr. Taylor often writes

CHAP. I. Chera for Travancore* and vice versa. In the collections from the Asiatic Journals, page 484, the same use of the term is made. Other facts can be adduced in favor of this view.

Almost all the southern possessions of Chera were included in the Travancore dominions till their conquest by the Madura rulers, and from them by the Carnatic Nabob. Several pagodas in Erode, Coimbatore and Tinnevelly which were once in the kingdom of Chera have still inscriptions on their granite walls commemorating the names of Chera, and Travancore kings; and besides, there is still a village called "Chera Maha Devi" in the Ambasamudram Talook of the Tinnevelly District, where we see, to the present day, the site on which the Chera king's palace once stood. In this locality, there are also villages built and presented to Brahmans by the Chera kings and in the possession of the descendants of the original recipients, deeds of grants are to be found.

In Chera Maha Devi, Thencasi, Kalacaud, Thrikanankudy, Valliyoor, &c., the Travancore Rajahs resided up to the seventeenth century, a fact clearly proved by documents and inscriptions.

Though there are numerous inscriptions of earlier dates in almost all the renowned pagodas between Coimbatore and Tinnevelly, we shall notice a few of the later ones, as our object is to prove the amalgamated state of Chera with Travancore, and its continuance in that condition :—

1. An inscription on the inner stone-wall of the Chera Maha Devi Pagoda, dated Malayalam or Kollum year 614 (1439 A.D.) commemorating a grant by the Travancore King Chera Oodiah Marthanda Vurmah to the pagoda at that place while the grantee was residing in the Chera Maha Devi palace.

* Pandya Desam is the Madura country; Sera Desam the Travancore and Malayalam country.

Taylor's Manuscripts Translation, Vol. I., page 51.

"2. $\frac{644 \text{ M.E.}}{1469 \text{ A.D.}}$ On the large bell at Thrikanankudy, denoting that the bell was presented by the Travancore king Adithiya Vurmah. CHAP. I.

"3. $\frac{685 \text{ M.E.}}{1510 \text{ A.D.}}$ Commemorating a grant to the pagoda by king Marthanda Vurmah while residing in the Veera Pandyan Palace at Kalacaud.

"4. $\frac{688 \text{ M.E.}}{1513 \text{ A.D.}}$ Commemorating a grant of land to the pagoda at Mannarkovil by the same king Marthanda Vurmah, and also making provisions for lighting a lamp in the palace where the king's uncle died.*

"5. $\frac{707 \text{ M.E.}}{1532 \text{ A.D.}}$ Commemorating a grant of land to the pagoda of Chera Chola Pandyswaram in Thrikaloor near Alwar Tinnevelly, by Marthanda Vurmah, Rajah of Travancore."

We have already said that the king of Travancore is styled "Thiruadikel" (sacred feet) to denote his sanctity, and his kingdom "Vanavanaud" (abode of Devas) which was corrupted into Venaud, a term now commonly used for Travancore. The antiquity of this appellation "Thiruadi" is seen from a copper plate in the possession of a Brahman in the village of Chera Maha Devi, one of the old capitals of the Chera king. The history of this plate runs thus: It would seem that a Telugu Brahman, commonly known by the name of Kunnadia, received a donation of a large number of gold coins from the Maha Rajah Prathapa Rudra of Veloor; that this Brahman, by the advice of the sage Agastyar, who resided on a hill in Thiruadi Desam (Travancore), built an anicut (still in existence) across the Thambraverni river, and opened an irrigation canal from that spot to the extent of about twenty-one miles; that with the surplus money he built a sathram at Chera Maha Devi for feeding a certain number of Brahmans daily; and that he

* It is customary in the royal family to keep a lamp continually burning for a long time in the room where the reigning king breathed his last.

appointed the holder of the copper plate as the perpetual manager of that institution.

A copy of the copper sasanum in question was procured by us. It purports to have been executed by Narayanappaya of the Kunnadian family of Bharadwaja Gothram (line) of Brahmans, professing the Rig Veda, and who received a donation called Kalapurusha Danum from Maha Rajah Gajapathi Prathapa Rudra Rayer, who reigned at Veloor; that he, the recipient, resolving to perform some charity with the money proceeded to Thrippathi, and on invoking Vencatachala Swamy, obtained that deity's blessing and in accordance with the commands of the swamy, he repaired to the southern kingdom called Thiruadi Desam (Travancore country) where on the Malayachala mountain, he met the sage Agastyar by whose order he excavated an irrigation canal for the benefit of the Brahmans: with the surplus money he resolved to institute a sathram for the daily feeding of Brahmans and accordingly constructed a building on the southern banks of the Thambraverni, and on the western side of Chera-Maha-Devi—Alakiyappen Swamy Kovil: Narayana Pillay, the son of Gopala Pillay, Brahman of Sreevatsa Gothram (line), professing the Yajur Veda, and residing in the old village or Brahman hamlet, built by Cheren Perumal Rajah, was entrusted with the management of this sathram, a perpetual grant being made to Narayana Pillay by this copper plate document, executed on Thursday, Shrawava asterism, Punchami Aushada month, Sowmmya Nama year of Kali 3342, (242 A.D.) for the maintenance of the sathram of certain lands purchased for 2587 Kali Yuga Ramen* Madura vella fanams, together with nine slaves of the soil at the rate of one hundred and thirty five-fanams accompanied by a scale of the daily expenditure to be made and mentioning a fixed sum as remuneration to the Superintendent Narayana Pillay.

* One Kali Yuga Ramen fanam is still the currency of Travancore.

The antiquity of this plate may be proved by the wording of the inscription. A Brahman is not called now-a-days Pillay, whereas such a term was used in ancient times.

To this sathram, pepper was to be supplied from Travancore as that spice was a produce of that country and could not be obtained without the king's permission. It was given gratis, and in the year 970 M.E. (1795 A.D.), three years previous to his death, the old Rama Rajah ordered a commutation price of one hundred and eighty Kali fanams to be paid to the sathram, which sum is paid to the present time.

Thus we have traced the history of the Travancore dynasty in an unbroken line, from the earliest period, and brought it down through all the four Yugams.

Ignorant of the foregoing history, and dwelling exclusively on local and untrustworthy information, many seem to have labored under mistaken ideas and have been misleading the public as to the antiquity and origin of Travancore, its dynasty, its caste, and its position amongst the present Hindu rulers of Southern India.

In narrating the ancient history of this peculiarly remarkable kingdom, in chronological order, various particulars have been left out, and as such may be interesting to the reader, and may tend to dissipate many false impressions, we shall go back to the earliest period once more.

The general impression in regard to the dynasty of Travancore appears to be that it is the creation of Cheraman Perumal, and that the kingdom was his gift to one of his sons named Veera Keralen from whom the dynasty originated. But no authentic accounts can be found to support this view in any reliable work.

Kerala Ulppathy is the only work which gives any information regarding the kingdom of Keralam, but the greater portion of this work seems to have been derived from Kerala Mahatmyam.

CHAP. I.

Kerala Ulppathy was composed by Thunchathu Ramanujen, commonly known as Ramen Eluthashan, who flourished about the seventeenth century of the Christian Era. This work, like many other Malayalam productions of this renowned author, is a compilation from the Mahatmayam above alluded to.

The original compilation of the author must have had several interpolations and changes made in it, especially as there appear now-a-days copies of several Kerala Ulppathies written in different styles, and each differing from the other in its account of Kerala. In such interpolations, numerous discrepancies and glaring mistakes are visible, for we find the interpolators, in their anxiety to prove the correctness of their accounts, confusing occurrences of modern with those of ancient days. For instance, Cheraman Perumal, who lived and ruled in the fourth century A.D., as recorded even in the version of the Kerala Ulppathy itself, and corroborated by Cona Thoma, an eye witness, is said to have fought with Anagoondy Krishna Row of Beejnuggur. The Beejnuggur dynasty flourished, or rather came into power, only in the ninth century A.D., while Krishna Rayer ruled Southern India in the sixteenth century.

Besides, in this work, many events of Parasu Rama's period have been introduced as if they occurred in the Perumal period.

It is obvious that on such a work as the Kerala Ulppathy, little reliance can be placed. But, however, we will try to sift out the trustworthy portion of its contents, and chronicle briefly the origin of the Perumal period.

It would appear that after the retirement of Parasu Rama from Keralam, the Brahmans rose in power, shook off the yoke of the Kerala kings and commenced their own rule within the limits of their sixty-four gramams. In the first century B.C., the people of the sixty-four gramams convened a congress and after holding a consultation, resolved to establish four divisions of their gramams, called Kalakams which division they denominated—Parinchaloor, Payennoor, Parppoor and Chenganiyoor respectively. Thus, the Brahmanical possession within the gramams was ruled for a very long time. But owing to dissension amongst them, anarchy and misrule prevailed, and the Brahmans again resolved to have a President called Rakshapumshen, appointed to each of these four Kalakams, for a term of three years. This form of rule continued for a considerably long period, and these Presidents who were also called Numpies (trustees), were paid at the rate of one-sixth of the produce of the land. But considering that they had each only three years tenure of office they availed themselves of their position to amass wealth for themselves and thus brought on ruinous results. The Brahman community finally resolved to introduce a system of elective Government and to appoint a ruler for a term of twelve years, but disputes having arisen at the election, they at last determined to apply to the king Cheren or Keralen and so proceeded to Ceyapuram (Coimbatore) and brought from thence a Viceroy called Ceya Perumal to Keralam.

The name of this Perumal, the Kerala Ulppathy says, was "*Cheraman Keralen*" a Kshatria, and he was the king of Malanaud (Malayalam). The date of his installation is said in the work, according to a certain astronomical mode of calculation, to have been in the Kali year 3316 (216 A.D.) It further observes that in all twenty-five Perumals ruled over Keralam. The last Perumal finished his rule as stated in this work, in Kali year 3528 (428 A.D.) and so the Perumal period we may consider to have been two hundred and twelve years.

Even in the Kerala Ulppathy, it is not said that the Travancore dynasty was descended from the Perumal or that the kingdom of Travancore was a gift from Cheraman to the present dynasty, neither does it say that the king of Travancore was a Sudra. We

CHAP. I. wonder therefore how, and upon what authority, the authors of the "Land of the Perumals" and the "Land of Charity" and other learned writers state that the Rajah of Travancore is a Sudra. If these authors will but search the Sanscrit works, wherein an account of Kerala or even of any other kingdoms in Southern India is given, they will be obliged to acknowledge that they are in the wrong as no mention is made therein as regards the caste of the Travancore sovereigns except that they are Soma Vamsa Kshatrias.

In the Kerala Ulppathy itself will be found, on careful examination, that the Travancore and Kolathnaud dynasties were in existence at the close of Cheraman's rule, and that Cheraman had simply recognized those dynasties but did not make a grant of the kingdom to them.

In the days of Parasu Rama and during the sway of the Travancore Kulasekhara Perumals as Emperors of Keralam, several local chieftains appear to have been nominated, partly by Parasu Rama himself, and partly by the Kerala emperor to assist him in the administration. So these chieftains were all holding their various possessions at the beginning of the Perumal viceroyalty.

The very fact of the Brahmans asking for a Viceroy from the king of Chera and that monarch appointing a Perumal (a member of his own family) as Viceroy, proves that the king of Chera was the legitimate owner of Keralam.

Kerala Ulppathy mentions the names of Pandya and Chola Perumals at intervals acting as Viceroys during the Viceregal period of two hundred and odd years. This may be correct, as there had been often wars between Chera, Chola and Pandya, and these three kingdoms have been ruled alternately by those powers, and hence perhaps the cause of the appointment of Viceroys from those kingdoms. Though there have been such changes of rule in the Chera country, the title of the Viceroys in Keralam was unchanged all along, as will be seen from the fact that the first and last Perumals retained the title of "Cheraman Perumals" they being members of the Chera royal family, for, as said above, the Kerala Ulppathy states that the first Perumal was from Ceyapuram (Coimbatore), and his name was "Cheraman Keralan" and that he was a Kshatria. The name of the last Cheraman Perumal was Bhaskara Revi Vurmah also a Kshatria by caste. Revi Vurmah and Kerala Vurmah are names borne generally by the members of the Travancore royal family. In the Cochin Rajah's family, which is believed to be descended from the last Perumal, such names are also commonly found.

Neither the Kerala Ulppathy nor any other work shows that the Travancore sovereign had ever been subject to the rule of the Perumals. On the other hand, the Perumals considered the sovereigns of Travancore as their superior authority.

Local and traditional information appears to have misled a good Sanscrit scholar, Pachu Moothathu, alluded to in the Preface; he has fallen into an error, as it would seem from his small pamphlet in the Malayalam language published by him in the Malayalam year 1043, wherein he says that the kingdom of Travancore was established under the auspices of Cheraman Perumal, that it was given as a gift to his son Veera Kerala Vurmah by his third wife in the Kali year 3412 (311 A.D.), and that since then the kingdom flourished. If he had only taken the trouble he would have found that Cheraman Perumal was installed in his vice-regal office not before the Kali year 3445, as has been shown. We do not know upon what authority our author has arrived at such an extraordinary conclusion. We have already shown that the kingdom of Travancore was in existence on the advent of the Perumals. The author appears to be laboring under a mistaken idea when he asserts that Cheraman Perumal is an individual title and that he was a king. He seems to have been ignorant of the

CHAP. I. fact that Cheraman Perumal is the name of the Viceroy sent out to Keralam by the king of Chera to govern his Kerala Province. The only inference one can draw from the author's erroneous statement is that he, like many other Sanscrit and Tamil authors of Southern India and especially of Keralam, derived his data, in composing his work, from local and hearsay information, embellishing it with ideas and statements supplied by his own imagination, a practice common among Sanscrit authors.

In Keralam, Cheraman Perumal was reckoned as the greatest and the most powerful emperor in the realm. He was a pure Kshatria of the solar race and to connect a royal family with such a personage was thought to be the highest honor in Keralam as was the case with the Cochin royal family. Consequently, under such an impression, our author must have composed his work. The Sanscrit scholars in Keralam generally begin their education from their earliest years. After mastering a little Grammar, they are taught the Kavyems, *i. e.*, poetical compositions founded upon the Puranas. In this study, they are made to pay attention to Grammar and none at all to facts. From Kavyem, the scholar turns to the study of the Natakum, Dramatical works, and afterwards to the Alumkaram and Tharkam, Logic and Rhetoric. When these studies are over, the scholar considers that he has completed his Sanscrit education and is perfect in all knowledge. He then begins to compose Shlokams (stanzas), not on facts, but simply upon fiction, as his ideas suggest to him. Acquiring at the same time a Puranic knowledge, he tries to become an author, and begins to write basing all his conclusions on his own fancies, while he is utterly ignorant of Geography or History. He draws profusely on the Puranic accounts of animals speaking, horses drawing chariots in the air, or going on wings in the firmament, and so forth. He is unable to speak as to historic facts which every man of intelligence ought to know, neither can he say how far the land he lives in, extends, and what nations inhabit the various countries of the world. But he is able to tell in a minute the names of the fifty-six kingdoms in the Bharatha Khandam. He would also repeat the names of the kings who ruled those kingdoms in the past three Yugams (ages), and the commencement of the present Kali Yugam so far as the Puranas describe them and beyond that he can go no further. He knows nothing of modern history and the existence of the European kingdoms and their kings, since the Puranas do not treat of them, neither does he know much of his own land nor any modern accounts concerning it. He is ignorant of the early visits of foreigners to India such as the Phœnicians, Egyptians, Greeks and Romans. He is in the dark as to who Alexander the Great was, when he lived, what were his achievements, and when he visited India; neither is he aware of the rule in India, of the Nunda, Mourya, Chalookya, Kalabhoorya, Chola, Chera, Pandya, Kadamba, Belala Raya and other dynasties, the Mohamedan conquest and rule, and lastly, the extraordinary enterprise of a handful of English merchants and their wonderful military exploits, by which they finally became the masters of this vast empire. To obtain such information and knowledge, English education is the easiest road, and a Sanscrit scholar of the present day, without any knowledge of English cannot, shine as an author of a useful work and procure the approbation of the public by a work like that composed by Pachu Moothathu.

Though we have clearly shown the origin of the Travancore dynasty citing unquestionable authorities, yet for the satisfaction of Pachu Moothathu, as well as of A. Sashiah Sastri, C.S.I., the late Dewan of Travancore, who, confiding in the statements of Pachu Moothathu sanctioned the publication of erroneous accounts in the English calendar of Travancore for the year 1877, we shall give further evidence and proof to show that the Travancore king was in existence and in power on the advent of the Perumals.

CHAP. I.

The ancient copper plates in the possession of the Syrian Christians of Cottayam and the Jews of Cochin (copies of which with reliable translations have been published in the Madras Literary and Asiatic Journals of Science and Literature, No. 30, pages 116 to 164) contain grants which were made by three of the Cheraman Perumals, including the last Perumal Bhaskara Revi Vurmah. They shew that the Perumals considered the king of Travancore the first sovereign in Keralam, so much so that the three Perumals, viz., Sree Veera Raghava Perumal, Sthanu Revi Guptha Perumal, and Sree Bhaskara Revi Vurmah Perumal (the last of these is the one commonly called the Cheraman Perumal), whose names the copper plates bear, invariably bring the name of the king of Travancore as the first power to witness their deeds; nay, one of them Sthanu Revi Guptha says that "that document, was executed with the sanction of the Travancore sovereign," and in making allusion to the king, uses the honorific term "Vanaud Iyean Adikel Tiruadikel." The prefix "Iyean" denotes the superior authority of the king.[1] In these ancient copper plates the names of all the subordinate chiefs are introduced with the exception of those of the Cochin Rajah and the Zamorin, who were therefore not then chiefs at all, *i. e.*, at the time when the documents were executed by the Perumals.

As the Cochin Rajah was the creature of the Perumal and is said to have been his heir[2] as authoritatively acknowledged, that Rajah could not have been in power at the time, a fact which the Jewish plate fully corroborates. The Eranadu mentioned in the document cannot be accepted as being the Zamorin of Calicut, if we are to place any reliance in the versions of the Kerala Ulppathy wherein it is distinctly said that

1. The Travancore king is still called Venad Adigal "the adorable feet of Venadu." Madras Journal of Literature and Science, No. 30, page 130.

2. Cochin Administration Report for 1875, page 4.

the Zamorin was created by the last Perumal who granted him his own sword and two small pieces of ground called Colicode and Chullicaud and invested him with regal power (Kerala Ulppathy, pages 42 and 43.) CHAP. I.

There appears to have been a good deal of discussion as to the dates of these documents, as well as to the use of such words as Anjuwannam and Manigramam in these plates. I think it will not be out of place here to say a few words on these relics of an ancient period. We find on consulting a learned Astronomer of Travancore, that the date of the first document is Kali year 3331 (230 A.D.) This was found by an astronomical process, calculated from the data given in the first document, the working of which cost no small labor to the Astronomer. The period and date specified in the plate is 21st Meenam, Saturday, Rohini Asterism, Jupiter in Capricornus. This phenomenon occurs once in 12 years. From this current Kali year, the Astronomer calculated back to the first day of the Kali year, and from that day he calculated forwards and ascertained the year in which Jupiter was in Capricornus on the 21st of the month of Meenam, Saturday, Rohini Asterism, and by this process, he fixed the Kali year 3331 to be the date on which all the given conditions were found to exist. From this, it may be inferred that this document was executed by the successor of the first Perumal Cheraman Keralen,* for the date given in the Kerala Ulppathy of the installation of Ceya Perumal is Kali year 3316 (216 A.D.), so that this document was executed fourteen years after the commencement of the Perumal Viceroyalty.

The author finds that the calculation of the Astronomer agrees with that of Kookel Keloo Nair, the late Munsiff of Calicut, as published in the Madras Journal of Literature and Science, Vol. 5, No. 9, New Series.

* Kerala Ulppathy, page 10, Cottayam C. M. Press, Edit., 1868.

CHAP. I.

Plate No. I shows that Veera Kerala Chuckravarthy was the first of the line, and the rule of this dynasty existed without interruption for many hundred thousands of years. Now in the face of this valuable evidence can any other power in Keralam claim having originated the title of Veera Kerala than the Chera or Travancore dynasty. It would be ridiculous to say that the title Veera Kerala belonged to the Cochin dynasty, whose origin is shown by the Kerala Ulppathy and corroborated by the Copper Plate No. 3, as well as the Cochin Administration Report to have been from the Perumal period.

Our account of Manigramam and Anjuwannam varies materially from those of numerous other writers. We think that Manigramam is a distinction given to the Syrian Christians by the Perumals, as they were then regarded as a class of respectable people. Parasu Rama divided Keralam into sixty-four Brahman "gramams" each having a particular name, but to the new community of Syrians, the second Perumal must have granted a gramam, denominated Manigramam, with the title of a Principality* as a distinctive name, the head of the community being invested with the dignity of citizenship. Mani in Tamil means a gem and is applied to all things of peculiar excellence. We find from the copy of the plate in Tamil inserted in the abovementioned Journal the following:—"Makothayer Pattanathoo Eravicorttenaya Cheramaneloka Peroomchattikoo Manigramaypatam Kooduthome" the literal translation of which is:—"We have granted to Eravi Cortten of Makothaperpatnom, the grand merchant of Cheraman world, the high office of Manigramamship." "Pattum" is a word used both in Tamil and in Malayalam and, according to Bailey's Malayalam Dictionary, means "ordination" "a high office or dignity."

* Still I thought myself justified in calling Manigramam a Christian Principality. The Revd. Peet, Madras Journal of Literature and Science, No. 30, page 146.

The translation of this plate by the Rev. H. Gundert as given in page 118 of the Journal appears to be correct, but with a slight difference. Mr. Gundert's translation is :—" We have given to Eravi Cortten of Maha Deverpatnam (henceforward to be called grand merchant of the Cheraman world) the lordship of Manigramam."

The original settlements of the Syrian community appear to have been at Makothayerpatnam, near the port of Cranganore, and Curakkeni Kollum at Quilon. This community continue to this day to call themselves the residents of Curakkeni Kollum and Makothayerpatnam. This last name may be linked with that of the Chera king styled Makothayer, as we find it stated in the Tamil Peria Purana, a celebrated work very popular in the Tamil countries, that the Chera king named Makothayer lived at Thiru Vunjeecolum, near Kodungalore, and ruled the Malanaud (Malayalam country) with great success, for a considerable length of time. Hence we conclude that a town near Kodungalore, must have been established in honor of this king under the name of Makothayerpatnam and probably it was there that the Syrian community established themselves at first.*

In like manner, the author is of opinion that Anjuwarnam, alluded to in the plate in possession of the Cochin Jews, is a distinction given to the Jews. Warnam is not here intended for colour as the Jews understand it, but caste. There were already four Warnams, Brahmans, Kshatrias, Vysias, and Sudras. The Jews, when they came to Keralam, were considered as a peculiar nation, and the Brahmans and others

* "Curakkeni Kollum." Tradition states that the Syrians came to this country in two bodies, one party landed near the modern Quilon at a place now engulphed by the sea, the other at Kodungalore or Maha Deverpatnam. The practice in documents observed till within the last 80 years was invariably to mark to which of these two bodies a Syrian belonged." Madras Journal of Literature and Science, No. 30, page 146.

The Revd. Peet of Mavalikaray.

CHAP. I. seeing their strict observances of religious rites and knowing not how to designate them, styled them Anjuwarnam, that is, the fifth caste. This, the last Perumal had publicly recognized in his grant by the third copper plate, creating one of the community as the head of their village. Plate No. 2 supports the conclusion that Anjuwarnam is a title of the Jewish Principality.

In Keralam the carpenter, blacksmith, goldsmith and brazier castes are all collectively called Nanku Warnum, (four sorts of castes.)

The Lubbays (Mahomedans) of the South, prefix Anjuwarnam to their names in all their deeds and documents. This the author thinks is a continuance of the Jewish designation adopted by the Southern Mahomedans, who must have been converts from the Jewish faith after the establishment of Mahomedanism in South Keralam.

The plates are properly arranged in the Journal No. 30. The last document was executed in the Kali year 3481, and Dr. Day seems to be correct in his calculations in this respect.

Cheraman Perumal assumed his viceregal power, according to the Keral Ulppathy and other accounts, in the Kali year 3445 (345 A.D.), and the copper plate document referred to above was executed in the 36th year of his reign. The "Yadir" 2nd year, mentioned in the plate, is not a cycle as has been supposed by many, but we conclude it to be the second century of the Perumal period, for this agrees with the fact that the Perumal period commenced in 216 A.D.; 100 years afterwards ends the first century of the reign of the Perumals. The last Perumal having come to the viceroyalty in 345 A.D. naturally wrote the document or rather executed it in the second century of the Perumal period, and in the 36th year of his rule in the Kali year 3481.*

* "Land of Perumals," page 342.

By the peculiar mode of calculating dates on astronomical principles in India, errors are very seldom likely to occur. For in a work, or in a stanza, a particular sentence is laid down for discovering the date on which such work or stanza was produced, and the calculation is made entirely by an astronomical process, every letter being numbered agreeably to the rules of Astronomy.

Primary education throughout Keralam commences with a study of the elements of Astronomy, and till the youth is taught Kavyem, his time is exclusively devoted to astronomical problems, and he thus learns to calculate the exact time of the rising of the sun, moon and stars. Even during the grammatical and Kavyem studies he is continually taught calculations regarding the planets and soon acquires the knowledge of finding out the dates of eclipses. Under these circumstances, the astronomical calculation of the Natives is considered to be generally correct and seldom wrong.

Thus we have cited additional proof that the dynasty of Travancore existed before the Perumal period; that the southern-most part of Keralam now known as Travancore, was not a division made at the time in favour of the Travancore dynasty; and that the origin of Travancore cannot be dated from the Kali year 3412, as Pachu Moothathu and the compiler of the Travancore calendar would have us believe.

Another fact deducible from these documents is, that the statement in the Kerala Ulppathy regarding the division of Kerala by the last Perumal is without foundation and here we cannot do better than quote the opinion of the learned Malayalam scholar, Dr. Gundert, on this important point:—

" That whole part of the Kerala Ulppathy in which
" the present dynasties of Malayalam are represented
" as dating their origin from the last Perumal's distribu-
" tion of the country, is fully disproved by this and the
" Jewish document, and the relation of the Kerala

7

CHAP. I.

"Mahatmyam, according to which the several families "were placed here and there by Parasu Rama for the "purpose of protecting certain temples and Brahmin "villages, comes much nearer to the truth, if we "understand by Parasu Rama the old time of Brah-"manical rule."

Indeed the Kerala Ulppathy is the only work which gives any account regarding Keralam down to the modern period, the Kerala Mahatmyam treating exclusively of Parasu Rama's period. Of this period, we have no other accounts whatever. The Kerala Mahatmyam says that Parasu Rama appointed a Samunda, as manager, to almost every pagoda in Keralam. The families of these governors of the temples assumed power in course of time, and became petty chiefs under the supreme sovereign, the king of Travancore, whom Parasu Rama had invited and installed as already shown. The families of these Kshatrias are still called Kovil Adhikarikel or Kovil of whom the Cochin Rajah is one. This Rajah's caste name is Koviladhikarikal or Kovil,* and in issuing his writ he adopts that designation. All the Kshatria families of his caste who are now found in Keralam, divested of royalty, are called Thirupaud.†

While we have histories of the Pandya and Chola kingdoms, we have no separate history of Chera apart from Kerala, a fact which proves that Chera being embodied with Kerala, a history of the former is unnecessary, and consequently the Kerala Mahatmyam and Kerala Ulppathy give only the history of Kerala.

In the Kerala Mahatmyam, as well as in the Halassya Mahatmyam, Kshatrias are called Samanthas, and allusions to the king of Chera and Kerala are often made as Samanthas. The newly created Numboory Brahmans, who are mostly residents of the locality

* Kerala Palama, pages 78 and 114.

† The Schatriya or (Tirripaud, Mal.) or royal caste is that from which His Highness the Rajah of Cochin has sprung. "Land of Perumals," page 312.

between Quilon and Korempulay, within which limits lay the sixty-four gramams established by Parasu Rama, seemed to have had no free intercourse with the royal family of Travancore, whose capital was originally established at Kerala Puram which subsequently was called by Parasu Rama, Sree Vardahana Puram popularly known as Padmanabha Puram.

In the division of castes by Parasu Rama, he does not appear to have aimed at anything like completeness, as he left the sections of the minor castes alone. But in the subsequent modifications by the renowned Sankara Acharyar,* there was established a particular class of people known by the name of *Samanther*, a degraded section of the pure Kshatrias who are found residing here and there between Quilon and Kolathnaud. These are also called Pandala, Unniayathiri, Thirupaud, &c., &c., according to the locality in which they reside.

The name of *Samantha* is mistaken for *Samanther*, and the Travancore family was considered by the ignorant to be included in the latter class. The Puranas describe two classes of Kshatrias, as has been already shown, viz., Soorya, Samantha, and Soma Samantha: but in our opinion the former are now not to be found in Southern India, though the Cochin Rajah is generally called a Soorya Kshatria. Kerala Mahatmyam calls the Cochin Rajah a Soorya Samantha, but the present dynasty having been descended from Cheraman Perumal, who being a member of the Chera family is a Soma Samantha, cannot be considered a Soorya Samantha, as is generally believed, and it consequently follows that the present dynasty of Cochin cannot be the same as that mentioned in the Mahatmyam.

Cheraman Perumal being a member of the Chera dynasty which is the same as that of Travancore, the

* Sankara Acharyar was born in Kerala and his mother's family is still in existence at Paloor near Poravem. This mendicant devotee's residence is still preserved in the neighbourhood of Alwaye.

CHAP. I. caste of the Cochin Rajah must of course be the same as that of the Travancore royal family, as the original stock was both one and the same.

Almost all the caste rites and observances of the Travancore and Cochin royal families are similar with the exception of marriage. The former adhere to the original custom of marrying their females to a Kshatria, whereas the latter have adopted the system of marrying their females to Numboory Brahmans. Both of these modes are sanctioned by the Sastras.

There is scarcely any difference in the observances of the Shodasa Kriya (sixteen ceremonies to be performed from birth up to marriage) between the Brahmans and the Kshatrias. These ceremonies are duly performed by the Travancore and Cochin royal families. The male members of both families wear the Brahmanical emblem called Poonunool.

A Samanthren of the class alluded to, cannot wear the Poonunool. For instance, the Zamorin being a Samanther is not permitted to wear the Brahmanical thread. He cannot, by caste observances, even touch a Brahman or Kshatria without the taint of contamination. Whereas the royal families of Travancore and Cochin, being both Kshatrias, move among and associate freely with the highest class of Numboory Brahmans and both have as their menial servants Numboories and other Brahmans.

The names of the male members of the Travancore royal family and those of the Cochin house are similar, and there is the striking fact that the name of Veera Kerala Vurmah, the first king of Kerala, is adopted by the Cochin dynasty on its coming to power.

That Veera Kerala was the name of the first Emperor of Keralam, who was of the Chera dynasty, has been already proved by various authorities. A modern writer (Kookel Kelao Nair Munsiff) observes in his memorandum to the Madras Journal of Literature and Science, that "it is difficult to learn the clear history "of the family of Veera Kerala, but from various

VEERA KERALA VURMAH KALI YEAR 3412. (311 A.D.)

"Sanscrit and other works such as the Mahatmyam, "Ulppathy, and others, it appears pretty clearly, if we "reject obvious fables, that Parasu Rama, a Brahman, "eventually gained possession of the country from "Veera Kerala's descendants and after improving it "to a great extent, introduced therein his own caste "people to whom he ultimately committed its govern-"ment."

Dr. Gundert, a generally acknowledged authority, is of the same opinion that Kerala was the appellation belonging to Chera (Travancore). He says that "Cheraman is the name of the whole dynasty of Chera "or Kerala rulers, for these two names are the same. "Kerala being only the Canarese pronunciation as "appears from the Deccan inscriptions of W. Elliot, "Esq., in which no Chera is associated with Pandya "and Chola but only a Kerala."

The failure in discerning the difference between the two words *Samantha* and *Samanther* has created a confusion in the minds of the people of Kerala, as has been already shown. It is generally the case that people are easily led away and deceived by first impressions without taking the trouble to analyze facts and ascertain their accuracy. We often find that writers rely much upon local accounts and regard them as being a chronicle of indisputable facts. For instance, Fra. Bartolomeo, a well informed writer on South Indian affairs, who had been residing in Travancore for a period of 13 years, says, in his work that "before "Veera Marthanda undertook his expedition, he "celebrated at Tiroovanadapurum a horrid festival "which I have described in my Systerna Brahminacum; "he had caused several of the pagan temples to be "burnt, and this crime, one of the most heinous "according to the principles of the Indians, could "not otherwise be atoned for, than by a very peculiar "kind of purification. He was obliged by the Brah-"mins to get a cow made of gold, under which he was "forced to creep in order to be freed from his sins.

CHAP. I.

"Niebuhr and Anquetil du Perron are therefore in "great error when they assert that the object of this "ceremony was to raise the king to the degree of "nobility. Both these authors ought to have reflected "that this tale was invented by the conquered people (to "whom the king behaved with great severity), merely "for the purpose of ridiculing him. The above golden "cow was preserved in the year 1787 in the royal "treasury at Padmanabhapoorum. I was at least told "so by M'Donardi, a Captain in the King's service "who had seen it."

This account of the Hirannya Garbham ceremony is surely incorrect as will be seen further on.

The notion, that by the performance of the Hirannya Garbham, an individual or a family would be raised in rank and caste, is simply ridiculous. A Sudra or a Samanther could not be raised to the rank of a Kshatria by any such process. If such a wished-for change could be effected, every rich and influential Sudra would have been raised to the rank of a Kshatria, and some of the Kshatrias would have thought of transforming themselves into members of the twice-born class, Brahmans.

The Zamorin Rajah, who had become himself Nadivirippu and latterly very powerful, and the richest among the Malabar sovereigns, would have been the first to avail himself of this means of becoming a Kshatria. He was highly influential in his kingdom, where almost all the great Numboory Brahmans such as Aloovancherry, Narary, Poovooly, and Kanhgnoor and other priestly jemmies were residing, and besides, the Zamorin proclaimed himself as the head of the sovereigns in Keralam in order to superintend the great national ceremony held at Theroonawaye called Maha Makhum. It must, therefore, have been to the interest of the Brahmans themselves to raise him, if possible, to a higher caste particularly as the Zamorin had to mingle much with the Brahmans during that festival.

It is said that the pure Kshatria is he who is born of parents of the Kshatria caste. He who is born of a Kshatria mother but by a Brahman father is a Soma Samantha or Soma Kshatria so that though the race of the Travancore royal house was of the latter description (Soma Samantha), yet it maintains a higher degree of purity in its marriage relations than does the Cochin Rajah and, therefore, in the social scale, the Travancore royal family may be considered better Kshatrias than those in the north.

So the king of Travancore does not appear to stand in need of performing any ceremonies to raise him either in dignity, or in caste and rank. Hirannya Garbham and Padma Garbham are two great danams (donations) which the kings of Travancore are bound by their religion to perform as coronation ceremonies. King Veera Kerala Vurmah, who reigned in the Kali year 3412, performed both of the costly ceremonies called Thulapurusha danam and Hirannya Garbha danam, at his coronation.

Tradition shews that on the 12th Magarom 3412, of the Kali year, corresponding with the 24th January 311, A.D., king Veera Kerala Vurmah, after assembling all the Brahmans of the several gramams, both Chowara Koor and Panniara Koor, and the family priest Tharanallore Numboory Paud, performed these important ceremonies, and was crowned by that high priest according to the rules of the Sastras, and, in accordance with the canon laid down by Sree Parasu Rama, he assumed the family titles of Kireetapathi and Kulasekhara Perumal.

A brief and clear account of the two ceremonies, Thulapurusha danam and Hirannya Garbha danam, will be given further on as many erroneous notions are prevalent in regard to the character and real object of these two ceremonies.

Thulapurusha danam is a ceremony performed by weighing the body of the king against an equal weight

CHAP. I. in gold, and distributing the same, among Brahmans.* For this purpose the required quantity of gold is procured, and after purifying it, it is coined in different sizes and weights with the inscription "Sree Padmanabha," the appellation of Vishnu and the household deity of the Travancore king, on one side.

A pair of ornamental scales of sufficient size is next constructed, and on the appointed day, the sovereign proceeds to the temple of "Sree Padmanabha Swamy," attended by all the learned Brahmans, not only of Travancore, but also of other parts of Malabar, Tinnevelly, Madura, &c., some of whom are specially invited while the rest crowd to the capital for the occasion. After the assembled Brahmans have performed the ceremonies according to the Vedas, the sovereign is seated on one of the scales, and the coined gold is heaped on the other till it rests on the ground and the other scale is raised into the air with the king. After the performance of this ceremony, the gold coins are distributed among the Brahmans, males, females and children. There is a difference in the weight of the coins given; learned Brahmans and such others have a more valuable coin than ordinary Brahmans, while children and females have coins of less value. To determine who are the proper men to receive valuable gifts there is a regular examination of the Brahmans in their knowledge of the Vedas, and those who pass successfully reap a good harvest. This ceremony and the distribution of the gold coins last about a week, during which time the Brahmans are sumptuously fed.

"Hirannya† Garbham or Padma Garbha danam" is a costly ceremony like the other, but performed

* Sevajee's Coronation. "He now determined to satisfy his pride and dazzle his followers by a formal coronation, modelled upon that of the Mogul, in which the weighing against gold and other childish ceremonies were not omitted. Gifts to an immense value bestowed on the Brahmans, gave lustre to this as well as to several other political festivals." Murray's History of British India, page 258.

† Note.—In Sanscrit, Hyrannya is gold, and Gurbhum, belly or inside, and so the real meaning of these words is "Golden womb."

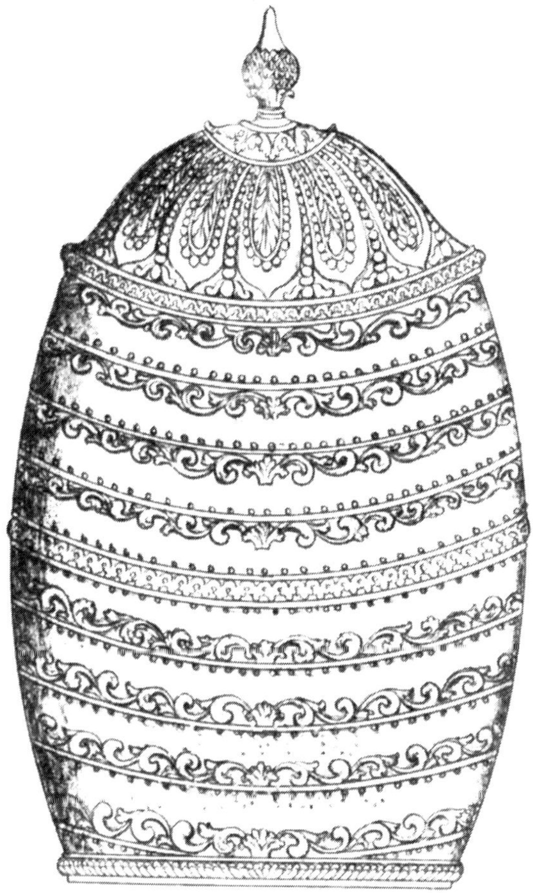

REPRESENTATION OF GOLDEN TUB FOR
PADMA GARBHAM CEREMONY.

PUBLISHED BY MESS^RS HIGGINBOTHAM & CO.   C. PAESENERY LITH: MADRAS.

by the greatest of Emperors only at their coronation. A vessel in the shape of a lotus flower, ten feet high and eight feet in circumference is made of pure gold, with a cover in the form of a crown, somewhat in the shape of a "Prize Cup," and this is half filled with punchagavyum, water mixed up with ghee, milk, and other substances; and the Brahmans perform their devotional prayers and hymns over the vessel according to the canon of the Vedas. The king, after performing his devotions, approaches the place where the vessel is kept, accompanied by all the high priests, Brahmans of note and learning in Malabar, Tinnevelly, Madura, Canara, &c., and gets into the golden vessel by means of a beautifully lined ladder, expressly made for the purpose. When His Highness enters it, the cover is put on and he dips himself into the holy water five times, while all the assembled priests and Brahmans continue praying and chanting Vedic hymns. This ceremony lasts about ten minutes, after which the king comes out of the vessel by the same ladder and after going through certain other ceremonies prostrates himself before the image of Sree Padmanabha Swamy, when the high priest, who is the chief celebrant of the ceremonies, and who acts the part of a bishop, takes the crown and placing it on the king's head pronounces the title "Kulasekhara Perumal." The place then resounds with Vedic recitations, prayers and hymns from the learned Brahmans. These ceremonies account for the Travancore kings being styled in Malayalam and Tamil "Ponnu Thumpooran" (Golden King). In giving an account of this ceremony, we cannot do better than quote in *extenso* a small pamphlet published in 1870, on this subject by "A Travancorean."

CHAP. I.

CHAP. I.

THE GREAT TULAPURUSHADANAM.

"His Highness Rama Vurmah, G.C.S.I., Maha-" rajah of Travancore, has performed the "great" Tulàpurushadánam," or, as it is more commonly" termed Tulabharam, a ceremony, which five of his" immediate predecessors have, without interruption," and several others before them, performed. Tulà-" purushadànam is a compound of three Sanskrit" words;—Tula (scales), Purusha (man), and dánam" (gift particularly of a religious character). The chief" part of the ceremony is the donation of a human" figure of equal weight with the donor. But on" account of the evident impracticability of construct-" ing a figure on the same day of weighing, a small" gold plate with the effigy of the donor raised in" relief on it, is given along with the whole quantity of" gold. It will be perceived that in the Sanskrit word" explained above there is no mention whatever of" the precious metal which forms the subject of dona-" tion. There is abundant proof that, in Malayálam" at any rate, Tulàbhàram is often performed with" other substances than gold. In several Pagodas" people perform it as a vow with sugar, molasses," sandal-wood, gingely-seed, pepper, plantain fruits," brinjals, &c. The Maharajah of Travancore of the" same name as the present ruler, who reigned forty" years, was a contemporary of George III, and was" Tippu Sultan's enemy, performed a golden Tulà-" bhàram in the beginning of his reign and a silver" Tulàbhàram by about the end of it. It may, how-" ever, be well conceived that, in the instance of a" sovereign Prince, and granting that the ceremony" takes place only once in his life as a matter of duty," the requirements of dignity and reputation among" a people proverbially fond of splendour and magni-" ficence, if not the strict prescription of religion, would

" render it necessary that the most precious substance " obtainable should be adopted. Religion itself pre- " scribes gold as the highest order of merit among the " various substances with which the Tulàbhàram " may be performed."

" The Tulàbhàram is not a ceremony peculiar either " to Travancore or the Malabar Coast generally. It " is one of the Shodasa (sixteen) Mahàdànams (great " donations) mentioned in Sanskrit works. A detailed " description of this great donation is said to be " given in the Pàdma Purànam, one of the eighteen " Purànas ascribed to Vyàsa. The sixteen Mahà- " dànams or great donations, as described in a " Sanskrit work, named Hemádri, are as follows :—

"	1	Tulàpurusha	Danàm.
"	2	Hiranyagarbha	do.
"	3	Brahmànda	do.
"	4	Kalpapàdapa	do.
"	5	Gosahasra	do.
"	6	Hiranyakàmadhenu	do.
"	7	Hiranyàsva	do.
"	8	Hiranyàsvaratha	do.
"	9	Hemahastiratha	do.
"	10	Panchalàngalaka	do.
"	11	Dharà	do.
"	12	Visvachakra	do.
"	13	Kalpalatá	do.
"	14	Saptasàgara	do.
"	15	Rathadhenu	do.
"	16	Mahàbhútaghata	do.

" The Tulàbhàram is, of course, one of the most " costly of these great donations and is, by its nature, " befitted only to Kings. That it was performed by " many Hindu Kings, not in the mythical but historical " ages, we have tangible proof. In the September " number of 1869 of the *Pandit*, a monthly Anglo- " Sanskrit periodical published at Benares, there is a " paper on a copper plate bearing old inscription, dug " up by a carpenter named Jagat when ploughing a " field in the village of Sivhàr near Benares. The

CHAP. I.

" copper plate purposes to be a grant of a village to a " Bràhman by Ràja Jaya Chandra Deva, king of " Kanouj in 1232, Samvat (1172 A.D.) The plate " is inscribed with a number of Sanskrit verses in the " way of preface to the actual grant—the verses tracing " the geneology of the royal donor and glorifying " each successive King. Among them is the follow-" ing verse:—

" 'Téirthàni Kàsikusikottarakosaledurasthàniyakà-
" niparipàlayatad'higamya,
" 'Hema Atmatulyam Anisam dadatà dvijebhyah,
" 'Yena Ankità Vasumatil Sàtasah tulàbhih.'
" 'It may be translated thus:

" 'The earth was marked with hundreds of scales by " him (name being given in a previous stanza) who, " going to Kàsi, Kusika, Uttarakosala and other " holy places, always distributed gold of his own " weight to Bràhmans.'

"As in all flights of oriental adulation, there is " exaggeration in the above; but exaggeration, though " it may magnify number and quantity, does not falsify " the mode of bounty. Hence we may safely assume " that the Tulàbhàram was performed by Hindoo Kings " in, or anterior to, the twelfth century. It is also well " known that the celebrated Mahratta Queen Ahalyá " Bhàyi performed the Tulàbhàram and other great " donations, and so also successive Peshwahs up to " Baji Rao. But what is really strange is that some " of the Mogul Emperors of the House of Baber " should adopt this purely Hindu mode of religious " gift. The "Calcutta Review," No. XCVIII, October " 1869, in an article headed 'The death of Jen-" hanger and the accession of Shahjahan' contains the " following passages: 'To-day Prince Khurram (Shah-" jahan) was weighed* * * *' (page 131). 'The " presents which Jotikrai received were enormous; he " was even once weighed in gold. * * *'

" It is believed that Cherumàn Perumàl, in dividing " his Malayàlam or Keralam Empire into four parts

" and assigning each to a separate chief gave a crown " to the Travancore king, and enjoined on him and " his successors the performance of Tulabharam and " the other great ceremony. Hiranyagarbham, as " preliminary to the wearing of the crown. Authentic " written records are extant which testify to their " performance by several of the ancient sovereigns " of Travancore. Since the reign of Raja Mârtánda-" varmá, who ascended the musnud in 1758-59, these " ceremonies have been performed in unbroken succes-" sion by every sovereign. In connection with the sub-" ject it may be worth mentioning that there is a " tradition that both the Zamorin and the Rajah of " Cochin have been unable to perform these cere-" monies as each of them could perform them only in a " pagoda situated in the heart of the other's territories, " which would always be jealously guarded against. " Trichùr is said, to be the Zamorin's Jerusalem, or " place to be won, and Taliparambu the Cochin Rajah's. " It is a fact known to history that the Zamorin " invaded the Cochin territories during the last " century, but whether he performed Tulàbharam at " Trichùr is not certain. That the Cochin Rajah has " a crown but does not wear it on his head is well " known. He carries it on his lap on the annual State " procession of Attachamayam in August."

" The two immediate predecessors (maternal uncles) " of the present Maharajah of Travancore performed " their Tulabharams in the years 1829 and 1850 res-" pectively. The first of them performed it in his " seventeenth year, and the second in his thirty-sixth " year. The present Maharajah has performed it in " the thirty-eighth year of his life and the tenth of his " reign. The Maharajah had long been desirous to " perform the ceremony as a preliminary to his coro-" nation, but the moral dissuasion which the outlay of " large sums of public money in ceremonies, the benefit " of which would not be admitted by any except " those who are within the pale of the most orthodox " Hinduism, must naturally meet both from the

"British authorities and from enlightened public "opinion, necessitated its postponement. The great "ease and buoyancy which the finances of Travancore "have, of late years, attained, and the unstinted allot- "ment of money to useful public works and other "purposes of public benefit, under the able adminis- "tration of Dewan Sir T. Madhava Rau, have served "to reduce the difficulty which must beset the perform- "ance of this costly religious ceremony. Moreover, "the British Resident, Mr. Ballard, with a broader "cast of mind than some of his predecessors, perceived "the propriety of letting the Maharajah act upon "the urgings of his religious solicitude to perform what, "from several generations past, has been considered "a matter of duty in his family, and what was looked "upon by far the great majority of his subjects as "calculated to promote the dignity and glory of their "sovereign to which they would gladly contribute. "Under this correct representation the Madras Go- "vernment had no objection; and in July last year, "the Maharajah issued formal orders for the per- "formance of the ceremony. The date first appointed "was the 7th of February, which was about a month "after the last day of the great Murajapam ceremony. "This arrangement, apart from the full cost of the "ceremony itself, would have entailed the great addi- "tional one of feeding *at least* ten thousand Bràhmans "twice a day during the interval of the two ceremonies "not to speak of the severe trials to which the sanita- "tion of the town would have been subjected during "the time. But these evils were obviated by a timely, "and masterly *coup* worthy of a Napoleon. About a "fortnight before the conclusion of the Murajapam "ceremony the date for the Tulàbhàram was suddenly "altered from the 7th February to the day following "the last one of the Murajapam. By this, almost the "whole expense of the seven days' preliminary feast "was saved, and also that of welcoming the great "Nampùri chiefs residing in Malabar and in the "Cochin State, who had come in for the Murajapam.

" If this saving of expenditure was in itself a very " gratifying achievement, doubly so was the saving of " trouble to the large body of *Viruttikárs* or service " land-holders. The Murajapam sheds were utilised " for the Tulábháram and in that too there was consi- " derable saving. Indeed, it may be said that the " expenditure was narrowed to the strictly religious " part of the ceremony and general distribution of " gold.

" Several months before the ceremony the Travan- " core Government, through its energetic Commercial " Agent, Mr. Hugh Crawford, purchased from Messrs. " Apcar and Co., of Calcutta, 7,808½ tolahs (about " 200¾ lbs. avoir. or 244 lbs. troy) of pure gold " at the rate of 15 Rupees 3 annas per Tolah or " 1,18,586 Rupees 13 annas 6 pie, for the whole. " Including the cost of freight, insurance, and duty " amounting to 3,011 Rupees 11 annas, 9 pice, the " total outlay was 1,21,598 Rupees 11 annas 3 pice " for the whole quantity or 15 Rupees 9 annas 2 pice " per tolah. This gold was received in sixteen rec- " tangular equiponderous (488 tolahs 2⅜ each) slabs or " ingots. Out of these, twelve slabs were taken for " coinage, the rest being reserved for use if required. " The work of the dies was commenced by about the " end of November. The device for the coin, on the " present occasion, underwent considerable changes " from that of these former Tuláb'háram—Illustra- " tions of both are appended to this narrative. From " these figures it will be seen that the coins of the " former Tuláb'haram consisted of circular pieces with " simply the letters "Srí Patmanábha" in Malayà- " lam, on the obverse, the reverse being a blank. " Whereas, those now coined contain those letters " encircled by a wreath on the obverse, and the conch " shell (the State device of Travancore) with a wreath " around it on the reverse. The wreath on the " reverse is a copy of that on the reverse of the old " Company's Rupee. Upon the whole, the new " Tuláb'háram coin is decidedly more handsome than

CHAP. I.

" the old. The gold, being of a superior quality, was " found sufficiently malleable to preclude the necessity " of melting; and so, chances of fraud were immensely " reduced. As shewn in the plate appended to this, the " coins are of four different sizes and weights.

" 1 Kalanju	=	78·65	grains,	approximately.
" ½ "	=	39·32	"	"
" ¼ "	=	19·66	"	"
" ⅛ "	=	9·83	"	"

" Of these, the work of the smaller pieces was first " undertaken, and as it proceeded in a leisurely man- " ner, the impressions have been sharp and complete. " But the change of date of the ceremony, which was " suddenly made, necessitated the hurrying over of the " coinage of the larger pieces; and consequently the " stamping turned out very imperfect. Subjoined is " the number of coins of each size struck:"

" Of 1 Kalanju pieces	...	3,564
" " ½ " "	...	7,904
" " ¼ " "	...	15,989
" " ⅛ " "	...	15,964
" Total	...	43,421

" They amount to 13,508¾ Kalanjus or about " 590,544 tolahs.

" The only preparation, besides the coining of gold, " which had to be made specially for the ceremony, " was the erection of the Tulámandepam, where the " scales were put up and the weighing and other rite " performed. The Mandapam was, as usual, built in " the south-east corner of the interior yard of the great " *Anantasayanam* pagoda. The Mandapam was a " strong shed, about 45×40 feet, thatched with " cocoanut leaves, and palisaded with split cocoanut " trunks, driven horizontally into vertical posts of the " same material. In the middle, a platform, about " 22×15 feet and a foot in height, was raised. It " was on this that the chief ceremony was performed."

" The religious preliminaries of the Tuláb'háram " extend over eight days—the weighing being on the " last day. To describe the several little religious " ceremones in detail would be neither intelligible nor " interesting to the general reader. However, they " may be very generally touched upon."

CHAP. I.

" First Day.—The Maharajah gets shaved, bathes, " dresses unbleached clothes, goes to the pagoda and " makes pecuniary and other offerings, then proceeds " to the Bhadradípamandapam, where he stays all the " while that the chief priest purifies and performs " púja to ten pratimas or golden plates with figures " in relief. These Pratimas represent Vishnu, Sïva, " Vinayaka, and the seven Mátrïs. Then twelve " Brahmins are specially fed and gifted with *Dak-* " *shinà*. The Maharajah then asks their permission " to perform the ceremony thus:—" Aham Tulá- " purushadánam kartum ic'hami"—They, in reply, say, " " Kriyatám," which means 'do so.' The Maharajah " then worships the pratimas and goes back to the " interior square of the pagoda. There the ceremony " of *Guruvarana* or the appointment of Rïtviks or " officiating priests is performed. Of these priests " they are 27. They are, one Acháryah, one Brah- " man, one Sadasyah, eight Rïtviks, eight Jápakas " (repeaters of Vedas) and eight Páthakas (readers of " Puránas). The Acháryah is the head priest and " occupies the place filled by the *Ad'hvaryuh* in " Yágam. Each of these twenty-seven is appointed " with all attendant religious ceremonies. After " *Guruvarana* the Maharajah returns to the Palace. " There are certain minor ceremonies that night, such " as the sowing of the nine grains" in silver flower " pots filled with earth and cowdung moistened with " milk."

" Second Day.—This day the high priest anoints " the Maharajah with sacred water. The water is " rendered red by boiling in it the barks of four " different trees of the ficus tribe. It is prepared on

CHAP. I.

"the previous evening, poured into a silver pot and "subjected to pújas and incantations."

"On the third, fourth, and fifth days, there are no "ceremonies excepting pújas to the pratimas already "mentioned."

"Sixth Day.—This day the high priest consecrates "the *Tulàmandapam* and propitiates with *Vàstu Bali*, "the spirits which are supposed to dwell in new "buildings."

"Seventh Day.—This day the Maharajah goes to "the pagoda as on the first day; and after worshipping "and making offerings, precedes to the Tulàmandapam "accompanied by the Achàryah or head priest and the "twenty-six others, and there stays till the Achàryah "performs pùja to the three pratimas of Vishnu, Siva "and Vináyaka, and returns to the Palace. After this "the Achàryah purifies the Tulàmandapam and "plants a *toranam* or ornamental arch at each of the "four entrances. The toranam post at the eastern "gate is made of *Asvattha*, (Ficus Religiosa), at the "southern of *Udumbara* (Ficus Glomerata), at the "western of *Vata* (Ficus Indica), at the northern of "*Plaksha* (Ficus Infectoria). These are further marked, "with one of the four weapons of Vishnu; viz., Conch "shell, Chackra or wheel, Gadá or Warclub, and the "Lotus. The Dhwajasor flag staffs are then planted at "the eight chief points of the compass, the chief one "being at the north-east corner. These are then conse-"crated. The high priest's assistants purify with "Mantras 120 pots of water of *Kolasas* to besprinkle "various parts of the Mandapam with. The "Achàryah or high priest then performs a Púja to "the goddess Lakshmi on the platform. Then the "scales and beam, specially made, are brought in "procession with attendant music, &c., and after "certain sacrificial *Homas* and purification with "*Kolasas*, the scales are put up. Inclusive of the "Tulàpurusha Pratimà there are 93 golden Pratimas, "and of these some are stuck on the beam with wax,

" others are placed on the scales, while the chief Pratimà " above mentioned is hung up in the middle of the " beam just beneath the index of the scales. Golden " pots, filled with water and covered with silk and " garlands, are placed beneath the scales. The eight " *Jápakas* repeat the four Vedas at the four gates in " the following order: Rig, east, Yajus, south, Sáma, " west, and Atharvá, north. The eight *Pàthakas* read " the PuràNas, among which are the Ramáyana, Maha-" bhàrata, and Bhàgavata. This night, in the presence " of the Maharajah, the Achàryah performs Púja to " the beam and scales, and after this, twelve Brahmins " are specially fed and presented with Dakshinas. " After this, the Maharajah, together with the Achàryah " and the rest of the priests returns to the Tulàman-" dapam and the Achàryah performs Púja to Indra, " Agni, Yama, Nirriti, Varuna, Váyu, Kubera, and " Isàna, the eight *Dikpàlas* in their due points of the " compass. Brahmà and Ananta are propitiated in " the S.W. and N.E. corners. The Maharajah per-" forms *Pushpàrchana* or bestowal of flowers to " these several deities and lastly to the scales, " accompanied with prayers, and then returns to the " Palace."

" Eighth Day.—This day, the Achàryah makes a " Púja early in the morning to the Tulàpurusha Pratimà, " after which the Maharajah goes to the Pagoda, bathed " and religiously attired. After worshipping and " making offerings he proceeds to the Tulàmandapam, " where in the south-east corner he is sprinkled with " *Punyáham* water. Thence he goes to the side room " where the "nine grains" are sown in silver flower " pots, where the Achàryah anoints him with nine fresh " water *Kolasas*. Thence the Maharajah retires to " the Palace, changes clothes, wears certain golden " jewels specially made for the occasion and, holding " the State sword in his right hand and the State shield " of black leopard's skin and a scimitar in his left, " he proceeds to the Pagoda, and having presented a " bull elephant at the foot of the great golden flag

CHAP. I.

"staff, and silks, gold coins, jewels and other rich "offerings in the interior, he walks round by the "Sivaimandapam and re-enters the Tulàmandapam. "He walks thrice round the scales, prostrates before "it, prays, performs certain preliminary donations, "bows before the priests and elderly relatives and "obtains their sanction to perform the Tulápurusha-"dánam. He then mounts the western scale, holding "*Yamás* and *Sùryás* Pratimàs in his right and left "hands respectively. He sits facing to the east on a "circular heavy plank cut out of a fresh jackwood "and covered with silk. The sword and shield are "placed in the lap. He repeats Mantras in this "position. The opposite or eastern scale then receives "the gold, both coined and in ingots, till it not only "attains equality but touches the ground, and the scale "occupied by the Maharajah rises high. The Maha-"rajah then comes down, and sitting facing to the "east, places the gold, the Tulapurusha Pratimá and "other Pratimás with flowers, sandal paste, &c., "in a basin of water, and meditating *Brahma* or "Supreme Being, he offers the contents to Bràhmans "generically. The Achàryah then dismisses with "Mantras the several deities invoked for the occasion, "and anoints the Maharajah with Avabhrï'ha Kalasám "in the north-west corner of the Mandapam. The Maha-"rajah is again sprinkled with *Punyâha*, and he then "prostrates before the Achàryah and other great men "and receives their benedictions. Leaving the "Tulámandapam he walks round the Pagoda in State "and having dismissed the Achàryah and other "priests near the golden flag staff, retires in the "Palace, after once more worshipping and offering "presents in the interior of the Pagoda. Thus ends "the *Tulàb'hárам* ceremony. One remarkable feature "in it will not escape notice. It is that it has more "of the Vaidik cast than that of later Hinduism. The "Vaidik Gods, Indra, Angi, Varuna, Váyu and others "are all propitiated. The priests who conduct the "ceremony bear, for the time, the several appellations

" given to those who take part in the Vaidik *Yajnam* " ceremony.

" Of the whole quantity of gold placed in the scale, " one-fourth is divided among the priests who conduct " the ceremony. The Division is thus :—

" 1. Achāryah gets .... ⅓ of the ¼th
" 2. The Brahman, Sadasyah and the eight Rītviks .... ⅓ " "
" 3. The eight Pāthakas and the eight Jāpakas together .... ⅓ " "

" In these, the third item is subjected to equi-divi- " sion, "—each of the 16 men getting 1/48th of the ¼th. " But the second is not so. Each of the ten does not " get 1/30th. The Brahmin gets about 1/18th, the Sadasyah " about 1/20th, and each of the eight Rītviks and Achàryah " (who again has a share in this also) gets about 1/39th,— " the whole making up about one-third. The whole " quantity of gold used in the scale to weigh the Maha- " rajah was 18,150 *kalanjus* and 19½ *machàties* or " 7934·80 tolahs approximately, which is 266 tolahs " in excess of the total gold specially ordered. This " excess was supplied by the Maharajah's private " Treasury in anticipation of payment from the public " Treasury."

" The shares of the 27 priests are approximately as " follows :—

" The Achàryah (major share)......... 661·07 tolahs.
" Do. (minor share)......... 50·9 "
" The Brahman .... 110·18 "
" The Sadasyah.......................... 94·43 "
" Each of the eight Rītviks at 50·91.. 407·28 "
" Each of the eight Jāpakas at 41·33.. 330·64 "
" Each of the eight Pàthakas at 41·33.. 330·64 "

" It will be seen from the above that the Achāryah " or head priest, has the lion's share of nearly 712 " tolahs, which, even at 15 Rs. per tolah, amounts to

CHAP. I.

"10,680 Rs. He has other emoluments besides this. "His family or Tarwád name is Tarunanallúr Nam- "púripád, and is the religious head of the great Pagoda, "and the head State priest.

"The remaining three-fourths of the gold is distri- "buted generally among Brahmans. On the former "occasion the rate of payment was as follows:

" Nampúri Bràhman *Adhyas* (Lords) of ordinary description	3	Kalanjus.
" Nampúri Bràhman *Karmis* (who have performed Yajnam)	3	„
" Ordinary Nampúri Bràhmans.........	2	„
" Canarese Bràhmans.....................	1½	„
" Tamil Bràhmans	¼	„
" Do. Women and Children	⅛	„

"From this rate a reduction was made on the "present occasion, by which the Adhyas and Karmis "got 2 k, ordinary Nampúris 1¼ k, and the Canarese "Bráhmans 1 k, no alteration being made in that "of the Tamil Bráhmans. Besides this, the great "Nampúri Lords receive varying quantities the "maximum being 100 k. Tamil Bráhmans who pass "an examination in Vedas and Sástras get extra gold, "about ¾ k. at an average. Great Pandits and "Vaidiks get much large quantities. On the former "occasion the maximum under this item reached 45 k, "but now this was kept down at 15 or 20 k. Certain "privileged families, hereditarily depending on the "court receive extra payments. The Maharajah "also makes discretionary gifts to friends and depend- "ants. But whenever a present of this gold is made "to any person not a Bráhman a deposit of its value "in money must be made, for the gold being the "property of the Bráhmans after the dánam cannot "be appropriated for other purposes. The late Maha- "rajah strictly adhered to this, and it is unlikely "that the present Maharajah has deviated from it.

" It may be mentioned that the Maharajah has, with " his wonted kind consideration presented all his " European friends with specimen coins. Lord Napier, " and probably H. R. H. the Duke of Edinburgh him- " self, must have had the addition of this curiosity to " their cabinets. The subjoined is a comparative state- " ment of the total distributions of gold on the recent " and the immediately previous occasions. It is given " in *kalanju* and *mancháti*. One *kalanju* is about 78·65 " grains or about ⅜th of a tolah, and one *mancháti* is " about 3·979 grains.

Items of Distribution of Gold.	*Tulábharám of 1850.*		*Tulábharám of 1870.*	
	K.	M.	K.	M.
" 1.—To the Acháryah and the twenty-six other priests who conducted the ceremony	5731	1	4537	14⅞
" 2—To the great Nampúri chiefs and heriditary grandees	846	5	712	10
" 3.—To Nampúri and Canarese Bráhmans generally	4778	10	3626	15
" 4.—To Tamil Bráhmans generally	3666	5	2845	15
" 5.—To do. Women and Children	1243	5	1416	5
" 6.—To do. Bráhman Pandits and those who were examined in the Vodas and Sástras	3707	0	2790	10
" 7.—To friends, dependents, servants and miscellaneous	2867	2¼	Not ascertained.	
" Total...	22924	8¼	* * *	***
" Total Gold used for weighing	22924	3	18150	19
" Gold unspent...	84	14¾	* * *	***

" It will be seen from the above that except in the " item of Tamil Bráhman women and children there " has been decrease on the present occasion. But " the total quantity of gold was smaller than on the " former occasion and the rates of distribution to the " Nampùri and Canarese Bráhmans and to the Pandits " have been considerably lowered. This, together " with the decrease of influx of people from distant

CHAP. I.

" parts of India, owing to the sudden alteration of " date, will account for the general decrease. The " chief saving, however, was in the items of feast, the " erection of sheds, and the travelling expenses of the " great Nampùri Chiefs, &c., which, owing to the " coincidence of the great Murajapam, were almost " *nil*. The whole ascertained expense amounts to " 155,427 Rs., and a few more unaudited items will " probably swell the total to 160,000 Rupees in round " numbers. The Hiranyagarb'ham ceremony, which " must be performed likewise before the Maharajah's " coronation, may cost about 140,000 Rs. Three " lakhs of rupees is doubtless a large sum in a small " State like Travancore, which has yet to undertake " many important public works and extend the bene- " fits of Education; but it is not too large to be spent " once in the lifetime of a Hindu Ruler, who has " seldom been oblivious to the just wants of his people " and never been misguided in the use of public " money, in religious ceremonies the performance of " which by the head of the State undoubtedly has the " exultant sanction of the whole Hindu population " in it.

" In the plate appended the figures in the line marked " A represent the coins or medals struck on the pre- " sent occasion, and those in the line B show those of " the last Tulábhâram."

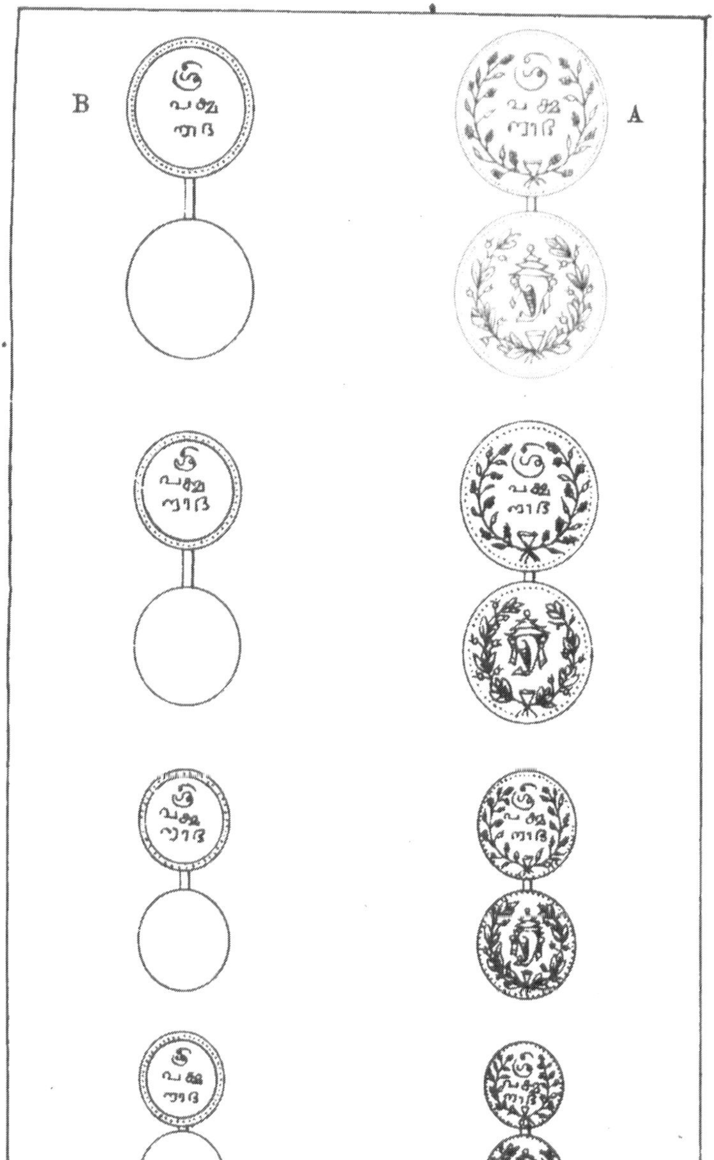

ALEX. BARREN, LITHOG.

FOR HIGGINBOTHAM & CO. MADRAS

Both of these ceremonies, Thulapurusha danam and Hirannya Garbha danam, are preliminaries to the coronation ceremony in Travancore. Parasu Rama himself performed Thulapurusha danum at Thiroonawaye, before he performed the great national feast Mahamukhum.

The chief actors in both of the above ceremonies are the Numboory Brahmans in whom Parasu Rama vested the duty of performing all the religious and Vedic ceremonies in Kerala.

Aluvanchery Samrattu, now vulgarly called Thamprakel, the supreme authority among the Numboory Brahman community, in regard to Vedic functions, is the chief preceptor to the Travancore royal family: he has to be present at all such ceremonies and is the principal person at the ceremony called Upanayanam, investiture of the young Princes with the Brahmanical emblem Poonunool, when they attain their proper age.

An account of this great Brahmanical chief will be found in Dr. Buchanan's work, wherein he is called Rajah. The denomination Thamprakel has led the people to call him Rajah, for Rajah is called in the Malayalam language, Thumpooran. The Numboory community was held in great reverence and high regard in Kerala, and none would venture to offend a Numboory, who is supposed to possess the power of imprecation and cursing.

Though several Rajahs and petty chiefs rose up subsequent to the Perumal period, still the Numboory community maintained its power within the sixty-four gramams, but owing to neglect of the devotional observances and religious performances, the prosperity of the community began to decline and the precepts and commands of Parasu Rama were indifferently attended to.

At such a period, the great and renowned Vedanthist, Sankara Acharyar was born. His birth-place is

CHAP. I. Kalady on the northern bank of the Alwaye river, and eight miles from the town of Alwaye; he was a Numboory of some rank and distinction.

We have only a traditional account of the period of Sankara Acharyar's birth, which is said to have been about half a century before the beginning of the Kollum era or the Malayalam year, and in the eighth century of the Christian era.

This account coincides with that given by the Author of the "South Indian Gods."*

Sankara Acharyar, while very young, began to criticise the religious proceedings of the Numboories and their Vedic knowledge and studies generally, and consequently the community was offended with the youth and began to persecute him in every possible manner. The community pronounced a verdict of excommunication upon the family (a cowardly mode of retaliation pursued by the Numboory community even up to this day.) The Brahmans were prohibited to associate with the family and even the lower orders were prevented from serving at Sankara's illum (house.)

When about sixteen years of age Sankara is said to have set out on a pilgrimage as a hermit.

An account of the pilgrimage, &c., of Sankara Acharyar is given in eight stanzas composed in Sanscrit, by one of his disciples. These verses are to the effect that Sankara Acharyar was born in the Brahman village Kalady in Keralam; that he became omniscient by the time he attained sixteen years of age, attained the religious degree of ascetism, proceeded to Baderikasramam where the Soothra Bhashya was composed that Vyasa, the great Rishi met Sankara Acharyar

* The most celebrated professor of the Vadanta was Sankara Acharya; and regarding him we learn from Professor H. H. Wilson's Hindu Sects, that he lived about the eighth or ninth century, and was, according to most accounts a native of Kerala or Malabar, of the tribe of Numboory Brahmans, and in the Mythological language of the Sect, an incarnation of Siva. South Indian Gods, page 114.

there; that the Bhashya was shown him, and that he fully approved of the work; that they resided there together for some years; that subsequently Sankara Acharyar returned to his mother to whom he administered spiritual aid in her last moments; that after her death, he returned to Baderikasramam and ordained a fit disciple there; that he set out from thence with his disciple, went to Gaya, and performed certain ceremonies for his deceased mother; that he was here engaged in a religious discussion with a learned Brahman whom he converted and made his disciple; that they came together to Gokarnam and converted there an unmarried Brahman who also became his disciple; that he proceeded to Kalastri and other holy places, accompanied by all his disciples; that subsequently he came to Kanchi, and after visiting Sreerangam, continued his pilgrimage to Ramaswarum and Sethu, and that finally, the Acharyar visited Trichoor, constituting several religious ordinations and establishments at various places during the pilgrimage.

Sankara Acharyar finished his worldly career at the early age of thirty-two years at Baderikasramam, or, as is generally believed, at Badrikadarum near the Himalaya and this is corroborated by the author of the "South Indian Gods," page 115. The Acharyar's disciples composed several works called Acharya Charitham, Acharya Vejayem, &c., but such works have now become very scarce.

Sankara Acharyar introduced various improvements amongst the Numboory community of Keralam, in modification of the laws and ordinances of Parasu Rama, which are now observed by the Brahmans as their religious bye-laws. He also made several divisions of caste in the lower orders, the particulars of which will be found detailed in Kerala Ulppathy, page 33.

At this period, the Numboory community continued as they were originally, in two sections, viz.: *Chowarakoor* and *Panniarakoor*.

The improvement effected by Sankara Acharyar was that each of these divisions should have a *Wadhyan* (spiritual Preceptor) called Thirunawaye Wadhyan and Thrishivaparoor (Trichoor) Wadhyan; that there should be under these two personages six *Wydeekens* (Vedic Judges) a set of *Meemamsakens* (expounders of spiritual laws,) and Smarthens (Professors of spiritual laws.) All spiritual affairs to be guided and conducted by these men in perfect accordance with the Vedic law.

Sankara Acharyar introduced also certain rules and observances regarding matrimony amongst the Numboory Brahmans, most rigid in their character. The married female is not allowed to be seen by any males even of the family or of her caste people. She is to move under the screen or cover of a large-sized umbrella purposely constructed with the Tallipot palm leaf, and is always to be attended by a female servant, who goes before her whenever she steps out of doors. She is not permitted to adorn her person with costly ornaments and clothes; her ornaments consist of a pair of golden ear-rings of a peculiar make and description, different from the pattern worn by females of other classes. She wears a string of neck ornaments called *Tholikoottam*, and a number of brass bangles on both hands. She wears a long country-made coarse cloth round her waist and covers her body from the neck downwards with a coarse sheet of cloth.

The costume, the ornament and the condition of the Numboory females continue to this day just the same without the least change from the original rules laid down for the sex by Sankara Acharyar.

The rules laid down for protecting chastity amongst the females are extremely rigorous and severe. The following is a brief outline of the mode of enquiry in cases of adultery among the Numboory Brahmans as established by Sankara Acharyar.

When a female member of a family is suspected of having violated the laws of chastity, the headman of the family generally takes the lead in an enquiry; he communicates the information to his kinsmen, and they together with some of the headmen of the neighbouring village assemble in the house and hold a private enquiry with the maid servant attached to the suspected female, as also with the other maid servants of the house. This enquiry is a very minute and searching one, and if the suspicion is found groundless, the enquiry is stopped and the matter dropped altogether. On the other hand, the suspected female is ordered to be located in a separate place which is called by the technical term *Anjampura*, and there she remains apart from the others. The owner of the house and his kinsmen, together with the elders, now proceed to the king and represent the matter in a particular form. The King, his family Priest, and other Pandits of the Court, assemble and the sovereign himself puts several questions to the complainant and his kinsmen as to the nature and grounds of the suspicion and their own knowledge of the matter, their opinion, &c. &c., and the courtiers also follow the same course, and then the king issues a writ to the *Smarthen* and deputes the king's agent or deputy in the person of a learned man and Vedic scholar of the Court. The prosecutor, together with certain men of the committee, go to the Smarthen, lays down a sum of money as a complimentary present to the Smarthen, and apprises him of the affair and of the king's order; the *Meemamsakens* are then assembled and all now proceed to the house of the suspected female, and the Smarthen, with all the respect due to a Numboory woman, standing at a good distance without being seen by the female, makes a maid servant his intermediary and commences asking a series of questions. If the Smarthen is satisfied that there is no ground for proceeding with the enquiry, he communicates the same to the Meemamsakens and to the king's agent, who are also present there. After mutual consultation and consideration of the nature of the questions and answers, should they agree with the Smarthen that the accused is innocent,

CHAP. I.

the enquiry, is discontinued and the ceremony known as *Kshama Namaskarum* is gone through, *i. e.*, lying prostrate before the suspected female and asking her pardon for the vexatious procedure to which she was subjected, and thus the female is honorably exonerated. On the other hand, should the suspicion be confirmed by her answers, and good reasons be found for believing the charge, the Smarthen shows himself before the accused female and confronting her, begins questioning her. From this stage, the female is called and addressed "*Sadanam*" (thing). This examination continues about three days, and by that time the guilt is likely to be completely established, mostly by confession strengthened by evidence, and then the case is summed up and considered by the Smarthen, Meemamsaken and others in the presence of the king's agent. At this stage, the female is closely watched, not only to prevent out-side advice from reaching her but also to frustrate any intentions of suicide which she may entertain. The result of the enquiry is reported to the king, who, after hearing all the facts sanctions the excommunication of the female and allows her a small pittance of rice and provisions to be issued from one of the Oottupurahs (feeding houses). The sentence of excommunication is announced by a foreign Brahman, called Patter. This person, standing on a platform erected for the purpose, declares in a loud voice the names of the adulteress, and the adulterer; he next announces that the crime has been proved against them and that they have both been excommunicated. For this service, the Patter gets the prescribed fee. The cost of this enquiry, which is generally called "*Smarthavicharam*," is somewhat considerable, and the whole is borne by the head of the family who is bound to go through certain ceremonies after performing the mock funeral ceremonies of the female, who is now considered as dead and severed from the family. This concluding ceremony is called "*Sudhabhojanam*" (messing after purification).

During the enquiry the assembled committee is sumptuously fed by the head of the family. CHAP. I.

This enquiry shows that the Numboory Brahmans depend solely upon the king for sanction in such cases, and that such an enquiry is essential to the Brahmans for preserving the purity of their race.

The Brahmans have to perform a most important ceremony in accordance with the canons of the Veda. This ceremony is called "Yagam" (sacrifice) and it is also to be performed with the sanction of the king, who, as in duty bound, is to attend the ceremony as a protector.

Parasu Rama himself respected and observed the above law when he performed the great Mahamakham sacrifices at Thirunawaye, where the Kerala Mahatmyam says that that great Brahman celebrated the ceremony with great pomp and in the presence of the kings, of whom the Travancore sovereign was reckoned the foremost.

We find that during the sway of the Numboories over each of the various Devaswams (temples of worship) instituted by Parasu Rama, a Samantha Kshatria called Kovil Addikarikal was appointed as manager. These Adhikarikals rose in power and in course of time established themselves as petty chiefs.

These Devaswams became possessed of immense wealth and landed property, to which latter numerous tenants were attached and who established themselves as ryots or subjects, so much so that the Devaswam managers and trustees enacted rules and laws for the management of the Devaswam property and began to enforce these laws, independent of the king, within the limits of their landed property.

Tradition shows that the life and property of the Devaswam tenants were at the mercy of the Devaswam community. In every pagoda, before the commencement of the annual Ulsavam festival, which generally begins by a flag being hoisted, such of the

CHAP. I. Devaswam tenants, as had committed any breach of the Devaswam rules were gibbetted before the hoisting of the flag and the commencement of the Ulsavam. By such arbitrary conduct of the Devaswam people the sovereign power was overshadowed, and the king became indifferent to the mode in which affairs were administered within the jurisdiction of Devaswam and Brahmaswam lands.

These powers of the Devaswam appear to have continued up to the early part of the eighth century, as will be seen from accounts of the Travandrum Devaswam.

The rise of the Devaswam to power greatly affected the military resources of the king, whose forces are chiefly constituted of militia trained out of the populace. Now, the Devaswam ryots became the largest portion of the people and they were not permitted to form a portion of the militia.

The military strength granted by Parasu Rama to the Travancore King as mentioned in the Kerala Mahatmyam was 3,50,000 men, and these were all militia.

We have already said that the art of war and the uses of warlike weapons were introduced by Parasu Rama.

The system of training soldiers adopted by that Brahman warrior and followed by the kings of Travancore and Kolathnaud was that every village should maintain its own militia. The name of every male child of the Nairs and others, six months after birth, was to be registered as belonging to the militia. Fencing and gymnastic schools, called Kalery, were established in every district under the superintendence of certain authorised masters, denominated Gurukals and Asans to educate boys in the art of war which consisted chiefly of sword exercises, arrow-shooting, spear, lance and dagger exercises, wrestling and the use of the shield, and several other arts of offence and defence. These masters were required not only to give the boys military education, but also to train them in gymnastic exercises, sword and rope-dancing for the entertainment of the public. CHAP. I.

For the command of the milita, trained men were expressly nominated, such as *Munnilakaren*, (one who stands in front of a company) *Cherumanakaren*, (the one behind or close to the first; ranking perhaps with the present grades Subadar and Jemadar). Over several of these men there were noblemen, with the titles of Karthavu (Lord), Kymal (nobleman), and such others like the old Barons and Knights of England. The head of the number of these noblemen was a petty chief of a State called raiah who had to appear before the king with his levee of fighting men in time of war. The *Gurukal* had *Writhi* (means of livelihood or maintenance), now called *Virithi*, allowed them by the king, which consisted of portions of lands. Similar privileges on a large scale were granted to all the chiefs for maintaining the militia. By the appointment of Parasu Rama, the king of Travancore and his relative the chief of Kolathnaud, had each 350,000 militia men, and these, were recognized even by the last Perumal. The Kerala Ulppathy[1] as well as the Kerala Mahatmyam[2] fully certify to this fact. The extent of the possessions of these two sovereigns, and the importance of Travancore and Kolathnaud may be justly and rightly judged from the strength of the militia, for to raise a militia of 700,000 men would undoubtedly require a large population, with an extensive area of land, and it is an additional proof that the whole of Kerala was in the possession of these two sovereigns, and that almost all the rajahs and chiefs and their nobles who were each head of thirty, fifteen, ten, five and three thousand men of the militia, according to the account in the Kerala Ulppathy (vide pages 41 and 42) were subject to these two kings of Travancore and Kolathnaud.*

1—Kerala Ulppathy, pages 40 and 41.
2—Kerala Mahatmyam, Chapter 86.

* The Kola conquest of the Belalas might be cited as an instance of the power of these kings.

CHAP. I.

We see remnants of the above system still in existence in Travancore, though not in its original form nor for the same purposes. Some of the originally established kaleries are to be seen here and there, with their privileged Asans or masters. Such kaleries are found now-a-days in the territories of the king of Travancore, where all such ancient relics are preserved and the services of the grade of men with their original title such as Munnilakaren and Charumanakaren, and the militia men as Virithicar are still retained, and they even to this day perform oolium services in the villages, and in the possession of lands allotted to them as Virithi. The aggregate number of such persons amounts to about 20,000 and the lands to the extent of about 14,000 acres and 5,000 gardens. In no country in India are such services found to exist.

That the supremacy of Keralam devolved upon the Travancore king we find borne out by the fact of the currency of Kerala.

We have already shown that Parasu Rama had minted a gold coin called Rasi, and that it was the sovereign coin of Kerala, till the commencement of the Kali Yugam. Though the coin Rasi has become almost extinct, since the last few centuries, still in all transactions relating to landed property in the northern parts of Travancore, this coin is to this day the standard for fixing the value thereof.

Travancore minted its coin from the earliest time in the Kali age and it is the principal currency of the kingdom and is called Kaliyuga Rajen fanam, which coin, though not current now, is the acknowledged currency in Travancore, like the star pagoda of the Carnatic. The old Kaliyuga Rajen fanam was a close imitation of the Madura Vella fanam (the Pandyan coin), and both had a faint resemblance to the Rasi fanam. These coins were certainly minted long after the coinage of the gold Rasi fanam by Parasu Rama. Subsequently, the Travancore mint issued gold coins the form and stamp resembling very much those of the Rasi, called Anantha Rajen fanam and Anantha Varahan (gold pagoda). A silver coin, under the designation of Chuckram, was issued from the Travancore mint from the earliest period and it was current even in the Pandyan kingdom.

Inscriptions and copper Sasanams show that the Kaliyuga Rajen fanam was the currency in the early part of the Kali Yugam. The Telugu Brahman Kannadyan's copper Sasanam already alluded to, corroborates the fact of Chuckram being the currency during that period.

All the designations by which Travancore coins were known had special meanings, viz., Kaliyuga Rajen fanam means the coin of the king who ruled Keralam in the beginning of the Kali age. Anantha Rajen fanam means the Travancore king's coin, so also Anantha Varahan; and Chuckram denotes the emblem or weapon of Vishnu, the household deity of the Travancore sovereign. Gold Chuckrams were minted in Travancore at one time, but they are not current now.

All these coins were current between Cape Comorin and Gokarnam. During the time of the Perumal period and that of the Brahmanical rule, the Rasi appears to have been the currency as also other coins which were minted and circulated in Keralam by the Travancore king. A few centuries subsequent to the Kollum era, Malayalam year, the Kolathnaud Rajah issued a gold coin of his own, resembling the Rasi and called the gold fanam. When the Zamorin flourished under the assumed title of "*Nadivirippu*," that potentate issued a coin of his own, being an imitation of the Kolathnaud Rajah's coin and he called it Veera Rayen Puthia fanam or Zamorin's new fanam, which, as well as the Kolathnaud Rajah's coin became the currency in all the northern countries and every one of the chiefs accepted them as such; but the Kolathnaud king's

CHAP. I. coin was now called Palaya fanam, old coin. Even the Perinpadappu king accepted the Zamorin's new fanam as legal tender in his country, a practise which still continues, and money transactions in the Cochin Rajah's territories are calculated chiefly according to the Zamorin's new gold fanam. But the Zamorin's coins were not a legal tender in the Travancore king's territories.

Perinpadappu latterly issued alloyed silver coin called Puthen, which appears to have scarcely been acknowledged out of his own territories.

The Travancore coins were current in Keralam up to the time the Zamorin rose to power. The Kaliyuga Rajen fanam and the Chuckram have been current in the kingdoms of Pandya and Chola from ancient times. Thus we have traced the currency of Kerala from the time of Parasu Rama up to the present day, and, though we have already shown that Kerala was no other than Travancore, yet it is necessary to refer once more to the subject and trace the names of localities in connection with our narration.

The coronation of King Veera Kerala Vurmah, Kulasekhara Perumal, in the Kali year 3412, has been chronicled above. This took place in the middle of the Perumal period and the coronation was attended by the then Perumal, and by all the chiefs and nobles of Kerala; the ceremonies of Hirannya Garbham and Thulapurusha danam were performed by the Numboory Brahmans of both Chowarakoor and Punniarakoor.

This sovereign occupied the Kerala throne for a long time and ruled his kingdom with prosperity and popularity.

The capital, where this monarch resided, was Veera Keralapuram close to Sreevalumcode, (Thiroovithancode) and Sreevurdhanapuram (Padmanabhapuram,) where Parasu Rama installed two of this king's ancestors.

CHERAMAN PERUMAL.

Published by Messrs. Higginbotham & Co.

[illegible] Lith. Madras.

Veera Keralapuram or Keralapuram is still in existence; there are the palace, the pagoda, the Brahman and Sudra villages. On the right side of this city is Sreevalumcode, and on the left, Sreevurdhanapurum, not far from each other.

This king appears to have ended his most praiseworthy career after an unusually long reign, during the Viceroyalty of Bhaskara Revi Vurmah, the last Cheraman Perumal.

There are many localities, capitals and towns in the eastern side of the Ghauts the names of which perpetuate the memory of the Chera dynasty and its kings, such as Chera Maha Devi, Marthandaswaram, Kulasekharapatanam, &c., &c., in like manner, in Keralam also similar names are abundantly found.

We find that besides Veera Keralapuram, the denomination connected with Kulasekhara is freely and largely adopted in Keralam, such as Kulasekharapuram, Kulasekhara Mangalam, &c. Keraladithyapuram and Keraleswaram are also used as denominations of pagodas, villages, &c.

Veera Kerala Vurmah, Kulasekhara Perumal, was succeeded by his brother, whose name is not very clear. No particulars of the reign of this king can be gathered from any reliable account; all that is known of him is that he was unable to follow in the track of his predecessor and that he did not perform the costly ceremonies and wear the sacred crown and become a Kulasekhara Perumal. This king's successor was the nephew of Veera Kerala Vurmah, whose name he bore.

It appears that it was in his reign during which nothing extraordinary occurred that the Perumal Viceroyalty ended.

The last Cheraman Perumal closed his worldly career at Thiruvanjicolam; the traditional account is that he disappeared suddenly from his residence. Certain Tamil accounts say that he ascended to heaven

CHAP. I.

with one Sundra Moorthy Swamy, while the Kerala Ulppathy narrates that Cheraman proceeded to Mecca, met the prophet Mahomet, embraced Mahomedanism, lived some years there, married the daughter of the Arabian king, had children by her, and died at that place. This statement, on the face of it appears to be utterly false, as the prophet was not born at the time when Bhaskara Revi Vurmah Perumal died.

Such statements strengthen the doubts as to the reliableness of the Kerala Ulppathy, which is the chief source of information respecting the Perumal's rule, subsequent to Parasu Rama's period; but the narration in this work (Kerala Ulppathy) subsequent to the Perumal period still further bewilders the reader, especially as almost all accounts therein related, are not annotated. There is no means of knowing exactly at what period the chronicles of this work end.

The division of Kerala; at the time of the last Cheraman Perumal's retirement as narrated in the Kerala Ulppathy, is generally disbelieved, and almost disproved, as has been said by Dr. Gundert. Besides, the Perumal as a Viceroy had no power to make territorial divisions of the dominions of his master, the Chera king.

It would appear from all accounts, that the Cochin chief, under the designation of Mada Bhoopathy or Madathin Kovil (vide Kerala Ulppathy, page 62,) also called Kovil Adhikarikel, as the relation of the Perumal, as a matter of course took possession of the Perumal's residence at Thiruvanjicolam (the original home of the Chera dynasty,) and enjoyed the Perumal's possessions and property as Ananthiravan (heir).

There is another account which says that the Cochin Rajah is not a real descendant of the last Cheraman Perumal, but that his family is descended from the fifteenth Perumal, called Mada Perumal (vide Kerala Ulppathy, page 18), and that they resided on the western bank of the broad back-water, Bampanaud Kayel, a few miles north of Alleppey, and in the Sharetalay district. The locality is still called Madathinkaray, and tradition shows that the Cochin Rajah had a residence there till the district fell into the Travancore sovereign's hands.

The above view was adopted by Kookel Kelu Nair, in his memorandum published in the Madras Literary Society's Journal already alluded to. He says: "Again "there is no ground to suppose that the Cochin Rajah "is descended from the said Veera Kerala, for, from "various authors, it is clear that the Cochin Rajah is "decended from Mada Perumal, one of the predeces- "sors of the last Perumal, and therefore, even up to "this day the Cochin Rajahs are called Mada Bhoo- "patis or Mada Rajahs." This may perhaps account for the general belief that the Cochin Rajah is a Soorya Vamsa Kshatria, for, if his family were descended from the last Cheraman Perumal, it must be a Soma Vamsa Kshatria, as that Viceroy was a Soma Kshatria, as has been already shown.

Kerala Ulppathy says in its forty-second page, that the last Perumal gave his sword and two small pieces of land to an attaché of his (an Eradi), with the title *Kunnala Konathiri* (Zamorin), and also that a few Arabs, residing at the locality were made over to him.

Such is the origin of the Cochin Rajah and of the Zamorin of Calicut, as narrated in the Kerala Ulppathy, which account appears to be fully corroborated by tradition.

The king of Chera (Travancore), had been till then the Emperor of Kerala, but the principal seat of royalty was gradually transferred to the southern part and embodied with its branch, as we have already stated.

The nephew of king Veera Kerala Vurmah ruled the kingdom satisfactorily during his reign; he established a residency at Kulladay, south-east of Quilon, where he consecrated a pagoda, and established

CHAP. I.

villages, &c. The successor of this king, whose name is unknown, did not govern his kingdom ably and well, and tradition has it that since that time other powers in the north commenced to rise and prosper in Southern India.

For the next two or three hundred years, we find no precise accounts of the affairs of north Kerala; it was the period of the flourishing dynasties of Kadamba and Chalukya, and northern Kerala had been subject to the supremacy of those powers. During this interval, there was an alliance between Travancore and the Kolathnaud Rajahs to repel the invaders of northern Kerala.

In the Kali year 3831 (731 A.D.), the Travancore king, Veera Marthanda Vurmah, performed Hirannya Garbham and Thulapurusha danam and ruled the kingdom for a long time. His nephew succeeded him as usual. This sovereign, whose real name it is difficult to find, died in the Kali year 3902 and was succeeded by his nephew, Udaya Marthanda Vurmah, who was an educated and highly accomplished monarch. His rule was very prosperous and more remarkable than that of many of his predecessors.

At this period, the Travancore royal family resided at different places and was commonly known by five different denominations, viz., (Vanavanaud) Venaud, (Sreevalumcode) Thiruvithancode, (Sreepatha) Trippappoor, (Sreevey) Sheravaye and (Jayuthunaganaud) Desinganaud Swaroopams.

All these five Swaroopams, when collectively referred to, were styled either Venadu, Travancore or Trippappoor, and sovereignty was assumed under these three designations only. Latterly they became to be known exclusively under one name, *i.e.*, Travancore.

In the Kali year 3926 (825 A.D.), when king Udaya Marthanda Vurmah was residing in Kollam (Quilon), he convened a council of all the learned men of Kerala with the object of introducing a new era, and after making some astronomical researches,

CHAP. I.

and calculating the solar movements throughout the twelve signs of the zodiac, and counting scientifically the number of days occupied in this revolution in every month, it was resolved to adopt the new era from the first of Chingam of that year, 15th August 825, as Kollam year one, and to call it the solar year.

This arrangement was approved of by all the wise men of the time, and every neighbouring country began to adopt the same. And this system of reckoning the year, continues up to the present day throughout Keralam, as well as in every part of the kingdom of Chera, then possessed by the king of Travancore. This era has been adopted by other kings also, as we see that in Madura, Tinnevelly, and other countries, the Kollam era is commonly used in reckoning the year. Stone inscriptions are generally found in Tinnevelly, and other localities, which corroborate this statement. The old records in the Trevandrum pagoda shew that on the 5th Chingam of the first Kollam year, *i.e.*, five days after the promulgation of the new year, the members of the five royal Houses of the Travancore family, the Swamyar, (ecclesiastical head), and all the nobility, &c., assembled in the Trevandrum pagoda and introduced certain new rules or ordinances for the conduct of the daily, monthly, and yearly performances of poojas and other ceremonies in the pagoda. These rules are still in force in the said pagoda.

In these old writings, it is found recorded that king "Cheraman Perumal" (not the Viceroy), laid the foundation stone of this pagoda, and that he passed all the ordinances appertaining to the pagoda, and appointed certain classes and castes of men for the different duties of the Devaswam.

In the Kollam year 5, (830 A.D.), Udaya Marthanda Vurmah, Kulasekhara Perumal died, but his successor's name and the particulars of his reign are not traceable from the records. The names and other

CHAP. I. particulars of many of the succeeding kings are also not in the records.

The Panthalam Rajah, now a pensioned feudatory chief of Travancore, was a subordinate Kshatria Rajah under the Pandyan king, and his family was privileged to wed the females of the Chera or Travancore royal family. This chief emigrated to Travancore under the sanction of the then sovereign, as is recorded in a copper-plate writing, dated 11th Purattasi Kollam year 79, (904 A.D.)

It was about this period that the combined army of Travancore and Koluthnaud drove out the Bellalas from Kerala, and pursued the fugitives into the Dravida country. Subsequently the kings of Travancore and Koluthnaud reverted to the enjoyment of their respective possessions originally assigned to them by Parasu Rama, *i.e.*, the former from Korempulay (the great river) to the south, and the latter from that stream to the north.

On northern Kerala being cleared of the outsiders, the local chieftains began to rise and much fighting amongst them resulted.

The Eradi, whom the Perumal called Kunnala Kon or Konathiri, as the Kerala Ulppathy calls him, and to whom the Perumal gave his sword, now rose up, and with the assistance of the Arabs, conquered almost all the northern chiefs, acquired large territories between Ponnani and northern Kollam, and established himself as a powerful monarch assuming the title "Nediviruppu Swaroopan" (the greatly spread power.)

Kerala Ulppathy narrates the particulars of the Zamorin's military exploits and victories (vide, pages 46 to 56.)

The last Perumal, Bhaskara Revi Vurmah, was, as stated above, far more popular than all the other Perumals, and he was held in such great veneration and affection by the people, as well as by all the chiefs throughout Keralam that he was considered by most of the people as an incarnation of Vishnu, and many even worshipped him as a deity. This Perumal's image, together with that of his wife, were cast in metal and placed in the Thiruvunjicolam pagoda.

The Cochin Rajah, being considered the legitimate heir to the Perumal, rose in the estimation of the people, especially of the Syrian community, who were rich and very influential, some of them being merchants carrying on business between Kodungalore and Quilon, and greatly attached to the chief ever since the end of the Perumal rule. In the course of a few years the Cochin Rajah also became a great power, and like the Zamorin, changed his title and declared himself Perinpadappu Swaroopam (the highly extended or stretched power). As almost all the northern subjects of Travancore acknowledged the Cochin chief as king, the title "Perinpadappu, applied to Cochin was not inappropriate." The then reigning king of Travancore being of a quiet and peaceable disposition, the ascendancy of Cochin was easily established. Hence, the king of Travancore lost his sovereignty over almost all his northern possessions, and the dominions of the Travancore sovereign were reduced to small dimensions, *i.e.*, between Edavaye near Vurkalay in the north, Erratta Malay (eastern side of Udayagherry) in the south, to a distance of about seventy miles in length and twenty miles in breadth: Nanjenaud and all other southern possessions having been assumed by the Pandyan king. Sree Vurdhanapuram (Padmanabhapurum), Sree Valumcode (Thiruvithancode) were at the time the capitals of the kingdom. This little possession, we find, was ruled without any disturbance, either externally or internally, for a long period. During this period, two members of the Travancore royal family were adopted into that of Madathinkoor Swaroopam (Mavalikaray,) which was originally related to the Travancore royal family, being a branch of the Kola family and thus the territories under that petty State, became again subjected to Travancore.

In the Kollam year 225 (1050 A.D.,) the ancient pagoda at Trevandrum was rebuilt by a Travancore sovereign, whose name is not known.

About this period, the Pandyan kingdom was invaded by the Mahommedans and the then reigning king Paracrama Pandyan was taken prisoner. Having sent him to Delhi, the Mahommedans took possession of Madura. On this occasion, the tutelary god of Madura was taken to Travancore for better security.* The king of Travancore afforded an asylum, without showing the least ill-will to the Pandyans for wrongs done to Travancore in appropriating territories which were parts of his dominions.

During the Mahommedan rule of the Pandyan kingdom, which rule appears to have continued for about half a century, one Nanja Koraven, a feudatory chief under Travancore obtained possession of Nanjenaud, the southern part of Travancore, and established himself there as a ruler. Subsequent to the conquest of Mysore by the Mahommedans and the relief of the Madura kingdom, Nanja Koraven and his confederacy were driven away by the king of Travancore in the Kollam year 292 (1117 A.D.)

In 345 K.E. (1170 A.D.,) the Panthalam family, to whom we have already alluded, appears to have received some territorial grants from the king of Travancore, in consideration of that family having taken up their residence in Keralam.

In like manner, the present Poonjat Rajah, who was a close relation of the Pandyan dynasty emigrated to Travancore, and the hill territories of Poonjar were assigned as the residence of his family, during the reign of king Adithya Vurmah of Travancore in 364 M.E. (1189 A.D.)

* Rev. H. Taylor, vol. 1, pages 33 and 35.

During the 5th century M.E., and in the reign of king Adithya Vurmah, the Travancore royal family was under the necessity of adopting two females from the Kolathnaud royal family, and a royal residence was constructed at Attingal,* for the residence of the two Ranees, and they were installed as Attingal Mootha Thumpuran and Elia Thumpuran, *i. e.*, senior and junior Ranees of Attingal. The country around Attingal was assigned to them, and the revenue derived therefrom was placed at their disposal.

King Adithya Vurmah extended his sovereignty over some of the northern Devaswams, as the accounts of the renowned pagoda at Vycome shew that in 505 M.E. (1330 A.D.,) that sovereign had assumed authority over the affairs of that Devaswam.

The reigning king died and the eldest son of the senior Ranee of Attingal, Sree Veera Rama Marthanda Vurmah, who was then in his 28th year was installed on the musnud in 510 M.E. (1335 A.D.)

This king reconstructed the palace near the pagoda at Trevandrum and built a Fort round it.

His government was most prosperous, and his reign which ended with his death in 550 M.E. (1376 A.D.,) lasted for a period of forty years.

He was succeeded by his third brother, Eravi Vurmah, who resided at Trevandrum like his deceased brother, and ruled the kingdom with great credit to himself and to the entire satisfaction of his subjects. His Highness was anxious to perform the coronation ceremonies and collected the necessary funds for the same. While the preparations were advancing for their performance, the sovereign died in 557 M.E., (1382 A.D.) after a reign of seven years; he was succeeded by his nephew, Kerala Vurmah, who, soon

* Attingal is the name of the maternal house of the Rajah of Travancore. In all Malabar, there is no queen-mother who possesses so much influence in public affairs as here.

Wis'scher's Letters from Malabar, by Major Drury, page 58.

CHAP. I. after he ascended the musnud, performed the coronation ceremonies, and became "Kulasekhara Perumal," but His Highness died three months after his coronation.

Kerala Vurmah Kulasekhara Perumal, was succeeded by his twin-brother Chera Udaya Marthanda Vurmah.

The reign of this sovereign was longer than that of all the Travancore monarchs.

His Highness ascended the musnud, while he was sixteen years of age, and died at the ripe age of seventy-eight after a reign of sixty-two years.

His reign was of a mixed character, partly attended with prosperity, and partly with troubles and annoyances, as is natural during such a long period, in which many vicissitudes must be expected.

His Highness Chera Udaya Marthanda Vurmah performed the coronation ceremonies, and was styled "Kulasekhara Perumal."

During the reign of this sovereign all the south-eastern possessions of Travancore on the Tinnevelly side were regained, and the sovereign often resided at Valliyoor and Chera Maha Devi.

In consequence of the mild and unwarlike disposition of this king, some of the subordinate chiefs in the East became refractory, and there was constant fighting and latterly, while this sovereign was residing at Trevandrum, the chief of Rettiapuram invaded Valliyoor, and the king's nephew being defeated in battle fearing disgrace, committed suicide.

In these places, several grants of lands made by this Kulasekhara Perumal, remain some of which we have already noticed. Chera Maha Devi was his favorite residence, and consequently, this sovereign was called Chera Udaya Marthanda Vurmah.

Towards the close of his reign, suspecting unfair proceedings on the part of the chief men of the Pandyan State, the residence of the royal family was

VEERA MARTHANDA ALIAS CHERA UDAYA MARTHANDA.

removed to Elayadathunaud Hottarakaray; and a Governor was appointed to rule Valliyoor and other possessions in the East. CHAP. I.

This sovereign died in 619 M.E. (1444 A.D.), at the ripe age of seventy-eight years. He was succeeded by Venaud Mootha Rajah, who reigned for fourteen years, and died in 633 M.E. (1458 A.D.).

From this year up to 855 M.E. (1680 A.D.), a period of about two and a quarter centuries, no detailed accounts of the reigns of the sovereigns can be found, except a list of their names, the dates of their accession to the musnud and the period of their reign.

His Highness Venauds Mootha Rajah was succeeded by Sree Veera Marthanda Vurmah, who after a reign of thirteen years died in 646 M.E. (1471 A.D.), and was succeeded by Adithya Vurmah whose reign lasted only seven years.

The successor of this sovereign was Eravi Vurmah, who was installed on the musnud in 653 M.E. (1478 A.D.), and ruled the country for twenty-five years, and the successor Eravi Vurmah Sree Marthanda Vurmah died in the very year of his installation.

In 679 M.E. (1504 A.D.), Sree Veera Eravi Vurmah assumed the sovereignty, and governed the kingdom for twenty-four years, and on His Highness' death in 703 M.E. (1528 A.D.), king Marthanda Vurmah succeeded him and ruled for nine years. He was succeeded by Udaya Marthanda Vurmah in 712 M.E. (1537 A.D.), who governed the kingdom for a period of twenty-three years, and died in 735 M.E. (1560 A.D.) This sovereign was succeeded by Kerala Vurmah, who ruled only for three years. On his death in 738 M.E. (1563 A.D.), he was succeeded by Adithya Vurmah who died in the fourth year of his reign. Udaya Marthanda Vurmah was then installed on the musnud in 742 M.E. (1567 A.D.), and ruled for a period of twenty-seven years, when he died.

CHAP. I.

In 769 M.E. (1594 A.D.), Sree Veera Eravi Vurmah assumed the sovereignty, and after performing the coronation ceremonies took the family title "Kulasekhara Perumal." Several of this sovereign's predecessors were unable to perform the coronation ceremony on account of difficulties in collecting the revenue, or in consequence of the obstructions thrown by the feudatory chiefs and nobles, as well as the Ettu Veetil Pillamars.

Sree Veera Eravi Vurmah Kulasekhara Perumal ruled for ten years and died in 779 M.E. (1604 A.D.), and was succeeded by Sree Veera Vurmah, whose rule having ended after two years, Ravi Vurmah ascended the musnud in 781 M.E. (1606 A.D.), and ruled for thirteen years.

Unny Kerala Vurmah was the successor of the last mentioned sovereign and he began to reign in 794 M.E. (1619 A.D.), and ruled the country for six years. His successor Ravi Vurmah, who commenced his reign in 800 M.E. (1625 A.D.), reigned six years and died, and was succeeded by Unny Kerala Vurmah in 806 M.E. (1631 A.D.), and he ruled the country for a period of thirty years.

King Adithya Vurmah succeeded in 836 M.E. (1661 A.D.), and died in the sixteenth year of his reign, under shocking circumstances, occasioned by the inhuman conduct of the feudatories and the combined artifices of the Ettoo Veetil Pillamar and the Devaswam association.

Some particulars are to be found concerning these events, and the disloyal proceedings of the feudatories against the king's government.

As has already been stated the re-organization of the ecclesiastical society in 225 M.E. (1050 A.D.) which was called Ettara Yogom amounted to this. A society was formed consisting of eight and a "half members" of whom eight were Potty Brahmans, each of whom pretended to have the privilege of a casting vote, and the sovereign who was considered half member, had no vote in the transactions of the Devaswam affairs. By such an arrangement, the affairs of the Devaswam became virtually vested in the hands of the eight Potty Brahmans, and they began to work the institution through their attachés the Etta Veetil Pillamar, who were the representatives of eight noble families. The sovereign had little or no influence over the Devaswam, and was simply required to be present at the usual periodical ceremonies.

CHAP. I.

The power of this Yogakar and the association become so great, that the records show that they even imposed heavy fines upon the sovereign for wrongs done to the Devaswam institution.

This Devaswam possessed extensive landed property, which was then called Sree Pundara Vaca (belonging to the holy treasury.) Its sole managers were the Yogakar, who had all the powers of despotic rulers over the Devaswam property, and over every one of the tenants and holders of the Devaswam lands. The Ettu Veetil Pillamar were entrusted with the collection of the Devaswam revenue, and the villages, where the Devaswam lands lay, were divided into eight Adhikarems. Each of the Ettu Veetil Pillamar was appointed a collector over the Adhikarem, with the powers of a petty chief.

The king having little or no authority over these men, they rose in power and importance, and gradually became supreme lords in their villages, and in time the Madempimar (nobles and petty chiefs,) who were not loyally attached to the crown, were also influenced by the Ettu Veetil Pillamar and the combination became a powerful one.

The principal royal residence was at Sreevalumcode about thirty miles from the Devaswam head station (Trevandrum,) which was solely under the despotic rule of the Yogakar and the Ettu Veetil Pillamar for a period of two hundred and thirty-five years, and so the re-construction of a royal residency at Trevandrum in 510 M.E., was not quite to the liking

CHAP. I. of the Yogakar, whose feelings were roused when the sovereign began to watch their proceedings and insist upon having the accounts, connected with the income and expenditure of the Devaswam submitted periodically to his inspection.

Though the king's command was resisted by the Yogakar, Sree Veera Marthanda Vurmah, from whom originated the proposal, quietly, but effectually, gained a step in the right direction, and, during his reign of forty years, His Highness established his authority, in a measure, over the Devaswam.

This sovereign's two successors maintained the policy of their predecessor Sree Veera Rama Marthanda Vurmah, in regard to Devaswam affairs; but subsequently the Yogakar and the Ettu Veetil Pillamar seem to have regained their ascendency, and they gradually began to oppose the royal power.

During the reign of seventeen sovereigns, (from Venaud Mootha Rajah downwards to Unny Kerala Vurmah) extending over a period of one hundred and eighty-seven years, the opposition and annoyance from the Yogakar and Ettu Veetil Pillamar and their confederates the Madempimars continued, and a hostile faction of the royalists and the confederates, existed, but through the vigilant and careful government of those sovereigns, no open outbreak occurred.

Adithya Vurmah, whose death in 852 M.E. (1677 A.D.), occurred under some noteworthy circumstances, was of a very quiet and mild disposition, and from his younger days, he led a retired and religious life, and became more like a spiritual minister than a king.

The confederates, taking advantage of this, began to oppose the royalists and to carry on every sort of oppression, to the extreme annoyance of the royal family, while the sovereign quietly submitted to all their misdeeds.

On a certain night, the king's palace at Trevandrum was found to be on fire, but not a single person among the villagers or the Devaswam people, who resided round the palace, would venture to come forward to extinguish the fire, and the whole of the palace and its out-houses were reduced to ashes before day-break.

King Adithya Vurmah and the royal family retired to a small palace constructed for the residence of the Elia Rajah, heir apparent, some years before on the top of a small hill on the western side of the river Killiar, and surrounded by a little fort called Puthencotta (new fort) built with mud walls, and His Highness resided here for some time; but soon after the burning of the palace, and the king's retiring to Puthencotta, the leaders of the confederates repaired in a body to Puthencotta, and requested an audience of the king which was granted. They pretended to know nothing of the fire that destroyed the palace, attributed it to mere accident, expressed their deep regret at the occurrence and professed to sympathize with the king.

His Highness being, as already said, a devotee, after expressing his resignation to the dispensation of Providence accepted the assurances of the confederates without tho slightest suspicion.

But this interview was sought by the confederates with the most diabolical intentions, for the Yogakar began to forward to the king, every day, *Nivedyams*, i. e., sweetmeat offered to the image of Padmanabha Swamy for pooja, and one day this being mixed with poison, the king, partook of it, became ill and died suddenly.

The whole royal family at the time of the king's death, consisted of one female, the king's niece named Umayamma Ranee, and her six male children, all under age.

On the death of the king the confederates went to Puthencotta palace, offered their condolences to the Ranee, and gave their assurances of allegiance to Her Highness and the young Princes; they then began to

CHAP. I. resort to the palace pretending to guard it against the intrusion of disaffected and rebellious subjects.

On a certain moonlight night, a few boys of the confederate party, who were of the same ages as the five Princes, were playing with them at the Puthencotta palace. One of the boys proposed to the Princes (doubtless at the instigation of the confederates), to go to a tank or reservoir, situated a few furlongs distant from the western side of the palace, and to play on a white sandy plain and bathe in the crystal water. The young Princes proceeded with the boys, without the knowledge of their unfortunate mother, and while they were bathing, shocking to relate, some men from the confederate party appeared there under the pretext of bathing, and seized the Princes and suffocated them under water: they left the bodies to float in the tank and went away, telling the boys to inform the people at the palace that the Princes were unfortunately drowned in the tank while bathing.

The tank, with which this tragical event is associated and which the confederates contemptuously called Kalippan Kulam (a reservoir for amusement), is at Manacaud, a few furlongs south of the Trevandrum fort, on the western side of Puthencotta.

The Ranee, on receiving this unexpected melancholy intelligence, though plunged in extreme sorrow, performed the funeral ceremonies of her murdered children by burning their bodies at the very spot where their late murdered grand uncle's body was burnt. The unfortunate Ranee now saw things in their true light and looking up to heaven, cursed the murderers of Her Highness' pious uncle and her innocent children.

There was now no male member in the royal family, except Umayamma Ranee's only son, aged nine years, to succeed to the musnud, and therefore Her Highness Umayamma Ranee became Queen Regent in 852 M.E. (1677 A.D.)

After a short residence in the palace at Puthencotta, Her Highness, finding the place unsafe for herself and the young Prince, abandoned it and proceeded to Neduvangaud, and resided in the little palace there, taking with her the royal Thavaree (the household priest), the palace Kariakar (Premier), Sumprathy (the Secretary), and other servants of the State, together with the palace establishment. This was done solely for the protection of Her Highness' son from the evil designs of the hostile confederates. CHAP. I.

It may be stated here that Providence heard the curse pronounced by the bereaved mother, for the spot where the castle and fort called Puthencotta once stood, and where the poisoned body of the pious Adithiya Vurmah Rajah and the bodies of the murdered Princes were burnt, was subsequently converted into a Hindu burial ground, where to this day numbers of dead bodies are daily cremated. The very race of the Ettu Veetil Pillamar and Madepimar, who caused those inhuman murders was, in the course of fifty-six years, extirpated in a more violent and atrocious manner. The reservoir originally a fine large tank, on the banks of which there was an extensive milk-white sandy plain bounded by cocoanut, cashewnut, jack, and other fruit trees, was the common resort of all the Brahmans and other residents of the village for the purpose of bathing and recreation but subsequent to the above event, it was abandoned, and became a desolate plain. People feared to approach the spot, and, ultimately, the tank was filled with sand and used for depositing the carcases of horses, cattle, dogs, and such other animals, as died in the town and the suburbs of Trevandrum.

The reigning Princess Umayamma remained for some time at Neduvangaud. She was obliged to cease interfering with government affairs from her fear of the confederates, who, if offended, the Ranee thought would injure her only son by some dastardly plot.

At this critical time dissensions broke out amongst

CHAP. I. the confederates, and each feudatory chief became sole master of his own possessions, and misrule and anarchy prevailed throughout every part of the country.

Taking advantage of this state of affairs in Travancore, in 855 M.E. (1680 A.D.), a petty sirdar, under the Mogul Emperor, wandering in the southern part of the Peninsula, with a number of horsemen and plundering the unprotected territories, invaded the southern part of Travancore and carried on depredations among the population. None of the nobles and chiefs being able to oppose the sirdar or arrest his progress, he advanced to Trevandrum and made his head quarters there.

The Devaswam Yogakar, fearing contamination, and the consequent loss of caste, shut the Trevandrum pagoda and fled for their lives. The Ettu Veetil Pillamar and Madempimar adopted the same course, leaving the country at the mercy of the Mogul sirdar, who was then at liberty to lay waste the country with fire and sword and compel the people to become Mahomedans. But fortunately for the kingdom, such a calamity was warded off by a few faithful Patans or Mahomedan servants attached to the Travancore house who remained after the flight of the Ranee to Neduvangaud.

These sirdars presented themselves before the Mogul and brought to his notice the circumstances that led to the proceedings of the confederates and of the departure of the bereaved Ranee from her royal residence. They seem to have been successful in persuading the Mogul sirdar not to demolish or contaminate the Trevandrum pagoda and other places of worship, or to convert any of the Hindus to Mohamedanism.

The Mogul sirdar exercised his power up to Edavaye in the north, and became sole master of the country between Thovalay and Edavaye on the coast line of Travancore, but he did not venture to proceed to Neduvangaud.

Possibly, out of some regard for the people and their sovereign, and also owing to the persuasion of the royalist Mahomedans, the Mogul chief encamped at Manacaud, outside the town of Trevandrum and remained there during his sway.

Though the sirdar did not attempt to convert the Hindus, still he insisted upon the Nairs adopting many of the Mahomedan customs, and they were compelled to do so. Some of these customs the Sudras still retain as useful and convenient.

The customs thus forced upon the Sudras, who reside between Vurkalay and Velavancode, and which are still observed by that community are the following:—

First.—Males to cover their heads and females to cover their bodies when they get out of doors.

Second.—Males to have the circumcision ceremony performed before they attain ten years of age.

Third.—That during the marriage ceremony, the relatives and the intimate friends of the family should sit like the Mahomedans in a circle and eat their meal from one vessel, having their heads covered while eating.

Fourth.—Sudra females should encircle their bodies with a cloth like the males, and abandon the mode of dressing in vogue among their sisters in the north.

Fifth.—Every child, on being weaned, should have a handkerchief tied round its head.

Sixth.—Females should have their forehead, chin, and hands tattooed; the designs being either of simple spots or plants, leaves, flowers, &c., &c.

All these are of common observance even now among the lower order of Sudras between Quilon and Kulculam; but the higher orders of Sudras seem to have shaken them off retaining only the first, viz., the covering of their head, by the males, and the shoulders, by the females.

CHAP. I.

Her Highness Umayamma Ranee, finding it difficult to recover her kingdom from the hands of the Mogul sirdar while her feudatories and militia were animated by a spirit of disloyalty towards her government, invited one Kerala Vurmah, a member of the northern Cottayam Rajah's family, a branch of the sovereign of Kolathnaud, and related to the Travancore royal house.

Rajah Kerala Vurmah was a brave warrior, perfect in sword exercise, arrow-shooting and in the use of other weapons of war.

This Rajah was appointed Her Highness' principal counsellor, and commander of all the militia then on the side of the royalists.

Kerala Vurmah lost no time in raising a force armed with bows and arrows, slings, swords and lances.

The Rajah, under his personal command led the army against the Mogul sirdar and attacked him unexpectedly at Manacaud near Trevandrum. As the sirdar had not a sufficient force near him, all his horsemen having been scattered about between Vurkalay and Thovalay collecting the revenue, he was unable to make a stand and was obliged to retreat precipitately to Thovalay. Kerala Vurmah pursued him and the sirdar was reinforced by a party of horsemen from Thovalay and the other southern districts. He made a stand near the side of a hill at Thiruvatar, and a severe battle ensued. While the jungles, and rocks with which the locality was covered, presented insuperable obstacles to the Mogul sirdar's cavalry and threw it into confusion; they afforded the Rajah's archers and slingers convenient positions for attack and defence. While the conflict was going on, many of the horsemen were killed and, unfortunately for the sirdar, a nest of wasps, on one of the trees under which he was fighting on horseback, was disturbed by the throwing of a stone from one of the slings and the insects came down in swarms, and stung him on his face and ears. On his attempting to dismount his horse, being stung by the wasps, threw its rider and ran away. Scarcely had the sirdar fallen on the side of the rock than hundreds of arrows pierced his body. Nor were the slingers idle, for they poured on the head of the great commander a volley of stones. The fallen chief was soon killed and his army was utterly defeated.

Kerala Vurmah arranged at once to capture the remaining horses, and to seize as many of the troopers as could be got. He succeeded in securing some three hundred horses and about a hundred prisoners with many swords, lances and other excellent weapons belonging to the enemy.

The Rajah marched victoriously to Trevandrum, which Her Highness the Ranee also reached with her son and all the palace establishment. They soon rebuilt the palace at Trevandrum.

Kerala Vurmah Rajah organized at once a battalion of cavalry with the three hundred horses secured at the battle, one regiment of archers, and one regiment of swordsmen and posted them in three different parts at Trevandrum.

After this, the Rajah found no difficulty in bringing to obedience all the refractory chiefs and nobles. The Yogakar and the Ettu Veetil Pillamar were cowed, and became obedient to Her Highness the Ranee.

The fort and palace at Puthencotta were broken up, and with the materials two buildings were constructed inside the Trevandrum fort. One was called Valia Koikel, and the other Thevarathu Koikel, and Kerala Vurmah Rajah occupied the former building.

The disaffected Madempimar and Ettu Veetil Pillamar and others perceiving that the strength of Her Highness the Ranee's Government rested with Kerala Vurmah, conspired against him. They concocted measures for his destruction and on a certain night he was assassinated in his own residence, but who the murderers were remains to this day a mystery.

CHAP. I.

In 859 M.E. (1684 A.D.), Umayamma Ranee's son, Prince Revi Vurmah, attained his sixteenth year, and in accordance with the custom of the country, the sovereignty was transferred by Her Highness Umayamma Ranee, to the Prince who was duly installed on the musnud.

As Kerala Vurmah had adopted all the necessary measures for the protection of the royal family from the inroads of the feudatories, the new sovereign found no difficulty in governing the kingdom and affording satisfaction to His Highness' aged mother, who had been a total stranger to the comforts of life from the earliest period of her career.

The Dowager Ranee being old, and there being no other member of the royal family, save the Ranee's reigning son, the adoption of some new members became necessary. The Kolathnaud sovereign was accordingly asked to send some members of his family as usual, but after hesitating a good deal, in consequence of the assassination of Rajah Kerala Vurmah, he ultimately acceded to the Travancore Ranee's wishes and sent two females and two males for adoption into the Travancore royal family.

The name of the elder male was Unny Kerala Vurmah and that of his brother Rama Vurmah. A year after this adoption, the Dowager Ranee died and was followed to the grave by the elder of the two adopted Ranees, and the junior Ranee was the only surviving female member of the royal family, who now became Attingal Mootha Thumpuran. This Ranee gave birth to a Prince in 881 M.E. (1706 A.D.) This Prince whose name was Marthanda Vurmah, distinguished himself above all other sovereigns and received the well-merited title of saviour of the kingdom of Travancore.

The reigning sovereign Revi Vurmah, was highly delighted at the birth of this Prince, and spent in commemoration of the event a good deal of money in charity, donations, &c., in accordance with the prescriptions of the Hindu Sastras.

In 893 M.E. (1718 A.D.), king Revi Vurmah died, and the eldest of the adopted Princes, Unny Kerala Vurmah was proclaimed king of Travancore. This sovereign was of a quiet and weak disposition, and consequently, the mischief-making confederates began to acquire strength. In the course of two years, they became once more powerful. To add to these misfortunes, all the organised forces of the able and wise commander Kerala Vurmah, which had been maintained by Revi Vurmah, during his reign of thirty-four years, were disbanded or scattered over the country, or took service under the feudatory chiefs.

Though he was only fourteen years old, Prince Marthanda Vurmah could not tolerate such a state of things, and His Highness therefore earnestly requested his uncle, the then reigning sovereign, to permit him to take an active interest in the affairs of Government, and the sovereign being pleased with the energy and intelligence of the youth, permitted him to do as he chose and make such arrangements as he found necessary, in consultation with the officers of the State.

Armed with such powers, the Prince lost no time in adopting measures for checking the rebellious spirit of the confederacy. The Yogakar, Ettu Veetil Pillamar and Madempimar, in their turn became inveterate enemies of the Prince, and began to seek measures for his destruction.

The confederates cared very little for the reigning sovereign, but were greatly afraid of the Prince; they were therefore determined to take his life at all hazards, and set to work for the attainment of this object.

Under these disagreeable circumstances, the Prince was obliged to shift from place to place to avoid falling into the hands of the assassins.

CHAP. I.

Finding it unsafe to reside always at Trevandrum, the Prince was obliged to proceed under disguise and to remain for short periods in the palaces of Sreevalumcode, Neduvangaud, Mavalikaray, Attingal, &c., &c.

At different times and places, this Prince was waylaid and was nearly falling into the hands of the confederates; but in every instance he providentially escaped.

On a certain occasion, the Prince had to conceal himself in the interior of a pagoda which was immediately surrounded by the confederate party, when his life was saved by the stratagem of the faithful priest of the pagoda. It was about dusk, and the escape of the Prince was miraculous. The priest quickly transferred his clothes and ornaments to the prince and putting a quantity of boiled rice in a brass vessel on the Prince's head, told him to walk out muttering manthrams, like a priest, and to whisper to the mob that the Prince was lying concealed inside the pagoda. As he walked out, the priest putting on the Prince's dress walked about inside the pagoda peeping here and there as if he was in a state of great anxiety. Seeing this the mob entered the pagoda, fell upon the counterfeit prince, dragged him out and killed him forthwith.

During his wanderings, the Prince had to sleep on the tops of trees, under the roofs of poor peasants, as well as in the midst of jungles, like Charles II of England.

After six years reign, Unny Kerala Vurmah died, and was succeeded by his younger brother Rama Vurmah in 899 M.E. (1724 A.D.), who was junior uncle to Prince Marthanda Vurmah.

Some time previous to the death of this Rajah, a female member of the Kolathnaud family was adopted as a Princess of Travancore, and Her Highness gave birth to a Prince in the Kollum year 899. This was the renowned Rama Rajah, generally called Dharma Rajah.

His Highness Rama Vurmah was more fond of his nephew than his deceased brother, and was also more resolute than several of his predecessors.

His Highness was a close observer of the difficulties and dangers to which his nephew was subjected by the Ettu Veetil Pillamar and Madempimar, and he was determined to punish them for their disloyalty and rebellious conduct.

His Highness, in consultation with his intelligent nephew, proceeded in 901 M.E. (1726 A.D.), to Trichinopoly with some of the officers of the State: he entered into a treaty with the Madura Government and secured its support by offering to renew the lapsed attachment to that crown, and to bind himself to pay a certain sum of money annually. At the same time, a suitable force was applied for to punish and bring to their senses the Madempimar and other refractory chiefs. After some discussion and preliminary enquiries, the sovereign was successful in obtaining a force consisting of one thousand cavalry, under the command of M. Vencatapathy Naiken, and two thousand Carnatic sepoys, headed by Thripathy Naiken, and others in charge of fifty sirdars, including Raghava Iyen and Subba Iyen, &c.

On the arrival of this force in Travancore, all the Madempimar and other refractory chiefs and insurgents fled, and consequently there was no work for the army which was however retained for the purpose of overawing the insurgents.

Though the refractory chiefs were thus kept under restraint, the Yogakar and the Ettu Veetil Pillamar at Trevandrum could not be brought to a sense of their duty, for they knew full well that the sovereign could not adopt harsh measures against the Devaswam community. They continued their arrogant conduct to the annoyance of the royal family, and consequently, Prince Marthanda Vurmah was obliged to reside at Mavalikaray and Attingal, with the senior Ranee and her son, the little Prince Rama Vurmah.

CHAP. I.

In 903 M.E. (1728 A.D.), when this Prince was being taken to Attingal from Trevandrum, a party of men, under the Ettu Veetil Pillamar met at a place called Calakoottem, headed by Ramanammadathil Pillay for the purpose of assassinating the Ranee and the Prince, but providentially both escaped unhurt by the vigilant measures adopted by Kilimanoor Koil Thumpuran, who was escorting the party. Koil Thumpuran, after sending away the Ranee and the Prince, under disguise to a neighbouring village, got into the Ranee's palanquin and moved forward, with all the attendants, and thus drew the attention of the party towards the palanquin. When the turbulent crowd neared the palanquin, and commenced the attack, the Koil Thumpuran jumped out sword in hand and cut to pieces many of the assailants. Unfortunately, however, the Thumpuran perished in the conflict.

In recognition of the faithful conduct of the Koil Thumpuran, grants of land, embracing a whole village called Kilimanoor, was given to the family of this distinguished hero and saviour of the Ranee's and Prince's lives. The grant is enjoyed by the family up to the present day.*

In the same year 903 M.E. (1728 A.D.), king Rama Vurmah died after a short illness, deeply lamented by the royal family, especially by His Highness' fondly attached nephew Prince Marthanda Vurmah.

The system of government and the mode of collecting the revenue appear to have been continued without any material change for a long period, but in the reign of the late king Revi Vurmah, who assumed the sovereignty in 859 M.E. (1684 A.D.), some alterations, in the existing system were introduced, which appear to be the following:

* A descendant of this Koil Thumpuran is now attached to the palace of the present Maha Rajah and has distinguished himself as an artist. For his drawings Revi Vurmah Koil Thumpuran has received gold medals awarded at the Fine Arts Exhibition at Calcutta, Madras, and Vienna.

The old system was that the revenue of every petty district should be roughly calculated, and the local chief was made responsible for the collection of the same, deducting the amount assigned for the performance of Devaswam and other religious ceremonies, for the maintenance of the militia and the collection of revenue.

The State establishment then consisted of one Valia Kariacar (Prime Minister), one Neetaluthu Pillay, one Rayasom Pillay (head clerk), and several Rayasoms and Kanacka Pillays (writers and accountants). The Minister and all his establishment held office in the palace, and the king presided over them. Every question, whether petty or important, was submitted for the king's decision, without whose order nothing was to be executed.

Commercial speculations seem to have engaged the attention of even the earliest Travancore kings; for Travancore seems to have had dealings with foreign nations from the remotest period, and pepper, cassia, areca-nut, &c., &c., were bartered for Chinese, Arabian, and Roman goods and manufactures.

The Greeks, the Egyptians, the Romans, the Danes, the Portuguese, the Dutch, the French, and the English were the nations with whom Travancore had commercial relations.

The Romans had from a very early period perfect toleration given them to promulgate Christianity throughout Travancore, and grants of lands were bestowed for erecting churches.

The Danes were permitted to erect a factory at Edavaye to carry on traffic.

The Portuguese were also allowed to establish themselves as merchants at Poracaud, Quilon, Neendacaray and several other petty sea-ports, soon after their arrival in India.

The Dutch received aid in their attempts to sup-

CHAP. I.

plant the Portuguese and establish themselves all along the sea-coast between Colachel and Cochin.

The English had a grant of some land at Anjengo for the opening of a factory contemporaneously with the establishment of their factories on the Malabar coast; and subsequently permission was given them for building a fort there. They always received warm support from Travancore in all their subsequent undertakings.

All these nations were treated very kindly and with respect by the kings of Travancore in times when European nations were but half-civilized. The kings cultivated the acquaintance and friendship of Europeans and gave to each and every one of them the valuable products of Travancore especially pepper, without showing partiality and without giving cause for quarrels among them, though at that period a strong spirit of rivalry prevailed among European nations and they were constantly at war with each other.

Various improvements were introduced by the king Revi Vurmah during his reign. The power of the local chiefs was curtailed and special agents appointed to various parts of the country, which was divided into districts called "Pacuthies," with power to collect the revenue, which was roughly estimated before their appointment. After defraying the expenditure on religious and other institutions, the agent was to pay the surplus into the king's Treasury.

All such agents were recognized as king's officers and thus the authority and influence of the Madempimar and petty chiefs were destroyed.

After the death of this sovereign, his successor Unny Kerala Vurmah was unable to enforce the above system generally, and consequently in many parts of the country, especially in the southern Districts of Nanjenaud, anarchy once more prevailed. It was this state of things that Rama Vurmah strove to remedy. Unfortunately, however, he died before he could fully carry into execution his intention to introduce a better system of Government, but left the kingdom in better hands, namely, in those of the able and the most noble Prince Marthanda Vurmah. CHAP. I.

Most of the Travancore kings have ruled the country with wisdom and valour, surmounting all oppositions both from the feudatory chiefs and from foreign invaders, and governing the kingdom satisfactorily.

Though there are no details of the reigns of some sovereigns on record, yet it may be stated without fear of contradiction, that the sovereigns of Travancore have been generally gifted with wisdom and a high sense of duty, and that almost without exception, their mental culture has been of the highest order.

Almost all the sovereigns of Travancore are distinguished, more or less, not only for their princely accomplishments, but also for the production of various Sanscrit works on Philosophy, Metaphysics, History, Religion, Music, the Drama, &c., while their governing abilities were and are seldom equalled by the native kings of India.

These sovereigns kept pace with other nations in the art of good government, and their wisdom and good principles were known and testified to by several European nations, in the earliest days of their intercourse with India.

CHAPTER II.

SREE PADMANABHA DASA VANJI PALA MARTHANDA VURMAH KULASEKHARA PERUMAL

CHAP. II.

SUCCEEDED his uncle, King Rama Vurmah, in 904 M.E. (1729 A.D.), he being the rightful heir to the musnud. When called upon to assume the reins of Government, His Highness was only twenty-three years old.

Though the Maha Rajah came to power under great many adverse circumstances, such as a highly depressed condition of the finances, a very disorganized state of the kingdom, caused by the long standing refractory conduct of the feudatory chiefs (Madempimar and Ettu Veetil Pillamar) approaching almost to a civil war, as was shown in the previous chapter of this work, yet the young Maha Rajah boldly faced all these difficulties and applied his resources, valour and sagacity with laudable firmness and fortitude in surmounting them.

The Maha Rajah's attention was first directed to the laying of the foundation of a good Government, and for this His Highness at once formed a ministry, consisting partly of the deserving and confidential servants of the late Maha Rajah, and partly of able men selected from among the people. Arumugam Pillay, who was the acting Dalawah when the late sovereign proceeded to Trichinopoly in 901 M.E. (1726 A. D.), was now confirmed in his office. Cumaraswamy Pillay was appointed Commander-in-Chief, and the Dalawah's brother Thanu Pillay, assistant to Cumaraswamy Pillay. Rama Iyen, a Brahman whom

MARTHANDA VURMAH MAHA RAJAH.

His Highness had brought up under his own care and patronage, was appointed palace Rayasom (Under Secretary of State), and several other deserving men were also employed for the performance of the various functions of Government.

Thus, the commencement of the Maha Rajah's reign was attended with such success, that the importance of the ancient mother kingdom of "Chera" (Travancore), may be said to have revived with this reign.

The late Rama Vurmah Rajah was compelled in 901 M.E. to proceed to the Pandyan capital (Trichinopoly), and to enter into an agreement with the Pandyan Government, by which he promised to pay an annual tribute of about 3,000 rupees and obtained from the Governor a force of 1,000 horse and 2,000 foot, for the purpose of overawing the turbulent chiefs and nobles.

The pay of this contingent, as well as the annual tribute, was in arrears for a few months, when the Maha Rajah ascended the throne, and on the demand of the troops for their pay and the tribute, His Highness referred them to his Dalawah, Arumugam Pillay, who, on delaying payment, was seized and removed to Thrikanamkudy by the force, whereupon he borrowed money from the Kottar merchants and others, and adjusted most part of the pressing demands. The Dalawah was however still detained by the force at Thrikanamkudy.

In the meanwhile His Highness commissioned Cumaraswamy Pillay, the Commander-in-Chief, and Thanu Pillay his assistant to raise an army of Maravers and a few hundred horse, to raise up barriers in the shape of mud walls between Kadakaray and Mantharamputhur Aramboly, and Cape Comorin; to construct special gates for passages, and to guard them by companies of Maravers and troopers. These arrangements were effectually carried out in the course of a few months, and Travancore was secured against the attacks of foreign invaders.

CHAP. II.

Cumaraswamy Pillay, with a force of Maravers, was then ordered by the Maha Rajah to proceed to Thrikanamkudy for the purpose of releasing the Dalawah, and that brave officer executed the command with promptness and vigour. The Maha Rajah was extremely pleased with him, as he had by this exploit extricated the Dalawah from a painfully embarrassing position, and removed the burden of care and anxiety that weighed upon his head.

The Maha Rajah then thought that he could safely do away with the Trichinopoly force and ordered it to march back to that town. His Highness communicated his resolution to the Pandyan Government, and requested the Governor to release His Highness from the conditions entered into with the former by the late Maha Rajah.

The feudatory chiefs and nobles, after the withdrawal of the Trichinopoly contingent force, began to rebel again, and as they had always been striving to get their independence, they combined and formed a confederacy as before, and were joined by the two sons of the late sovereign, known by the names of Kunju Thambies *alias* Papu Thamby and Ramen Thamby, who held high rank among the nobles, during the life-time of their father and were in affluent circumstances. But they were now reduced to the level of the ordinary nobles of the country and they felt their degradation keenly. The confederates sympathised with them, and considering them proper instruments for overthrowing the royal authority, they persuaded them to claim their father's throne; and one of them (Papu Thamby), being furnished with sufficient means, proceeded to Trichinopoly in 905 M.E. (1730 A.D.), and represented to the Pandyan Governor his imaginary grievances, saying that great injustice was done to him by the kingdom being forcibly usurped by Marthanda Vurmah. He entered into certain terms with that chief to put him in possession of the kingdom. The Governor, annoyed by the refusal of payment of the Peishkush, and the dismissal of the contingent forces by Marthanda Vurmah Maha Rajah, readily listened to Papu Thamby's false representations. CHAP. II.

The Governor ordered one of his agents Alagappa Moodelliar to proceed with a sufficient number of men and horses to Travancore, and institute enquiries into the claims of Papu Thamby, giving him authority to enforce the same if found valid.

The Moodelliar set out from Trichinopoly, accompanied by Papu Thamby and arrived at Udayagherry, where he commenced to institute the enquiry into the claims of the Thamby. The Maha Rajah, on learning this, deputed the State Secretary Rama Iyen and his assistant Narayana Iyen to the Moodelliar, and they were furnished with valid documents to prove the absurdity and fictitious character of Papu Thamby's claims.

While Papu Thamby was utterly unable to produce any documentary evidence in support of his pretended rights, Rama Iyen fully proved the claims of the Maha Rajah to his uncle's throne. The Moodelliar was very indignant with Papu Thamby, and his false complaint was at once rejected. He was told that he should be loyal and obedient to his king in accordance with the customs of the country.

The Maha Rajah informed the Moodelliar of the renewed outbreak of a rebellious spirit among his chiefs and asked him to place one-half of his force at His Highness' disposal. The Moodelliar complied with this request and returned to Trichinopoly loaded with presents.

Though the Maha Rajah was enraged with the conduct of the Kunju Thambies and the chiefs and nobles, yet His Highness pretended to be indifferent about the matter. As His Highness had the strong support of the Trichinopoly force, besides his own Maraver troops, he directed his attention to certain important affairs of Government in which he was engaged before the peace of his kingdom was menaced by the plots of his

CHAP. II. enemies. The Thambies and the Ettu Veetil Pillamar were all quiet and matters continued so for some time.

While Elia Rajah (heir apparent), His Highness had in view the repairing and re-constructing of the pagoda at Trevandrum which had become old and dilapidated. In the very year of His Highness' accession, the pagoda work was commenced, and though its progress was impeded by the mischievous proceedings of the Ettu Veetil Pillamar, yet with active and energetic supervision, the whole work was completed by the next year, 906 M.E. (1731 A.D.)

Twelve thousand salagramams, (sacred stones representing the incarnations of Vishnu, obtained from the bed of the river Gunduck, north of Benares) were procured, and with these the idol of Sree Padmanabha Swamy was re-consecrated. At the same time, a huge piece of granite slab cut out of a rock at Thirumalay, about four miles north of Trevandrum, measuring 20 feet square and 2½ feet thick, was brought and placed in front of the idol in the month of Edavom 906 M.E. (June 1731 A.D.), and it was called Ottakel Mundapam.

In addition to the irregular army of Maravers and Nairs already organized, regiments of infantry with fire-arms were formed and maintained, fortifications were constructed at all the important frontiers and garrisoned by detachments. His Highness himself moved from place to place accompanied by the Dalawah, and His Highness' confidential and intelligent Secretary, Rama Iyen. Thus, in the course of a couple of years, the country enjoyed the benefits of perfect peace and tranquillity, and the Maha Rajah was able to recover most of the longstanding arrears from his chiefs and nobles, who were all now overawed by the sight of the new army and of the Trichinopoly cavalry.

After paying off the pressing demands of the State debts, the Maha Rajah was enabled to keep a surplus in the Treasury.

With the view of making a good use of the money in the Treasury, His Highness set to work for the improvement of Nanjenaud, the most fertile part of the country, by undertaking certain gigantic irrigation works which are still to be seen as the monuments of His Highness' wisdom, the efficient government of that period, and the anxiety and desire of the Maha Rajah for the welfare of his subjects.

Foremost among these works were the Poymanay and Puthenu anicuts, which latter, while it irrigated several miles of lands in Kulculam, also supplied drinking-water for the inhabitants of Padmanabhapuram and the people around it.

These works are certainly gigantic, and are the result of no ordinary courage, enterprise, and engineering skill. Indeed, these works were very expensive, laborious and useful; for the surplus water running from the western range of the ghauts where there is an anicut called Pandyan anay, constructed in time immemorial for the irrigation of lands in Nanjenaud, became a river known by the name of Kulithurayar, and the water of that river ran waste into the sea; and the wise Maha Rajah, recognising the practicability of utilising this for irrigation purposes, commenced to build the granite stone anicut across the river. This anicut is called the Poymanay Puthen anay. The structure of this work will vie with any of a similar kind constructed on scientific principles and under professional supervision. Connected with this canal, tanks and reservoirs were also excavated, and feeding channels opened from the main one to fill those tanks with water for irrigating the lands. Thus, the lands which were dependent entirely upon rain for cultivation, and which yielded only one crop in a year, now became rich; an unfailing supply of river water was secured and the lands began to yield two crops annually. Public roads were opened, markets and thoroughfares and various other useful institutions established, and revenue measures introduced.

CHAP. II.

As the Maha Rajah's military force was now considered equal to the requirements of the country, the Trichinopoly troops were sent back.

On the return of the Trichinopoly force, and the detaching of the Maha Rajah's troops to different stations, to watch the frontiers, to preserve peace in the several districts, and to assist the Revenue Officials in the collection of revenue and the execution of the maramuth works, &c. &c., the restless and turbulent Kunju Thambies, and the chiefs and nobles renewed their schemes and plots against the Maha Rajah's life, for which purpose they assembled at different places and consulted upon the measures to be taken for accomplishing their object.

Their leader was Papu Thamby, and through him, all the chiefs and nobles between Padmanabhapuram and Attingal were invited to join in the confederacy. The Maha Rajah received private intelligence about their foul designs upon His Highness' life, and employed spies to move about in disguise, and to procure information regarding their treacherous proceedings.

On a certain night, two men of the Ettu Veetil Pillamar, named Kalacoottathu Pillay and Kodamun Pillay, convened a meeting of the confederacy in a building at Venganoor, some distance from the town of Trevandrum, and held a consultation as to the best plan to be adopted for effecting the assassination of the Maha Rajah; the assembly agreed "that on the day of the Aurratt procession, in the month of Thulam, the Maha Rajah would have to walk on foot, preceding the carrying of the idols at some distance; that every one of the Ettu Veetil Pillamar, viz., 1st, Ramanamadathil Pillay; 2nd, Mathanamadathil Pillay (leaders); 3rd, Kolathoo Pillay; 4th, Kalacoottathu Pillay; 5th, Chempalathil Pillay; 6th, Pallichel Pillay; 7th, Kudamun Pillay, and 8th, Venganoor Pillay; as also Moothadathu Pandaram, Elumpale Pandaram, Elumpilli Pandaram, and Edatharay Potty, (four Brahman chiefs connected with the Yogakar) should attend the Aurratt procession, accompanied by their men (militia), armed with swords, lances, daggers, &c., under the pretext of attending the Aurratt procession; that when near the sea beach and when the idols are housed as customary for the pooja, and when the Maha Rajah retired to the shed after sunset, a party of men should suddenly attack and assassinate him there, and all the nobles should stand by as spectators and pretend to know nothing about the matter; and that should the royalists attempt either to rescue the king, or to retaliate on the assassins, the whole confederacy should fall in and execute a wholesale murder." This resolution was committed to writing on ola (cadjan or palmyra leaf on which all documents were made in Malabar during that time), and several copies were drawn up for the information of the absent chiefs. In order to ensure secrecy, these were put inside the soles of the messengers' slippers and were so despatched to various places.

An old Pandaram who was living in that building, which was a public inn, overheard the consultation and witnessed all these treacherous transactions. This man was one of the Maha Rajah's spies, and the chiefs blindly ignorant of the fact, took no heed of his presence there, as the old man was in the employ of Venganoor Pillay.

Soon after the breaking up of the meeting, the old Pandaram revealed the matter to one of the Maha Rajah's confidential servants who was also moving about under a similar commission. His Highness received this extraordinary information before day-break: persons were immediately despatched in pursuit of the men who carried the written resolution of the aforesaid meeting, and fortunately two of them were apprehended, and the documents discovered in the soles of their slippers. These men were quietly taken to the Maha Rajah, without the knowledge of any one. Every particular connected with the conspiracy

CHAP. II.

was divulged by them, and exactly corresponded with the contents of the two olas detected on their persons.

The Maha Rajah was very much excited at this singular occurrence, but did not think it proper to take any active action at the moment. The two men were kept in private confinement, within the walls of the palace, and the two olas were secured in the Maha Rajah's own desk; and thus the matter was hushed up for the time.

The Maha Rajah was a well-trained warrior, tall, possessing a powerful frame and long arms: he learnt from his boyhood gymnastic exercises in all their branches, and was a perfect master in the use of the sword, lance and dagger, besides being a precise marksman. His Highness was equal to any single man in combat, and he was able to command a whole army in the field. Possessing an indomitable and fearless disposition he was not alarmed at the conspiracy which he was determined to trace to its origin, and then extirpate the race of the conspirators.

Secret arrangements were now made through His Highness' confidential Secretary, Rama Iyen, to detach parties of trustworthy sepoys and troopers, to watch the movements of the nobles and chiefs, and to secure a strong force composed of infantry and cavalry to accompany the Aurratt procession.

The Utsavam festival commenced in the month of Alpasy, when the military began to concentrate in the capital. On the Aurratt day, an unusual force escorted the idols, both in front and rear, while the Maha Rajah fearlessly walked in front of the idols, with a glittering broad sword in hand and a favourite Persian dagger in his girdle.

On seeing such preparations and precautions adopted during the procession, the chiefs and nobles were cowed and none had the boldness to strike the premeditated blow.

Soon after the Aurratt festival, the Maha Rajah

made all the necessary arrangements for the protection of the capital, and for defending himself against the nobles and chiefs. Detachments of his force were privately posted and subsequently strengthened on the Aurratt day.

In 908 M.E. (1733 A.D.), the Maha Rajah proceeded from Trevandrum to Nagercoil. While there, His Highness resolved to extirpate his old enemies and to punish their leaders, the Kunju Thambies. Secret instructions were conveyed through the State Secretary, Rama Iyen, to the military officers to seize, on a signal being given, all the nobles and chiefs simultaneously, and to post horses between Nagercoil and Trevandrum for conveying the signal.

One morning, while the Maha Rajah was sitting upstairs in the palace at Nagercoil on a swinging cot, Papu Thamby came to see His Highness. When he observed the Thamby coming, His Highness' attendants were instructed to stop him at the door leading to the staircase; to resist him should he insist on going up and to cut him down if he drew his sword. The attendants prepared themselves and guarded the staircase with drawn swords. Papu Thamby came in and walked to the staircase; being the son of the late Maha Rajah, he had the privilege of going to the royal presence without special permission, but the attendants stopped him and told him that they would not let him go without special orders. The Thamby being irritated and affronted, a quarrel ensued, which resulted in a bloody conflict. Papu Thamby drew his sword, and as he was aiming a blow at one of the attendants, he received several cuts on his neck and hands from behind, which brought him to the ground. His brother Ramen Thamby witnessed the tragedy, but without waiting to remonstrate, or confront the attendants, or notice his fallen brother's condition, he rushed upstairs with his sword and approached the Maha Rajah who was still seated on the swinging cot, pretending to know nothing of what was going on down-

CHAP. II. stairs. Ramen Thamby aimed a deadly blow at His Highness with his drawn sword, but providentially the point of the sword struck against the low beam of the roof and missed its aim. The Maha Rajah instantly and dexterously sprang upon the Thamby, seized the sword before he could raise his hand for a second thrust, threw him down, and having seated himself on his breast, took his favourite dagger which always hung at his girdle and plunged it to the hilt into the traitor's heart. During this scuffle, the Maha Rajah's body and clothes were besmeared with blood: rising up, he opened the window, showed himself to his officers and men and gave them the pre-arranged signal, telling them, at the same time, that now that the leaders of the confederacy had been punished, the remaining work should be executed with all possible expedition.

Some of the followers of the Thambies who flocked to the spot on hearing that their masters were in trouble were cut down, and others escaped.

Before daybreak, every one of the Madempimar and Ettu Veetil Pillamar, together with the three Pandarams and the Potty alluded to above were apprehended, and the next day they were arraigned before the Maha Rajah, who was then at Kulculam.

The Maha Rajah presided at their trial, the two "olas" were produced, and both the men on whose persons they were found and who were in confinement at Trevandrum, were called as witnesses.

Each of the nobles and chiefs so arraigned was called upon to answer the charge of treason on which he was indicted. The two witnesses were confronted with the prisoners and the olas read to them. Forty-two of the nobles and chiefs and their confederates were tried, pleaded guilty and were sentenced to death. They were all hanged at a place known by the name of Mukhamandapam, a few miles north-west of Kulculam. The four Brahmans and a few others of the same caste were also tried and found guilty, but the punish-

ETTU VEETIL PILLAY.

PUBLISHED BY MESS.RS HIGGINBOTHAM & CO.

C. PACZESNY LITH: MADRAS

ment of death in the case of Brahmans not being allowed by the laws of Manu, by which the Hindus are governed, the Maha Rajah sentenced them to be banished the country, after making them out-castes by branding their foreheads with the figure of a dog.

Though the total destruction of these inveterate enemies of the royal house was seriously resolved upon by the Maha Rajah, still His Highness would not tolerate the massacring of women and children; orders were therefore given to seize the families of the traitors, and make them over to the fishermen who lived on the sea-beach, so that they might become out-castes and the race of Madempimars and the rebellious Ettu Veetil Pillamars might not be revived in this age. All their houses and landed property were confiscated and taken possession of by the Sircar, the former were broken up and the materials used for erecting certain buildings attached to the Trevandrum pagoda, and the latter was annexed to the Sircar lands. Thus ended a race of chiefs who had been guilty of rebellion against the royal house for many hundreds of years, and at whose hands the royal family had suffered injuries and wrongs of the most inhuman and atrocious character.

Perfect order and peace now prevailed in the country between Aramboly and Edavaye, and the Maha Rajah began to entertain ideas of extending his dominions towards the North, His Highness being then in possession of only isolated localities in the North, such as Kullada, Mavalikaray, &c.

The royal family of Quilon, designated Dasinganaud or Jayathungnaud (which Visscher calls signate in his letters) and of Kottarakaray (Elayada Swaroopam) were collaterally related to the Travancore royal house, or rather, they were branches of the Travancore house, as has been already said.

In 906 M.E. (1731 A.D), the Rajah of Dasinganaud (Quilon) formed an alliance with the principality of Kayemkulam, by adopting some members of the ruling

CHAP. II. family of the latter. This adoption was in direct opposition to the Maha Rajah's wishes and it consequently offended His Highness.

His Highness led a powerful army towards Quilon, under his command, and after several battles at the Quilon frontier, the Maha Rajah's force being victorious, His Highness advanced to the capital of Dasinganaud, and the Rajah of the place, finding resistance impossible, sued for peace. The Maha Rajah acceded to the proposal, but compelled the Quilon Rajah to cancel the adoption, and break off the alliance with the Kayemkulam principality. Moreover as the Quilon Rajah was related to Travancore, His Highness decided that Dasinganaud should be annexed to Travancore, on the death of the only remaining Rajah of that family.

All the conditions proposed by the Maha Rajah were agreed to by the Quilon Rajah; his army was withdrawn, and it afterwards joined the Travancore force. All the fortifications were destroyed and a detachment of the Travancore army was stationed there under the command of Arumugum Pillay. The Maha Rajah then returned to Trevandrum bringing the Quilon Rajah with him.

The Quilon Rajah was accommodated in one of the palaces called Valia Koikel, with liberal provisions and supplies and every comfort of life, and he lived there in a more luxurious style than the Maha Rajah himself.

The Kayemkulam Rajah (a relative of Travancore) was alarmed at the success of the Maha Rajah, and began to concert measures to prevent further territorial acquisitions by Travancore. A consultation was held by all the northern principalities, presided over by the Cochin Rajah, and they resolved upon assisting the Quilon Rajah restoring his principality, and re-establishing Dasinganaud. To effect this, spies were sent to Trevandrum under disguise, and the Quilon Rajah was called away to Kayemkulam; and thence he was sent under a strong force to Quilon. The Dalawah resisted, but his detachment was no match to the combined army of Kayemkulam and Quilon, and therefore, after a severe battle, the Dalawah was obliged to retreat. Reinforcements were soon sent from Trevandrum and the Maha Rajah himself proceeded to re-conquer Quilon, but the fortifications raised and the defensive measures adopted there, with the assistance of the Cochin Rajah, supplemented by European fire-arms procured from the Dutch Governor of Cochin, made success on the part of the Travancore army doubtful. Great loss of life was suffered on both sides, and the Maha Rajah considering it inexpedient to venture further and sacrifice more men, wisely retreated to Trevandrum.

The Quilon Rajah now became powerful, and emboldened by the retreat of Travancore from the field, assumed the offensive. Together with the Kayemkulam Rajah, he attacked some of the territories belonging to the Travancore sovereign situated at Kulladay and Mavalikaray.

The Maha Rajah enraged at the conduct of the Quilon Rajah and irritated by his late defeat, took measures to teach the Quilon Rajah and his ally, the Kayemkulam chief, a wholesome lesson. The Travancore army was strengthened with additions of cavalry and infantry, new fire-arms were procured through the English merchants then trading at Anjengo and Edavaye, and in 909 M.E. (1734 A.D.), a powerful army was despatched against those principalities, under the chief command of Thanu Pillay and Sthanapathy Cumaraswamy Pillay, aided by the able Secretary, Rama Iyen.

Quilon and Kayemkulam were invaded simultaneously and a severe conflict commenced. The Kayemkulam Rajah applied for assistance to the Dutch, but the Governor of Cochin refused his aid on the plea that this war was brought on by the aggressive

CHAP. II.

conduct of the Kayemkulam towards Travancore. He was however still supported by the Cochin Rajah, but after several battles no advantage was gained by either side. At last, finding the Kayemkulam army could not hold out much longer, the Rajah of that State, a very bold and powerful personage, took the chief command of his army and pushed it forward against the Travancoreans and a severe and sanguinary battle ensued. It lasted for many hours and during the heat of the fight, one of the Travancore mounted sepoys fired at the Kayemkulam Rajah and brought him down to the ground. The death of the Rajah was not known at the moment and so the battle continued for some time longer, but when the loss of their sovereign became known, all the other commanders were disheartened and gradually retired from the field.

Notwithstanding the death of the Rajah, the spirit of the Kayemkulam army was not thoroughly broken, for the fallen Rajah's younger brother succeeded and he being more obstinate and courageous than his late brother, the war was continued with redoubled vigour. The Maha Rajah repaired to Quilon, accompanied by the heir apparent, who infused fresh courage into the Travancore army. A special body of recruits was raised for the war with Kayemkulam. Secretary Rama Iyen, finding that the army in the field could not successfully withstand the Kayemkulam force without sufficient reinforcement, proceeded to Tinnevelly, brought a regiment of Maravers under the command of Ponnam Pandya Deven, procured a thousand mounted sepoys from some of the Palayapattucar (Poligars), and marched the reinforcement by the hill roads through Kottarakaray. After holding a consultation among the officers, including the Dalawah and the Sthanapathy, Rama Iyen assumed the chief command of the army. In the battle, the next day he distinguished himself with signal success, and the Kayemkulam force met with a defeat for the first time. But the war continued, and Rama Iyen's army began to gain ground slowly and to advance into the Kayemkulam territories day by day. CHAP. II.

The Kayemkulam Rajah finding it impossible to hold out any longer against the Travancore army, applied again to the Cochin Rajah to procure him the aid of the Dutch Governor, but seeing that no aid could be expected from either party and knowing that the Dutch Governor had declined to interfere, the Kayemkulam Rajah sued for peace. With the permission of the Maha Rajah hostilities were suspended and the war came to a close.

In 909 M.E. (1734 A.D.), the Maha Rajah annexed Elayada Swaroopam, embracing Shencottah, Clangaud, Kerkudi, Valliyoor, on the Tinnevelly side, and Kottarakaray, Pathanapuram, &c., on the northern limits of Travancore. The Rajah Veera Kerala Vurmah, who was in charge of those territories was a relative of Travancore and died leaving as his successor a princess. The administration of the State was conducted by a Survadhikariakar, a very unscrupulous person, and anarchy began to prevail in the province. The Maha Rajah called the minister to Trevandrum and pointed out to him various instances of mal-administration and banished him from the country in disgrace. A proper and fit man was appointed to the responsible post of Survadhikariakar to the State, and the Maha Rajah took the government of the principality into his own hands, advising the Ranee to come and reside at Trevandrum, or to remain at Kottarakaray in her own palace as she pleased. The Ranee preferred the latter course.

In the meanwhile 909 M.E. (1734 A.D.), the Rajah of Quilon died and his country was taken possession of by the Kayemkulam Rajah, on the plea that he had established a claim upon that State by adoption. But the Maha Rajah remonstrated with the Kayemkulam chief on this unlawful conduct, on the ground not only that the family of Dasinganaud Rajah was collaterally related to Travancore but that in 906

CHAP. II. M.E. (1731 A.D.), the adoption in question was cancelled by the deceased Quilon Rajah.

The Kayemkulam chief being now well supported by his friend the Cochin Rajah, and having through him secured the aid of the Dutch at Cochin, paid no regard whatever to the remonstrances of the Maha Rajah and the result was the declaration of a second war.

The Dutch East India Company's Government, which had hitherto always observed a neutral policy in regard to the quarrels between Travancore and Kayemkulam, began to assume a kind of dictatorship in dealing with all these principalities, with the express view of establishing a check against the progress and extension of the Travancore kingdom, which the Dutch saw fast rising in power.

The Dutch Governor, M. A. Maten, sent a messenger to the Maha Rajah, desiring him not to go to war with the Kayemkulam chief; the Governor considered that even the annexation of the principality of Elayada Swaroopam was an unjust act on the part of the Maha Rajah, and that the Ranee should be allowed to rule that State. The Maha Rajah received the message with great courtesy, though his feelings were hurt. He sent a reply to the Governor by the same messenger to the effect that His Excellency need not trouble himself with questions which do not concern the commercial speculations and interests of the Dutch East India Company, and that while the Maha Rajah was friendly and paid all possible attention to the promotion of commercial prosperity of the Company, he greatly regretted to find the Governor attempting to interfere with the internal affairs of Travancore.

Little expecting an answer of this description the Dutch Governor, M. A. Maten, was highly displeased, and he professed to feel that an insult had been thereby offered to the Dutch Company.

RAMA IYEN DALAWA.

About this time, Arumugam Pillay Dalawah died, and his brother, Thanu Pillay, was appointed Dalawah, but he did not hold the appointment long, for he died in 912 M.E. (1737 A.D.), and the very able and meritorious Rama Iyen, who had been, soon after the Kayemkulam victory, raised to the post of Deputy Prime Minister, was appointed Dalawah. He began a brilliant career in his joint office of Prime Minister and Commander-in-Chief.

Great preparations to attack Kayemkulam were now set on foot; a large force was collected at Trevandrum, and arms and ammunition procured in abundance through the English merchants trading at Anjengo. The English were friendly to Travancore for a long time, and now offered to assist the Rajah with a number of their men in the campaign against Kayemkulam, but the Maha Rajah, wishing to obtain the victory single-handed, of which he was almost sure, politely and thankfully declined the offer. For a similar reason, the Maha Rajah refrained from obtaining assistance from the Pandyan kingdom.

Along with the preparations for war, Rama Iyen Dalawah was engaged in making several improvements in Trevandrum. Palaces, chuttrums, storehouses, &c., were constructed, rules were introduced curtailing the independent power of the Yogakar in the great pagoda at Trevandrum, and reserving supreme power to the sovereign over that Devaswam. The old reservoir called Padmatheerthum was drained and enlarged; flights of granite steps on the four sides of the tank down to its bottom, in the shape of ladders, for the convenience of people going down and coming up from the tank were also erected.

In 914 M.E. (1739 A.D.), when the Travancore force marched against Kayemkulam, the Dutch Governor of Ceylon, M. VanImhoff, came to Cochin and learnt the above facts and also that Travancore had risen to a high position from its success in the late war with Kayemkulam, and from the annexation of the terri-

CHAP. II.

tories of such neighbouring States as Elayadathunaud, Quilon, &c. He believed that the Travancore Maha Rajah was acting under the hostile counsels of the English, and that for the commercial interests of the Dutch, a proper balance of power among the native princes should be maintained and Travancore prevented from rising higher. In order to carry out this policy he thought that measures ought to be taken at once to check the progress and curtail the power of the Travancore Maha Rajah, and he confidently expected the full approbation and concurrence of the Rajahs of Cochin, Kayemkulam, and all the other northern petty chiefs.

M. VanImhoff deputed two persons from Cochin to the Maha Rajah with a message similar to the one sent by the Cochin Governor, M. A. Maten, but the answer of the Maha Rajah was just the same as before. M. VanImhoff was incensed at the obstinate resolution of His Highness and he wanted to take action at once against Travancore, but having no sufficient force at hand, to command respect and enforce authority, he considered it prudent to try conciliatory measures once more. Espousing the cause of the Ranee of Elayada Swaroopam, M. VanImhoff sent a protest in 915 M.E. (1740 A.D.) to the Maha Rajah, against the retention of that territory, but finding that the protest had no effect, he requested an interview with the Maha Rajah, and after a good deal of discussion on the subject, he failed in his mission and satisfied himself as to the difficulty of bringing about an amicable settlement of affairs. M. VanImhoff irritated and indignant, threatened His Highness with an invasion of Travancore. The Maha Rajah calmly replied that he was perfectly at liberty to do so, and reminded him of the unlikelihood of such an undertaking being crowned with success, and added that even if it should succeed, there were forests throughout Travancore into which the Maha Rajah could retire in safety. M. VanImhoff scornfully said that the Dutch could follow His Highness wherever he went.

The Maha Rajah closed the interview with the ironical retort that if M. VanImhoff could carry into execution his threats, His Highness would also think of invading Europe with his Munchees (native boats) and fishermen!

There being no prospects of an amicable settlement, M. VanImhoff had no alternative left but to proceed against Travancore. He wrote to Ceylon for a detachment of infantry and artillery and prepared his force at Quilon for immediate action.

In 916 M.E. (1741 A.D.), the Ranee of Elayada Swaroopam was installed sovereign of that State by the Dutch Governor, who obtained tracts of land and other advantages from her.

When the proceedings of the Dutch came to the knowledge of the Maha Rajah, His Highness directed the Travancore forces to take the field against them. The small Dutch detachment, with the large allied forces which supported the Ranee in her possession, were attacked by the Travancore army with complete success. Many Dutch soldiers were killed; the allied forces fled at the approach of the Travancoreans; and the Ranee herself escaped and reached Cochin, placing herself under the protection of M. VanImhoff. After taking possession of the territories of Elayada Swaroopam, the Travancore force turned against the Dutch possessions, captured Dutch out-posts in Travancore, attacked the factories, and took possession of the goods stored therein. After this signal defeat, the Dutch retired to Cochin, and the Travancore force besieged Kayemkulam, where a severe contest ensued.

While matters were thus in the north, the reinforcement which the Dutch Governor called from Ceylon, effected a landing at Colachel, and commenced to attack the villages and the small Travancore garrisons posted there. They committed many depredations and atrocities, plundered all the valuables in the bazaars and houses of rich people, fortified a place near the

CHAP. II.

port with wooden posts and garrisoned a portion of the Dutch force in it. The rest proceeded and attacked the Travancore out-posts on the coast, such as Tengapatnam, Midaulom, Kadiapatnam, &c., &c., and advanced to the opulent city of Eraneel.

On receiving this unexpected intelligence, the Maha Rajah, who was then at Trevandrum, hastened to the south with all the force at his command, and directed Rama Iyen Dalawah, who was then engaged in the north, to march with a sufficient force and join His Highness at Padmanabhapuram.

On the Maha Rajah's reaching Kulculam, he adopted measures to arrest the progress of the Dutch who being, at the time, in possession of almost all the villages between Colachel and Kottar, and contemplated an attack on His Highness' palace at Padmanabhapuram, but this was frustrated by the Maha Rajah's timely arrival at Kulculam, where he raised a levy of Nairs, and reinforced the regular infantry already in service in that part of the country. The Maha Rajah strongly remonstrated with the Governor of Cochin and even wrote to the Government in Batavia a letter of remonstrance and complaint.

An embassy was with as little possible delay sent to Pondicherry to treat with the French Governor, to render military aid to His Highness against the Dutch. A treaty was concluded, by which the French bound themselves to assist the Maha Rajah against the Dutch and his other enemies, and the Maha Rajah, engaged to grant them certain lands at Colachel and other parts of the coast, for building factories; and allow them to carry on commerce with Travancore.

Rama Iyen Dalawah reached Kulculam from the north, with a large reinforcement, consisting of infantry, cavalry and artillery, and the Maha Rajah, in consultation with the Dalawah planned an attack upon the Dutch invaders. A number of Munchees (native boats), properly manned, with a mixed force of trained sepoys and militia, and a full complement of seamen as rowers, organized for the purpose of watching the movements of the Dutch ship which landed the detachment, was kept in readiness at sea. Rama Iyen marched his troops and stationed them between Nagercoil and Eraneel: each army was commanded by tried officers, and the Dalawah, as the chief in command, placed himself in the centre. All these arrangements were completed in the course of a few months, and in the month of Chithiray, fighting commenced and lasted full two months. CHAP. II.

It appears from the Thiruvattar Devaswam accounts, that the Maha Rajah who was then at Eraneel, a place near the seat of war, proceeded on the 29th Vykasi (10th June) to Thiruvattar, the shrine of the Travancore family-deity, and after worshipping and invoking the god to aid him against the Dutch, placed his sword before the idol of the pagoda, and performing poojas, received back the sword from the officiating priest. He then returned to the seat of war, after making a donation of 500 fanams to the pagoda.

The Maha Rajah appears to have conducted the war in person.

On the morning of the 27th Audy (10th August) the battle of Colachel was commenced by the Travancore line. The Munchees surrounded the Dutch ship, anchored in the Colachel roads, and watched the landing of men and arms to assist the Dutch detachment then engaged in the battle. Rama Iyen Dalawah's army charged the Dutch line which was drawn up in fighting order against the Travancoreans. The Dutch line was broken through, the officers and men were driven from their positions and the whole force thrown into confusion and disorder. The Dutch having no cavalry, of which the Maha Rajah's force formed the largest portion, were placed in the greatest peril and after suffering much, they effected a precipitate retreat to the fort, leaving behind them several of their comrades dead, wounded, and prisoners. Of the last, there were 24, consisting of both officers and privates,

CHAP. II. who were sent to Udayagherry and taken great care of. The names of only nine of these prisoners are found in the Malayalam account of this war.

On the 31st Audy, the siege of the Colachel fort took place. In the course of a few hours, the fort was taken and the enemy driven to their ships which sailed to Cochin. In this siege, 389 muskets, with a few pieces of cannon, and a number of swords were taken by the Travancoreans from the Dutch.

Before the ratification of the French treaty, the battle of Colachel was fought and won, and the assistance of the French not being needed, the stipulations of the treaty were not carried into effect.

Of the Dutch prisoners, two men who attracted the Dalawah's notice, were taken before the Maha Rajah, who pitied their condition, but was unable to communicate with them, as there was nobody present who understood their language. His Highness being a good physiognomist, was struck with the appearance of one of them, who, His Highness thought, was brave and bold, and destined probably, to become a man of note. His Highness ordered Rama Iyen to take great care of them and treat them as gentlemen. The Maha Rajah made it a point to see them occasionally, and succeeded at last, in getting a man who understood their language.

The Dutch prisoners were so overcome with the kind treatment they received at the hands of the Maha Rajah, that they resolved to serve him in any capacity, and were enlisted in the Maha Rajah's army. Most of them distinguished themselves in His Highness' service as Captains, Majors, &c., &c., and some of their descendants are still to be found in Travancore.

The two men whom the Maha Rajah took special notice of were Eustatious D'Lanoy and Donadi, both of Flemish origin. Of these two, the one on whom His Highness fixed his particular regard was M. Eustatious D'Lanoy, and he was selected to discipline a few companies of sepoys, whom His Highness

GENERAL D'LANOY'S MILITARY SEPOYS.

PUBLISHED BY MESS^RS. HIGGINBOTHAM & CO.

G. PACKENHAM LITH: MADRAS

looked upon as the flower of his army, for his body-guard. D'Lanoy trained the sepoys so satisfactorily in a few months, that His Highness, delighted with his ability and military knowledge, appointed him Captain of His Highness' body-guard battalion, and subsequently he was vested with the power of controlling the garrison stationed at Padmanabhapuram. D'Lanoy's companion held the appointment of a Captain in the army. Captain D'Lanoy was engaged in getting an efficient magazine organized and ammunition arranged, and the Maha Rajah seeing his extraordinary skill and superior knowledge, authorized him to superintend the construction of a strong fort round the hill at Udayagherry. Here Captain D'Lanoy resided, and here he closed his earthly career.

Captain D'Lanoy was also entrusted with the onerous task of organizing and disciplining the Travancore army on European principles, and inspecting every garrison and out-post. He executed his task most creditably to himself and beneficially to the Maha Rajah's force.

About this time, a strong party of marauders, headed by Chunda Sahib and Bada Sahib, relatives of Dost Ali Khan, the Nabob of Arcot, who were permitted to wander about for the purpose of securing a principality for the Nabob's son, and also on plunder for themselves in the dominions of the native Princes, entered the territories of Travancore by the Aramboly gate. They took possession of Nagercoil, Sucheendrum, and the rich town of Kottar: they plundered the shrine at Sucheendrum; burnt the great car; mutilated many of the images of the pagoda; and perpetrated many other deeds of atrocity and devastation, the favourite process generally adopted by the Mussulman chiefs.

Rama Iyen Dalawah was ordered to march an army and drive the marauders out of Travancore, but on meeting them he found them powerful in horse, and his own force no match for the Mussulmans.

CHAP. II. However, the Dalawah challenged them and commenced a battle, but his exertions were not attended with his usual success. But the Dalawah had reason to know that the object of the party was principally to secure pecuniary gain, and consequently, they were made to retreat without offering resistance to his army. After making arrangements for further strengthening the Aramboly garrison, Rama Iyen returned to Trevandrum, and thence he was ordered to march to Quilon, accompanied by Captain D'Lanoy, who was appointed his chief assistant in command of the field force then engaged against Kayemkulam.

Many battles were fought without either side obtaining the victory, and the war continued for an unusually long time, the Dutch rendering every support and assistance to the Kayemkulam chief and also attacking certain parts of the Travancore country. The only actual defeat that the Travancore army met with was towards the end of 916 M.E. (1742 A.D.), when 6,000 men of the Travancore troops attacked the Dutch port at Quilon, which was defended by a number of Nairs under the leadership of one Autchutha Warrier, a Kariakar of the Kayemkulam Rajah, who commanded the fort garrison and fought with such desperate courage that the Travancore troops were obliged to retreat. But still the war continued.

In the early part of the year 917 M.E. (1743 A.D.), the combined forces of the Kayemkulam Rajah and the Dutch began to assume the offensive. They marched to Kilimanoor (within the limits of Travancore), and attacked and captured the fort. The Maha Rajah, who was at Sucheendram, started immediately to Attingal, near the seat of war, and adopted measures, not only to arrest the progress of the combined army, but also to give them a sanguinary battle there. His Highness raised an army of about 5,000 Nairs, and a corps of Sappers and Miners; procured arms and ammunition from the English at Anjengo and the French at Mahe; collected all the best guns from his forts at Udayagherry, Kulculam, Trevandrum, &c., &c.; and after forming a junction with the main army, under Rama Iyen Dalawah, he divided the army into three divisions. The Maha Rajah assumed the chief command, the prince (heir apparent), Rama Iyen Dalawah, and Captain D'Lanoy were appointed to the command of each division, and they were posted at different stations. CHAP. II.

After making these arrangements, the siege of Kilimanoor fort was commenced. The enemy held out most desperately for sixty-eight days, when the Maha Rajah succeeded in overpowering the enemy and recapturing the fort. After this defeat, the remnant of the Dutch and Kayemkulam forces retreated with great loss to Quilon.

The Travancore army now advanced towards Kayemkulam, and though opposed for some time, proved ultimately victorious, and the Kayemkulam Rajah sued for peace. In the latter part of the year 917 M.E. (1742 A.D.), the Kayemkulam Rajah concluded a treaty with the Travancore Maha Rajah ceding the greater portion of his country to Travancore and binding himself to be a tributary and ally, paying annually a tribute of one elephant and 1,000 rupees, and solemnly pledging his word that every State inimical to Travancore shall be regarded as his own enemy.

The Maha Rajah did not stop here. Finding that the Rajahs of Cottayam and Vadakankoor had rendered assistance to Kayemkulam and to the Dutch, His Highness directed the army under the command of the prince to attack those two principalities. Here the prince distinguished himself. The war against these two Rajahs was carried on and several battles fought, in the course of which the Cottayam fort was captured and the Rajah taken prisoner. In consequence of the fall of Cottayam, the Vadakankoor or Yetmanoor Rajah fled to Calicut, leaving his country at the mercy of the prince. Cottayam and Vadakankoor were annexed to Travancore by Rama Iyen Dalawah,

CHAP. II. and the heir apparent returned with his army to his uncle.

The Quilon Rajah, after the fall of Kayemkulam, disconnected himself from the fallen chief, and with the secret aid of the Dutch, defied the Maha Rajah's authority. The Maha Rajah sent his army against the Quilon Rajah, designated king of Desinganaud, and after several battles at Quilon, that country was also annexed to Travancore.

The chief of Ambalapulay rendered assistance to the Maha Rajah during these wars and his spiritual minister, Thekadathu Bhattathiry, appears to have come to the Maha Rajah at Chowray, at the head of a large number of Nairs and boats.

A diary of the Maha Rajah's movements, in connection with this year's war with Kayemkulam and other principalities, was found among a mass of old and worn out cadjans in a corner of the Padmanabhapuram palace, and the particulars therein recorded correspond with the history of events already given. The perusal of the substance of the same may be interesting to the reader :—

SUBSTANCE OF THE DIARY.

On the 28th Dhanoo 917 M.E. (10th January 1742 A.D.), the Maha Rajah left Sucheendram.

On the 1st Makaram (12th January), the Maha Rajah arrived at Trevandrum.

On account of the illness of the prince (heir apparent) the Maha Rajah stayed at Trevandrum 17 days. In the meantime, he was engaged in making preparations for war and organizing an encampment of troops at Attingal.

On the 18th Makaram (29th January), the Maha Rajah left Trevandrum and halted at Kalakootam.

On the 21st Makaram (31st January), His Highness visited Anjengo and after arranging for ammunition and appliances of war returned by boat to Attingal.

On the next day some of His Highness' European military officers arrived at Attingal and were accommodated in the east fort of the town.

The Maha Rajah concentrated his force and made all necessary preparations for the impending war.

The combined army consisted of his own military troops, called Kunchoottakar, his cavalry and 4,000 and odd Nairs newly enrolled for military service from Eraneel, Kulculam, Velavancode, Neyattumkaray, Neduvangaud, Trevandrum and Sheraingheel districts.

There was also a good number of labourers with mummatties (spades) for clearing jungles, and artisans, such as smiths, sawyers, &c., for repairing guns and also making rails in the east fort at Attingal.

Rama Iyen Dalawah arranged for victualling the troops, and appointed Panchangam Appa Perumal, Panchangam Appa Krishnen and Ponnum Pandya Devan as Commissary Generals.

The ammunition and munitions of war were obtained from Kulculam, Trevandrum and Anjengo, and from Mahe, through the French.

The contest commenced on the 23rd Makaram (3rd February) at the fort of Kilimanoor. On that day there were 13 wounded amongst the Travancore troops.

The Travancore army encamped in different localities, some at Attingal, and some at Avanancherry. Besides, there was a division quartered at Vamanapuram and another at Perumathura. There was an encampment at Nagaroor and another at Kadinenkulam.

The prince (heir apparent) commanded the division at Vamanapuram. The enemy attacked this place, but it does not appear that they met with success.

On the 24th Meenam (4th April), the prince proceeded to Kottarakaray and organized encampments at Anchel and Koomil. Ponnum Pandya Devan was at the head of this division.

CHAP. II. The contest at the Kilimanoor fort lasted 68 days. It began on the 23rd Makaram (3rd February) and terminated on the 30th Meenam (10th April).

There were several wounded in the Travancore army, but the number of men killed was only four or five. On the 27th Meenam (7th April) some of the wounded Europeans of the enemy's forces, and on the 28th idem (8th April), 293 Nairs of the Kayemkulam army were taken prisoners. Proper arrangements were made for their maintenance.

On the 30th Meenam (10th April), the Kilimanoor fort was completely taken possession of when the Rajah of Kayemkulam and the Commodore of Cochin were present.

The enemy's ordnance and ammunition, &c., which were in the Kilimanoor fort, consisting of 5 pieces of cannon, 43 muskets, 2 drums, ammunition filled in 28¾ barrels and 121 sacks, 142 shells, 20 cannon balls, and some weapons were captured.

On the 3rd Madom (14th April), the Maha Rajah left Attingal for Kottarakary. On the 6th (17th), the young prince (heir apparent) encamped at Yenathimangalam.

On the 8th (19th), the Maha Rajah left Kottarakaray for Kunnathoor. On the 16th (27th), the Maha Raja marched to Kayemkulam and took possession of Kayemkulam fort.

Simultaneously, preparations seem to have been made to conquer the petty States of Vadakankoor and Cottayam.

On the 18th (29th), the Maha Rajah left Kayemkulam for Karthigapilly. On the same day the young prince marched to Vegayapuram. On the 20th Madom (1st May), siege of the Vegayapuram fort commenced.

A large number of labourers and artisans were collected on the spot from Vattapparambu, Karunagapilly, Kottarakaray, Manchoor, Kulladay, and other places to execute the preliminary works for action. CHAP. II.

Excepting the portions of the army placed at Attingal, Kilimanoor and Kayemkulam, to guard those forts, all other available forces of the Maha Rajah, including men, horse, and Nairs enrolled for military service, were engaged in the conflict at Vijayapuram. The guns of Kayemkulam were taken to Vijayapuram.

On the 28th Madom (8th May), a number of elephants was taken from Ambalapulay to Vijayapuram.

From the 1st Edavem (10th May), Vadakankoor Rajah's name is found in the pension list.

When hostilities were going on with the Cottayam and Vadakankoor Rajahs, the Maha Rajah was in and about Kayemkulam.

Till the 23rd Edavem (4th June), the Maha Rajah was at Karthigapilly, when he moved on to Mavalikaray.

From Mavalikaray, the Maha Rajah proceeded to Pathiyoor and thence again to Kayemkulam.

The Maha Rajah next waged war against Quilon.

On the 25th Edavem (6th Juno), the Maha Rajah left Kayemkulam for Quilon.

On the 20th Edavem (1st June), the battles of Palakel Peringanaut and east Quilon were fought.

On the 3rd Mithunam (15th June), the battle of Kureepula in west Quilon was fought.

In these successive battles, the Travancore troops consisted, amongst others, of men enrolled from districts south of Kulculam, and also from Ambalapulay, Mavalikaray, Ashtamani, Kuttianikaud, Karthigapilly and Perinaut. Many were wounded.

A body of slaves of the soil was collected from Kulladay, &c., and set to work to raise two earthen mounds, as batteries, one at the landing place at Kureepula and another at the landing place, near the bridge.

CHAP. II.

The landing places near the bridge and at Kureepula were the scenes of conflict for several successive days until 19th Karkadagam (2nd August).

During this time, the Maha Rajah was in constant motion, with the view, as might be supposed, of taking diverse measures to ensure success.

On the 22nd Edavem (3rd June), the Maha Rajah marched from Kilialloor to Kureepula.

On the 1st Mithunam (13th June), the Maha Rajah left for Kilialloor.

Thence the Maha Rajah proceeded to Ambalapulay.

On the 10th Mithunam (22nd June), the Maha Rajah visited Iyencovil.

On the 18th and 19th Mithunam (30th June and 1st July), Thekadathu Bhattathiry arrived at Chowray with a number of men and boats.

On the 22nd Mithunam (4th July), the Maha Rajah reached Chowray.

On the 26th Mithunam (8th July), an encampment was formed at Chowray.

On the 31st Mithunam (12th July), Nairs in the service of Palikara and Madathinkoor reinforced the Travancore army.

At Chowray a sanguinary battle took place.

On the 31st Mithunam (12th July), the Maha Rajah paid a flying visit to Trevandrum to worship at the temple for Karkadaga Sewali.

On the 3rd Karkadagam (17th July), the Maha Rajah returned to Kilialloor.

He sent a large quantity of shot and ammunition to the field of battle at the landing place near the bridge.

On the 6th Karkadagam (20th July), the Maha Rajah himself took the field.

On the 11th Karkadagam (25th July), twenty boats arrived there from Attingal.

On the 19th Karkadagam (2nd August), the Maha Rajah visited Vurkalay for Audy Amavasi.

On the 30th Karkadagam (13th August), Quilon fell. The army was paid batta up to this day.

After the fall of Quilon, and the treaty of Mannath with Kayemkulam, the Dutch were disheartened and further hostilities with Travancore being considered unadvisable, they were inclined to make peace. Rama Iyen Dalawah made the Dutch understand, through the Kayemkulam Rajah, that he was prepared to direct his formidable army against the Dutch, but that the Maha Rajah had no objection to come to terms with them, provided the East India Company would submit to the reasonable conditions which Travancore might propose to them. The Dutch were overjoyed at this message, as they had been considerable losers by the unnecessary hostilities in which they took part, and they regretted their imprudent conduct chiefly on account of their commercial interests having suffered greatly during the war.

The Dutch next requested the Rajahs of Cochin and Thakankoor to effect a settlement with Travancore, through their means, and though these chiefs gave their word that they would do so, still they delayed fulfilling their promise, thinking that Travancore had already become powerful and had extended her territories to Poracaud, in the west, and Menachil, in the east, and that should the Maha Rajah enter into a treaty of alliance with the Dutch, whom lately, through their stratagems, they had rendered hostile to Travancore, she would become still more powerful. The Dutch now discovered these Rajahs' secret intentions, and the Cochin council resolved to manage the affair for themselves, without waiting for the assistance of their allies. The Dutch Governor of Cochin then addressed himself directly to the Maha Rajah, proposing an amicable settlement of their misunderstanding.

The Maha Rajah received this communication

CHAP. II. favourably, and informed the Dutch Governor that His Highness had authorized Rama Iyen Dalawah to hold a conference with the Dutch, and that the Dalawah, together with Thalavidi Cunju Moothathu Kariakar, had been delegated for the purpose. The Dutch East India Company's Council at Cochin despatched Ezekiel Rabbi and Silvester Mendes, the latter a Captain in the Dutch Service, to Mavalikaray. After a protracted conference and discussion, they drafted a treaty, the terms of which though mostly favourable to Travancore, were objected to by the Maha Rajah. Some stringent clauses were proposed, which restrained totally not only the interference of the Dutch Government with Travancore, but also their countenancing and aiding the native princes in Malabar. The Cochin council was about to depute one of their members to Mavalikaray for the purpose of ratifying the treaty, when their Commissioners sent them this revised proposal of the Maha Rajah. While they were hesitating about sending a reply, as they required permission from the Batavian Government, before they could do so, they received information from the Rabbi and the Captain, that His Highness the Maha Rajah would not enter into the proposed treaty at that time and that the consideration of the matters in dispute was postponed.

The Dutch now resumed their hostile attitude against Travancore, though with much reluctance, as they were not then in a position to withstand the Travancore army.

Some time later, the negotiations were re-opened by the Maha Rajah and the parties that had assembled at Paroor, south of Quilon: they discussed again all the questions, but the Dalawah held firm to the original proposal and consequently the conference was broken up, this time by the Dutch. A few days afterwards, the Dutch revived the negotiations a third time and the party met at the same town, simply to break off again. In this manner, the Dutch continued these negotiations without any favourable results.

At this period, the Rajah of Kayemkulam put forth every endeavour to shake off the Travancore yoke, but he was utterly unable to carry out his intentions as he could not expect any aid from the Cochin Rajah, who was now in constant fear of losing his own country by a sudden attack of the Zamorin's troops, and as the Dutch refused their assistance on the ground that they were already negotiating for peace with Travancore. He then applied to the neighbouring principalities of Ambalapulay and Chunganacherry, and they promised their co-operation.

The Kayemkulam Rajah had not paid the tribute since the ratification of the treaty, evidently considering it degrading and beneath his dignity to do so. He continued to withhold the payment, principally at the instigation of the two neighbouring Rajahs.

The Maha Rajah had reason to believe that there existed a confederacy between the chiefs of Kayemkulam, Ambalapulay, and Chunganacherry, and that this was the cause of the non-payment of the tribute by the first named prince. His Highness therefore directed Rama Iyen Dalawah, in 921 M.E. (1746 A.D.), to proceed to the north with a sufficiently strong army and enforce the conditions of the treaty with the Kayemkulam Rajah.

The Dalawah came to Mavalikaray and demanded from the Kayemkulam Rajah the payment of the arrears of tribute due by him, and apprised him of the Maha Rajah's decision that on his failing to do so, the conditions of the treaty would be enforced. The Rajah was obstinate and resolved rather to abandon his country than to submit to the indignity of paying the tribute.

The Rajah sent a reply to the Dalawah, asking a few days time, either for paying the tribute or giving up his country, and the Dalawah acceded to the Rajah's wishes by allowing him the required time.

This chief who possessed rare firmness and resolution sent off very privately, by night, all his family, his

CHAP. II.

treasure, jewels, and all that could be conveyed to the north, in covered boats, accompanied by trustworthy attendants, with orders to proceed beyond Trichoor. He was now left alone in his palace. Every night he collected what was left, such as silver, brass and copper vessels, which are to be found in profusion in the residencies of Oriental princes, and all valuable arms, such as brass guns, silver and brass pistols, swords of great value, and loaded them in large baggage boats, called Kattu Munchee or Kolla Munchee. These boats were despatched secretly to the deep back-water known by the name of Ashtamudikayel at the mouth of the Neendacaray of Quilon bar and their contents were consigned to the deep. This the Rajah continued doing for a week, and by that time, his palace and other establishments were completely emptied. On the 8th day, placing his private and official correspondence in the custody of the neighbouring chiefs of Ambalapulay (Chempacaserry), Chunganacherry (Thakankoor), Yetmanoor (Vadakankoor) Rajahs, he left his desk in his bedroom and stole away from the palace to the north.

After the expiration of ten days, Rama Iyen Dalawah sent a messenger to the Rajah, but to his utter surprise the Rajah's palace was found desolate and the whereabouts of the Rajah himself was unknown. In searching the palace, the Rajah's desk was discovered and its contents proved the combination of the chiefs against Travancore. Besides this, a number of swords with the inscriptions of Deva Narayanen, the name of the Ambalapulay deity, was found heaped in one of the corners of the palace. These circumstances led to the war against those principalities.

The Dutch seeing the final fall and annexation of Kayemkulam, and finding that they could not get pepper from Travancore, their rivals, the English having almost monopolised this article in the Maha Rajah's territory, became more anxious to ratify the treaty. They accepted the draft prepared and sent by the Dalawah and forwarded the same to Batavia for sanction. At the same time they continued their friendly relations with Travancore as if the treaty had already been confirmed. This was in 922 M.E. (1747 A.D.) CHAP. II.

In 923 M.E. (1748 A.D.), the draft treaty was sanctioned by the Batavian Government, and the Cochin Governor was instructed to get it ratified without delay, but the Cochin Council having made some slight modifications, the Maha Rajah started fresh objections and the treaty was not adopted before a further reference to Batavia. In 928 M.E. (1753 A.D.), it was finally ratified, and the following were its principal conditions:—Travancore and the Dutch should be mutual friends; Travancore should not permit any other European power to acquire a footing in its territories, should leave undisturbed the English factories at Anjengo, Edavaye and Vilinjam, but that the English should not be allowed greater advantages than they were entitled to, under existing treaties; that the Dutch should assist Travancore, both by land and sea, in case of an attack from a foreign power; the Dutch should not in any way aid the enemies of Travancore or give them refuge; the two contracting powers should apprehend and deliver up deserters to each other; Travancore should afford every protection to the Dutch resorting to its territories; that Travancore should restore to the Dutch such goods and men as belonged to them and may be wrecked on the Travancore coast; Travancore should compel its subjects to fulfil mercantile contracts with the Dutch and abstain from levying any unusually heavy duty on the goods of the Dutch who should renounce all their engagements with the Malabar princes and particularly with those against whom Travancore intended to go to war; the Dutch should supply Travancore with the munitions of war annually, to the value of 12,000 Rupees at cost price; Travancore should sell every year to the Dutch a stated quantity of pepper, at certain fixed rates, from territories then in the possession of Travancore, and also another stated quantity from

CHAP. II. those territories which Travancore might conquer thereafter. This treaty was concluded at Mavalikaray, where the Dutch Commandant, F. Cunes, prevailed upon the Rajah of Cochin to meet the Maha Rajah. A vigorous but unsuccessful attempt was made by the Rajah to introduce a clause in the treaty for the protection of the Cochin Rajah's territories, but all that could be obtained from the Travancore sovereign was a promise that the Maha Rajah would be friendly with the Cochin Rajah, provided no cause of offence was given. The Cochin Rajah made his own assurances to the Maha Rajah, promising to be friendly to Travancore in future.

In the year 923 M.E. (1748 A.D.), the adoption of female members into the royal family was found necessary, as there were no hopes of any offspring from the neices of the Maha Rajah. As usual on such occasions, two young princesses from the Kolathnaud family (Cherakel house), were selected and brought from Kolathnaud to Mannath and entertained there for some months till a propitious hour for adoption arrived. They were then removed to Trevandrum and formally adopted into the royal family with pompous ceremonies and festivities.

In the same year, the marriage ceremony of one of the adopted princesses was performed at Attingal.

The Maha Rajah now directed Rama Iyen Dalawah to proceed against the Ambalapulay Rajah, and a large force marched against that chief, who, though a petty Rajah, had a well-trained force, armed with bows and arrows as well as match-locks. When this chief received information of the approaching invasion of his country, he ordered his force, under the command of Mathoo Paniker and several others, to garrison his southern frontier town, Thottapilly, where the Travancore army, under Rama Iyen Dalawah, met them and a severe action commenced. This Ambalapulay Rajah was an ingenious chieftain and had invented different kinds of arrows, the points of which were all poisoned, so that any little wound inflicted by these arrows communicated the poison to the blood, and death followed within a couple of hours. Rama Iyen's troops suffered severely from these arrows, and when the loss of men had become considerable, his force was obliged to retreat, and the next day, a panic seized the Nair troops, under the supposition that Deva Narayanen, (popularly called Krishna Swamy) the household deity of the Rajah, had been personally conducting the war. None of the Hindu portion of the force could be persuaded to continue in the field, and consequently, Rama Iyen Dalawah had to wait for Captain D'Lanoy, with his Artillery and the Mussulman and Christian corps. On the arrival of this reinforcement, the Dalawah renewed the battle, and Captain D'Lanoy working his artillery with deadly effect, threw several balls amongst the ingenious Rajah's archers. In the course of a few hours, great loss was sustained by the enemy. The Nairs and the other Hindu portion of the Travancore army were encouraged, and the battle became general, so that the best portion of the Brahman Rajah's force was slain. Mathoo Paniker, the Commander-in-Chief, and Thekadathu Bhattathiry, the family priest of the Rajah seeing their inability to resist the Travancore power, advised the Rajah to yield and negotiate for peace, but the Rajah would not listen and placing too much confidence in his inventions and in his archers, ordered the battle to be continued, whereupon the action was renewed and the Travancore Army proved victorious and advanced towards the capital. The Rajah, was as resolute as ever, but the Paniker and Bhattathiry came over to Rama Iyen Dalawah, and asked for a truce, suspending action on their part at the same time. When the Rajah was informed of their conduct, he calmly turned to his favourite game of chess, but the Dalawah pushed forward his army to the Rajah's capital, approached the palace, took the chess-playing Rajah prisoner, and sent him to Trevandrum under a strong escort.

CHAP. II.

The defeated Rajah's remaining force was at once disarmed, and the Dalawah took possession of his territories.

The prudent behaviour of Thekadathu Bhattathiry and Mathoo Paniker having been brought to the Maha Rajah's notice by Rama Iyen, His Highness was pleased to confer all the privileges exercised by the late Rajah of Ambalapulay over the great pagoda of that place upon the former, and large grants of lands, in addition to a title of nobility upon the latter. These gifts and privileges their families enjoy to the present day.

After the fall of Ambalapulay, the Maha Rajah contemplated the invasion of the Chunganacherry Rajah's territories, because that chief assisted both the late Kayemkulam Rajah and the now-deposed Ambalapulay Rajah, while they were at war with Travancore, and the Maha Rajah's project was expedited by the Chunganacherry Rajah's own conduct. But the Elia Rajah (heir apparent), the immediate brother of the Rajah, was more sensible and far-seeing than his brother the reigning Rajah; for looking at the fall of Ambalapulay, he expected that a similar fate was in store for Chunganacherry, as the military power of that principality was far inferior even to that of Ambalapulay. This wise prince advised his brother to offer to the Rajah of Chunganacherry as the only condition of peace the submission of the latter as a vassal to the Maha Rajah of Travancore, but the Rajah was haughty, and like the Kayemkulam chief, refused to listen to his younger brother, and consequently a misunderstanding arose between them.

The Elia Rajah proceeded to Trevandrum and represented matters to the Maha Rajah, who kindly accepted his offer and promised to treat him as a tributary.

The conduct of the young prince incensed his brother, who repeatedly applied to the Maha Rajah to send back the prince. On the Maha Rajah's refusal to comply with his request, the Rajah had recourse to stratagems for inveigling his brother. He contrived to give currency to a rumour to the effect that the mother of the young prince was extremely ill and at the same time sent a requisition for the attendance of the prince at his mother's death-bed. When this news reached him, and when the Maha Rajah ordered him to return to his native place, the prince represented that the news of his mother's illness was false, and that the object of the Rajah in sending such a message was to entrap him. But the Maha Rajah disbelieved the prince's assertion and told him that he ought to respect his mother's wish to see him, whereupon the prince left Trevandrum for Chunganacherry, with many presents from the Maha Rajah. The fears of the young prince were but too true, for as he approached Chunganacherry, the senior Rajah sent his people to seize the poor prince and caused him to be strangled, spreading a report that the Elia Rajah had died by the bite of a snake.

When this intelligence reached the Maha Rajah, Rama Iyen was directed to make preparations for war against the principality of Thakankoor (Chunganacherry). Some new corps of Nairs from Kulculam, Eraneel, Velavancode, Kayemkulam and other places were raised, in addition to the standing army, and Rama Iyen proceeded to Arrummolay, when a number of Telugu or Gentoo Brahmans, dependants of the Rajah, flocked together and placed themselves before Rama Iyen's army, in the belief, that in Travancore the life of a Brahman was sacred, and consequently that they would not be in danger of being killed. But Rama Iyen, though himself a Brahman, determined to do his duty, and in the first instance told the Brahmans that they had no business with the politics of the country, and that they had better look to the performance of their religious ceremonies, instead of unnecessarily endangering the safety of their lives. But heedless of the Dalawah's

CHAP. II. advice and remonstrances, the Brahmans began to shout and throw sand and stones at the army and to curse both it and the sovereign of Travancore. On this, Rama Iyen requested Captain D'Lanoy to do his duty without shrinking. This brave officer, calling a few companies of his detachment, consisting of Christians, Mauplays and fishermen, directed them to drive away the mob of Brahmans and clear the way for the march. By the confusion created by the Brahmans, sufficient time was afforded to the cowardly and weak Rajah, who was at a place near Arrummolay, to flee from his country to the north.

On the 28th Chingum 925 (11th September 1750), Rama Iyen Dalawah took possession of Chunganacherry, the seat of the Thakankoor Rajah. The State treasury, jewels, arms and accoutrements and property of a considerable value, fell into Rama Iyen's hands, among which were some brass guns and mortars of European manufacture, besides some clocks and timepieces, 28 in number. The latter, together with several arms of European manufacture, testify to the connection of Travancore with European nations from ancient times.

At this time the Maha Rajah appears to have come to Chunganacherry, as many of the nobles and chiefs called Karthavu, Kymul, Elayadam and Paniker, under the Chunganacherry Rajah, as well as those of Ambalapulay and Vadakankoor, are said to have presented themselves before the Maha Rajah at Chunganacherry and acknowledging His Highness's sovereignty, paid homage with large nuzzers. Rama Iyen marched to the north, and after fortifying the positions between Thakankoor and Vadakankoor from Komarakam to the east up to the hills at Koondoor, marched towards the north to settle the northern boundary, which was extended to the southern bank of the Periar which runs to the west by Alwaye. The newly acquired territories included those lying on the south-east and north of the Cochin Rajah's capital Thripoonithoray, with the exception of Alangaud and Paravoor, which petty States were in the possession of their respective chiefs. All the country south of the Dutch possessions at Cranganore thus became the Travancore Maha Rajah's dominions. In the course of about fifteen years, the Travancore Maha Rajah extended his country from Edavaye to the Periar, and brought all the Rajahs, petty chiefs, and nobles, who had hitherto tyrannized over their subjects, treated them often like slaves or wild beasts, into subjection. The inhabitants of the kingdom between the Periar and Thovalay were relieved from forced military service and compelled to abandon their weapons of war for spades and ploughs and other agricultural implements, and cultivate their lands which had been lying waste for ages past. Fra Bartolomes says:—"Thus ended the dominion of the petty Malabar sovereigns; thus was humanity avenged, and thus were crimes punished, and the licentiousness suppressed, by which this country had been distracted ever since the tenth century."

By the last conquest the Travancore territories surrounded that of Cochin, and the out-posts of the former had become greatly intermixed with those of the latter. The critical position of the Cochin Rajah was to him a source of great alarm for he was placed between two formidable powers, the Zamorin on the north and Travancore on the south, both eagerly ambitious of extending their conquests.

About this time, the deposed Rajah of Ambalapulay escaping from Kodamaloor, where he was placed by the order of the Maha Rajah proceeded towards the north. He there was joined by the Thakankoor and Vadakankoor Rajahs, and in concert with them resolved upon adopting measures for the recovery of their respective countries. They appealed for support to the then most influential nobleman, the Paliathu Menon, (generally known as Paliathu Autchen), and to other nobles, such as Kodasherry Karthavu, Koratee Kymul, &c., who were feudatories of the Cochin Rajah, and they

CHAP. II. all in a body went to that sovereign, and persuaded him to break the alliance concluded by him with the Travancore king in 929 M.E. (1753 A.D.), on the occasion of the Dutch treaty at Mavalikaray, and to assist the three deposed Rajahs in trying to recover their territories. The Cochin Rajah being a man of an easy disposition, was soon prevailed upon, and his consent was obtained for hostilities against Travancore. Many disaffected Nairs from Kayemkulam, Ambalapulay, Chunganacherry and Yetmanoor, were invited privately to assemble at Cochin, Palluthuruthi, Undikadvu, &c. Large numbers of militia were collected by Paliathu Menon, Kodasherry Karthavu, and other nobles, and a fleet of Munchees with guns and ammunition was got ready to convey the men by sea. While these preparations were going on, the Dutch Governor at Cochin, though a friend of the Rajah of that place, conveyed private information to the Maha Rajah, who, making the necessary preparations to meet the enemy, proceeded at the head of a large army to Mavalikaray, accompanied by the prince and Rama Iyen. At Mavalikaray, the Maha Rajah was slightly indisposed and the prince (heir apparent), together with Rama Iyen and D'Lanoy, were ordered to lead the expedition. The Dalawah, with his characteristic activity and promptitude, proceeded with Captain D'Lanoy and a strong force supplied with all kinds of arms, and reaching Poracaud, prepared to meet the enemy on their landing, while the prince remained at Kandeyoor with a reserve force. The Cochinites arrived and landed at Poracaud, and as their large army securely moved forward, squadrons of Travancore cavalry poured in by their right, took up their position to the rear, and prevented the enemy's retreat to the sea. At the same time a good number of Travancore Munchees destroyed and disabled the Cochin fleet. Rama Iyen Dalawah and Captain D'Lanoy now commenced the attack. Their army being drawn up in front of the Cochinites, the first charge threw the whole of the enemy into disorder and confusion and the greater part of them were killed or wounded, while many ran to the sea and perished there. The Cochin Commanders, Paliathu Menon and Kodasherry Karthavu, and several nobles of minor importance, were taken prisoners and sent to Trevandrum.

CHAP. II.

The Dalawah detected many Nairs from Kayemkulam and other places in Travancore among the enemy's force, and orders were issued to search out all such and visit them with the punishment they deserved. This order was carefully executed under the superintendence of Captain D'Lanoy.

Rama Iyen thence proceeded to the north, and the prince joined him at Anandaswaram, which place he reached, during the battle, from Kandeyoor. Here the army was split up into two divisions; the division commanded by the prince marching to Komarakam, crossing the Bempanaud Lake; and that commanded by Rama Iyen through Ambalapulay, Alleppy and Ariyad. The army of the prince was joined on its march by the third prince of Vadakankoor and the chiefs of this part of the country viz., Navakat Kymal, Vettiyathu Thampan, &c. At Komarakam, a large number of boats having been collected at the spot as well as from Veliyanaud and the neighbouring villages, the prince proceeded by land and a portion of his force went by backwater, and both reached Vycome and Vadayar, crossed the Vycome Lake and encamped at Sharetalay, opposite to Vycome. Rama Iyen went at first to Madathumkaray, the southern boundary of the Cochin Rajah's dominions, about five miles north of Alleppy, where the Cochin Rajah had a palace which was considered the original seat of the Cochin dynasty and from which the Rajah takes his title "Mada-Bhoopathi," as said in the first Chapter.

No member of the royal family resided at the time in the palace: it was guarded only by a few sepoys and other servants, and therefore the Dalawah found no difficulty in taking possession of it and capturing the guards.

CHAP. II. Rama Iyen afterwards proceeded northwards, driving away or seizing every servant of the Cochin State found in the locality, and marched as far as Arookutty, where he pitched his camp.

By this time, the Cochin Rajah became alarmed and sent an express messenger to Trevandrum, with a full apology for the mistake committed by him, and requested that the further advance of the Travancore army should be stopped. He promised to enter into a treaty of alliance and friendship upon favourable terms to Travancore. The Dutch Governor of Cochin also requested the Maha Rajah to order the Dalawah to respect their limits, which, it was stated, extended two miles south of Cochin. On the receipt of this communication from the Cochin Rajah, Rama Iyen was immediately ordered to return to Mavalikaray, without making any further conquests. Though Rama Iyen returned at once, yet he took care to retain possession of the part of the country between Alleppy and Arookutty, through which he marched, and which extends to about 24 miles. This piece of territory was sufficiently garrisoned by the Dalawah before he left.

In the middle of the year 929 M.E. (1754 A.D.), the people of Ambalapulay, Chunganacherry, Cottayam, Yetmanoor, and almost all the people of the northern districts exhibited symptoms of rebellion. They appeared to be acting under the instigation of the Zamorin and the late potentates of Thakankoor, Vadakankoor, &c. Rama Iyen Dalawah was therefore compelled to advance to these districts with an army sufficient to overawe the rebels. With all his ability and energy, being embarrassed and perplexed by the confused state of affairs, he requested the Maha Rajah to visit the disaffected districts. The Maha Rajah, not being in good health, deputed his nephew, the heir apparent, to the rebellious province with his army. Nevertheless, there appears to have been great cause for anxiety, as even the brave Rama Iyen Dalawah continued to show signs of uneasiness and again requested the Maha Rajah to visit these places and stay there at least for ten days. The Maha Rajah did so. Though the rebellious spirit of the people subsided on the appearance of the Maha Rajah and peace was restored, still the Maha Rajah's prudence dictated to him the necessity of adopting more effectual and decisive measures to check a recurrence of rebellion in the northern parts of the kingdom.

With this view, the Maha Rajah wrote to Hyder Ali at once, asking him whether he would render assistance with his troops if His Highness was in need of it. The rising Mussulman chief of Mysore received the Maha Rajah's communication with due respect, and promised to send a portion of his army from Dindigul, viâ Cumbum and Goodalore.

This private arrangement of the Maha Rajah with the dreaded Hyder Ali having come to the knowledge of the chiefs of the disaffected provinces, they were all frightened and never showed the least propensity to rebel.

The Maha Rajah did not avail himself of the assistance promised by Hyder. The Maha Rajah kept silence on the subject for, on re-consideration, it suggested itself to His Highness that the admission of the Mysoreans into Travancore would ultimately prove injurious to the kingdom. Hyder appears to have written to the Maha Rajah, saying that his troops were ready, and asking why His Highness did not call for their aid. The Maha Rajah very politely and respectfully declined the profered assistance, informing Hyder Ali that his country was fortunately then enjoying tranquillity and that the assistance asked for, and so readily granted, was not needed. The drift of this reply the Mysore chief understood and thus was sown the first seed of enmity between Mysore and Travancore.

During the continuance of war in north Travancore, several changes took place in the government of the

CHAP. II. Pandyan provinces, including Madura, Trichinopoly, Tinnevelly, &c., and the sovereignty finally fell into the hands of the Nabob of the Carnatic. The Maha Rajah's attention having been directed, for a long time past, to the management of the internal affairs of his kingdom and the suppression of the rebellion in the north, he had neglected adopting measures for the protection and maintenance of his eastern possessions, including Valliyoor, Kalacaud, &c. The Nabob's Governor at Trichinopoly took advantage of this opportunity and annexed those tracts to the Madura province, and thus the Maha Rajah was deprived of those places for a long time.

In 927 M.E. (1752 A.D.), Moodemiah, the Nabob's Viceroy at Trichinopoly, growing powerful established himself as an independant chief, and being a very covetous man, disposed of villages and territories on receiving sufficient consideration for them. The Maha Rajah, understanding this disposition of Moodemiah, deputed Rama Iyen Dalawah to Tinnevelly, where Moodemiah had arrived on a visit. The Dalawah represented the Maha Rajah's ancient claims to the territories in the east. Possession of the country lying between Cape Comorin and Kalacaud, to the extent of about 30 miles, including Valliyoor, was obtained for a sufficiently large consideration. Rama Iyen Dalawah returned to Trevandrum after stationing about 2,000 of the Travancore Maha Rajah's force at Kalacaud, for the protection of the districts thus purchased by Travancore.

In 930 M.E. (1755 A.D.), Mahomed Ali, the Nabob of the Carnatic, wished to supplant Moodemiah, who had proved refractory and had proclaimed himself the sole ruler of the Pandyan empire. The Nabob appointed his General, Maphuz Khan, to supersede Moodemiah, and sent him with a small force requesting the Nabob's allies, the English at Madras, to send a detachment to assist the Khan, not only in assuming his office, but also in bringing the inhabitants into subjection. Colonel Heron, with 500 Europeans and 2,000 Natives, was ordered to Trichinopoly under the pretext of assisting Maphuz Khan, but probably the English too had an eye on the beautiful and highly productive Pandyan empire, comprising the rich countries of Madura, Trichinopoly and Tinnevelly. The allied forces arrived at Tinnevelly about Kumbham 930 M.E. (March 1755 A.D.), after having reduced Madura on their way. When this intelligence reached Kalacaud, the Travancore garrison, consisting of 2,000 sepoys stationed in that fort, was alarmed and finding that they were no match for the combined forces of the Nabob and the English, the Travancore commandant abandoned the fort and Kalacaud, and withdrew the garrison to Thovalay. In Meenam-madom (April), Maphuz Khan after taking charge of the fort and establishing his authority there went to Tinnevelly and Colonel Heron returned with the English force to Trichinopoly.

Moodemiah, who fled from Tinnevelly after his defeat, found an asylum under the protection of Pulithaver, a Poligar, and on the departure of the English troops from Tinnevelly to Trichinopoly, he applied to the Maha Rajah for assistance and urged on him to take back the lost territory of Kalacaud. Pulithaver also offered his assistance, as that Poligar was for a long time dependent on Travancore. A strong force, consisting of 2,000 infantry and an equal number of cavalry, was despatched from Travancore, accompanied by the prince and Moodemiah, and without much resistance Kalacaud was taken. The Maha Rajah, however, thinking that such a proceeding would offend the English Government, ordered the withdrawal of his troops for some time, and postponed all operations till he made himself sure that the retaking of his usurped territories would not offend the English. The Maha Rajah subsequently ordered back a sufficient force, under the command of Captain D'Lanoy assisted by the Poligar Pulithaver. Maphuz Khan's troops were defeated, the Kalacaud fort cap-

CHAP. II. tured and the 500 infantry and 200 cavalry, who defended it, were taken prisoners. Thus the Maha Rajah once more recovered Kalacaud and all the territories appertaining to it. The Travancore kingdom now extended from Periar in the north, to Kalacaud in the south.

Towards the middle of 930 M.E. and the beginning of 1755 A.D., the Zamorin of Calicut sent a formidable army, under the command of some of his subordinate princes, to invade the Cochin Rajah's territories. All the countries north of Cochin were taken possession of and military stations at Trichoor, Cranganore and Paravoor established. On the remonstrances of the Dutch, the further progress of the army, which was on its way to Thripoonithoray to attack that place, was arrested. In the following year 931 M.E. (1756 A.D.), the Zamorin met the Dutch Governor and informed him that he would spare the Dutch ally, the Cochin Rajah, and his country, provided the Dutch join him in his intended invasion of Travancore. The Dutch Governor very cunningly said that he would give this proposal his best consideration, provided the Zamorin would give back all the Dutch estates of which he had assumed possession, and enter into a treaty of perpetual alliance with the Dutch. The Zamorin also sent a reply similar to the one sent by the Governor, *i. e.*, that he would give the matter his best consideration.

While matters stood thus, the Dutch Governor having written to the Maha Rajah of Travancore, informed His Highness that the Zamorin was about to send down his troops by the backwater, as well as by sea, every preparation was made by His Highness to meet the invading army at Arookutty as well as at Poracaud. The Zamorin's army came by sea in a large fleet of native craft, and as it was being landed, Captain D'Lanoy's force, accompanied by Rama Iyen Dalawah, met the enemy and after a vigorous encounter, compelled the Zamorin's force to retreat with great loss of life and ammunition. Many of the enemy's boats were captured and destroyed and a portion of the force was drowned. CHAP. II.

This defeat greatly checked the Zamorin's haughty and arrogant spirit. But, chagrined and humiliated as he was, he again began to prepare for another invasion, and collecting another army of Arabs and Nairs, he was about to start when he was compelled to relinquish his object and hasten back for the protection of his own dominions from the claws of the Mysore lion, Hyder Ali Khan, who then made a descent on Malabar.

In 932 M.E. (1757 A.D.), the Cochin Rajah, who was solicitous for an interview with the Travancore Maha Rajah, ever since he learned his mistake and suffered the mishap at Poracaud, and was now desirous of entering into a treaty with His Highness, repaired to Mavalikaray, where the Maha Rajah then was, and tendered in person his apologies for his reckless proceedings at Poracaud, which he attributed entirely to the ill-advice of his friends and ministers. A new treaty was drawn out, by which the Cochin Rajah declared perpetual alliance with Travancore; voluntarily ceded all those portions of his territories which the Travancore army had conquered; relinquished all his claims to the northern petty principalities, with the exception of Allangaud and Paravoor; and bound himself to refrain from all intercourse with the deposed Rajahs of Ambalapulay, Thakankoor and Vadakankoor.

In narrating a train of events, connected with battles and conquests, in chronological order, many useful plans and systems of administration which were introduced and promulgated by this wise Maha Rajah and his meritorious minister, have been reserved for special mention, and these shall now be noticed.

After the conquest of Kayemkulam and Ambalapulay, and the signal victories over the Thakankoor and Vadakankoor Rajahs, Captain D'Lanoy was

CHAP. II. raised to the rank of General and appointed Commander-in-Chief of the Travancore army. He was ever afterwards known to the Travancoreans as the Valia Kappithan, the Great Captain, and in his latter days was specially employed in strengthening the fortifications of the country.

The Maha Rajah finding it an imperative necessity to adopt strong and efficient defensive measures authorized Rama Iyen Dalawah to have forts and other necessary defensive works constructed under the sole care and superintendence of General D'Lanoy.

The construction of all the fortifications was finished with great speed and economy. Strong forts, with granite walls, were constructed enclosing the Maha Rajah's residence at Padmanabhapuram; a still larger one, surrounding a hill at Udayagherry; and a third at Cape Comorin, on the sea beach at Aluwakaray, south-east of the Cape Comorin pagoda. From this last, a strong wall was built up to the hill at Aramboly, fortifying in a great degree the earthen works already thrown there, as a barrier between the sea and hills. Bastions, batteries and powder magazines were also constructed at intervals. An iron foundry was established at Udayagherry where cannons, mortars and balls were cast, and all the batteries were supplied with the necessary pieces of artillery. After completing these works in the south, D'Lanoy proceeded to the north, and erected batteries on the sea coast at different places between Cape Comorin and Poracaud. The fortifications at Quilon, Mavalikaray, Chunganacherry, Cottayam, Yetmanoor and Muvattupulay were also strengthened. He repaired many of the old forts of the late chiefs of the localities and constructed new batteries and forts with laterite, some of which are still to be seen partly in ruins, and others in a damaged state, overgrown with brushwood, such as those at Karuvannoor in Thodupulay, Komarakam in Yetmanoor, Lalam in Meenachil, and Peravom in Muvattupulay.

PADMANABHA PURAM FORT AND THE POWDER MAGAZINE.

After successfully completing all these fortifications, General D'Lanoy's praiseworthy exertions were directed towards the further improvement of the Travancore army, which now numbered above 50,000 trained troops of all branches, such as infantry, cavalry, artillery and irregular troops, trained and drilled according to European discipline under the chief command of the General. They were mostly armed with European weapons, procured through the Maha Rajah's friends, the English and the Dutch. This large force was divided into regiments, battalions, &c., and commanded by Europeans, Eurasians, Nairs and Pattans. The garrison, from Aramboly to the north as far as Thodupulay, was fairly arranged, and the main army was divided and cantoned at Padmanabhapuram, Trevandrum and Quilon, and from these stations monthly relief was sent to the garrisons, as well as to the numerous outposts, while strong detachments were made to march from place to place, for securing internal peace.

While General D'Lanoy was entrusted with the military arrangements, the Maha Rajah did not relax his usual attention towards the improvement of the revenue administration.

In the first place, Rama Iyen Dalawah was ordered to establish a commercial system, and the Iyen who always foresaw his sovereign master's views, commenced his energetic labours in this direction. Warehouses or commercial stores were opened at Padmanabhapuram, Trevandrum, Quilon, Mavalikaray and Aurakolay in the Muvattupulay district, under the designations of Pandakasala and Thorum. Each of these houses was superintended by an officer called Vijarippucaren or Thoracaren, and the store was guarded by detachments of military men. In these depôts, pepper, tobacco, cassia, arecanut, and other articles of commerce were purchased and stored on account of the sircar, at fixed rates of price which were then introduced and established throughout Travancore by

CHAP. II. special royal proclamation. These articles were to be sold afterwards by the sircar to the merchants, wholesale as well as retail. Rules were framed and established for the guidance of the commercial department and special royal proclamations were issued, legalizing the monopoly of all such articles by the sircar and prohibiting all private dealings in them. By these enactments, it became the law that no one could sell these articles, even if produced by him, to any one but the sircar and that no one could purchase these articles, even for private comsumption, from any other quarter, save from the sircar stores.

The Dalawah then introduced the system of Chowkeys, for levying duty on all articles transmitted and transported from place to place. For this purpose, rules were framed fixing tariff rates for all the articles and the duty to be levied thereon. Stations were also fixed and persons appointed for the performance of the functions of each department.

A methodical plan for manufacturing salt was adopted, and the sale of that necessary article was restricted to particular stations, where salt-stores and selling-houses called Pandakasalas, were opened. Rates for the purchase and sale of salt throughout the country were at the same time fixed. To ensure the successful carrying out of all these measures and to give effectual support to the agencies employed in connection therewith, Rama Iyen Dalawah was continually moving about, with a large retinue, from Padmanabhapuram to Muvattupulay and vice versâ, and in the course of a couple of years, all the above systems were peaceably and permanently established, without any great discontent amongst the populace.

The second step adopted by the Dalawah was to regulate the expenditure of the State in proportion to its income which had been previously accurately ascertained. In order to secure the expenditure on a fixed scale, without considerably exceeding the income, the Dalawah had drawn out a Pathivu Kanaku (fixed

PAGODA TOWER TREVANDRUM

TREVANDRUM SEEWALIPURAY.

account), with great care and precision, noting down the expenses for the Devaswams, Oottupurahs, palace, revenue and military establishments, pensions, purchase of goods, and for meeting all the contingent charges. This valuable and masterly Pathivu Kanaku met with the full approbation of the Maha Rajah and the officers of the State. Most of these rules are even to this day in observance.

Rama Iyen Dalawah repaired and constructed palaces for the Maha Rajah within the Trevandrum fort. In order to give additional strength to the Trevandrum fort, the old mud wall was partly enclosed by a granite wall. Before the work was finished, Rama Iyen died.

Several other works of importance were executed under the personal superintendence of the Maha Rajah and his Dalawah, the greatest of which was the Sewalipuray, a building surrounding the pagoda measuring 420 feet from east to west and 226½ feet from north to south. The breadth and height of this structure are respectively 20 and 23 feet. It is supported by 368 pillars, each measuring 13 feet in height and 2½ feet in diameter. The terrace is paved with granite slabs, each 25 feet long, 2½ feet broad, and 1¾ feet thick. The great merit of this undertaking is that it was completed in the seventh month after its commencement. There were 4,000 masons daily at work who were brought down from Madura, Trichinopoly, Tinnevelly and other places, and to assist them there were employed daily 6,000 coolies and 100 elephants.

Similar to the above work was the eastern Gopuram (gate tower of the pagoda), the foundations of which were laid in 741 M.E. (1565 A.D.). It was undertaken and executed up to its fifth story in a very short time.

The golden Dhwajam (flag staff) was constructed and planted in front of the pagoda. The teak-wood for this work was cut from the Kakachel forest, some thirty miles east of Trevandrum, and according to the Hindu Sastras, the wood was not allowed to touch the

CHAP. II. ground, but was supported by men and elephants when it was felled and thence it was carried to Trevandrum, without its once touching the ground.

The palace at Padmanabhapuram and that at Krishnapuram, as also several Oottupurahs (feeding-houses) and other useful buildings, were constructed under Rama Iyen's superintendence.* And all these are now living monuments of the versatile talents of the renowned Maha Rajah and his able minister.

Mavalikaray being a place highly suited for commercial purposes, especially for collecting and storing pepper produced in the neighbouring districts, Rama Iyen made that place his head quarters, and in addition to the store-houses, a set of large and spacious buildings was constructed and Mavalikaray was made the centre of the commercial department.

After the subjection of the petty Rajahs, chiefs, Madempimar, and Ettu Veetil Pillamar, the Maha Rajah initiated certain measures in accordance with the prescriptions of the Vedas, not only for expiating the sin incurred by war, but also for the prosperity of the kingdom and its inhabitants. His Highness therefore convened an assemblage of all the learned Brahmans of Malabar, Tinnevelly and Madura, and desired them to make researches in the three Vedas and the six Sastras and find out therefrom the most effective form of prayer to be adopted for the above purpose. The Brahmans, after examination, recommended the Bhadradeepam and Murajapom ceremonies and the prayers prescribed in the Vedas as observed by one of the Kshatria kings of a former age, (Karthaveerarjuna). This ceremony consists in the lighting of a sacred lamp on the 1st of the month of Magarom (13th January); after seven days prayers

* Feeding-houses were mostly established in the vicinity of roads or renowned pagodas and are generally for the benefit of Brahman travellers as also for the support of the poor of all castes. Every Oottupuruh has a provision for feeding the poor with a meal called *conjee* (boiled-rice water) besides these, special poor-houses were also established in different parts of the country.

PUBLISHED BY MESSRS HIGGINBOTHAM & CO. G. PACCERELY LITH. MADRAS

PADMANABHA PURAM PALACE.

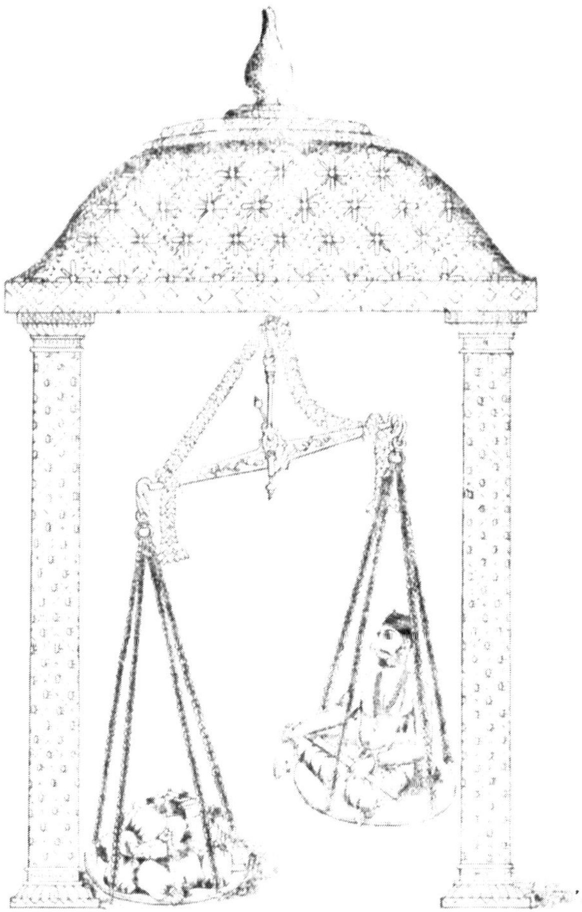

MARTHANDA VURMAH MAHA RAJA
PERFORMING THULAPURUSHA DANUM

PUBLISHED BY MESS.RS HIGGINBOTHAM & CO.

and offerings, this is to be repeated on the 1st Karkadagam (15th July), for five consecutive years. In the sixth year, the grand ceremony of Murajapom is to be performed. It lasts eight weeks or fifty-six days, and on the concluding day, one hundred thousand lamps are to be lighted. The literal meaning of the word *Murajapom* is prayer by turns; *mura* is turn, and *japom* is chanting prayers, and so Murajapom is the praying by turns of a large number of Brahmans, who assemble at the great Pagoda at Trevandrum and repeat the prayers from six to ten in the morning, and from eight in the evening. The *Murajapom* also means a chanting of the Vedas. This is intended, as has been already said, for the express purpose of devoutly imploring the blessings of Providence on the country and the royal family. This ceremony will, possibly, be considered an extraordinary one by the modern world of the west, but when the true and real intention is taken into consideration, it need excite no wonder or ridicule, for it is entitled to admiration, as the act fully testifies the godly disposition and piety of the sovereign and the depth of his own religious convictions. Prayers and praises of God, whether they be repeated in Hebrew, Greek, Latin, English, Syriac, or Sanscrit are all the same in intention, as long as we thereby supplicate the Creator for mercy and forgiveness of sins. No sensible person would therefore deride them.

This general prayer and thanksgiving ceremony, which had not been performed by any of the Hindu kings and princes on such a scale for ages, was commenced by the Maha Rajah on the 23rd Mithunam 919 M.E. (5th July 1744 A.D.), though it is recorded that ceremonies of this kind, on a minor scale, had been performed in the pagodas at Thiruvattar and Valwachhagoshttam near Padmanabhapuram, Sucheendrum, Kalculam and Attingal, from time immemorial by the ancestors of this Maha Rajah.

In the 6th year, 925 M.E. (1750 A.D.), the first

CHAP. II. Murajapom was celebrated in the grandest possible style, at an outlay of about two lacs of rupees. In the next year, 926 M.E. (1751 A.D.), the coronation ceremony (Hirannya Garbham donation) was performed, Thulapurusha danam having been already celebrated in 924 M.E. (1749 A.D.). In 928 M.E. (1753 A.D.), the remaining 14 danams were performed at a cost of 8½ lacs of fanams or 1,21,000 and odd rupees.

Though Travancore was now perfectly freed from the long continued molestations and opposition of the Ettu Veetil Pillamar and their confederate chiefs, and the recurrence of oppression on their part had been rendered impossible by the subjugation of the insurgent feudatories; though all sources of danger from neighbouring principalities had been removed by the expulsion of the petty Rajahs from their strongholds; and though success had attended all the acts of the Maha Rajah in enforcing order and regularity in the kingdom, constructing fortifications, introducing a scheme of military organization, promulgating a sound system of administration, and bringing about a reign of perfect peace throughout the Maha Rajah's dominions, still His Highness' prudence and wisdom suggested his resorting to further measures for the protection of his ancient house and his dearly acquired possessions. Consequently, this wise and remarkable sovereign, who had latterly become more of a religious devotee than a despotic king, adopted a most important precautionary measure as a lasting and powerful check on any future internal commotion in the country. This was effected by connecting the government of the State with religion, and making the kingdom sacred in the eyes of all Hindus, in the manner following:

After the conquest of Kayemkulam, and taking possession of Dasinganaud, Elayada Swaroopam, and re-establishing the Travancore dominions up to Valliyoor in the east and Thricunnapulay in the north, the Maha Rajah proceeded on the morning of the 5th

MARTHANDA VURMAH MAHA RAJAH
ENTERING INTO THE TUB.

MARTHANDA VURMAH MAHA RAJAH

MAKING OVER THE KINGDOM TO PADMANABHA SWAMY.

Madom 925 M.E. (17th January 1750 A.D.), to the great pagoda at Trevandrum, accompanied by the heir apparent with the other male and female members of the family, and the prime minister Rama Iyen. After assembling all the priests and the Brahmanical body attached to the pagoda called the Yogakar; the Maha Rajah with great reverence and devotion laid his State sword on the Ottakel Mandapom, in the presence of the image of Sree Padmanabha Swamy, and made over the kingdom of Travancore to the Devaswam, declaring that from that day forward, he was the vassal or agent of the deity, Sree Padmanabha Swamy, and that he would conduct the affairs of the kingdom as a trustee of the Devaswam. From this day, the Maha Rajah assumed the title of "Sree Padmanabha Dasa," *i. e.*, a servant or minister of Sree Padmanabhan. This measure, we may reasonably believe, had the desired effect, for since that time the people of Travancore have had a devoted attachment* and sacred regard for the royal house, and this has continued unchanged up to this day. This religious regard for the sovereignty is so great that the people of Travancore both high and low would not dare to speak ill of the Maha Rajah or the royal family, for they hold that by doing so, they commit a sin known as "Swamydrohum," which means doing mischief to the Swamy (the deity or lord).

Thus, this wise Maha Rajah strengthened the position of his heirs with every support, religious, political or military.

* "But although the entire system can only thus be developed, some of its leading features and characteristic principles discoverable from their manifest effects, and the first of those is a devoted attachment borne by all descriptions of people to the Rajah to whose character they are taught to attach an idea bordering on the sacred, from this principle their obedience to his commands, whether imposed direct or through the agency of his minister, who is generally known to them by the title of Dalawah is implicit."

Selections from the records of Travancore, Part II, page 16. Lieutenant Arther's Report forwarded to the Madras Government by Colonel Munro, 25th December 1810.

CHAP. II.

It has been already said that during the reign of the former Rajahs, Travancore had made an agreement with the Governor of the Pandyan empire at Trichinopoly, promising to pay a nominal annual tribute for obtaining military aid, but subsequently, the Nabob of the Carnatic having taken the direct government of that empire, the Maha Rajah considered it wise and prudent to renew this treaty directly with the Nabob, which was accordingly done upon more favourable terms and conditions. By this treaty, the powerful aid of one of the greatest potentates of Southern India was secured to Travancore, which was bound to pay to the Nabob 6,000 rupees, and a tribute in the shape of an elephant annually, the Nabob promising to afford every protection to Travancore from foreign and local enemies. Thus Travancore became perfectly secure, having two powerful allies to guard and protect her, the Nabob in the east and the Dutch in the west, while the English merchants at Anjengo were also ready to assist her when needed.

After making the kingdom of Travancore the property of Sree Pandara Vagay, and converting all denominations of the State servants into Sree Pandarakariyum Chaywargal (men who perform the duty of the holy financial administration), the name of the talooks (districts) was changed and styled Mandapathomvathukal (the gate or presence of the pagoda,) and all business was now carried on under the new titles. The Maha Rajah having next ordered Rama Iyen Dalawah to frame regular accounts and rules for fixing permanent taxes on lands and gardens, that official commenced a survey of them in 926 M.E. (1751 A.D.), and conducted and completed this laborious work throughout Travancore in 929 M.E. (1754 A.D.) The first Auyacattu account (assessment) in Travancore was clearly framed out after this survey, and the holders of lands and gardens were furnished with a Pathivu (registry).

Several good roads and water communications for

the convenience of passengers as well as for the convenient march of troops, were opened during this reign, under the supervision of Rama Iyen Dalawah. The most remarkable of these were the canal which connects the backwaters of Quilon and Kayemkulam through Chowray and Ponmannay, the canal by which the Karthigapilly river is joined with the Kayemkulam broad backwater at the north eastern end of it, passing through the village of Kayemkulam and Pathiyoor to the north up to the above river, and the Paroor canal, south of Quilon by which a passage was opened between the backwaters of Paroor and Edavaye.

While Rama Iyen Dalawah was thus carrying on his most successful administration, he fell ill at Mavalikaray, in Dhanu 931 M.E. (1756 A.D.) and when his recovery was despaired of the Maha Rajah felt exceedingly sorry and directed the Elia Rajah, Bala Rama Vurmah, to proceed to Mavalikaray and visit Rama Iyen, and ascertain from him his wishes as to the mode in which His Highness could perpetuate the memory of so trustworthy and upright a minister, and one who had proved himself a veritable hero. The Elia Rajah had also been commissioned to convey the Maha Rajah's expressions of sympathy with the sick minister.

The prince started at once to Mavalikaray and found the Dalawah in a sinking state, and on communicating to him his uncle's wishes, Rama Iyen disclaimed any personal right to the proposed honor, saying that he was merely an instrument in the hands of his royal master. Rama Iyen observed at the same time that he had accomplished all his aims for the good of the kingdom, but the only matter in which he was disappointed was, that he was not permitted to conquer and annex the whole of the Cochin Rajah's territories and add that Rajah's name to the Travancore pension list, along with the names of all the other princes conquered and pensioned by the strong hand of the Maha Rajah.

CHAP. II.

His Highness the Elia Rajah returned to Trevandrum, and soon afterwards Rama Iyen Dalawah expired. The Maha Rajah on hearing from the prince all that had transpired, as well as the sad intelligence of the Dalawah's death, was overwhelmed with sorrow, and His Highness took it so deeply to heart, that ever after, His Highness' mind became a prey to melancholy reflections.

It was reported, as a matter of great surprise, that no private property of any considerable value was found in the deceased Dalawah's residence, though he had been closely attached to the Maha Rajah from his boyhood, and had held the most responsible appointments of secretary to the Maha Rajah for eight years, and latterly that of prime minister for the long period of nineteen years.

The death of Rama Iyen Dalawah cast a gloom over every heart, and the whole administration seemed to have been under the shadow of a dark cloud for a time.

No successor was appointed in the room of Rama Iyen for the next two years, but the functions of prime minister were discharged by Iyappen Marthanda Pillay, Sarvadhikariakar. The Maha Rajah, though only 53 years of age, began to feel unwell and gradually became weak and infirm and died on the 27th Mithunam 933 M.E. (1758 A.D.), without the least pain or agony, in perfect consciousness and in the full possession of all his faculties.

The Maha Rajah expired, sinking quietly as if he fell asleep, in the presence of all the members of the royal family, and a large crowd of attendants, officers, &c., &c. But a few hours before his death, he called the heir apparent before him and gave that prince his last advice on the following points :—

1. "That no deviation whatever should be made in regard to the dedication of the kingdom to Sree Padmanabha Swamy, and that all further territorial acquisitions should be made over to the Devaswam."

2. "That not a hair's breadth of alteration or deviation should be made in the established charities and the institutions connected with the same."

3. "That no family dissension or quarrel should be allowed in the royal house."

4. "That the expenses of the State should not be allowed to exceed the income."

5. "That the palace expenditure should be defrayed from the profits of the commercial department."

6. "That, above all, the friendship existing between the English East India Company and Travancore should be maintained at any risk, and that full confidence should always be placed in the support and aid of that honorable association."

On the solemn assurance of obedience by the prince to all these really valuable instructions, the dying Maha Rajah exhibited signs of perfect satisfaction, and with a happy face, blessed his worthy nephew. After a few minutes' silence, he committed his soul to his Creator by repeating prayers and hymns in praise of the supreme Spirit.

There have been numerous instances in which it was clear that divine succour had been extended to this extremely pious Maha Rajah from his boyhood, some of which were described in this and in the preceding Chapter, but a very noticeable one, the writer thinks, has not been brought into prominence in the narration of the train of events, and this omission he will now try to remedy here.

During the long continued war with Kayemkulam, the Maha Rajah's treasury was completely drained and a serious financial embarrassment ensued, when, to the help of the Maha Rajah, was found by divine blessing, in a village called Kulashekhara Mangalam, attached to the Vattookavu Adhikaram, in the Trevandrum district, mines of valuable gems consisting of cat's-eye and ruby of an inferior quality called Thalum by the natives. This was followed by the

CHAP. II.

discovery of similar mines about Trevandrum, Arumanay in Velavancode, Kodaman near Attingal, and Karumankunnu in Sheraingheel.

The incidents in and recollections of the career of this Maha Rajah and his prime minister Rama Iyen, who flourished in times when western civilization and education were unknown in Travancore, and when the Europeans considered the natives a barbarous nation, are found not only in the annals of Travancore and its official records, but have also formed the themes of the songs of the peasantry. The boatmen, as well as the day labourers and even native performers, have their songs founded upon the doings of this Maha Rajah and many of his ministers, of whom Rama Iyen's name stands foremost.

There are various anecdotes often related with delight, about this famous Maha Rajah and his heroic ministers, but many being unauthenticated by records are not noticed in this work. Nevertheless, a few of the reliable ones concerning the Maha Rajah and his meritorious minister, may suffice to show how that monarch and his prime minister were ever ready to sacrifice their own comforts, while contributing to the welfare of the country, and also how strict and impartial they were in the promotion of the public weal.

During the time the water channel from Ponmanay towards the south, as mentioned above, was being opened, a part of the locality was found rocky, and the channel had to be cut through the middle of it. The process of blasting not being known in those days, manual labour was the only agency whereby the work could be effected. It was conducted under the personal superintendence of the Maha Rajah. In a most difficult part of the locality, the work was once stopped for several days. On this, His Highness proceeded to occupy a block of rock which served for a throne on one side of the channel, and sat there from eight in the morning till six in the evening, taking only one meal during the whole day. A servant used to hold a large umbrella of palm leaves, with a long pole, after the Malabar fashion, over the Maha Rajah, in order to protect the royal person from the rays of the scorching sun, but thinking that the services of this servant could be utilised for the canal work, the Rajah ordered one of the stone cutters to pierce a deep hole in the rock. This having been done, the Maha Rajah ordered the servant to fix the pole of the umbrella in the hole, and seated himself under its shade, directing the servant to work in the canal along with the coolies. This hole in the rock, and the place where the Maha Rajah was seated, are still seen at a place between Ponmanay and Padmanabhapuram as a monument of the perseverance and energy of this wise sovereign.

It is also said that after completing the construction of the granite building called Seewali Puray, fragments and chippings of granite were left about the place, and there was scarcely any spot within the wall of the pagoda that was not disfigured by such rubbish. The festival in the pagoda being near at hand the Maha Rajah ordered the clearing of the place with all possible haste, but the work was somewhat of an Herculean nature, and could not be finished quickly. But one day, the Maha Rajah himself attended the place, and found one thousand men at work. His Highness quietly set himself among the workmen, spread his handkerchief which he had in his hand, and picking a small quantity of granite chippings, carried them on his head and threw them outside the wall, and walked away to the palace. This so stimulated not only the working men, but also the spectators, that before evening the spot was perfectly cleared of all the rubbish.

The strictness of the Maha Rajah, in economising his time, is also highly commended, an instance of which is the following. Once upon a time, two ambassadors of the Carnatic Nabob came to His

CHAP. II. Highness on certain business, but before commencing with their errand they entered into a long preamble, when the Maha Rajah interrupted them gravely and said "men, don't be too tedious, life is short."

It may not be out of place to narrate here another a very instructive anecdote, regarding the Maha Rajah and his minister Rama Iyen, exemplifying the strict and rigorous discipline exacted from the royal family, even from the heir apparent to the throne, and showing likewise how rigidly the established rules were enforced and how independent the position of the prime minister himself had been made. During his minority, the Elia Rajah, Bala Rama Vurmah (the heir apparent), was very fond of dramatic and theatrical entertainments. On a certain night, while the performance was going on, the oil in the lamps running short, the prince ordered his attendant to go to the pagoda store and fetch a quantity, but the store-keeper said that he could not give the oil without the sanction of the Dalawah. The prince enraged at this, ordered his servants to enter the store, and forcibly take the required quantity of oil.

The next day the matter was reported to Rama Iyen, and through him it reached the Maha Rajah's ears. Rama Iyen suggested to His Highness the imperative necessity of adopting such measures as would check the young prince's propensity to carry out his arbitrary orders, and the decision arrived at was to deport the prince at once to the palace at Cape Comorin, where he was to reside and perform penance and devotion to the goddess, and implore her mercy for righting his understanding and sense. The prince walked out, without a murmur, either from himself, or from his good mother, the senior Ranee of Attingal, or from the other members of the family, for it had always been one of the peculiar virtues of the Travancore royal family to be strictly obedient to their head, whose order the rest consider as solemn law. A junior member, even the immediate heir to the throne, behaves himself in the presence of his senior as an ordinary member of society in his bearing, address, and deportment. The junior member, in addressing the sovereign, says "your holy self" and in speaking of himself "your vassal." None would dare to say "you" or "I." Such are the forms enjoined by the rules of this royal family from time immemorial, and any instance of departure from this sacred observance or presumptuous speech on the part of any member, has been unknown in this kingdom.

Rama Iyen Dalawah, though a Hindu Brahman, continued an unmarried man, and kept aloof from all family connections from the day of his entering the service up to the day of his death. He is said to have laughed at his friends' telling him that a Brahman's soul could not be saved according to the canons of the Vedas, unless his son performs his funeral rites, and that consequently he should enter into the matrimonial state. He observed that he had to look to a better and still more important and primary matter concerning himself in this world, than the one in the next, that is, his service to his sovereign and his duty to his fellow creatures. Should he bind himself into a relationship with any family by marriage, he said he should find himself entangled in a net, restraining his free movements, and thwarting him in the conscientious discharge of his public functions. In consideration of these points, he resolved to remain an unmarried man through the whole course of his life.

It also appears that the Dalawah had a Sudra woman near Mavalikaray as his concubine and that at his death he left a packet in her hands, with instructions to produce the same before His Highness the Maha Rajah, after the Dalawah's death. This poor woman was unable to present herself before the Maha Rajah during that sovereign's life-time, but it is satisfactory to find that in the next reign, she went to Trevandrum, and that fortunately the packet reached the hands of the Maha Rajah, who, on opening it, was

CHAP. II. astonished to find a cadjan ticket, in the handwriting of Rama Iyen, stating that the custodian of that ticket was a poor woman and an old dependant upon him; that she deserved His Highness' charitable notice; and that the tax of a few chuckrams on the garden in which she had her cottage and on the acre of land adjoining it, which was also hers, might be made the royal grant of Anubhavam to her. His Highness after perusing the ticket, handsomely rewarded her, over and above the recommendation of the late minister.

It was during the reign of this sovereign that an order akin to that of knighthood, was established as a kind of stimulus to those in the public service. Distinguished services were rewarded by this honor. It was denominated *Chempakaramen.* The ceremonies observed on the occasion of conferring such a title are as follows:—The recipient of this distinguished honor when selected, is presented before the Maha Rajah on a propitious day fixed for the ceremonial. His Highness then, delivering a short speech in the presence of all the officers of State, expressive of the satisfaction afforded by the knight-elect to justify His Highness' bestowing such an exalted title on him, gives him some special presents and names him by the title Chempakaramen after his name. The knight then proceeds to the gate of the palace followed by the prime minister and other officials. At the gate, in a hall attached to it, takes place the subsequent ceremony which consists in the presentation of a new piece of a peculiar kind of silk, eight yards long, called Veeravaly Pattu and the wearing of a suit of new clothes. The knight being dressed properly, after the Travancore fashion, one end of the silk is tied round his head, leaving the other end to the extent of two and a half or three yards loose, like the train of a long robe. He is then placed on an elephant and behind him three nobles or other persons invested with similar titles, seat themselves bearing the train of the knight's turban. The knight is then carried in procession, accompanied by a native band, a small detachment of military, together with all the State peons, karikarahs, and other servants. The procession moves round the four streets inside the fort, and returns to the gate, where the knight dismounts from the elephant and proceeds with the prime minister who is waiting for him to the latter's seat where the knight then enjoys the privilege of being seated with the minister. The new knight is now presented with a quantity of betel leaves and arecanuts, together with a few ripe limes in a silver plate, called thattom or thampalam, and thus ends the ceremony. From this day the title Chempakaramen Pillay is always added to his name.

The Maha Rajah adopted several other measures for rewarding meritorious men, by giving titles, presents, lands, &c., &c., too numerous to be detailed here. Suffice it to say, that every encouragement was held out to the members of the various services, and while toleration was impartially extended to the people in general without reference to caste or creed, Hindus, Christians, Mahomedans and Jews were all allowed the exercise of their respective religions freely and without being molested or disturbed by any one; but they were not allowed to exhibit the least spirit of rivalry or disaffection amongst themselves. In short, by this wise and impartial government, the people of Travancore in general, as well as all the sirkar officials held the sovereign in great veneration, and looked upon His Highness as a common father to them.

The Maha Rajah was most economical, and knew well the value of public money; consequently every pie collected from the people, and from His Highness' country was usefully spent. His Highness did not build any magnificent palace, like the Thirumala Naick's palace at Madura for his own personal accommodation and comfort; no valuable jewels were purchased or made for his personal adornment, nor was the private treasury loaded by an accumulation of

CHAP. II. public money. All the wealth the Maha Rajah acquired during a reign of about thirty years, was applied to honorable and useful purposes, to the consolidation of his kingdom by territorial acquisitions and vast improvements; which, to this day, proudly and eloquently proclaim the renowned Maha Rajah's incomparable wisdom and justice and the grandeur and splendour of his Government.

The following observations on the talents and heroism of this sovereign, described by Fra Paolinoda San Bartolomeo, in his "Voyages to the East Indies" are here transcribed, as corroborative of what has been detailed in this history :—

" The kings of Travancor had hitherto been insigni-
" ficant princes, whose territories extended only about
" fifteen or twenty miles up the country from Cape
" Comari; and were, besides, not very fruitful. The
" sovereign of this district, at that time *Vira Martanda*
" *Pala*, was uncle to the present king *Rama Varmer*.
" He was a man of great pride, courage and talents;
" capable of undertaking grand enterprises, and from
" his youth had been accustomed to warlike operations.
" As he had concluded an alliance with the king of
" *Madura*, it needs excite no wonder, that, agreeably to
" his character, he should conceive the idea of mak-
" ing conquests, and of enlarging his unproductive
" dominions by the acquisition of new provinces. For
" this purpose he crossed the river *Palur* in the year
" 1764; fought a decisive battle with king *Ciangaceri*,
" and, having entirely subdued him, laid waste his
" territories with fire and sword; caused all the
" palaces, and even some of the Pagan temples, to be
" demolished; and took prisoners the neighbouring
" petty princes. The latter had been called in by
" *Ciangaceri* to his assistance; but they were at open
" variance with each other, and too much occupied
" with their own feuds to unite in one common cause
" against *Vira Martanda Pala*, who advanced to *Airu-*
" *cutti*, which is only three leagues distant towards

" the south from Cochin. His commander in chief, " *Martandapulla*, laid siege to the place, and con- " tinued his conquests, which were completed by M. " Eustatius de Lanoy, with whom I formed an ac- " quaintance at *Curriapalli* in the year 1777. He " drove *Samuri* on the other side of the river from " *Alangatta* and *Codungalur*; assigned a small spot to " the king of Cochin for his support; made himself " master of all the fortresses; put the king's troops " on the same footing as the European; divided among " them the conquered lands; caused them frequently " to march through the country with full military " parade, in order to keep the people in subjection to " their rulers; and after *Vira Martanda's* death, gave " the kingdom, in which perfect tranquillity was now " restored, to the present sovereign *Rama Varmer*, " who had just entered the twenty-fourth year of his " age. Thus ended the dominion of the petty Malabar " sovereigns and princes: thus was humanity avenged; " and thus were the crimes punished, and the licenti- " ousness suppressed, by which this country had been " distracted ever since the tenth century.

" Of a great part of the above events I was myself " an eye-witness: the account given of the rest is " taken from the information of persons worthy of " credit, and in particular from the valuable manu- " scripts of Father Cruz Fernandez, a Malabar priest, " which contain a minute relation of the war carried " on by *Vira Martanda Pala*. I had an opportunity " also of consulting a great many original documents, " quoted in this work, which were preserved among " the archives of the missionary establishment at " *Verapole*. I conversed likewise on this subject with " the present king and his generals *Martandapulla* and " M. de Lanoy, who all three often came to *Verapole*, " and to whom we were indebted, besides other marks " of kindness, for freeing our convent, church, and " surrounding district, from the payment of all taxes."

In fine, the writer of this history feels proud that

CHAP. II. his accounts and observations are fully corroborated by the recorded opinions of Rajah Sir T. Madava Row, the late Dewan of Travancore, who, as the head of the administration for many years had the opportunity of ascertaining every fact connected with the kingdom of Travancore and its internal administration, both from records and from enquiries. This able native knight, who is widely known, has undertaken the work of writing a History of Travancore, and the opinion given by him about this sovereign, as published in the Malayalam translation of his unpublished work, may be here quoted as fully corroborating the writer's observations regarding one of the greatest of Travancore's kings.

"The Maha Rajah whose reign has been brought to "a close is certainly one of the most remarkable "figures in the history of Travancore. He came to "the throne while yet young, and amid difficulties "and dangers. He inherited a small territory, full of "anarchy and disorder. In the earlier days of his "rule, his life was often exposed to the hand of the "assassin. He had to wander in disguise and narrowly "escaped violent death. But his energy and decision "enabled him to establish internal tranquillity. His "sagacity felt no difficulty in selecting the most effi- "cient instruments for carrying on the administration. "His ambition and enterprizing spirit led him to "extend his dominions almost to the present limits of "Travancore. His wisdom and moderation made it "easy for him to consolidate his conquests and to "endear himself to his subjects. Barring some of the "early acts of his reign, which were dictated by the "stern necessities of a struggle for existence, he was "undoubtedly a just and humane ruler. He con- "siderately rewarded those who had assisted him in his "adversity. His benevolence was unbounded, though "of course it flowed in the channels which the Hindu "Shastras prescribed or the Hindu public admired. "It was that very benevolence that induced him to "exact the practise of it from others. Tradition "relates that he in disguise solicited alms from a rich "niggard subject and on being rudely refused, the dis- "gusted sovereign confiscated the miser's accumulated "hoards and dedicated them to the support of a charit- "able foundation for the benefit of the neighbouring "poor. It was that very benevolence that induced "a life of frugality and abstemiousness as a means "of increasing the resources to be employed in the "exercise of that virtue. The Maha Rajah was far from "indulging in that magnificence which is the charac- "teristic of Courts oriental. His tastes were simple. "His dress and equipages were almost primitive; his "mansions displayed no great architectural splendour; "and his court and all that appertained to it showed "that what was useful was decidedly preferred to what "was showy or gorgeous. He was so intensely pious "that he may be regarded as a religious devotee in "the purple. Yet he by no means neglected the "numerous and daily duties which sovereign power "devolved on him. These he got through with "application and despatch. It is said that, on the "occasion of an audience given to two ambassadors "from a neighbouring State, one of them began a "long harangue which the other was preparing to "continue. "Be not tedious" said the Maha Rajah "with an austere brow, "life is short." The most "memorable feature of his reign was the uniform and "unvarying good fortune that attended him in all his "enterprises for the benefit of his country; a good "fortune which the orthodox Hindu of the period "fondly ascribed to the sincerity of the incessant "protection accorded to temples, Brahmins, women "and cows."

CHAPTER III.

SREE PADMANABHA DASA VANJI PALA RAMA VURMAH KULASEKHARA KIREETAPATHI MUNNAY SULTAN MAHARAJ RAJAH RAMARAJAH BAHADUR SHAMSHEERJUNG MAHARAJAH.

CHAP. III.

HIS Highness Rama Vurmah was the late Maha Rajah's nephew and heir apparent to the musnud. He succeeded his uncle when he was 34 years of age. His Highness had been trained and brought up by his uncle so that he should leave behind him one worthy to be his successor. This training, together with the extraordinary talents which nature had bountifully bestowed upon him, made the new sovereign's character remarkable in his exalted position. Having been closely attached to his uncle from his boyhood, and having taken great interest in the administration of the country, His Highness was quite in his element in his new sphere, and found no difficulty, in carrying on with firmness, the system of Government established by his uncle, and in conducting it on the principles, rules and regulations already adopted and introduced.

These rules and regulations had not been fully established in the newly acquired territories in the north, and therefore, His Highness inaugurated his reign by adopting measures for that purpose. He next turned his attention to the further improvement and remodelling of the forces, training and disciplining additional men under various denominations, and bringing the Travancore army to an equal footing with that of the Carnatic Nabob and the English, of whose forces the Maha Rajah was a particular admirer.

RAMA VURMAH MAHA RAJAH.

PUBLISHED BY MESS.RS HIGGINBOTHAM & CO. C. [illegible] LITH. MADRAS.

Sepoy regiments, Pattan or Mogul battalions, Sikh and Rajput battalions, artillery and cavalry regiments, and artificers, consisting of all castes of volunteers, which were organized in the late reign, were now furnished with new accoutrements and arms. The garrisons between Thovalay and Kuriapilly were increased.

The revenue and judicial administration of the kingdom was improved. The acting Dalawah, Iyeppen Marthanda Pillay Valia Sarvadhikariakar was confirmed in his appointment, and the position of a number of efficient and select officers, who were holding various appointments under the deceased sovereign, were improved by their promotion to responsible and more important offices, and the entire system of administration was again improved and re-modelled, without materially violating the principles of the late Government.

The whole kingdom was made into three divisions,* viz., Vadakaymukham (northern division), Padinjaraymukhan (western division), and Theckaymukham (southern division); each of these divisions was placed under the control and supervision of a Valia Sarvadhikariakar, and these again were subdivided and placed under Sarvadhikariakars, and the same were again made into districts, and over each of the districts a Kariakar was appointed. The districts were, moreover, subdivided into Maniums, Kelvies, Adhikarems, and

* Under the Dalawah or Dewan, there is a chain of officers, all dependant on each other in regular gradation for the management of the revenue and all other affairs of Government; thus the whole country is parcelled out into a certain number of grand divisions over each of which a principal officer termed Valia Sarvadhikariakar presides and his authority extends to all matters of a revenue, commercial and judicial nature. These great portions of the country are again divided into a certain number of parts, each under the secondary controlling management of a Sarvadhikariakar and these again are subdivided into districts, under the management of a Kariakar, who has a residency in certain principal places in his district. Other officers termed Proverticars are the last in gradation among the managing officers of respectability: but under them again there are several inferior officers called Chundracars, Toracars and Villacars or Peons, who have each a distinct and separate office. Besides the above, there

CHAP. III. Proverthies and placed under charge of Manikarens, Adhikaries and Proverthicars. All these officers had a staff of sub-officials such as writers, accountants, rayasoms, peons, &c.

The Zamorin of Calicut, who still retained possession of the Cochin Rajah's northern frontiers from Trichoor down to the south, up to the fine tributary districts of Paravoor and Alangaud, threatened further encroachment on the Cochin principality; consequently, the Cochin Rajah sent his minister, Paliathu Menon, to Trevandrum and applied for assistance to drive away the Calicut Rajah and recover the lost territory. He promised to pay every expense attending the march of an army for that purpose, and to relinquish for ever the rights and claims of Cochin upon the Karapuram territories, and offered to cede the tributary Districts of Paravoor and Alangaud, with all the privileges enjoyed by the Cochin Rajah in those Districts. It was added that should Travancore succeed in taking from the Zamorin any territories beyond those which he had wrested from the Rajah, such acquisitions should exclusively belong to the Maha Rajah himself. The Maha Rajah acceded to this proposal, and His Highness the Rajah of Cochin repaired to Trevandrum in Dhanu 937 (1685 A.D.) and entered into a new treaty, embodying all the above particulars, and renewing the substance

is an officer appointed in each of the three great divisions who is entitled the Maluvejarippoocar and the nature of his office is partly judicial; but in what particular cases his interference is required I have not learned. Each of the principal officers named above has an office establishment of writers, &c., for keeping the accounts of his Cutcherry. The head writer in the Cutcherry of the Kariakar is entitled Theroomukompedecha Pillay and all those inferior officers, Pillays. " Lieutenant Arthur's Report," page 16.

" He keeps two *Valia Sarvadicdriacdrer*, the *Vadakemugham* and the *Tekmugham*, one of whom is established in the north and the other in the south. Each of these has under him four other officers, called only *Sarvadicdriacdrer*. These have inspection over four subalterns or *Cariacdrer;* and these subalterns have under them *Pravarticdrer*, *Ciandracdrer* and *Torracarer;* or collectors of the taxes, overseers and judges." Bartholomeo's Voyage to the East Indies, page 173.

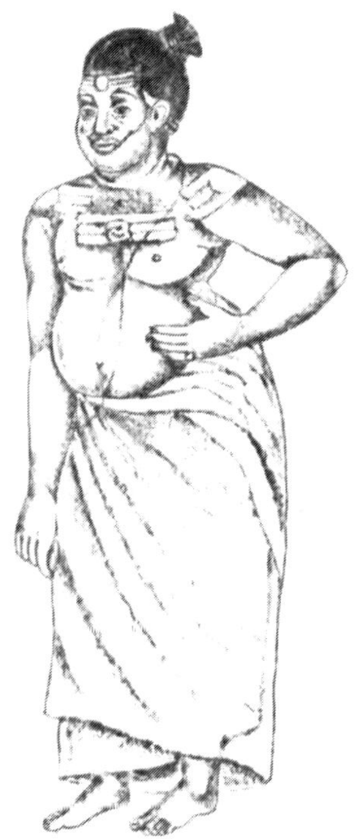

THE RAJAH OF COCHIN.

PUBLISHED BY MESS.RS HIGGINBOTHAM & CO. C. [illegible] LITH: MADRAS

of the former treaties. This having been ratified on the 12th Dhanu (26th December 1761) the Cochin Rajah returned to his capital. But warned by past experience, the Maha Rajah hesitated to place full confidence in the Cochin chief, and delayed to take action against the Zamorin, whereupon the Cochin Rajah sent his nephew, Rohani Thirunal, the Cochin Veera Kerala Vurmah Rajah to Trevandrum, and made the conditions of the treaty still more binding upon himself. For this purpose, the Rajah proceeded to the most sacred and renowned pagoda of Sucheendrum, and made a solemn declaration, before the deity, swearing perpetual alliance with Travancore in the following terms :—

Translation of a solemn declaration made by the Cochin Rajah at Sucheendrum, on the 25th Karkadagam 937 (1685 A.D.)

"We, Veera Kerala Vurmah Rajah, born under the "Star Rohanee of the Perimpadapu Swaroopam, "declare in the presence of Sthanu Moorthy, deity of "Sucheendrum, that neither we, nor our heirs, will do, "or cause to be done, any act against Sree Padmana-"bha Dasa Vanji Pala Rama Vurmah Kulasekhara "Perumal Rajah of the Tripappoor Swaroopam, born "under the Star Kartiga, or against his heirs. We "will not join with those who are his enemies, neither "will we correspond with them. Truly resolved and "solemnly declared upon the feet of Sthanu Moorthy."

This declaration was in the hand-writing of Powathy Ambady (the Cochin Rajah's recorder).

His Highness the Maha Rajah then directed his prime minister, Iyeppen Marthanda Pillay, to proceed with an army to the north, under the command of General D'Lanoy.

The Dalawah accordingly set out at once, and after him marched a large force which, on reaching Paravoor, drove away the Calicut Rajah's garrison stationed there. The army was then divided into two

CHAP. III. divisions, one under the direct command of the Dalawah, and the other under General D'Lanoy. The division of the army led by the Dalawah proceeded to Trichoor by Karoopadanay, while the other, under General D'Lanoy, marched towards Chowghaut and commenced the attack upon that place. Though the Calicut Rajah's force resisted obstinately for a time, still it was no match to General D'Lanoy's disciplined army and it was therefore compelled to retreat.

General D'Lanoy pursued the retreating force, taking prisoners and killing those who resisted, and by the time D'Lanoy reached Trichoor, he had the satisfaction of seeing Iyeppen Marthanda Pillay sole master of Trichoor; the Zamorin Rajah and the Trichoor garrison having retreated, after a great struggle with the Dalawah's force encamped at Chalakaray.

The divided force, after forming a junction, marched to the north, driving the Calicut Rajah's army from its stronghold at Chalakaray and pursuing it as far as Kakadu, and while the Dalawah contemplated marching to Calicut to attack the Zamorin's capital, that chief sent an express messenger to Trevandrum and sued for peace. The wise Maha Rajah of Travancore accepted the offer and directed the minister's return. This policy of the Maha Rajah appears to have been apparently founded upon the consideration that the Calicut Rajah had given no offence or provocation to Travancore in the present instance, and the only duty Travancore was bound to perform was to drive off the Zamorin and his forces from the Cochin Rajah's territories. The Zamorin subsequently came to Padmanabhapuram to meet the Maha Rajah in the same year 938, and a treaty of alliance was entered into on the 26th Edavem 938 (1763 A.D.), by which the Zamorin agreed to indemnify the Maha Rajah for the expenses of the war, by paying the moderate sum of one-hundred and fifty-thousand rupees, promising at the same time perpetual friendship and fidelity. This treaty efficiently protected the interests of the Cochin

State by providing that it was to be left unmolested by its ancient enemy, and that any disputes that might arise between it and the Zamorin, should find a peaceful solution by the friendly and impartial mediation of Travancore. CHAP. III.

After stationing a strong garrison at Chalakaray, at the expense of the Cochin Rajah, under the command of a European officer, the Dalawah and the General returned with the force to Paravoor, detaching at the same time other portions of the army to Trichoor and to different places in the Cochin country, to defend those territories against any further molestations from the Calicut Rajah.

The Dalawah on his arrival at Paravoor assumed formal possession of the petty States of Paravoor and Alangaud, not only in virtue of the Cochin Rajah's treaty, but also on the more powerful ground of his having taken them from the hands of the Zamorin after driving him away from those localities. He also made arrangements for collecting the revenue of those States. As the Dalawah had observed every one of the conditions of the Cochin Rajah's treaty, and that Rajah was highly pleased with his heroic conduct, he gave him the grant of a village called Puthencheray, but the Dalawah very nobly and honestly annexed the said village to Travancore and made the same a Proverthy under the Alangaud district.

The Maha Rajah had it in contemplation to construct a barrier at the northern frontier, like the one erected at Aramboly, between the sea and the hills, during the late reign, and as the northern frontier of Travancore was now extended to Kanjerapulay (Cranganoor bar) the construction of a barrier between the Dutch settlement at Palliport and the eastern range of high hills was considered imperatively necessary, in order to prevent the advance of enemies into the Travancore territories, especially at this time, when Hyder Ali Khan's power was rising in the north and when he entertained no friendly feelings towards Travancore.

CHAP. III. The Maha Rajah repaired to Annamanaday, a famous Brahman village near the northern frontier, the sovereignty of which rested with the Zamorin, but had been transferred to Travancore by recent arrangements. After a personal inspection, in conjunction with Iyeppen Marthanda Pillay, Dalawah, and General D'Lanoy, both of whom were at Paravoor after their victorious return from the north, the Maha Rajah commissioned those two able officers to superintend the construction of the frontier fortifications and returned to Trevandrum. The Maha Rajah had also a conference with the Rajah of Cochin at Annamanaday, as many parts of the said barrier had to pass through that chief's territories and obtained the cession of the lands necessary for carrying on the work alluded to.

The chief motive which influenced the Maha Rajah to hasten on the completion of such a precautionary measure was the visit of Hyder Ali Khan to North Malabar, and the probability of that Mussulman chief's progress towards the south. The apprehensions of the Maha Rajah were not altogether groundless, as subsequent events showed.

The Dalawah and the General consulted together and devised the plan of the fortification, and after tracing out a line from Kuriapilly on the southern bank of the Cranganoor bar, to the east up to the chain of hills to a distance of about thirty miles, the work was commenced at once. A strong fort of laterite was built at Kuriapilly, and from that a mud wall, 20 feet thick and 12 feet high, ran to the east having stone batteries and bastions at intervals and also small forts at certain localities adjoining the barrier. On the left side of the barrier, a ditch measuring 16 feet broad and 20 feet deep was dug, while on the right a road of similar breadth and on a good level was opened. On the side of the ditch close to the wall, bamboo and other thorny shrubs were planted.

IYEPPEN MARTHANDA PILLAY DALAWAH.

PUBLISHED BY MESS^{RS} HIGGINBOTHAM & CO. C. FABERNORY LITH: MADRAS.

This was called Nedumcottah or Vittiacottah, the traces or rather the ruins of which are still seen extending from the fort at Kuriapilly in the west, to the foot of the ghauts in the east. CHAP. III.

General D'Lanoy was stationed at Paravoor in command of the force and the several garrisons stationed both at the new fortifications and in the Cochin Sircar's territories, as well as on the Travancore frontier.

General D'Lanoy adopted a most effective measure, by causing military detachments to march frequently through the country in full military parade, in order to keep the people in subjection to the rulers. All the lawless characters in the northern parts of the Cochin territories were kept in great awe by the movements of this great General.

While General D'Lanoy was thus employed at Paravoor, Marthanda Pillay Dalawah was engaged in establishing the Travancore laws and regulations in the districts of Alangaud and Paravoor. He then returned to Trevandrum, and on his way encamped at a place called Krishnapuram. This place he found well suited for a military station and so he set to work to erect a fortress with strong mud walls, and to build magazines and other military stores near the palace constructed there during the former reign. The residence of the sovereign was improved in a becoming style, and a public road from Quilon to the north viâ Krishnapuram to Poracaud was opened, and a causeway through the marsh between Aripaud and Poracaud raised with several bridges at different places over rivers and canals. On his return from Krishnapuram, he ordered the clearing of a piece of waste land east of Neendacaray, and planted thereon cocoanut and other fruit trees. This was converted into a Government garden called Dalawapuram. On the Dalawah's arrival at Varkalay, he improved that town, and had twenty-four houses built there. All of them were given as gifts and grants to Brahmans under the authority of the sovereign, and thus the place was

CHAP. III. raised from its obscurity into a populous and important town.

Maphuz Khan Sahib, the Governor of the Pandyan empire, under the Carnatic Nabob, who was stationed at Trichinopoly, rebelled against his master and made a descent on Kalacaud, the eastern possession of the Maha Rajah, at the western frontier of Tinnevelly. He attacked the Travancore garrison stationed there and drove them into the Aramboly lines, following them up with the Khan's forces. The Maha Rajah hearing this, ordered one of his native commandants named Thamby Kumaren Chempaka Ramen Pillay, who was then stationed at Trevandrum, to march with his force to meet the invading army. He started at once and the battle which took place when this worthy warrior met the enemy was so severe and decisive, that the Mahomedan chief was obliged to beat a retreat from the Aramboly lines; but the Khan not only retained possession of Kalacaud, but assumed possession of the district of Shencottah and all the other eastern districts belonging to Travancore.

The Maha Rajah represented this matter to the Nabob, who was already so seriously displeased with the Khan, on account of his disobedient and refractory conduct, that he had it in contemplation to appoint a new Governor in the room of Maphuz Khan. A very able man named Yusuff Khan was appointed and sent as successor to the rebellious Maphuz Khan.

Yusuff Khan on coming to Trichinopoly found it difficult to subdue the refractory Governor and sought the Maha Rajah's assistance. The Carnatic Nabob and the English East India Company at Madras requested His Highness, at the same time, to co-operate with Yusuff Khan in the subjection of the refractory Khan and the Maha Rajah gladly acceded to their wishes.

Five thousand men, under the command of Thamby Kumaren Chempaka Ramen, then stationed at Thovalay were ordered to join Yusuff, and 10,000 men from Quilon were sent through the Ariencavu Pass to Shencottah. Yusuff was now at the head of a powerful army consisting of 20,000 men, which enabled him to drive away the Poligar of Wadakaray, and subsequently Maphuz Khan fled from the position he hitherto held and Yusuff established his power.

As a grateful acknowledgment of the readiness with which the Maha Rajah lent his assistance, Yusuff Khan restored all His Highness' eastern possessions, and Kalacaud again became a part of His Highness' dominions.

The Maha Rajah however did not retain possession of Kalacaud for any lengthened period; for His Highness lost this portion of his territories, under very peculiar circumstances. Yusuff Khan, the Nabob's Governor, in his turn became disobedient to his master and began to endeavour to shake off the Nabob's authority and establish himself as an independent chief; to accomplish this object Yusuff secured aid from the French in India.

In 937 M.E. (1762 A.D.), a joint force of the Nabob and the English was sent against Yusuff, and the Travancore Maha Rajah was also requested to co-operate with this army, which was to take possession of Madura and Tinnovelly and capture Yusuff Khan. The Khan had already applied to the Maha Rajah for assistance, offering all the territories west of the town of Tinnevelly, including Palamcottah which had once belonged to Travancore, in return for the help His Highness would give him towards the retention of the Pandyan provinces under Yusuff's independent possession; but the wise Maha Rajah declared that whatever may be the prospect of gain before him by aiding Yusuff, His Highness would not go against his old ally the Nabob, and would not take arms against the English.

The Maha Rajah sent a strong force to Trichinopoly to co-operate with the combined force against Yusuff, and that rebel finding that resistance would be of no avail gave himself up and was hanged by the Nabob's order in 1762 A.D.

CHAP. III.

Yusuff Khan's successor thought it proper to assume possession of all the countries lying on the eastern side of the ghauts, as belonging to the Pandyan empire, and accordingly not only Kalacaud, but also Shencottah and all the other eastern possessions of Travancore were annexed to the Nabob's dominions.

The Maha Rajah despatched a special messenger, Manik Lalla by name, to Madras, and represented the injustice of the Nabob's officers in unlawfully annexing territories belonging to Travancore, but the Mussulman potentate, intoxicated with his recent victories and the punishment awarded to Yusuff, would not listen to the representations of the Maha Rajah's agent, and His Highness was therefore under the necessity of seeking the mediation of the Governor of Madras, who, though he once confirmed the claims of the Maha Rajah to the districts of Kalacaud and other eastern possessions, now wavered in his opinion. After a good deal of discussion, the Nabob agreed to restore some of the Travancore territories including Shencottah, Cape Comorin, &c.

The Mahomedan chief did not appear to be satisfied with the unlawful annexation of the Kalacaud district, which was the legitimate possession of Travancore from time immemorial, and was recently acquired by purchase from Moodemiah. That purchase was confirmed by two of his successors, the Nabob himself, and by the Honorable East India Company. The Nabob now pressed a demand for the few previous years' revenue on the Kalacaud district.

A settlement was effected by the intercession of the Governor of Madras, Mr. Robert Palk, who, after arranging matters with the Nabob, wrote to His Highness in 1765 A.D. in reply to a communication from the latter, to the effect that the English Company had taken some steps in restraining the victorious Nabob from further hostilities, in putting a check to his demands, and also in advising him to conclude the treaty. For such services Travancore was reminded of the debt it owed to the Honorable East India Company and the Governor hoped that the Company would be amply rewarded for their assistance.

The sagacious Maha Rajah saw the desirability of adopting the Governor's suggestion and the necessity of entering into a treaty with the Nabob against whom resistance was at that critical period almost impossible.

The principal conditions of the treaty with the Nabob were, that Travancore should renounce all claims to the Kalacaud district; that His Highness should increase the tribute to 15,000 rupees; that he should pay two lacs of rupees in liquidation of some pretended demands on the Maha Rajah in connection with the Kalacaud district; that he should never assist any of the Poligars against the Nabob; that the Maha Rajah should assist the Nabob with an army in his war against Madura and Tinnevelly; and that the Nabob should assist Travancore against all her enemies foreign as well as internal.

It is necessary to mention here that Pala Rama Vurmah Kulasekhara Perumal, the Maha Rajah of whom we are now speaking, had when His Highness was Elia Rajah, taken a warm interest in a young man and brought him up under his own patronage, training him for the public service, just in the same way as his uncle had brought up Rama Iyen, Dalawah.

This fortunate youth, whose name was Ramen Kasaven or Kasava Pillay, gradually grew up under His Highness' paternal care and support and became a most intelligent and deserving man.

When about twenty-four years of age, Kasava Pillay was appointed as a rayasom (writer) in the palace under the Samprathy (the State Secretary). He now became most influential and proved himself a highly efficient State servant, so much so, that His Highness' secretary as well as the prime minister, used to consult him and seek his advice on questions of the greatest importance.

CHAP. III.

Kasava Pillay was much attached to D'Lanoy and to several Mussulman and Pattan officers in the military service. He was trained in the military art and was competent to command a whole brigade in times of emergency. He learnt the Dutch and Portuguese languages under General D'Lanoy and the Persian and Hindustani under the Pattan officers.

At this period, the Maha Rajah sought for, and procured a Portuguese, by name M. Pedro da Veigas, and appointed him the king's interpreter and State clerk. A Persian moonshee was entertained and one or two able Hindustani writers of the Lalla caste (Rajputs) were also employed under His Highness.

Kasava Pillay was specially entrusted with the management and supervision of commercial affairs and a regular correspondence was opened and kept up with the Dutch and the English East India Company, established then at Cochin and Anjengo respectively. The former had their commercial factories at Poracaud and Colachel, while the latter had a flourishing trade at Anjengo.

As usual, pepper, cassia, cinnamon and other articles of which the Sircar had the monopoly, were sold to these allies, and in return, iron, copper, sugar, arms and ammunition were purchased from them.

General D'Lanoy's iron foundry at Udayagherry continued in full working order and supplied cannon, balls, &c., &c.

By the long continued intercourse with the Dutch and the English, supplies of arms, accoutrements and other military articles were secured and stored in abundance, while the Government of the Nabob of the Carnatic furnished swords, shields, lances and other Indian arms. The whole army of the Maha Rajah was now remodelled and brought into a state of greater efficiency in respect to their dress and arms. The number of European officers in the military service was also increased.

In 938 M.E. (1763 A.D.), soon after his victorious return from the north, Iyeppen Marthanda Pillay Dalawah died, and he was succeeded by Varkalay Subba Iyen (a native Brahman of Travancore) in 939 M.E. (1764 A.D.), who commenced a career which appeared to be as full of promise as that of his predecessor, and His Highness placed great confidence in his ability and integrity.

In this year, 939 M.E. (1764 A.D.), this able Dalawah persuaded the Rajah of Paravoor to resign formally his sovereign rights in the Paravoor State in favor of Travancore and retire on a pension. Accordingly, the Rajah signed an agreement, by which he gave up entirely his sovereign rights to Travancore, and accepted a family pension.

Subba Iyen Dalawah then made a similar proposal to the Alangaud Rajah, who, though he hesitated to part with his sovereign rights at first, signed an agreement, like his neighbour the Paravoor Rajah, and accepted a family pension.

Thus Subba Iyen Dalawah finally completed the work most energetically commenced by the late Rama Iyen Dalawah. The defensive works commonoed by the late prime minister Marthanda Pillay were finally completed by this able Dalawah Subba Iyen. Many other useful works were also undertaken and completed during Subba Iyen's administration.

About this time, 941 M.E. (1766 A.D.), Hyder Ali Khan of Mysore invaded and took possession of all the northern countries of Malabar, and the opposition of several Nair chiefs and the resistance of the Zamorin of Calicut having proved ineffectual to check his rapid progress, the Zamorin committed suicide by burning himself with some of his relations and courtiers in his own palace. Hyder took possession of all the petty States, as well as the whole of the Zamorin's dominions, and thus became master of the country between Cannanore and Ponnany.

CHAP. III.

The Cochin Rajah, fearing the approach of Hyder Ali, offered his allegiance and paid a sum of two lacs of rupees and eight elephants, binding himself at the same time to be a tributary to the Mysore chief.

Having thus humiliated the Cochin Rajah, Hyder directed his attention to Travancore, but the Dutch who were friendly both to Hyder and Travancore, had established themselves at the very northern frontier of Travancore, and thus proved a barrier to Hyder's progress. On this, Hyder wanted the Travancore Maha Rajah to follow the Cochin Rajah's example and pay fifteen lacs of rupees and thirty trained elephants.

To neither of these proposals did the Maha Rajah accede, but made Hyder to understand that the Travancore sovereign was already a tributary of the Carnatic Nabob and had besides formed an alliance with the Honorable East India Company.

Hyder having allowed sufficient time for the Maha Rajah, through the medium of the Dutch, to consider the proposal, returned to Mysore, and the Maha Rajah informed the Governor of Madras and the Nabob of the Carnatic of what had occurred.

At the same time General D'Lanoy and Subba Iyen Dalawah were ordered to the north to fortify the barrier, strengthen the several garrisons, and replenish the magazines with fresh ammunition in order to meet any emergency. The Dalawah, and the General made all the necessary arrangements and the Dutch also rendered assistance.

In the meanwhile the meritorious Dalawah Subba Iyen's labors were terminated by his death, which occurred in the year 943 M.E. (1768 A.D.). Gopala Iyen (a Travancore Brahman,) was appointed Dalawah; but having been found unequal to the work, he was simply allowed to retain his office, and the able Commandant, Thamby Chempaka Ramen Pillay, was appointed Valia Sarvadhikariakar or deputy prime minister to conduct the duties of Dalawah. Kasava Pillay was appointed palace Samprathy or State Secretary.

The appointment of these well known able men afforded general satisfaction as they were particularly fitted for the posts.

The Maha Rajah was pleased to find that the frontier fortifications, with which the late Dalawah had been engaged, were very satisfactorily completed under the joint supervision of these officers.

The strength of these fortifications which cost several lacs of rupees during a period of nearly three years was fully tested by subsequent events.

The arrogance and tyranny of Hyder Ali had received an effective check from a superior power, for about this time he had the mortification, for the first time in his career, of being defeated by the East India Company's soldiers in several engagements with them. This sobered him and convinced him that he was not supreme in India and that there was a power mightier than his own to the will of which it was expedient and necessary that he should bow.

Hyder unhesitatingly sued for peace and a treaty was concluded at Madras with the Honorable East India Company in 1769, in which ample and special provisions were secured by the Company for the future safety of the kingdom of Travancore from the tyrannical hands of Hyder Ali Khan.

The Madras Government communicated to the Maha Rajah this pleasing intelligence, which no doubt relieved His Highness of a good deal of uneasiness. But still, the Maha Rajah being wise and far-seeing did not rest satisfied with these results, as His Highness knew well the ambitious and faithless character of Hyder Ali Khan.

The Maha Rajah considered it necessary to depute an officer to the Court of Mysore to be stationed there to watch the further movements of Hyder, and this was viewed by the latter in no unfriendly light. An

CHAP. III. officer under the designation of sthanapathy* (ambassador) was appointed and sent to Mysore. The Maha Rajah had also such "sthanapathies" stationed in the Carnatic Nabob's Court, in the Cochin and Zamorin Rajah's Courts, as well as in Tinnevelly and Madura.

His Highness subsequently proceeded to the north, and arrangements were made with the Dutch East India Company and with the Cochin Rajah, to combine their armies and render assistance to the Travancore force stationed at the northern barrier, in case of Hyder violating the conditions of his treaty with the Honorable East India Company.

These arrangements were initiated during the administration of the able Valia Sarvadhikariakar Thamby Kumaren Chempaka Ramen Pillay, assisted by Samprathy Kasava Pillay, but in the course of two years Valia Sarvadhikariakar died and was succeeded by an equally able man, Mallen Chempaka Ramen Pillay (a Sudra native of Travancore,) who was then holding the post of a Sarvadhikariakar. Valia Sarvadhikariakar conducted the administration as efficiently and satisfactorily as many of his predecessors had done.

Mallen Chempaka Ramen Pillay, Valia Sarvadhikariakar, obtained His Highness' permission soon after his appointment, to commence the survey of the whole kingdom. In the year 948 M.E. (1773 A.D.), the survey was completed, a clear assessment was made, and registry given to the ryots accordingly for lands and gardens throughout the whole kingdom from Thovalay to Paravoor. Thus was a second survey of all the lands and gardens made in Travancore. A new town and village were established at Parachalay, a few miles south-east of Neyattinkaray, bordering the road, and a charitable institution (ootupurah) was opened there. The road between Trevandrum and Padmanabhapuram was widened and repaired.

* Descendants of such sthanapathies appear to still exist in Travancore and are in the service.

In 955 M.E. (1781 A.D.), Gopala Iyen the nominal Dalawah died, and the Valia Sarvadhikariakar, Mallen Chempaka Ramen Pillay, was appointed to the vacant office of Dalawah, but unfortunately, he did not hold the office long, for he died a year afterwards, 956 M.E. (1781 A.D.) CHAP. III.

One Vadeveeswaram Subrahmanian who succeeded Mullen Chempaka Ramen Pillay, died the year after he was appointed and Nagercoil Rama Iyen succeeded him. He was Dalawah for a period of about six years; but he as well as his predecessor (native Brahmans of Travancore) held the office nominally; for the administration was conducted by the then deputy minister Valiasarvadhi one Chempaka Ramen Pillay (a native Sudra of Travancore). This able officer also followed the example of Mullen Chempaka Ramen Pillay Dalawah, for in the course of his first year of office, he commenced many useful projects the foremost of which was a most important irrigation work, an anicut (granite stone dam) across the Kodayar, with the view of irrigating a large tract of waste land. This though not completed, certainly shows that he was a man of considerable ability and spirit. The unfinished granite works are still to be seen.

In 949 M.E. (1774 A.D.), Hyder Ali again entered the province of Malabar, and began to commit devastations. The then Zamorin of Calicut fled from his country, together with all his relations and dependants, and placed himself under the Maha Rajah's protection.

On hearing of the Zamorin's flight to Travancore, Hyder became enraged and commenced his march towards that country; but as on the previous occasion, the Dutch East India Company stood in the way, and objected to his marching through their territories.

Hyder Ali remonstrated with the Dutch and threatened to force an entrance. The Dutch declared that they could not give the Mussulman chief a free passage through their possessions without special permission from Batavia, and at the same time they communicated

CHAP. III. with the Maha Rajah and asked him if he was prepared to join them in offensive operations against Hyder. His Highness replied that the conditions of the treaty of Madras, precludes his joining the Dutch in any such operations, without the knowledge and permission of the Nabob and the English. His Highness added that he had already adopted measures for the protection of his frontiers, and for that purpose only he would willingly join them.

Hyder had therefore to seek a route by the Cochin Rajah's country. He ordered a large army, under the command of one of his Sirdars, to proceed through Trichoor. The Cochin Rajah not being protected by the late Madras treaty (as he was then an ally of the Dutch Company and not a dependant of the English), acknowledged his vassalage to Hyder, paid an additional sum of four lacs of rupees and four elephants and bound himself to pay an annual tribute of one and a half lacs of rupees.

The Maha Rajah, on hearing this, set to work with his army in conjunction with that of the Dutch, and strongly resisted the progress of Hyder's force through the Dutch frontier.

General D'Lanoy's health failed at this juncture, and consequently the Valia Sarvadhikariakar, samprathy Kasava Pillay, and the several able commandants of His Highness' army were the persons principally engaged on this occasion.

Intimation of the unwarrantable proceedings of Hyder Ali Khan was given by the Maha Rajah to the Governor of Madras, as also to the Bombay and Bengal Governments, and a general war against Hyder resulted.

The Maha Rajah was asked by the Government of the Honorable East India Company to co-operate with the Company's army and His Highness most willingly consented to do so entailing thereby great loss of money and life.

The war was continued by the East India Company and the Maha Rajah assisted them to the extent that lay in his power. Travancore regiments of infantry and cavalry placed at the disposal of divisional Commanders of the Company were taken to distant places, such as Calicut, Palghaut, Tinnevelly, &c., &c., and they were "universally allowed to have behaved remarkably well."

After strongly fortifying the northern and eastern frontiers of Travancore, the Maha Rajah sent a portion of his army under able officers to the north, to co-operate with the Bombay army, under Major Abington at Calicut. His Highness' troops were engaged in the war and were successful in their united actions. Another portion of the Travancore army which was despatched to co-operate with the British army in Tinnevelly against Hyder, was stationed at that town for a period of two years.

The following abstracts of letters addressed to the Maha Rajah by the various officers commanding the English forces at the time of the war establish the accuracy of the above facts.

Abstract of the letter of Major Abington, Commander of the Bombay detachment at Calicut:

"Your Highness is embarked in the same cause with us and the rest of the Malabars and already too far engaged to observe a neutral conduct any longer. The only safe way is now to exert every means to shut the door against the enemy and Your Highness is sensible that that cannot be effected while the passes of Canom are left open and Palghautcherry in their possession. It might be easily reduced, and I am informed, that a number of Your Highness' troops are now lying inactive at Paravoor. Two thousand sepoys acting with vigour, in junction with the Zamorin Nairs and the people, I have already sent to the southward will be more than sufficient for this purpose. The Zamorin Nairs in particular will then act with great spirit when they are backed by Your Highness' troops

CHAP. III. and when they are assured that no means in any power will be neglected to support and assist them."

Abstract of a letter from Colonel Humburstone :— " I am well informed how steady and sincere an ally Your Majesty has ever been to the English nation."

Abstract of a letter from Colonel Fullerton, the English General, who commanded the southern countries :—" I will relate to the Governor in Council the great friendship you have shewn and the services you have rendered to the English interests in general and to the army that I commanded in particular."

This war continued for several years, and in the interval Hyder Ali died in 957 M.E. (1782 A.D.), and his son Tippoo succeeded him, and for a couple of years matters were in *statu quo*.

During this war, General D'Lanoy fell ill at Udayagherry and died in the year 952 M.E. (1777 A.D.), deeply lamented by the Maha Rajah and the whole military of Travancore, while his loss was universally felt in the country. He may be called the founder of European discipline in the Travancore army and to his genius the country was indebted for most of the granite forts between Thovalay and Paravoor. He had been a hero in the reigns of the late Maha Rajah Marthanda Vurmah, and this Maha Rajah died in the service leaving behind him an imperishable and brilliant renown. He was buried with military pomp in the church in the fort of Udayagherry, constructed under his own superintendence. The Maha Rajah very gratefully ordered the following inscription which is still to be seen to be engraved on his tomb :—
"Hic jacet Eustathius Benedictus de Lannoy qui
" tanquam dux generalis militiæ Travancotidis præfuit
" ac per annos XXXVII fermi summâ felicitate regi
" inservüt cui omnia regna ex Caiamcolum usque
" ad Cochin vi armarum ac terrore subject. Vixit
" annos LXII menses V et mortuus est die 1 Junni
" MDCCLXXVII.

Requiescat in pace."

In the year 959 M.E. (1784 A.D.) a fresh treaty was concluded by the Mysore chief with the Honorable East India Company at Mangalore, when all hostilities ceased; in this treaty too, the Company secured sufficient guarantees for the protection of Travancore from the invasions of the tiger of Mysore.

The Commissioners, Messrs. Staunton and Huddlestone, landed at Anjengo on the 22nd March 1784 on their way to Madras, after concluding the treaty of Mangalore. They addressed the following letter to the Maha Rajah.

"Being on our return to Madras from Mangalore " and finding ourselves near the place of your residence, " we do ourselves the honor to inform you that peace " between the Honorable East India Company and " Tippoo Sultan was concluded and signed on the 11th " instant near Mangalore. The Company did not on " this occasion forget your fidelity and the steady " friendship and attachment you have uniformly shown " them in every situation and under every change of " fortune. You are expressly named and included in " the treaty as their friend and ally; and as such we " can assure you on the part of the Company that " your interests and welfare will always be considered " as protected as their own."

The Maha Rajah on receiving the above favorable intelligence from the Madras Government and the Commissioners engaged in drawing out the treaty, was relieved of a good deal of anxiety. Though conscious, from past experience, of the worthlessness of the Sultan's professions, still he hoped for rest, at least for some time, and freed from the annoyances of this tyrannical chief he wished to look after the internal affairs of his kingdom.

In the year 959 M.E. (1784 A.D.) His Highness the Maha Rajah, partly to perform a religious ceremony and partly to satisfy his curiosity to see some other parts of the country in the east and south of Travancore, proposed making a pilgrimage to Rama-

CHAP. III. swaram and seeing the districts of Tinnevelly and Madura on his way to and from that renowned resort of Hindu pilgrims.

But before starting from Trevandrum on this pilgrimage, His Highness had to take the precaution of effecting some arrangements through the means of His Highness' allies, the English East India Company and the Nabob of the Carnatic. The districts through which His Highness had to travel to Ramaswaram, viz., Tinnevelly and Madura, though subject to the sovereignty of the Nabob, were divided and were in the possession of Palayapattacars (Poligars), the majority of whom were rude and lawless chieftains.

His Highness obtained the assistance of a few companies of sepoys of the English East India Company and some responsible officers from the Nabob's Government to escort him to Ramaswaram. With these and a large portion of His Highness' own army and a number of followers, he set out with all the pomp and grandeur, usually attending the movements of Indian sovereigns of the rank and celebrity of the Maha Rajah.

His Highness took great care to inspect and examine all the important irrigation works, roads and bridges, sathrums or choultries built for the comfort and convenience of the public in Tinnevelly and Madura this being the chief object for which he undertook the tour.

His Highness reached Ramaswaram in good health and performed the ablutions and other ceremonies there: and after spending a large sum in ceremonies and charities, returned, taking care to visit every place of note, to his own capital (Trevandrum), quite delighted with all he saw during a very agreeable journey.

His Highness lost no time in turning to account the knowledge of irrigation works, &c., he had acquired during the tour, and introduced improvements in

CRANITE PADDY STORE AT MANACUDY.

several works of this description in the southern districts comprising Nanjenaud, &c. CHAP. III.

By this time, His Highness had set aside all unnecessary religious scruples and prejudices usually predominant among high caste Hindus and contracted a habit of free intercourse with Europeans. He made himself perfectly accessible to the resident missionaries of the Roman diocese and to the others who wished to have interviews with him.

His Highness took advantage of the various interpreters employed in his Court and studied the Dutch, the Portuguese and the English languages, and though he did not attain any proficiency therein, he could converse in those languages tolerably well. He spoke fluently the Hindustani and the Persian languages.

Several public roads were opened about Trevandrum, and in order that uninterrupted communication might be secured between the garrisons at Paravoor and Thovalay, the main road between these two places was improved and extended. Several other roads were also constructed for facilitating the marching of troops. The Government unjéll (post) was improved and established on better principles.

The kingdom of Travancore at this time was in a most flourishing condition and the comfort and prosperity of the people were greatly increased. Trade and agricultural pursuits engrossed the attention of the inhabitants, and safety of life and property throughout the country was perfectly ensured. In short, the villages and roads which thieves and plunderers formerly infested and where travellers could hardly move in safety, with any valuables even in the day time, were watched and patrolled by the military so that a banker or trader who brought his money with him could sleep with perfect safety on the public road the whole night. The rule in regard to theft and robbery in those days was that the villagers, watchmen and guardians of each of the villages, should be responsible for the detection of all crimes and should

CHAP. III.

always apprehend the criminals with the stolen property; in default of this they were compelled to make restitution to the loser in an equivalent sum.

In 963 M.E. (1788 A.D.), the Dalawah Rama Iyen died and was succeeded by one of the Sarvadhikariakars Krishnen Chempaka Ramen (a Sudra native of Travancore.) This minister was not a very able man; but was selected for the post on the ground of his seniority. He was not quite equal to the duties of Dalawah, and so, Samprathy Kasava Pillay who was the first officer for the post of Dalawah, was appointed Sarvadhikariakar, and entrusted with the actual performance of the functions of the prime minister.

Here, we must observe that though Kasava Pillay was generally acknowledged to be the fittest man for the important post of Prime Minister, though there had been frequent opportunities for promoting him, and though he was a favourite and protége of the Maha Rajah, still His Highness would not appoint him to the post, simply because such a selection would have been an injustice to Kasava Pillay's seniors in office and a deviation from the established rules. This grand principle must bear strong and clear testimony to the Maha Rajah's impartiality and high sense of justice.

Sarvadhi Kasava Pillay began to distinguish himself in a very remarkable manner. His attention was directed for a long time towards the strengthening of the alliance with the English East India Company, and accordingly he commenced a friendly correspondence with the several English officers in the presidencies and other places in India. The conditions of the commercial treaty with the Anjengo factory, which was then under the Bombay Government were punctually observed and performed.

A few months after Kasava Pillay's appointment to the post of Sarvadhikariakar, His Highness the Maha Rajah took another tour to the northern districts of Travancore, and while at Alwaye he was so delighted with the place principally on account of the

TIPPOO SULTAN.

PUBLISHED BY MESS[RS]. HIGGINBOTHAM & CO.

C. FOOZENOY LITH: MADRAS.

crystal-like clearness of the water of the river at that season, that His Highness resolved upon remaining there for some time. During His Highness' stay at Alwaye he performed a particular Hindu ceremony called *Yagom* (sacrifice) at an immense expenditure. He bestowed several grants upon Brahmans of note and respectability and distributed valuable presents to educated persons who came to pay their respects to His Highness from Calicut, Palghautcherry and the Cochin Rajah's country. The expense attending His Highness' stay at Alwaye was enormous, but Sarvadhi Kasava Pillay without the least difficulty, managed affairs so economically in regard to the necessary funds, that the Maha Rajah was quite pleased and delighted with the manner in which he performed this important duty. At this time, the Dalawah fell ill and his recovery being doubtful, the Maha Rajah contemplated appointing Kasava Pillay in his place.

This officer was a man of great ambition. He wished to have a more high sounding name than that of Dalawah, a title which he thought was too antiquated for him. On this point he consulted his English friends and also the Nabob's officers at Madras and came to the resolution of adopting the title of *Dewan* as in the Courts of the Mogul monarchs.

His Highness returned from Alwaye to Mavalikaray and fixed his residence there for the Dassora festival of the year 964 M.E. (1789 A.D.), and the post of Dalawah having then become vacant, Sarvadhi Kasava Pillay as the legitimate claimant for the office, was appointed as the first Dewan on the 8th Kanni 964 (22nd September 1789), the last day of the Dassora festival. Thus was the title of Dewan first introduced into Travancore.

Tippoo, who had been watching with an eagle's eye, the proceedings of the Travancore Court, became jealous of the growing prosperity of the Maha Rajah and of his reputation which had spread throughout the whole of India. He again began to concert measures for bringing Travancore under his sway.

CHAP. III. In the Malabar year 963 (1788 A.D.), he renewed his incursions into theMalayalam territory, his depredations being accompanied with additional violence and cruelty. He proclaimed martial law between Ponnany and Cannanore.

The worst of Tippoo's tyrannical proceedings was that he ordered the conversion of all the Hindus indiscriminately, whether of high or low caste, male or female to the Mussulman faith, and all who objected to acknowledge the prophet were menaced with death.

All the high caste Hindus fled from Malabar: but where could they find shelter? In the Cochin Rajah's country they could not get an asylum as that potentate was a tributary of the Sultan.

The Hindu portion of the population of Malabar including the royal family of the Zamorin of Calicut, and every one of the opulent Numboories resorted to Travancore and begged for protection at the hands of the Maha Rajah.

The generous Maha Rajah, without the least hesitation or fear of the consequences, stretched his charitable hand of protection to the helpless refugees, and housed and fed them according to the deserts of each family. Many of these families settled in Travancore, and took a pride in becoming naturalized in the country which afforded them protection at a time of necessity.

This noble and generous behaviour of the Maha Rajah offended Tippoo Sultan still more highly, and he sent a message to His Highness through some of his confidential Sirdars, asking the Maha Rajah to order back all the refugees on the ground that they were deserters from his dominions.

The Maha Rajah sent a polite and friendly message in reply, to the effect that His Highness was ready to comply with the wishes of the Sultan, provided the people who had come from the northern countries to reside within His Highness' dominions were willing to return; for it would be unjust, as well as unlawful, for His Highness to cause them to leave Travancore under compulsion. CHAP. III.

This message no doubt displeased the Sultan the more; but concealing his anger, he tried again in soft and persuasive terms to attain his object as he was very desirous to get back and punish certain persons on whom his Sirdars wished to wreak their vengeance. Of these, one Mandayapurathu Ramunny Menon, a Mussulman convert from Vettathnaud called Meeravoonny, ancestor of the present Eloor Mooppen of Varapulay, was the foremost.

Tippoo summoned the Cochin Rajah before him, and his obedient tributary proceeded to Palghautcherry and there paid his homage to his liege lord. The Sultan appears to have found fault with the Rajah for the lateness of his appearance. After accepting the Rajah's apologies, Tippoo advised him to discover some pretext to provoke the Maha Rajah of Travancore to a war. To effect this, the Sultan suggested to his vassal that he should claim the districts of Paravoor and Alangaud, and that on refusal, he should commence hostilities in which he would be strongly assisted by the Mysore army. This proposal embarrassed the Cochin chief, who said that those districts were ceded to Travancore for important assistance given in the defence of his country and that they were ever since in the possession of Travancore. The Sultan, laughing to scorn the timidity of his vassal, told him that he could reduce Travancore in a week; that the Maha Rajah's friendship with the English would avail him nothing; and that the Cochin Rajah would do well to advise the Travancore king to become a vassal of Mysore. Anxious to free himself from such a dangerous superior, the Cochin Rajah readily offered his mediation, promising to put forth every effort to bring matters immediately to an issue; and the Sultan promised to send commissioners to the Maha Rajah with a friendly letter.

CHAP. III.

Before the Cochin Rajah could convey the subject of the Sultan's message to the Maha Rajah by a personal interview, His Highness received every particular connected with this conference.

After his return from Palghautcherry, the Cochin chief met the Maha Rajah at Annamanaday in the northern part of his country, where His Highness had proceeded on a tour of inspection of the military stations and conveyed to His Highness the Sultan's pretended friendly message, which was that that potentate was willing to enter into a treaty of alliance with the Maha Rajah; that he, the Sultan, expected the Maha Rajah to pay him a proper tribute at once and make preparations for the treaty; and that Tippoo's messengers are on their way to meet the Maha Rajah with letters and presents. But the Maha Rajah said that he was not prepared to negotiate with Tippoo, without the knowledge and consent of His Highness' allies, the Honorable East India Company and the Nabob of the Carnatic. The Maha Rajah, with his usual prudence and faithful attachment to his allies the English, resolved to see no messenger of the Sultan or receive any communication from him, except in the presence of a British officer. His Highness wrote to the Governor of Madras, Sir Archibald Campbell, to depute an officer of integrity and ability to the Maha Rajah's court, with whom His Highness might consult on some important points connected with the Sultan's mission. The Governor was quite delighted with the Maha Rajah's prudence and wisdom and ordered Major Bannerman, then stationed at Palamcottah, to proceed to the Maha Rajah's court with a small detachment under his command.

The messengers Goola Moadien and Dada Row arrived and were received in durbar in the presence of Major Bannerman and every respect was paid to the Sultan's Khareeta, which was read in open court. It ran thus:—"I learn from Rama Vurmah Rajah of

"Cochin that you are a good and a great prince "and that you desire to cultivate friendship with our "Sircar. As you are wise and well informed it must "be manifest to you how advantageous my alliance "will be to your interests. My trusty servants, Meer-"goolam Moadien and Dada Row, are charged with "this letter and will convey to you my present of a "dress, some jewels, and a horse. They come to you "on a friendly mission and will communicate full par-"ticulars." Notwithstanding all the regard and attention shown by the Maha Rajah on the occasion, the Sultan's messengers were far from being pleased, owing to the presence of Major Bannerman. The Maha Rajah accepted the presents, though reluctantly.

The messengers were dismissed with suitable presents the Maha Rajah promising to send his own officers with the reply and return presents to the Sultan.

This occurred in the year 964 M.E. (1789 A.D.). The Maha Rajah forwarded a very polite answer to Tippoo Sultan, conveying His Highness' thanks for the Sultan's consideration and his proposal for an alliance but intimating at the same time, his total inability to form an alliance, without the knowledge and consent of His Highness' ally, the East India Company, under whose support and protection the Maha Rajah had placed himself for several years past. Several valuable presents accompanied the letter, which was sent in charge of His Highness' Hindustani Interpreter, Chandrabhanu Lalla, and one of the native commandants of His Highness' brigade.

True copies, with English translations of the Sultan's letter and His Highness' reply, were forwarded to the Governor of Madras, with a solemn assurance that what was stated at the commencement of the Sultan's letter was incorrect or that it might have arisen through a blunder on the part of the Cochin chief. Sir Archibald Campbell was quite pleased with His Highness' policy and resolution, as well as, with this

CHAP. III. fresh proof of his true and unfeigned attachment to the Honorable East India Company.

Major Bannerman had also reported all the particulars connected with the interview of the Sultan's messengers. The Governor sent to the Maha Rajah several letters containing the expression of his full approbation and appreciation of His Highness' conduct in this intricate and troublesome affair. The Governor also tendered his valuable advice and counsel to His Highness.

The Maha Rajah's envoys returned from their visit to Tippoo Sultan, who was then near Coimbatore. Though the Sultan received them and the presents with due courtesy, the envoys had still every reason to believe that the Mussulman chief was offended with the tenor of the Maha Rajah's communication. The envoys informed the Maha Rajah that the Sultan was making great preparations for war.

As already stated the Maha Rajah had no confidence in Tippoo and he continued to pay great attention to the strengthening of his fortifications and the increase of his military forces so as to be prepared to meet any emergency.

With the view of ensuring the efficiency of his forces, which lacked the advantage of effective supervision since the death of General D'Lanoy, His Highness thought of placing them under the direction of English officers. He had full confidence in the courage, truthfulness and integrity of Englishmen and was convinced that he could not place his army in better hands than the English East India Company whose friendship had been cultivated in the time of his ancestors and properly and unfeignedly fostered by His Highness' renowned uncle, the late Maha Rajah.

The Maha Rajah wrote to Sir Archibald Campbell and requested four English officers and twelve surgeons from the Honorable East India Company's Army should be placed at the disposal of His Highness'

Government. But that acute politician, while appreciating the confidence reposed in him by the Maha Rajah, a confidence at the time unusual in the case of Indian princes thought this an opportunity to step in with a political object; for he informed His Highness that "the Honorable Company's officers "are brave and good men and will always discharge "their duty with zeal and ability; but it is contrary "to the system now laid down for the management "of the English Company's affairs, to lead their "officers to command any troops, except such as "are actually in their own pay and under their "own authority. Great inconvenience has been "found to arise from pursuing a different line of "conduct which I hope will reconcile to your mind "my declining to comply with the proposal. If you "can suggest any plan by which one, two, or even "three battalions of the Honorable Company's troops "can be employed to advantage in securing your "country against any sudden attack from Tippoo, I "shall very readily take the same into consideration "and if practicable, form an arrangement that will "afford safety to your possession without deviating "from the rules of our service." The Maha Rajah, though he knew well the drift of the Governor's proposal, and its ultimate result gladly availed himself of the offer and determined to have two regiments of the English East India Company stationed within His Highness' dominions and he accordingly replied:—"The friendship and attachment I bear to the English Company are known to "the whole world. I call the Almighty to witness "that I rest my whole dependence on them for support "and therefore most willingly acquiesce in the proposal in your Excellency's letter of having some "battalions of the Company's troops with me. Your "Excellency will be pleased to shew me your favor in "any manner that can tend to the security and protection of my country."

CHAP. III.

In reply to this frank communication, Sir Archibald

CHAP. III. observed: "You may rest assured that the confidence "you repose in the friendship of the English Company is not ill-placed. They regard you as their "faithful ally and consider your interests the same as "their own. Your having acquiesced in the proposition I made, of having some battalions of the Company's troops stationed on the frontier of Travancore, is a wise and judicious measure: it will ensure "the safety of your country against the ambitious "views of any persons who may be ill-disposed towards "you and cannot fail to convince them of the danger "they would be exposed to in attacking a Prince supported and protected as you are by the English, "whose arms, by the blessing of God, are too powerful "for them to combat with. At the same time I am "anxious to see your country in a complete state of "security. I am not less so in effecting it in such a "manner as will render your expenses easy; for this "purpose, I would recommend that in time of peace, "two battalions of the Company's native infantry "should be stationed on your frontiers at your expense "and that the amount may be either paid by you to "the Company in cash or pepper as may best suit your "convenience. That if an additional force of Europeans and natives are required to strengthen your "frontier against the designs of an enemy, these shall "be maintained at the Company's expense entirely; "with this proviso, that you will order them to be "supplied with provisions and the necessary articles "for erecting buildings to lodge them in and then "paying for the same at the usual rates of your "country." The Maha Rajah gladly acceded to this proposal and this was the origin of a British subsidiary force stationed in Travancore.

According to the agreement, two regiments commanded by Captain Knox were stationed near Aycottah in the northern frontier of Travancore in the year 964 M.E. (1788 A.D.). At the same time, as a medium for communicating between the Maha Rajah and the Madras Government, Mr. George Powney, a civil officer under the English East India Company, was also stationed in Travancore. He may be reckoned as the first Political Resident and British representative in the Maha Rajah's Court. CHAP. III.

Although the Maha Rajah was by these arrangements relieved of a good deal of anxiety in regard to the threatened invasion of Tippoo Sultan he did not relax precautionary measures.

About this time Tippoo arrived at Palghautcherry with a large force, with the intention of marching against Travancore. He sent for his tributary, the Cochin Rajah. On the receipt of Tippoo's summons, the Rajah was perplexed. He apprehended that the Sultan who was then in the zenith of his power, angry at the ill-success of his negotiations with the Maha Rajah of Travancore, would punish him either by imprisonment or by compelling him to renounce his religion for that of Mahomedanism. He thought that Tippoo was incensed against him for allowing a number of refugees to pass through his territories to Travancore and might probably extort a grant from him, ceding his dominions to Mysore and banish him from the Cochin territories.

The Cochin chief conveyed the Sultan's requisition for his appearance to his allies the Dutch and the Travancore Maha Rajah, both of whom considered the Rajah's apprehension as justifiable, and advised him to excuse himself from responding to the Sultan's call.

The Cochin Rajah addressed the Sultan, humbly asking him to excuse his attendance, stating that he had already paid his tribute and that he was ready to obey any further orders from his suzerain, but that ill-health put it out of his power to undertake a journey in an unfavorable season. The Sultan professed his sympathy with the Rajah in his illness, and deputed his envoy Kader Khan, partly to ascertain the extent of the Rajah's illness, and partly to press him to send his heir apparent or at least a minister possessing his confidence. Kader Khan arrived at Thripoonithoray.

CHAP. III. The Rajah shut himself up in his room as his illness precluded his seeing the envoy, who continued to reside in the capital for some time.

During Kader Khan's stay he procured every information connected with the frontier fortification and other military arrangements of the Travancore Maha Rajah as well as the Dutch at Cochin, and communicated the same to his master at Palghautcherry. After the return of Kader Khan, Tippoo threatened the Cochin Rajah with the forcible seizure of his person and the annexation of his country. But the Travancore Maha Rajah soothed the fear-stricken Cochin Rajah, gave him every assurance of protection and support and informed him that he need not fear the Sultan, so long as he was south of the Travancore lines.

The Maha Rajah sent his Dewan Kasava Pillay to Cochin to consult and arrange with the Dutch Governor M'Van Angelbic for the further fortification of the frontier.

The Dutch forts of Aycottah and Cranganore were situated at the very northern frontier of Travancore. After the construction of the barrier works and the connecting fortifications, these forts were regarded as the best defence against the approach of an army to the frontier, and consequently the Maha Rajah had been treating with the Dutch Government for the last two years for the purchase of these two forts. By the arrangements lately entered into with the Madras Government, it had been settled that the British force posted in Travancore would only be available for the protection of *Travancore territory*, and so, if those forts belonged to the Dutch and Tippoo Sultan's army captured them and entered Travancore by that road, the Maha Rajah could not expect any assistance from the Honorable Company's regiments stationed at the northern frontier. Moreover, the Maha Rajah now heard that Tippoo himself was thinking of purchasing these forts.

The Maha Rajah at once authorized Dewan Kasava Pillay to enter into immediate negotiations with the Dutch Governor for the purchase of these two forts. By this measure, His Highness thought that he would station the two English regiments in those forts and thus protect the frontiers. As the Dutch had already sold many of their minor possessions to Travancore, and as the negotiations for the purchase of Monambam and all the northern Dutch possessions including the forts of Aycottah and Cranganore were now pending, the Dewan found no difficulty in coming to a speedy settlement. CHAP. III.

On the 3rd July 1789, the Dewan concluded the bargain. M'Van Angelbic executed the title deeds on the part of the Dutch, to Dewan Kasava Pillay, on the part of the Maha Rajah. The Dutch possessions were sold for three lacs of Rupees, to be paid in several instalments, and the property was to change hands after receipt of the first instalment, which was paid on the last day of the week in which the deed was executed, and according to the terms of the purchase deed, the Dutch Governor transferred the property to Kasava Pillay in the presence of Mr. Powney, the British representative at the Travancore Court. This transaction of the Governor was subsequently ratified by the Batavian Government.

The Maha Rajah viewed the whole transaction with great satisfaction and apprised the Government of Madras of the same. His Highness observed in his letter that he hoped "the measure would prove a source of as much pleasure to that Government as it had been to himself." But before this letter reached Madras, Mr. Powney had written to Governor John Holland, who succeeded Sir A. Campbell, on the subject. On the receipt of this letter, Mr. Holland addressed the Maha Rajah as follows on the 17th August 1789:—" Mr. Powney has informed me that "you are on the point of concluding a negotiation "with the Dutch for purchasing Aycottah and the

CHAP. III.

"fort of Cranganore which they hold under the Rajah "of Cochin. Although I shall at all times be happy to "hear of your increasing prosperity, yet, at the pre-"sent juncture, I think any purchase of lands and "forts from the Rajah of Cochin, who is a tributary "to the chief of Mysore, will tend to irritate this chief "against you, and may have the appearance of a "collusive transaction. I have expressed these to Mr. "Powney in answer to his letter, and I have desired "him fully to state to you the serious consequences "which may result from engaging, at this time, in any "measures that may produce discussions between the "chief of Mysore and yourself. I think it necessary "to inform you that this Government will not support "you in any contests you may engage yourself on, "beyond the limits of your own possessions." The Maha Rajah received this letter only after the transaction was over. It has been already observed that the Maha Rajah had himself addressed a letter to the Governor at the close of the transaction. The Governor replied to His Highness on the 30th August. The letter ran thus:—"My last letter to you was dated "the 17th of the present month and was written in "consequence of the notification which I had received "from Mr. Powney of your being on the point of con-"cluding a negotiation with the Dutch for purchasing "Aycottah, &c. In the letter abovementioned I gave "you my opinion fully upon the measure which "you had in view and stated the impolicy of it. I "told you also, in plain terms, that this Government "would not support you in any contests in which you "might engage yourself beyond the limits of your own "possessions. Being thus furnished with my opinion "and declarations respecting the negotiations, you "cannot but expect that the news of your having con-"cluded it and of your being in possession of Aycottah, "and the fort of Cranganore is far from agreeable to "me. Your letter therefore of the 10th instant, lately "received, which you expected would give me pleasure, "has had a different effect. I lament that you have "taken the indiscreet step which may possibly involve "you in much embarrassment, if Tippoo should be "disposed to wrest from you these late acquisitions. "I cannot approve of your having entered into a "treaty with the Dutch for extension of territory "without the consent of this Government. This very "impolitic conduct makes you liable to a forfeiture of "the Company's protection, for you cannot expect "that they will defend territory of which you were "not possessed when their troops were sent into your "country, and which have since been obtained without "their assent. I therefore think it necessary you "should immediately give back to the Dutch the "places you have thus indiscreetly received from "them, and thereby establish your affairs precisely "upon their former footing. I again recommend to "you the greatest caution in your conduct towards "Tippoo." Thus was the transaction condemned by the Madras Government, and His Highness discouraged from adopting measures absolutely necessary for the protection of his kingdom. But the Maha Rajah, though disheartened at first, was encouraged by his firm belief that the Honorable East India Company would do him justice when the true bearings of the case were laid before them.

The Maha Rajah submitted his vindication to the Governments of Bengal, Bombay and Madras, and showed them the propriety of his conduct in purchasing the forts. He pointed out that the forts of Cranganore and Aycottah were at first in the possession of the Portuguese, who at the time of their settlement in India obtained possession of Cochin by conquest, and made it their capital; that Cranganore and Aycottah were their dependencies and the forts were built by the Portuguese so far back as 1523; that the Dutch having conquered the Portuguese in the year 1663, they held uninterrupted possession of the same till the date of the transaction, a long period of 126 years; that the Dutch were therefore quite competent to sell and the Maha Rajah to purchase them, without reference to

CHAP. III. either the Cochin Rajah or the Sultan of Mysore; that the purchase was not, as was erroneously supposed, from the Rajah of Cochin, the Sultan's tributary; that neither the Cochin Rajah nor any other prince had any right to the property in question; that the Maha Rajah had not, as was also erroneously supposed, concluded the bargain without the knowledge of the Madras Government; that independent of the circumstance of the sale having been conducted in the presence of Mr. Powney, Major Bannerman, whom Governor Campbell had delegated to Travancore as an adviser to the Maha Rajah, on the part of the English Government, had inspected the locality and the forts, and had suggested the advisability and stern necessity of the Maha Rajah's purchasing the forts, to prevent the great danger that Travancore would be exposed to, in case those forts should fall, by force or purchase, into the possession of the Sultan, a danger which even the assistance of the English would find it difficult to avert; and that the late Government of Sir A. Campbell had concurred in the opinion of Major Bannerman, that the Maha Rajah's object in purchasing the forts was not extension of territory or increase of revenue, but simply the security of his dominions. The Maha Rajah solicited the Bengal Government to do him the justice of appointing a Commission to enquire into these statements, as well as the points urged by him, adding that should he be required to surrender the forts he would do so to none but the English Government.

When the Sultan heard of the proceedings of the Madras Government, he thought that this was too good an opportunity to be lost. So he put forth his claims to the forts of Cranganore and Ayacottah, alleging that they belonged to his tributary, the Cochin Rajah, and that therefore their purchase by Travancore was unlawful.

Although the arguments contained in Mr. Holland's letter were fully answered *seriatim*, that gentleman was not satisfied with the defence put forth by the Maha Rajah. When Mr. Holland represented his one-sided views to Lord Cornwallis, his Lordship entirely disapproved of the transaction; but when his Lordship received the Maha Rajah's defence, he suspended his judgment and proposed to send Commissioners to investigate the subject. CHAP. III.

Mr., afterwards Sir Thomas Munro, Governor of Madras, remarked thus on the argument of Mr. Holland. He said: "The distinction made between recent acquisition and ancient territory appears to be a subterfuge of Government to cloak their dread of war, under a pretended love of peace." When these discussions were going on, His Highness was strengthening his defences to meet Tippoo. He concentrated all the forces and appointed Kasava Pillay the Commander-in-chief. The two forts of Aycottah and Cranganore were fortified and the Travancore army was garrisoned in and about them.

Meanwhile, Tippoo started from Coimbatore with a large army, consisting of infantry, cavalry and artillery, with a detachment of pioneers numbering in all 30,000 men, 5,000 horse and 20 cannon. He sent one of his Sirdars to the Maha Rajah with a threatening letter, accompanied with some presents. The Maha Rajah being then engaged with the celebration of the Dassara festival, he deputed Dewan Kasava Pillay to meet the Sirdar who had arrived at Paravoor.

The Dewan met Tippoo Sahib's Sirdar, and after the usual complimentary exchanges, the Sirdar was taken to Mavalikaray, and introduced to the Maha Rajah, who received Tippoo's letter and presents with his usual grace. The purport of the letter was; (1), a requisition for the immediate surrender of all the chiefs of Malabar who had taken refuge in the Maha Rajah's dominions; (2), that, as the Dutch had sold to him places to which they had no right, he should at once withdraw his troops from Cranganore; and (3), that he should demolish that part of his

CHAP. III. fortifications which crossed the territory of Cochin, because it belonged to the kingdom of Mysore."

Though the Maha Rajah felt indignant at the unjust and menacing tone of the Sultan's letter, and the haughty spirit of the envoy, he replied with great equanimity, and said (1), "that the Rajahs, against whose protection the Sultan complained, had obtained an asylum in his country several years back, because they were his relations; that no objection to their residence had ever been taken before, but to prove his amicable disposition they would nevertheless be removed; and that no refractory subject of the Mysore Government had ever, with his knowledge, been protected in Travancore; (2), that the fort and territory which he had purchased from the Dutch belonged to the Dutch, and was in no respect the property of the dependant of Tippoo; and (3), that the ground on which he had erected his lines was ceded to him, in full sovereignty, by the Rajah of Cochin, before that Rajah became tributary to the sovereign of Mysore, and that the lines existed at the time when he was included in the late treaty between the English and the Sultan and were sanctioned by the silence of that important deed." The envoy declared that the persistent refusal of the Travancore Sircar to be guided by the directions of the powerful Sultan, cannot but go much against the king, and a war with Travancore would be the result. He then left the place abruptly.

The Maha Rajah lost no time in transmitting a suitable reply to the Sultan laying before him strong arguments in support of the legality of His Highness' purchase of the two forts, and expressing his extreme desire to maintain peace between them, which His Highness pointed out should be reciprocated under the treaty of 1784. The Maha Rajah also forwarded some valuable presents to the Sultan in return.

Tippoo was infuriated at the contents of the Maha Rajah's letter, and forthwith despatched a rejoinder

NAIR AND SIKH SEPOY AND ROCKET BEARER.

PUBLISHED BY MESSRS HIGGINBOTHAM & CO. [illegible] LITH: MADRAS.

couched in severe language. The Sultan said that the Maha Rajah's reply was incorrect and made without proper inquiry, that from the tenor of his reply he acknowledged that he had allowed the Malabar Rajahs to escape from his country; that the Maha Rajah was responsible to Mysore for their liabilities, unless he recaptured and delivered them over; and that it was highly improper on his part to have purchased Cranganore without the assent of Mysore, in whose territories that fort lay. The Maha Rajah on receiving this haughty and arrogant communication thought it prudent to drop all further correspondence with the Sultan and submitted all the papers to the Madras Government, with a detailed account of Tippoo's warlike preparations.

On the 11th Dhanu (24th December), Tippoo encamped at a place four miles distant from the Travancore lines, where he began to erect batteries on the 12th (25th).

On the night of the 15th Dhanu, 964 M.E., (28th December 1789 A.D.), Tippoo's powerful army, under his personal command, attacked the Northern frontier of Travancore and attempted a breach of the barrier; but the attack was ably and gallantly resisted by the troops on duty, generally known by the designation of "Paravoor Battalion."

On the morning of the 15th Dhanu (28th December), the Sultan's force, consisting of 14,000 select infantry and a body of 500 pioneers, paraded in front of the line. The pioneers were ordered to clear a part of the ditch where the wall was not guarded, and they proceeded with the work which was not successfully completed during the night. However, the Sultan ordered the force to proceed and effect an entrance within the walls during the night. By day break on the 16th Dhanu (29th December) he gained an entrance and succeeded in possessing a considerable extent of the ramparts. The troops of the Maha Rajah, occupying those ramparts, retreated before Tippoo's army as the

CHAP. III. latter was marching by the side of the wall with the view of reaching the gate. The Travancore garrison opposed their progress. Tippoo found it necessary to bring in a reinforcement to afford help to the leading corps. In the hurry of the moment, the order was misunderstood and ill-executed. In this confusion, a party of twenty men of the Travancore garrison, who were stationed at a corner of the rampart, threw in a regular platoon on the flank which killed the officer commanding, and threw the corps into inextricable disorder and flight. The advancing relief was met and checked by an impetuous mass of fugitives.

The panic now became general and the retreating men were borne on to the ditch, while others were forced into it by the mass which pressed on from behind. Those that fell into the ditch were, of course, killed. The rear now became the front. The bodies that filled the ditch enabled the remainder to pass over them. The Sultan himself was thrown down in the struggle and the bearers of his palanquin trampled to death. Though he was rescued from death by some of his faithful followers, yet he received such injuries that he never forgot in this episode in his invasion of Travancore. Tippoo's State sword, signet ring, and other personal ornaments fell into the hands of the Travancore army; several officers and men were taken prisoners, and of the former, five were Europeans, and one a Mahratta.

Tippoo retreated with great shame and chagrin, and Dewan Kasava Pillay returned to Trevandrum in triumph, bringing with him Tippoo's sword, shield, &c., as trophies. The Maha Rajah communicated the news of his success to his friends the English and the Nabob, and received their warm congratulations. The Nabob requested the Maha Rajah to send Tippoo's sword, shield, dagger, belt, palanquin, &c., and they were accordingly forwarded.

In the interval, the Governor of Madras, Mr. Holland, wrote the following letter to the Sultan under date the 1st January 1790:—"We wrote to you on "the declaring our intention of inquiring into the "grounds of your claims concerning the forts of "Cranganore and Aycottah and assuring you, if they "should appear to be equitable, that we would cause "those forts to be returned to the Dutch and placed "on the same footing on which they were previous to "the late purchase of them by the Rajah of Travan-"core. We have now heard that your army has "approached to the neighbourhood of those forts and "that the Rajah is under alarm from an idea of its "being your intention to take them by force. You are "not unacquainted with the circumstance of the Rajah "being an ally of the English and you are no doubt "sensible that any hostility towards him would be "contrary to the faith of the treaty subsisting between "us. The forts in question are of no value to us; "but we think it necessary to inform you that we shall "consider any attempt to take them by force on the "present footing of affairs as an act inconsistent with "the fair and liberal sentiments of honor and friend-"ship subsisting between us and tending to create "hostilites between the two Governments. It is our "firm intention to do you justice on this occasion: and "it is scarcely necessary for us to say that we are "equally determined to do justice to our own reputa-"tion and honor, and it will be wise for you to wait "the issue of a fair inquiry. If you are desirous of "settling the points in contest by the investigation of "commissioners, we will appoint one or more to meet "such persons as may be appointed by you at any conve-"nient place on the borders of our respective countries, "and you will then judge whether our intentions are "fair. In the meantime, we shall state the whole of "the proceedings to the superior Government in "Bengal and wait their orders on them. On the "justice and equity of their decision you may safely "rely, as well as on the firmness of the British "Government to retaliate with their whole force any "injury they may receive either on their honor, or "territories and possessions."

CHAP. III. This letter reached the Sultan soon after his defeat. But it would appear that he wrote a letter to the Governor, some days after, ante-dating it and pretending to have written it before the receipt of Mr. Holland's communication. In this, Tippoo concealed all the facts and falsely represented to the Governor that his troops were employed in searching for fugitives; that the Maha Rajah's troops fired upon them and that his own troops retaliated and carried the lines; but that on his being informed of this, he ordered his troops to desist and return; and he requested the Governor to direct the Maha Rajah to observe the treaty.

Tippoo now determined on retaliating on Travancore. He remained in the vicinity of the northern frontier and concentrated a large army there which consisted of infantry, cavalry and artillery, which would have been enough to conquer the largest portion of India, rather than the small kingdom of Travancore. The Madras Government was duly informed of the above proceedings of the Sultan, and the Maha Rajah received assurances of assistance from the Governor, in the event of Tippoo's invasion of his country.

In the meantime, the Maha Rajah was not idle. The northern frontier line was repaired and all available troops were concentrated there. Recruits were enlisted, and guns, stores and ammunition were stored in the arsenals. The anxiety of the Maha Rajah was a good deal increased by the disparity between his means of defence and the Sultan's immense army and military resources.

No measures were adopted by the Madras Government till the beginning of March, though the Maha Rajah had repeatedly communicated to the Government intelligence of the close approach of Tippoo at the head of a large army, and their commencing to raise batteries and fill ditches. Still no active measures were taken by the Madras Government. On account of the inactivity and feeble policy of Mr. J.

Holland, which have been the theme of public comment, the Maha Rajah of Travancore was exposed to the mercy of the relentless tiger of Mysore. The very subordinates of the Governor condemned his policy. Some idea of the perilous situation of the Maha Rajah at this juncture may be realized from the following letter written at the time by T. Munro, a subaltern in the Madras army, (afterwards Major-General Sir Thomas Munro, Governor of Madras): "A second attack is daily expected; and if the king (of Travancore) is left alone, all his exertions against a power so superior can delay but for a very short time his ruin. The English battalions were behind the lines, but not at the place attacked; and it is said that they have orders not to act even on the defensive. If such be the case, the Rajah ought to dismiss them with scorn, for the present is the only moment in which the aid of such a handful of men can be effectual. The barrier once forced, orders for them to act, will arrive too late."

Tippoo's force commenced action. The opening of hostilities was a skirmish between a party of Travancoreans and Mysoreans, outside the wall, on the 20th Kumbham 964 M.E. (2nd March 1790, A.D.), and Tippoo's artillery began to work on the 24th Kumbham (6th March). Finding no perceptible effect on the wall, a few more batteries were erected close to the northern wall and the largest guns were mounted, which opened a destructive fire. The wall resisted the fire for nearly a month and in Madam (April) a practicable breach of three-quarter of a mile in length was effected. By this time, the Travancore army abandoned the defence as useless, and retreated. A portion of Tippoo's army, under Lally, attacked the fort of Cranganore, which was defended by the Maha Rajah's troops under Captain Flory. Finding that the defence of the fort against the enemy was impossible, and an English Engineer of the Company's regiments stationed then at Aycottah whom Captain Flory consulted being of the same opinion, he abandoned it to

CHAP. III. the enemy, who demolished the fortifications the next day. Lally now proceeded to Kuriapilly, which fort was also abandoned by the Travancoreans. The whole line thus fell into the hands of the Sultan, together with 200 pieces of cannon of various sizes and metal and an immense quantity of ammunition and other warlike stores, which were forwarded to Coimbatore as trophies.

While this destructive warfare was going on, the two English regiments stationed at Aycottah and another brigade consisting of a European and two native regiments just landed from Bombay under Colonel Hartlay at Monambam and Palliport, remained passive spectators of all these disasters and depredations on the plea that no orders had been received by them, from the Governor of Madras, to fight against the Sultan.

It is to be observed here that the orders of Government to co-operate with the Travancore army were at last received by the Officer Commanding the British force: but their receipt being just at the time of Tippoo's entry into the Travancore lines, the commander considered that his force was no match for the victorious army of the Sultan, and that therefore it would be injudicious to sacrifice his men.

Seeing that the English force stationed at Aycottah did not venture to assist Travancore, Tippoo was encouraged to march on to the interior committing devastation on his way.

Dewan Kasava Pillay was at Paravoor, at the head of a strong force of the Travancore army with its European officers. But the further advance of the invaders could not be arrested and so the Dewan thought it prudent to retreat.

The Sultan's first object was to destroy the "contemptible wall" and fill up the ditch, and so he took a pickaxe himself and set an example which was followed by every one present and the demolition of the wall was completed by his army without much delay.

After this, the lawless force was let loose in the villages. They committed various atrocities and the country was laid waste with fire and sword. Some of the inhabitants fled for shelter to the wild hills of Kunnathnaud, while many were taken captives. Hindu temples and Christian churches were equally desecrated by the followers of Mahomet. Towers of pagodas, the houses of the rich, and the huts of the poor, all were burnt to ashes, and the scenes throughout the districts of Alangaud and Paravoor were heart-rending. The ruins which may be seen up to the present day testify to the ferocity of the invaders. Records of antiquity, secured in the archives of pagodas, palaces, churches and the houses of the nobles were all committed to the flames. CHAP. III.

All these cruelties and atrocities were perpetrated with the express sanction of the Sultan, who, with his main army marched southward, and reached Alwaye, the celebrated watering place where, a few years ago, the Maha Rajah had performed the vedic sacrifice (Yagam) at a considerable expenditure as mentioned in page 211.

Fortunately for the country, the south-west monsoon broke out with unusual severity and the beautiful Alwaye river, a stream which usually rises after a few showers, filled and overflowed its banks causing Tippoo's army great inconvenience and rendering their march almost impossible. The current, during the freshes in this river is so strong, that even the permanent residents of the adjacent villages find difficulty in crossing it at this time. As the country around is mostly intersected by numerous rivers and streams, and intermixed with large paddy fields submerged under water at this season, Tippoo and his army were surprised at a scene which they had seldom witnessed before, and were bewildered by their critical situation.

Tippoo was certainly in a very awkward predicament and one for which he was not prepared. He had no idea of what a Malabar monsoon was. His army

CHAP. III. had no shelter; no dry place for parade; all their ammunition, accoutrements, &c., got wet. Even the very necessaries of life were washed away by the impetuous current of the flooded river. These untoward events exercised a depressing influence in the mind of Tippoo. If he had ever repented of his cruel actions in his life, it was at this moment. He repented his having reduced to ashes large pagodas, churches and other edifices which could have now afforded him and his army shelter and protection from the severity of the rains. Cholera, small-pox and other epidemics broke out. Provisions became scanty, and the scarcity was followed almost by famine. Numbers began to perish by disease and hunger. The lawless people took advantage of the time and commenced plundering every thing that they could get hold of, and in fine, the state of the country had become so desolate, that even the pen of Sir Walter Scott, the great Novelist, would find it difficult to give an adequate description of it.

Kasava Pillay, after leaving Paravoor, strengthened the garrison at every military station, both at the sea beach and at Arookutty and other places, erected stockades, at every backwater passage, fortified the line and batteries between Kumarakam and the Kundoor hills at Poonjar. All the responsible officers, both military and revenue, were posted at different places and the divisional revenue authorities were directed to remain at intermediate stations and raise irregular militia, armed with whatever descriptions of weapon the people could get at the moment, such as bows, arrows, swords, cudgels, &c. The Dewan then went to Trevandrum. He found the Maha Rajah, who was already advanced in years, in an extremely melancholy state of mind. His Highness, when he saw the Dewan exclaimed in a very low voice:—"We have now lost every thing. Our safety is in the hands of Providence. Padmanabha Swamy alone should protect us in this perilous predicament. It is now impossible to check Tippoo's progress. We have trusted the English and placed every confidence in them. But now, it is our misfortune that the Sultan should be thus allowed to encroach upon our territory." Dewan Kasava Pillay, though equally perplexed at the situation, consoled the Maha Rajah by the announcement that he had learnt from the Dutch as well as from his English friends, that the Bengal Government had taken the matter into their hands and a war against Tippoo was at hand, and he added that by the mercy of Providence, the Maha Rajah would be soon relieved from all fears, as regards the Sultan. At the same time, the Dewan informed the Maha Rajah that Tippoo's progress from Alwaye was totally impeded on account of the rain, that any attempt on his part to march with his army from Alwaye to up-country, must be thwarted by the natural defences of the country, that his cavalry as well as his infantry could not find road-way for a free march, that the backwater had been properly stockaded at different places so much so that no canoes or boats could be taken from Alwaye, up the river to the south, without encountering the stockades and the backwater garrison, and that the line between Kumarakam and Kundoor hills had been strongly barricaded while a regular militia lined the hills and the sea, so that till the opening of the rumoured English war, nothing would occur to Travancore.

The Dewan's assurances and representations encouraged the Maha Rajah a good deal, and the first order His Highness gave the Dewan was to go back to the north and adopt further measures for the increased protection and safety of the numerous families who had taken asylum in the Maha Rajah's territories. His Highness displayed greater anxiety about these families than about the safety of his own kingdom and person.

The Cochin Rajah had already sent his royal family to Trevandrum with the following letter to the Maha Rajah :—"Tippoo has come to Paravoor, and Cranga-"nore is being cannonaded. I therefore desire to "send my family and children to your capital. Take

CHAP. III. "them safely over. God is witness that to you I con- "fide my all."

The Dewan returned to the north. News of Tippoo's first attack on the Travancore lines and his defeat on the 29th December 1789 reached Calcutta on the 26th January following. Lord Cornwallis wrote at once to the Madras Government expressing his hope that the Government had already declared war against Tippoo, and that every exertions was being made to conduct it to a satisfactory issue. His Lordship declared that he was determined "to exact a full reparation from Tippoo for this wanton and unprovoked violation of treaty." This letter does not appear to have had the desired effect upon Mr. Holland. The Governor-General repeatedly urged war as the only honorable alternative left. "We had dissembled," the Governor-General wrote, "our sense of Tippoo's failure in the performance of several stipulations in the last treaty of peace, as well as of many insults and injuries that he had offered to us in the course of the last three or four years, and we are now resolved to curb his insolence and exact signal reparation for the many injuries that we and our allies have sustained."

In a letter dated the 8th February, Lord Cornwallis blamed the Madras Government for neglect of duty and disobedience of orders, and for having, in their correspondence with the Maha Rajah, "discouraged a faithful ally in the defence of his country against an enemy who was within a few miles of his frontiers, and with the insolence and violence of whose character they had long been fully acquainted." On the 8th March, the Governor-General forcibly observed "good policy as well as a regard to our repu- "tation in this country, requires that we should not "only exact severe reparation from Tippoo, but also "that we should take this opportunity to reduce the "power of a prince who avows upon every occasion so "rancorous an enmity to our nation."

Mr. Holland, Governor of Madras, still persisted in

his mischievous and perverse policy of inaction and delayed hostilities, and the Government of Lord Cornwallis wisely determined to assume the Government of Madras themselves; but the supercession of Mr. Holland by the appointment of General Meadows, as Governor of Madras, in succession to Sir Archibald Campbell relieved them from the necessity of resorting to such an extreme measure.

On the 30th March, Lord Cornwallis addressed the following letter to General Meadows the new Governor:—"So far am I from giving credit to the late "Government for economy in not making the necessary "preparations for war according to positive orders of "the Supreme Government, after having received the "most gross insults that could be offered to any nation, "I think it very possible that every cash of that ill-"judged saving may cost the Company a crore of "rupees, besides which I still more sincerely lament "the disgraceful sacrifice which you have made by "that delay, of the honor of your country by tamely "suffering an insolent and cruel enemy to overwhelm "the dominions of the Rajah of Travancore which we "were bound by the most sacred ties of friendship "and good faith to defend."

General Meadow's assumption of the Madras Government was inaugurated by the declaration of war against Tippoo.

In his reply to General Meadow's formal announcement of his arrival and assumption of office, Tippoo took exception to the military preparations made by the Madras Government and he intimated his wish to send a person of suitable dignity, who would explain to the Governor his views on the subject, bring to the notice certain important matters, and state the circumstances which led him to object to the menacing attitude of the Madras Government.

To this communication, the Governor's reply was short and decisive. He said:—"The English equally "incapable of offering an insult, as of submitting

CHAP. III. "to one, have always looked upon war as declared "from the moment you attacked their ally, the king of "Travancore." The Governor of Madras addressed the Maha Rajah, assuring His Highness that preparations were in progress for punishing the Sultan for his wanton violation of the treaty, and at the same time requesting the Maha Rajah to prevail on the Malabar princes and chiefs who had taken refuge in Travancore to join the English, in bringing about the humiliation of the tyrant of Mysore. While Tippoo was in his uncomfortable encampment at Alwaye, as has been already described, intelligence of the commencement of hostilities and the assembling of a large English force at Trichinopoly reached him. Harassed on all sides, the Sultan was under the necessity of beating a precipitate retreat. But he was in a position full of danger and anxiety. The rivers were all full. The country was under water. The Cranganore bar rose high with a swift current seawards. Except boats, no other means of communication could be used in that part of the country at that time. There was no time to be lost. He divided his army into two portions and ordered one portion to march viâ Annamanaday and Chalakudy to Trichoor and thence to Palghaut, and the other viâ Cranganore and Chowghaut to Palghaut. This hasty retreat was attended with the loss of the great portion of the army and bore some resemblance to the disastrous retreat of the great Napoleon from Moscow. This calamity was accelerated by the Travancore army under Dewan Kasava Pillay following in close pursuit.

The Travancore force joined the British army at Palghautcherry, Coimbatore and Dindigul, and fought under the command of British officers, such as Colonel Stuart, Lieutenant Chalmers, Major Cuppage, &c.

The Travancore army remained and fought with the British force against Tippoo, up to the conclusion of the war and the treaty of Seringapatam, where the Dewan Kasava Pillay was present.

The treaty of Seringapatam and the reduction of Tippoo's power was no small source of satisfaction and relief to the Maha Rajah. But he was destined not to enjoy peace of mind, even at a time when he considered himself freed from all troubles and mental pains, for the contribution of a large amount of money was demanded by the English East India Company, for the expenses incurred by the Company's military department in protecting Travancore against Tippoo Sultan, while by the agreement of 1788, the Honorable East India Company had bound themselves to station two regiments in Travancore, at the expense of the Travancore State, for its protection and they expressly provided that "*If an additional force of Europeans and Natives are required to strengthen your frontier against the designs of an enemy, these shall be maintained at the Company's expense entirely.*" The Maha Rajah therefore little expected such an extraordinary demand from the Governor of Madras. However, a sense of delicacy and friendship dictated to his mind not to discuss the question at such a time with his ally, notwithstanding the empty condition of His Highness' treasury and the embarrassed state of his finances. The Maha Rajah managed to pay seven lacs of rupees by several instalments. But still, the Governor of Madras, Sir Charles Oakely, thought it right to impose upon the Maha Rajah the payment of ten lacs of rupees per annum, as a contribution towards the expense, independent of the charge of His Highness' troops employed with their (English) armies. On a just and fair representations being made by His Highness, Sir Charles rejoined "Your Excellency's "mind is, I doubt not, fully impressed with the justice "of the Company's Government in standing forth at a "critical juncture to protect you against the designs of "a tyrant who had drawn the sword for your destruc-"tion and must have instantly effected it, but for the "powerful interposition of your friends. The war "thus undertaken upon your account has been carried "on with all the forces of the Company and at an

CHAP. III.

CHAP. III. "enormous expense. Not only the revenues of this "presidency but those of Bengal and the greatest "part of the resources of the Carnatic and Tanjore "have been appropriated to this great undertaking, "and on the ultimate success of our arms, Your Ex-"cellency must trust for all that is valuable to you, "your territory, your honor, and even your personal "safety." He also said that the demand of the Company was "calculated upon a fair and moderate estimate." Mr. Powney, the British resident, at His Highness' Court also represented the matter in the strongest terms.

The Maha Rajah, now pressed for money, consulted with his faithful Dewan, Kasava Pillay, who suggested that a moiety of the amount should be paid again, and he promised to exert his utmost endeavours to raise funds for meeting this unexpected demand.

The Dewan applied his energies to this difficult task and made up a sum of about seven lacs of rupees and paid it without any great delay.

On a further requisition of the Madras Government for a payment of the Maha Rajah's contribution at the rate of ten lacs of rupees per annum, during the late war, the Maha Rajah felt his situation most keenly. The Dewan was not at the time at the capital and the Maha Rajah's feelings of embarrassment are disclosed in a private and confidential letter he wrote to his minister:—"I have not in any way bound myself to "contribute to the expenses of the war; yet the Com-"pany presses for payment. I have raised loans and "paid fourteen lacs; yet they make further demands. "My previous debts remain unpaid. I have raised "money by doing what I ought not to do. I never was "in such anxiety and distress before. The Company "care more for money than for their friend."

When the Dewan appeared before the royal presence, the Maha Rajah exclaimed that His Highness little expected his old ally, the Honorable East India Company, would thus persist in their demand and trouble him in his old age; that the Madras Government ought to have recollected and respected their solemn engagement with Travancore in 1788 (963 M.E.); that that Government could not be ignorant of the immense expenses Travancore had undergone while entertaining a large force from the time of Hyder Ally's aims upon Travancore, a period of about twenty-five years, and also for assisting the military operations of the Company and of the Carnatic Nabob both in Tinnevelly and Calicut; that the Company's Government ought to have also considered the irreparable loss and disgrace to which Travancore was subjected owing to the persistent obstinacy of Governor Holland of Madras, by which alone Tippoo's army was enabled to attack and enter the northern limits of Travancore and devastate the country: that this loss of the Maha Rajah was not taken into consideration when the last treaty of Seringapatam was concluded, where the East India Company had obtained three crores and thirty lacs of rupees and one-half of the Sultan's newly acquired territory, which latter was divided and appropriated between the Company and their allies, the Nizam and the Mahrattas; and that it was highly to be regretted that the Governor of Madras gave a deaf ear to all the Maha Rajah's representations of the difficulties he had to encounter. The Dewan, Kasava Pillay, suggested to His Highness, that a full representation of the subject to Lord Cornwallis would probably relieve the Maha Rajah from such extravagant demands. The suggestion of the Dewan was adopted, and the Governor-General after mature consideration, gave a just and favorable decision freeing the Maha Rajah from the obligation of meeting in full the demand of the Madras Government.

As has been already said, the Governor of Madras, General Meadows, requested the Maha Rajah in May 1791, "to prevail on the Malabar chiefs who had taken shelter in Travancore to join the English" against Tippoo. But subsequently, the Government

CHAP. III. vested the Maha Rajah with the power of controlling all the Malabar principalities and restoring them to their respective princes and chiefs.

The work assigned to His Highness by the Madras Government was certainly a very honorable one, though not unattended with difficulties, for the country was still in an unsettled state. Many of its princes and chiefs fled at the approach of the dreaded Sultan, leaving their countries at the mercy of the Mysore tyrant; others preferred suicide to an ignominious conversion to Mahomedanism. There were many of the ruling princes and chiefs of Malabar whose territories had been given by the Sultan to his Mussulman Sirdars and others of his caste. The whole of Malabar was in a state of chaos. The selection of His Highness to arrange the restoration of the countries to their respective rulers gave universal satisfaction. Everybody acknowledged the stern impartiality and the calm judgment of the Maha Rajah. Moreover, most of these princes and chiefs had received an asylum in Travancore, and knew the liberality, justice, kindness and truthfulness of His Highness, and they were all satisfied with the choice of the Company's Government.

The princes and chiefs who were then in Travancore, were called before the Maha Rajah, and after receiving His Highness' kind advice and suitable presents, were sent back to the north, with instructions to go to the Dewan who was then stationed at Palghautcherry with a large army.

The royal family of Cochin was sent back to Thripoonithoray as soon as Tippoo re-crossed the Travancore frontier.

The Zamorin, who was then past seventy years of age, wished to remain in Travancore for some time longer. The Maha Rajah allowed the septuagenarian to do so and deputed his heir apparent Krishnen Rajah to Calicut to act for the Zamorin.

The Rajah of Cherakel remained at his head-quarters after despatching his family to Travancore, in the hope of gaining the favor of the Sultan, through the medium of Ally Rajah of Cannanore, but being disappointed "he died either by his own hand or by that of a friendly Nair whom he is said to have required to perform this last mournful office for him." No successor to the deceased Rajah was nominated, as there were two claimants, and in accordance with the prevailing custom the Maha Rajah elected the elder of the claimants as successor to his deceased uncle.

The names of some of the Rajahs and Chiefs who took refuge in Travancore are—

Rajahs (1) Zamorin.
(2) Cherakel.
(3) Cottayam.
(4) Kurrumpanaud.
(5) Vettathnaud.
(6) Beypore.
(7) Tanniore.
(8) Palghaut, &c., &c.

Chiefs (1) Koulaparay.
(2) Coringotte.
(3) Kowgat.
(4) Etatharay.
(5) Mannore.

Dewan Kasava Pillay was now delegated by the Maha Rajah to the onerous duty of restoring these Princes and Chiefs to their respective countries and this appears to have taken up the time of this officer, for about a year, during the war. He had to move between Cherakel and Palghautcherry to investigate the claims of each of the Rajahs and nobles to the territories, as there had been many encroachments on the villages and lands. He visited the capitals of all the Rajahs and Chiefs and reinstated every one of them in his respective possessions.

CHAP. III.

As many of these Princes and Chiefs were ignorant and unable to conduct the administration of their States, the Dewan was obliged to appoint Kariakars (ministers) to manage their affairs.

For the Zamorin (who was then absent at Travancore and for whom Krishnen Rajah was acting), the Dewan selected an able and influential Palghaut Brahman, named Saminatha Patter, as Kariakar.

After making all these arrangements, the Dewan came to an understanding that every one of these States, according to its ability, should supply the British and Travancore Commissariat departments with grain.

Every Kariakar was made responsible for the due performance of his functions, with the threat, that the least remissness on the part of any these officials would result in his dismissal from office.

By this wise arrangement of the Dewan, a sufficient supply of grain was secured for the forces stationed on the Malabar coast and also at Palghautcherry and Coimbatore.

Kariakar Saminatha Patter displayed great zeal and activity, and the acting Zamorin, Krishnen Rajah, experienced some difficulty in the free exercise of his despotic power to which he had been accustomed from infancy.

Krishnen Rajah's junior now proceeded to Trichinopoly and appeared before General Meadows and succeeded in obtaining a cowle from the Madras Government, recognising him as the legitimate successor of the old Zamorin. On the strength of this cowle, Krishnen Rajah began to act independently of Dewan Kasava Pillay, and the result was a deficiency in the supply of grain and other necessaries which were to be sent up from the Malabar coast. Dewan Kasava Pillay reported the cause of this to General Meadows, who remarked: "It was never intended the cowlenamah forwarded to him (Krishnen Rajah) should convey any authority independent of the Rama Rajah (Travancore) but that the old Calicut Rajah, who has long resided in the Travancore country, or persons properly authorized by him should administer the revenue of the country under the control and direction of Rama Rajah, whose protection to the dispossessed Rajahs and exertions for the prosecution of the war entitle him to take a lead in the affairs of the coast." General Meadows again said that "in the execution of such authority as he might be vested with by the old Rajah (Zamorin) he is to be guided by the instructions he shall receive from the minister of the Rama Rajah, now at Palghaut, and consider himself in all respects subject to his command and authority."

After the above peremptory order of the Madras Government, the Malabar province was under the sole control of the Maha Rajah, whose minister, Kasava Pillay, now became dictator of the Princes and Chiefs of Malabar. He held this important office and controlled all affairs connected with the war till the treaty of Seringapatam.

During this time the Cochin Rajah brought forward a claim against the petty State of Koulaparay. He contended that the Nair Chief of Koulaparay was a tributary of his and that the Travancore Dewan's reinstating the Nair as an independent Chief was a matter of grievance to him. The Madras Government, after a careful and impartial enquiry, (into the details of which it is not our province to enter) pronounced Dewan Kasava Pillay's act just and right.

By the treaty of Seringapatam, Tippoo was bound to cede one-half of his dominions to the Honorable East India Company, and in his schedule of the districts to be ceded, he for a similar object included the Travancore districts of Alangaud, Paravoor and Kunnathnaud as belonging to him.

When Commissioners were appointed to take charge of the ceded territories, Dewan Kasava Pillay informed

CHAP. III. the Bombay Commissioners so early as May that these districts belonged to Travancore, and subsequently Mr. Powney, the British Resident in Travancore, reported that "the hobilies in question had appertained to the Travancore Rajah ever since 1755, having been at that time made over to him by the Rajah of Cochin when the latter was at war with the Zamorin, and that these being included in cession was therefore altogether unwarrantable."

The Maha Rajah laid the whole matter before Lord Cornwallis and the Governor-General said, "With "respect to the talooks of Alangaud, Paravoor and "Kunnathnaud, the justice of the cession of them to "the Company must be decided by the period of the "commencement of the war, when if they were in the "possession of the Rajah of Travancore by whatever "means and more especially if it shall appear that the "Rajah of Travancore had acquired these districts "from the Rajah of Cochin before the latter became "tributary to the Hydery Sircar, it would be an act of "great injustice on the part of the Company to deprive "him of them."

After a good deal of correspondence between Tippoo, the Indian Government, and the Commissioners, two of the Commissioners, Messrs. Page and Boddam, were specially deputed to hold an inquiry to ascertain the facts of the case. When it was found by the Commissioners that Tippoo had no right to include those districts among those ceded to the Company, the Rajah of Cochin came forward and claimed the very same districts. He alleged that the Maha Rajah "having only assisted his ancestor in the recovery of part of the conquest thus made from this his country, from the Zamorin and therefore left incomplete the performance of the consideration for the cession of the three talooks in question, the Rajahs of Cochin have ever since annually continued to require their being relinquished by the Travancore Rajah who had frequently promised a compliance but never performed."

He (the Cochin Rajah) therefore contended that he was entitled to the talooks in question. This was really quite an unfounded claim, probably invented in a moment of weakness or temptation under the instigation of unprincipled advisers. The able and painstaking Commissioners obtained a full explanation from the Travancore Dewan Kasava Pillay, who joined them during the time of the investigation, and being quite satisfied with the justice and validity of the Maha Rajah's claim to those districts, called upon the Cochin Rajah for evidence in support of his claims. Finding that he had very little to offer as a convincing proof of the justice of his claim, he judiciously abandoned his suit. The Commissioners in their report to the Government wrote as follows:—"At "length the Rajah came and with tears in his eyes "requested them not to insist on making any further "scrutiny into the points in question as he had now "become fully convinced that he did not possess any "rights to the said districts which had been ceded to "the State of Travancore with other parts of his "country some years previous to Hyder Ally's "conquest." The Cochin Rajah's candid and frank declaration, though made at the eleventh hour, enabled the Governor-General to give a final and just decision, confirming the Maha Rajah's undisputed claim to the districts of Alangaud, Paravoor and Kunnathnaud.

Though throughout the greater part of the Maha Rajah's reign the country was plunged in war, the improvement of the internal administration of the country was not in the least neglected.

The first step taken was to improve all the seaports for the purpose of increasing traffic. The Dewan entertained extensive views in commercial affairs, and was convinced that the prosperity of Travancore depended in a great measure on its commercial resources, and that there would be increased security to the kingdom by affording facilities for vessels to anchor at the various ports.

CHAP. III.

Dewan Kasava Pillay accordingly proceeded to visit the coasts and seaports from Cape Comorin to the north, and after arranging for the introduction of certain improvements to the port of Colachel, he came to Poowar and thence to Velingium,* in whose road-steads vessels could anchor in perfect safety. Being resolved to establish a port in the neighbourhood of Velingium, arrangements for building a large ware-house, a store godown and a spacious bungalow at Poonthoray were made. In the course of a few months, the beach at the latter place was dotted with various buildings, the property of private individuals and fishermen, and several other classes of industrious people also began to inhabit the place, so that the prospects of the new port appeared bright.

After the opening of this port, the Dewan continued his progress to the north, and while at the port of Poracaud (where the Dutch had a factory), his enquiring and energetic mind was directed to the singular state of the sea at Alleppey, a few miles north of Poracaud. He ordered a survey of the sea by some experienced persons about him, and finding the existence of a good anchorage protected by a bank, he resolved to open a port there also.

This important resolve was communicated to His Highness, who was only too willing to approve of all such useful measures. The necessary sanction was at once accorded for undertaking the work, with the necessary outlay.

Dewan Kasava Pillay commenced by getting the beach cleared of jungle, for it was thickly covered with wild thorny bushes, which were the habitation of jackals and other wild beasts. The beach was cleared in the course of two months and made fit for erecting buildings on.

A warehouse and a few shops were built at the Sircar expense, and merchants were invited from

* Here the English East India Company had a factory.

PUBLISHED BY MESS[RS] HIGGINBOTHAM & CO — C. FALZENSKY LITH. MADRAS.

CLOCK TOWER TREVANDRUM.

various places in Travancore to establish themselves at the new port. CHAP. III.

The Dewan communicated with his friends at Bombay, and induced a couple of rich and influential Cutch and Sind merchants from thence to come and settle at the new port.

To effect the permanent settlement of Hindus at the place, a pagoda was built in the interior, and Brahman cloth merchants who were invited from Tinnevelly and other commercial towns established themselves at Alleppey.

All this while the Dewan remained at Alleppey, with his official establishment, and as an additional proof, to the new settlers, of the Sircar's intention to make the place one of some importance, the Dewan ordered the construction of a spacious building for the Huzzoor Cutcherry, and a palace for the residence of the Maha Rajah, whenever His Highness visited the locality.

A Vijaripucar (manager), was appointed and all the hill produce was ordered to be brought to Alleppey and stored there, under the charge of the Vijaripucar.

The timber grown in Malayattoor and other forests was given out on contract to an influential native Christian (Mathoo Tharagan), who was directed to bring his timber to Alleppey and sell it there.

Thamby Naicken and other Vijaripucar were appointed and stationed in various parts of the forests, such as Combum, Goodaloor, &c., to collect and forward to Alleppey, all the hill produce, viz., cardamom, bees-wax, honey, ivory, stick lac, &c., and thus a system of forest conservancy was introduced for the first time in Travancore.

With the view of clearing the State-debt, which was still unpaid, the Dewan adopted another measure, viz., the building of ships for conveying the staple produces of the country to Bombay and Calcutta, and thus the Sircar embarked in trade and commercial speculations.

CHAP. III. Three ships were built and they carried to favorable markets such produce as were monopolised by the Sircar. In the course of two or three years a large amount of profit was realized, a circumstance which afforded additional satisfaction to the sovereign.

Several canals were opened to facilitate and extend communication from the back-water to the new town of Alleppey.

The Dewan, after accomplishing so much returned to Trevandrum, and commenced his improvements there. The public road leading to the east from the eastern gate of the Trevandrum fort was further widened. Bazaars or shops were built on the side of the road at Chalay, and a regular traffic and market established there. A bridge over the Killiar river and another over the Karamanay river with granite stone and several other public works were constructed, besides further irrigation works at Nanjenaud.

The Dewan also introduced improvements into the town of Kottar by inviting a number of weavers, dyers, painters and other industrious workmen from Tinnevelly and Madura to settle there; and thus this town became a very rich and important one, and formed the grand depôt for the supply of cloths for the whole kingdom of Travancore.

The great pagoda of Trevandrum was repaired, and the large flag-staff beautified and gilt. A golden vehicle for carrying the image of Sree Padmanabha Swamy, called Indra Vahanam, was made and an admirable granite work called Kulasekhara Mandapom, as well as several other valuable works were constructed.

Gold coins called Anantharayen fanam, Chinna fanam and Ananthavarahen were coined in the Travancore mint, in addition to a large quantity of silver bullion, coined as chuckrums. A new contribution called Nilavary, upon Sircar pattam lands, was raised which yielded a good round sum of money.

KULASEKHARA MUNDAPAM.

Thus the Dewan succeeded in clearing away the greater part of the State-debt contracted in consequence of war and other emergencies. CHAP. III.

All the fortifications were improved, a few more were newly constructed; and the manufacture of guns, shots and other warlike stores at Udayagherry was pushed on with great vigour. Palaces were built in different parts of the country, and the official buildings at Mavalikaray received much attention. The pagoda tower at Trevandrum was successfully completed. The temples throughout the country were repaired or improved.

The Madras Government, though on the most friendly terms with the Maha Rajah, had been making strenuous efforts to strengthen treaty stipulations and conditions with Travancore. After the treaty of Seringapatam, the Maha Rajah considered that the services of the two battalions of the Company's forces stationed at Aycottah might be dispensed with. But on communicating this view to the Madras Government, Sir Charles Oakely observed that the military forces kept up by the Company extended to the protection of their allies, who should therefore take a share of the ordinary expense of this establishment, adding: "In estimating the advantage which your country derives from the Company's protection I have recurred to the transaction which passed between your Excellency and this Government in 1788, at which time two battalions of our Sepoys were by your own desire stationed in your country. The expense of such a force I doubt not your Excellency will now be very willing to defray, upon the assurance that it shall be ready to move when required for your defence, and I propose to limit the contribution to the precise sum agreed to be paid by you in 1788 being star pagodas (42,768) forty-two thousand seven hundred and sixty-eight per annum."

On the appointment of the Earl of Mornington as Governor-General, the Maha Rajah opened a

CHAP. III. friendly correspondence with that august personage, who held the Maha Rajah in great regard and esteem. The Dewan Kasava Pillay had many European friends in the persons of the Governors of Madras and Bombay, as well as in most of the Members of Councils, and he was also well acquainted with several military officers in the army under the two presidencies. He was in the habit of corresponding with the Governor-General, who looked upon him as one of the first Statesmen in India. In 970 M.E. (1795 A.D), the Governor-General proposed to the Maha Rajah a revised treaty on more liberal and detailed terms, and after a good deal of correspondence between the Dewan and the Indian Government, a new one was drawn out and submitted to the Maha Rajah. This treaty consisted of nine articles.

First.—"That the Company has renounced every claim to the three Travancore districts which Tippoo had ceded and which undoubtedly belonged to the Maha Rajah."

Second.—"If any power or States, near or remote, by sea or land, shall without aggression on the part of the Rajah of Travancore, attempt or begin hostility and war upon the country of the said Rajah or of his successors; under such circumstances the expulsion of, and the protection of, the country against such enemies rest with the Company's Government."

Third.—"In consideration of this stipulation the Maha Rajah bound himself and his successors to pay both in peace and war a sum equivalent to the expense of three battalions of the Company's troops."

Fourth.—"Should it so happen that the aforesaid force and the Rajah's own army be at any time found unequal to cope with, and defend the country against, the superior force of the enemy, the expense of such further troops as it may be necessary and requisite for the Company to furnish in such instances, is to be altogether at the said Company's cost; nor shall their

Government anywise object to furnish such additional force, the expense of which shall in no respect be chargeable on the Rajah or his successors; nor shall the Company ever apply for or demand any sum on that account nor possess any plea or claim to make any further requisition for pecuniary aid from the Rajah or his successors, by reason of any warfare or hostility that may hereafter eventually occur."

The *Fifth* clause imposed upon the Maha Rajah the obligation to abstain from all aggression towards any other State whether Indian or European and that "in the event of the Rajah or his successors having any disputes of a political nature or tendency, it is necessary that the same shall be transmitted by the latter to the Honorable Company's Government, who will determine thereon according to justice and policy and mutual concert."

Sixth.—"The reigning Rajah of Travancore for the time being shall not keep in his service, in any civil or military capacity nor allow to remain within his dominions as merchants or under any other plea or pretext, the subjects or citizens of any nation being at war with Great Britain or with the East India Company; nor under any circumstances of peace or war allow any European nation to obtain settlements (*i. e.*, territories or places under his own authority) within the same, nor enter into any new engagements with any European or Indian States without the previous concurrence of the British Governments in India."

Seventh.—"When the Company shall require of the Rajah of Travancore any aid of his troops to assist them in war, it shall be incumbent on the said reigning Rajah for the time being, to furnish such aid to such extent and in such numbers as may be in his power, from his regular infantry and cavalry exclusive of the native Nairs of his country, which succours, thus furnishable by the Rajah as far as shall be consistent with the safety of his own country, shall be

CHAP. III. liable to be employed as far by the Company's Government on either side of the Peninsula, as to Madura and Calicut; and to be, during such service at the Company's expense and under their orders."

The *Eighth* clause comprised a contract for the supply of pepper for the Company's investment.

Ninth.—The Company engage not to impede in any wise the course of the rule or of administration of the Rajah of Travancore's Government "nor at all to possess themselves nor enter upon any part of what regards the management of the present Rajah's or his successor's country."

This treaty was duly ratified in 1797 A.D. (972 M.E.) by the Court of Directors, and the Governor-General was exceedingly pleased with the Maha Rajah and the Dewan Kasava Pillay.

About this time, the English having conquered the Dutch and annexed Cochin, the Dutch connection with the Travancore kingdom ceased, and Tangacherry and other Dutch possessions passed into the hands of the English. The services of all the Europeans in the army, excepting the English, were dispensed with at this time.

Though an enhancement in the amount of tribute had been obtained by the English by this treaty, still great advantages were justly expected to be derived by securing the permanent protection of one of the greatest rising powers in the world, and the Maha Rajah and the Dewan congratulated themselves on the success which had attended these negotiations, but the ignorant and lower orders of the country began to murmur on account of the increase of the tribute. The Maha Rajah observed that His Highness' great uncle had secured the kingdom from internal commotion by connecting it with Sree Padmanabha Swamy's Devaswam, but the Maha Rajah had followed in the footsteps of his renowned uncle, and had secured the kingdom to His Highness'

RHYE KASAVA DASS DEWAN.

PUBLISHED BY MESS.RS HIGGINBOTHAM & CO.

C. PACZENSKY LITH: MADRAS.

heirs from the invasion of foreign enemies, by insuring the support of a nation, which he prophesied would become in time, a power whose supremacy would extend throughout the world. The annual tribute had now become a little above two lacs and forty thousand rupees. But since the ratification of this treaty, the Maha Rajah enjoyed perfect peace of mind to which His Highness had been a stranger for a very long period, and began to devote his exclusive attention to the improvement of the country and the promotion of the welfare of its people.

The kingdom of Travancore now flourished, with a peaceful and contented population, devoting their attention to agricultural, commercial and other industrious pursuits with greater zeal and vigour and with increasing prosperity, and the country soon occupied a conspicuous position amongst the south Indian principalities. There was a large number of rich and opulent Sowcars, residing, with immense capital for traffic, between Aramboly and Paravoor, and trade flourished under the wise rule of the sovereign and the able administration of the Dewan Kasava Pillay, who, besides proving himself to be a minister of versatile talents was a remarkable warrior, his skilful hands managing the sword and pen alike.

In recognition of the Dewan's merits and his valuable services, the Maha Rajah wished to grant him a jageer or some such royal gift, but as a proof of his disinterestedness the minister most honorably declined the boon under the plea that he was a man already amply provided for by his sovereign master and therefore stood in no need of such a grant.

This Dewan had not drawn any fixed pay during the tenure of his office, as he made it a point to receive from the treasury whatever money he wanted for his expenses, and to pay into the treasury whatever surplus income he obtained, and consequently, he was perfectly right in declining the proposed royal gift.

The Earl of Mornington conferred on this Dewan

CHAP. III.

the title of "Rajah Kasava Dass," in recognition of his merits and fidelity.

Lord Mornington had a very high opinion of his "ability and prudence" as well as "his attachment to the interests of the Company," and the Dewan was besides held in high estimation by the Governments of India, Madras and Bombay, as has been already stated.

The people of Travancore looked on him as they looked on the Maha Rajah, with a kind of filial regard and esteem and he is known up to this day among the people as "Valia Devanjee," the Great Dewan.

The family residence of this renowned Dewan was a place called Kunathoor, near Velavencode, about twenty-two miles south-east of Trevandrum, where his descendants are still residing, in ordinary circumstances.

This Maha Rajah was one of the best and most faithful Indian allies of the Honorable East India Company, and he was treated with uniform regard and esteem by the Company and the Nabob of the Carnatic. The title "Munnay Sultan Maharaj Rajah Rama Rajah Bahadur Shamsheer Jung" was offered by the Carnatic Nabob and accepted by the Maha Rajah, and the same was subsequently adopted by the succeeding sovereigns of Travancore.

It was in this Maha Rajah's time that the present long title, "Sree Padmanabha Dasa Vanji Pala Rama Vurmah Kulasekhara Kireetapathi Munnay Sultan Maharaj Rajah Rama Rajah Bahadur Shamsheer Jung" was introduced.

The reputation of this Maha Rajah had rapidly spread throughout the whole of India. It was in his time that the Travancore Rajah was known and generally styled "Rama Rajah" and "Dharma Rajah," which names are quite familiar to travellers who journey from Benares and other northern parts of India to Ramaswaram or Ramanad.

ASWATI THIRUNAL (ELIA RAJAH.)

The Hindustanee pilgrims from northern India, who often traverse the country between Ramaswaram and Benares, are provided with free meals and halting places throughout the territories of the Maha Rajah, and up to this day, these people exclaim loudly "Jeya Rama Raj Jeya Dharma Raj!" *i.e.*, success to Ram Raj and prosperity to the land of charity, and continue doing so at every halting place, till they pass Aramboly. CHAP. III.

The Maha Rajah had the misfortune to lose his younger brother (the heir apparent), a prince of uncommon qualifications and natural talents, in the year 961 M.E. (1786 A.D.); and another brother, an accomplished Sanscrit scholar, also died in the year 963 M.E. (1788 A.D.).

At this period, there remained only a young prince of six years and having no prospect of issue from the Ranees, it was necessary to have recourse to adoption.

In the year 964 M.E. (1789 A.D.), two princesses were adopted from the family of Kolathnaud, who then resided at Mavalikaray.

This remarkable sovereign, of happy memory, ruled for the long period of forty years. He lived to the advanced age of seventy-three and closed his worthy career on the 6th Kumbham 973 M.E. (1798 A.D.), between one and two P.M., on the remarkable Hindu holy day called Sivarathri, leaving only one male member in the royal family, aged sixteen years, as heir to His Highness' throne.

The population, of every caste and creed, high and low, unanimously lamented the loss of this sovereign, so much so, that each family appeared to have looked upon it in the light of a personal calamity, as if it had been deprived of its own parental head. Never before had there been seen such demonstrations of mourning and sorrow in Travancore on a similar occasion.

All the public places and bazaars in the towns, as well as isolated shops, were closed for a week, and the

CHAP. III. people adopted the usual symbols of mourning voluntarily, even in the most distant localities in Travancore.

As in the former reign, there are numerous incidents and recollections concerning this Maha Rajah and His Highness' ministers, but for the reasons already stated in the last Chapter, we would not attempt to embody them all here. Nevertheless, one or two very interesting incidents may be noticed, which, while they show how attentively judicial matters were looked into, at the same time illustrate the great wisdom and foresight of the Maha Rajah and the tact of some of his subjects at that period.

On one occasion, when the Maha Rajah had assembled a party of men as usual, as a sort of jury, headed by himself as president, to consider and decide a case involving some most important claims put forward by a certain opulent and distinguished family, the Maha Rajah was seated on a chair, and the assembly formed two lines and stood on either side of the chair as customary, but before commencing business, an old man, a member of the assembly, arrived late, and standing in the centre, between the lines, put his right hand across his forehead and looked round, as if he were short-sighted from old age, and lifting his head direct to the spot where the Maha Rajah was seated, called out in a low voice "*Aividay yenta Thampuran Alunnally Irickunu,*" i. e., "where is my sovereign seated?" The Maha Rajah said smiling, "*Mooppinai! nhane narayana irrickunu*" i. e., "O! old man! I am sitting just in the right." The drift of the old man was to sound His Highness' position in the affair, but the sagacious Maha Rajah was not in the least offended, but expressed much delight at the old man's wit and straightforwardness.

On another occasion, Tippoo Sultan sent Brahman spies to His Highness' Court, and they, assuming the character of great sastries (learned men), repaired to Trevandrum, and were one day seated in the mandapom, inside the pagoda, along with many other Brahmans, when the Maha Rajah entered the pagoda to worship. His Highness looked on the assembled persons as usual, and returned to the palace. After reaching the palace, the Maha Rajah ordered one of the attendant hurikarahs, to call in the two sastries, and when they came before him, they began to repeat several verses and poems composed by them in honor of Sree Padmanabha Swamy, and also in praise of His Highness, and of the highly renowned administration of the State, and lastly, of the strength and condition of His Highness' army and of the strong fortifications of Travancore. When they finished this display of their eloquence, the Maha Rajah calmly and with a pleasant countenance and tone, asked them whether Tippoo Sultan Sahib was quite well and if the Sultan was then engaged in warfare! The Brahmans were struck with admiration and fear, but the Maha Rajah soothed them with kind words, and told them plainly that they need not be afraid of any injury, as long as they stayed within the jurisdiction of His Highness; that they should have full permission to move about the country and make all the observations they possibly could. The Brahmans were so overcome by the Maha Rajah's kindness and goodness, as well as by his courage, that they at once acknowledged the true character of their mission, and much valuable information was obtained from them. The spies were allowed to return, not only unmolested, but with such presents as were usually given to learned Brahmans who resorted to the Maha Rajah's Court.

To show how particular this Maha Rajah was, how minutely he looked into affairs even in his old age, and the familiarity that existed between the Sovereign and his ministers, we annex here a translation of an autograph letter addressed to His Highness by Kasava Pillay Dewan, while he was at Dindigal with the Travancore force. It appears that the Dewan delayed a little to move on with the Travancore army to join that of the Honorable East India Company, and that the delay at such a critical time, was not only injudi-

CHAP. III. cious, but was also attended with additional expenditure. The Maha Rajah wrote to the Dewan a sharp letter, to which the latter addressed the following reply:—

"I received and perused the royal writ forwarded to me by Kariakar Venctaswara Iyen and others conveying instructions for my guidance. They also delivered into my hands Your Royal Highness' letter to Lord Cornwallis."

"I shall embrace an early opportunity of meeting His Lordship at the camp and after holding a conference, shall personally present the letter."

"As some delay has occurred on the road, after I took leave of Your Highness, I have not been able to accompany the General to this place, but by the grace of the Almighty, I expect Your Highness' force will form shortly a junction with theirs."

"Pecuniary difficulties had in a measure caused the delay, but that is a matter not to be made public."

"As it is necessary that Your Highness' force should move in good style and neatly dressed, that was also a cause of the delay."

"I am led to infer from several incidents, that Your Highness considers the expenses I am incurring extravagant. When my present engagements, which I have undertaken by Your Highness' command, prove successful, all such delays as are caused by me will, by the mercy of God, turn to Your Highness' own advantage; but on the other hand, Your Highness may consider that such have been the result of my indiscretion."

"Anyhow, no act on my part will ever be calculated to prejudice Your Highness' dignity, while all my acts are calculated to promote Your Highness' glory."

"I write at this length, as I cannot allay my anxieties, unless I communicate all my grievances to Your Highness, and I solicit that this may not be taken amiss."

"I am not wanting in energy, nor by Your Highness' gracious condescension, shall suffer even its diminution."

"The creatures born on the Maha Meru (a supposed golden mountain sustaining the world and the sky), cannot but have, even in some slight degree, a reflection of its greatness; so born as I, though humble and poor, am in Your Highness' auspicious realm, which is the ocean of Your Highness' glory, and supported as I am, by Your Highness' glory, cannot but reflect on myself by Your Highness' merciful countenance in whatever clime I may be; like the sun's rays to which I shall compare Your Highness' kindness."

"As Your Highness is the sovereign disposer of adequate reward and punishment for good and evil, I, Your Highness' servant, prostrate myself before Your Highness' lotus-like feet, which I always bear on my head and implore that Your Highness' good blessing and unceasing mercy and benediction may be extended to me, at all times and places, like the rays of the sun. Awaiting Your Highness' further commands.

I beg to subscribe myself,
Your Highness'
Vassal, KESHAVEN."

Such has been the relative position of master and servant in Travancore, and the above letter and the sentiments expressed therein are well worth the study of the present generation. There are numerous accounts concerning this reign, which may be brought into this work, but instead of increasing the bulk of the volume with facts, the accuracy of which may be open to question it would be preferable to quote here passages from Fra. Bartolomeo's works, as this remarkable author gives a full description of the renowned Maha Rajah, and of his administration, from personal knowledge:—

"The military forces of the present king of Travan- "cor consists of 50,000 men, disciplined according to

CHAP. III.

"the European manner; and 100,000 Malabar *Nayris* "and *Cegos*, armed with bows and arrows, spears, "swords, and battle-axes. He keeps two *Valia Sarva-* "*dicàriacàrer*, the *Vadakemugham* and the *Tekmug-* "*ham*, one of whom is established in the north and the "other in the south. Each of these has under him "four other officers, called only *Sarvadicàriacàrer.* "These have inspection over four subalterns, or *Caria-* "*càrer;* and these subalterns have under them *Pràvar-* "*ticàrer*, *Ciandracarer*, and *Torracarer;* or collectors of "the taxes, overseers and judges. The troops are "always marching up and down through the country, "to change their cantonments, to enforce the collection "of the taxes, and to preserve peace and tranquillity. "Public security is again restored throughout the "whole country; robbery and murder are no longer "heard of; no one has occasion to be afraid on the high- "ways; religious worship is never interrupted; and "people may rest assured that on every occasion "justice will be speedily administered. The present "king has caused several canals to be constructed, in "order to unite different rivers with each other and "with the sea. By his desire also a very beautiful "road has been completed between Cape Comari and "*Cudungalur;* so that in the course of 24 hours he "can be informed of everything that takes place "throughout his whole kingdom. After deducting "the expenses of Government, his yearly income may "amount to half a million of rupees, arising from trade, "duties, and various kinds of fines. One-half of this "revenue is deposited in the royal treasury, and "never touched but in cases of the utmost necessity. "The king, as well as all the other pagan Indians, the "chief men even not excepted, live according to the "manner of the Pythagoreans, and use no other food "than rice, milk, fruit and herbs. He generally wears "a turban of dark blue silk; a long white robe, fastened "at the breast with a string of diamonds; long white "drawers, of red silk; and shoes, the points of which "are bent backwards like those of the Chinese. A "sabre is suspended from his shoulders; and in the "blue girdle bound round his loins is stuck a "poniard, or Persian dagger, which can be used either "for attack or defence. When he shows himself to "the people in full State, he is attended by 5,000 or "6,000 men, together with a great number of palan- "quins and elephants. At the head of the procession "is a band of musicians, and two court poets, who "celebrate in songs his great achievements. He is "borne in a palanquin; and the principal gentlemen "of his court must walk on each side of it. In my "time he was very much attached to the Catholic "missionaries. As often as he passed by the parson- "age house at *Angenga*, where I resided two years, "he always sent two of the gentlemen of his bed- "chamber to enquire after my health.

"This sovereign had two powerful enemies: one in "the north, Tippoo Sultan, now prince of *Maïssur* "and *Concam;* and another in the south-east, the "prince of *Arrucate*, Mohamed Aly Khan, of whom "I have already spoken in the preceding Chapter. "The latter has it in his power to make an attack, by "*Tovala*, one of the fortresses which lie near Cape "Comari, towards the east; and the former can "attempt the same thing in the district of *Palaca-* "*ticeri*, the last city in the kingdom of *Concam*, "towards the west. Through a dread of these two "dangerous neighbours, the king of Travancor found "himself obliged to conclude a treaty of alliance with "the English, and to make a common cause with them "both in peace and war. As long as he enjoys the "friendship of these allies, from whom he pur- "chases freedom and security at a sufficiently dear "rate, and as long as he pays regularly what is due "on that account, his dominions will be protected and "defended; but if ever a quarrel should arise between "him and the Governor of Madras, he is one of the "first Indian princes that will fall a sacrifice. The "annual tribute which he is obliged to pay to the "English, amounts to half a lack of rupees or 25,000

CHAP. III.

" Roman scudi. In the time of war he must supply " them, over and above, with horses, cannon, soldiers, " and rice. He is an affable, polite, contented, pru- " dent, and friendly man. On account of the inte- " grity of his character, and his many good moral " qualities, it is the more to be lamented that he is so " zealously attached to idolatry, and is so much blinded " as not to perceive the value of the Christian religion. " It cannot, however, be denied, that nothing tends so " much to rivet the affection of subjects, as when the " sovereign adheres to the established religion, and " worships the deity in the same manner as his people. " *Rama Varmer* never omits being present at the " ceremonies and devotional exercises of the pagans, " as will be seen in the following Chapter.*

" Pope Clement XIV by an apostolical letter had " recommended, in a particular manner, the Christians " of Malabar to the protection of the king of Tra- " vancor. This letter, dated July 2nd, 1774, arrived " at *Verapole* just at the time when the *Pravaticarer* " of that place took possession of our rice-fields and " gardens, under a pretence that the missionaries, as " well as the Bishop, ought to pay the usual imposts " and taxes, which all other subjects were obliged to " pay for their lands. We insisted, however, on our " immunity, and represented to him, that *Martanda- " pulla*, the commander-in-chief and prime minister of " the former king *Vira Martanda Pala*, had declared " us free from all public burdens whatever: but the " *Pravaticarer* paid no regard to our remonstrances; " endeavoured to enforce payment by violent means, " and for that purpose caused our convent and church " to be beset by fifty Mahometans, who suffered no " person to go out or to enter. These people, who at " all times are sworn enemies of the Christians, behaved " in so indecent a manner, and made so much noise,

* This information is of the utmost importance to the modern history of India; and the author is entitled to thanks for having communicated it to the public. *F.*

"that our Bishop and Apostolic Vicar, Carolus à "Sancto Conrado, was half dead with fear. I tried "to compose his mind as much as possible; and as I "knew that the deed by which immunity from all "imposts was secured to us, as well as the Pope's "letter, were to be found among our papers, I "sent for the *Pravarticarer*, and, in the presence of "more than 30 Christians, protested against his con- "duct, and summoned him to appear before the king. "At the same time I wrote to Father Clemens à "Jesu, requesting that he would repair to *Verapole* as "soon as he could. When he arrived, we submitted "the whole affair to mature discussion, and at length "resolved to appeal immediately to the king.

"We therefore purchased without delay two Euro- "pean paintings, a large mirror, fifteen pounds of "red sandal-wood, and 12 bottles of Persian rose "water; articles which, according to the established "etiquette, must be presented to the king by those "who wish to obtain an audience. On the 20th of "June 1780, we proceeded to *Tiruvandaburam*, and "immediately made the prime minister acquainted "with our intention.

"As M. Adrian Moens Governor of Cochin, and "M. John Torless Governor of *Angenga*, had both "written letters to the king in our favour, the "minister embraced the earliest opportunity of grati- "fying our wishes; and the more so as we had taken "the precaution to announce ourselves as delegates "from the Pope, and procurators of the missionary "establishment.

"As soon as we made our appearance before the "gate of the castle, the guard presented his arms, and "the minister sent a guide to conduct the persons "who bore our palanquin to the door of the palm- "garden in which the king resided. Here our "coolies, or palanquin-bearers, were obliged to remain "behind us, lest, being people of the lowest caste, "they might contaminate the royal palace. At this

CHAP. III.

"door we were received by the king's commander-"in-chief, who conducted us through the palm-garden "to a second door, where the king was waiting for "us. He received us standing, and surrounded by a "great number of princes and officers. Near him "stood his son, with a drawn sabre in his hand; and, "in a shady place were three chairs, one of which was "destined for the king, and the other two for me and "my colleague. When we had all three taken our "seats, the attendants formed a circle around us. I "then produced the Pope's letter, which I had hitherto "carried in a pocket-book richly embroidered accord-"ing to the eastern manner; raised it aloft; applied "it to my forehead in order to show my respect for "the personage in whose name I presented it; and "then delivered it to *Sampradi Keshavapulla*, the "Secretary of State. The latter handed it to the "king, who also raised it up, and held it to his fore-"head as a token of respect for His Holiness. At "the moment when the Pope's letter was delivered "there was a general discharge of the cannon of the "castle. After the king had asked us some common "questions respecting the naval war between the "English and the French he enquired of me, in parti-"cular, how long I had been in Malabar; and how I had "learned to speak the language of the country with "so much fluency. "I have often observed," added "he, "that other Europeans are either unacquainted "with it, or, for want of the proper pronunciation, "express themselves so badly that they can scarcely "be understood." I immediately replied, that I had "carefully studied the Brahmin book *Amarasinha*. "The king, on this answer, seemed highly pleased. "“What!” said he, "do you read our books?"—This is "the real and principal cause why the king, during the "whole time of my residence in Malabar, behaved to "me with so much kindness. He entertained the "utmost reverence for the writings and religion of his "people; and as he saw that they were studied by the "Europeans, this paved the way for my obtaining from "him afterwards many favours, which were of the "greatest benefit to the Christian religion. CHAP. III.

"When the king had conversed for some time on "various topics, he ordered his minister and secretary "to give such an answer to our petition and such "relief to our grievances, which we had specified on an "*ola*, that we might return home perfectly satisfied "and easy. For my part, I could not help admiring "the goodness of heart, affability, and humanity of this "prince, as well as the simplicity of his household "establishment and way of life. At that time he and "all the persons of his court, according to the Malabar "mode, had nothing on their bodies but a small piece "of cloth fastened round the loins; and the only "mark of distinction by which his royal dignity could "be discovered, was a red velvet cap with gold fringes. "At our departure he accompanied us as far as the "door. Next morning the prime minister, *Cumàren* "*Cembaga Ramapulla*, sent for us to his apartments, "and enquired very minutely respecting the behaviour "of the *Pravaticarer* at *Verapole*. Being informed "that this officer, with the assistance of the Mahome-"tans, had prevented the Christians from frequenting "our Church, he was highly displeased; and immedi-"ately wrote to the *Cariacarer* at *Parur* to remove "him from his office as an inconsiderate man, who "was little acquainted with the king's interest. A "new instrument was expedited in our presence, by "which immunity from all imposts whatever was "secured to our convent in future. The king then "sent to us by a Brahman, who acted the part of "household steward, and who was accompanied by "another officer, a service of dishes prepared after the "Malabar manner, and which were paid for out of the "royal treasury. These particular marks of favor "are shown only to such persons as give the king "distinguished proofs of their respect.

"The king had learned English for several months, "and spoke it exceedingly well. As he observed that

CHAP. III.

"the English was as familiar to me as the Malabar he "sent to me in the evening his chamberlain, *Payam-* "*palli Curipu*, to request that I would explain to him, "in the Malabar language, the parts of speech of the "English grammar, because he was always at a "loss respecting them. He had indeed an English "master; but he was not able to give him a proper "explanation, in the Malabar language, of the precise "meaning of these technological terms. I immedi- "ately wrote them down on a piece of paper, and "arranged them in two opposite columns, the one in "English, and the other in the Malabar language. "The king found my explanation perfectly clear, and "ever after called me always his *Guru* or preceptor. "He was extremely desirous to retain me at his "court; but the crafty Brahmans found means to "dissuade him from his design. My companion and "I therefore returned home; the *Pravaticarer* was "displaced; and our convent, as well as the Mis- "sionary establishment, was suffered to remain in "peace and tranquillity. The Christians of *Alapushe* " and *Muttam* were so rejoiced at the deposition of "the *Pravaticarer*, that they came to meet us, as we "returned, with drums and other musical instruments.

"Some time before I sailed for Europe, being "desirous to obtain an answer from the king to the "letter which had been written to him by Clement "XIV, I at length received one by means of *Payam-* "*palli Curipu*, before mentioned. It was addressed "to the present Pope Pius XVI, and contained, besides "other things, an assurance from the king that he "would take under his protection the Missionaries and "Christians in general, who had been recommended "to him by His Holiness. M. Pietro de Veigas, "who instructed the king in English, and who had "the care of the correspondence with foreign courts, "translated it into Portuguese. The king subscribed "it with his own hand, and, according to the oriental "custom, caused it to be inclosed in a bag, in which I "transmitted it to M. Antonelli, the director of the

" *Propaganda*. The present Pope returned an answer " in an Apostolic letter, dated February 24th, 1790, " and at the same time sent him his portrait, which " arrived safely on the coast of Malabar, and was deli- " vered to His Majesty in the month of March, 1793, " by my agent Franciscus à Sancto Elisæo, a bare- " footed Carmelite. This ecclesiastic, in a letter " dated *Verapole*, May 13th, 1793, informed me that " the king had received him in the politest manner, " and had testified the utmost satisfaction on account " of the letter, as well as the Pope's portrait; so that " he expected the best consequences from them. The " king, indeed, soon after, took such measures that " all the grievances of the Malabar Christians were " redressed in the kindest manner; and he presented " Father Franciscus with a gold bracelet worth one " hundred rupees. There is reason, therefore, to hope " that Christianity on the Malabar coast will acquire " new strength, and be again raised to its former state " of respectability.

" In the year 1783 some of the clergy on the coast " of Travancor thought proper to impose certain fines " on the Christian fishermen belonging to their congre- " gations. The fishermen complained to the king, who " was then at *Padmanaburam*, and requested he would " expel these ecclesiastics from the kingdom. The " king, in consequence of this application, sent a letter " to the Bishop and Apostolic vicar, Carolus à Sancto " Conrado, in which he informed him that he had " resolved to separate totally seventy-five congregations " from the diocese of Cochin, and to place them under " the inspection of the Apostolic vicar, that he might " commit the charge of them to his Missionaries belong- " ing to the *Propaganda*. He therefore desired that " the Bishop would immediately repair to *Patnam*, to " examine into the conduct of the above Portuguese " clergy; and that he would dismiss those found " culpable, and take possession of the before-mentioned " churches.

CHAP. III.

"The Bishop being at that time sick, I was obliged "to supply his place, and to proceed to *Padmanaburam*. At *Tiruvandaburam* my coolies or palan-"quin-bearers ran away; so that I was obliged to "travel twelve miles on foot on the king's high road, "named Madacava, which none but the Brahmans and "nobility dared to tread. As soon as I approached "*Padmanaburam*, I repaired to a very small church "on the south side of the castle; for the gates were "shut, and no person belonging to the inferior casts, "in which the Europeans are commonly included, "was suffered to enter the city. This took place on "the 23rd of September 1783. Scarcely, however, "had the king heard of my arrival, when he resolved "to make an exception in my favor from the severity "of this law. He therefore sent to me, next morning, "four of the nobility of his court to conduct me into "the city. They accompanied me to the habitation of "the king's secretary, where His Majesty was waiting "to receive me; for on that day he could not give me "audience in his own palace, lest it should be defiled.

"When I approached the place, the king's guard of "honor, consisting of 500 men, came under arms to "meet me; and formed themselves into two lines, "between which I was obliged to pass. The king, "who was sitting in an European arm-chair, received "me with great friendship, and addressed me as "follows: "I have sent for you, father, that you may "settle the disputes between my Christian subjects "and your clergy. It is my will that the clergy have "a sufficient maintenance, and a proper income for "their support; but I will not suffer them to oppress "my subjects by the imposition of fines. Look," "added he, "here stands my minister (the *Survadicari-"acàrer Nagampulla*), and there my secretary *Sam-"pradi Keshavapulla*), devise with them what is best "to be done, and then let me know the result." We "did as the king desired; and as I had no great "inclination to undertake the very difficult and bur-"thensome administration of seventy-five congrega-

"tions, I endeavoured to prevail on the ministers to "write to the Archbishop of Goa, and accommodate "the matter in an amicable manner. Some of the "clergy complained of were obliged to pay a certain "sum of money, by way of punishment; and a new "*Padiòla* or tarif, was established, to settle once more "the fees which the Christians should pay to the "clergy for discharging their sacred functions, and "which the latter should be authorized to exact.

"As the king would not suffer me to depart till this "business was completely settled, I was obliged to "remain sixteen days at *Padmanaburam.* During "that period His Majesty sent to me every day the "Kopu, which is a certain dish prepared in the Mala-"bar manner. As the festival of the goddess Saras-"vadi was then celebrating, (on which account, as I "have already said, the gates of the city were shut), "I employed a part of my time in observing the "religious practices of the Brahmans." * * * *

"As the *Cassanar* or clergyman of the Christians "of St. Thomas at Callurcada, whose name was "*Ciandi*, had applied to me to get some abuses "reformed which had crept into his congregation, I "conversed on that subject with the prime minister "*Cumàren Chembaga Ràmapulla*, and procured from "him a letter to the officer at *Ambálapushe*, to whose "jurisdiction *Cullurcada* was subject. I shall here "subjoin a copy of it, translated word for word from "the Malabar language:

"" The business respecting which I write is this: "Father Paolino appeared before His Majesty at "*Padmanaburam*, and informed him that some Map-"pulians (so the Christian women are commonly called) "in the parish of *Callurcada*, which is subject to the "jurisdiction of the Governor of *Cembacolam*, indulge "in criminal intercourse with various Shuddras (pagan "nobility of the fourth cast), and condescend to live "with them as concubines. Now, as this is the case, "continued the Father in name of the Bishop of *Vera-*

CHAP. III.

"*pole*, the distinction between the casts will be des- "troyed and nothing but confusion will prevail among "the different classes of the inhabitants; which gives "him great uneasiness.

"" Some person in the neighbourhood, and particu- "larly the Governor, ought certainly to have commu- "nicated by letter an account of these irregularities, of "so much importance to be known. When the Father "transmits to you a list of those who keep concubines, "you will immediately cause them to be arrested and "imprisoned. If they are convicted of the crime, send "them hither under a military guard, that they may be "banished from the country, and transported beyond "the boundaries of *Tovàla*. The effects of the *Map-* "*pulians*, who condescend to be kept as concubines, "shall be seized and confiscated; and an account of "their immoveable goods shall be delivered in to His "Majesty's exchequer.* Such is the will of His Ma- "jesty.

"" The Father states further, that when the Mappu- "lians (christians of St. Thomas) assemble to attend "divine service, the *Pravaticarer* (receiver of the king's "revenue) seizes the boat in which they arrive, drags "the people by force from the church doors, and "compels them to serve His Majesty. In the last "place, the Father has complained to His Majesty, "that some Magistrates at *Ambalapushe* borrowed "money, a long time ago, from the church, and have "paid neither principal nor interest; and also that a "large copper kettle borrowed from them had received

* It is here evident, that confounding the different casts was assigned as a reason by the Roman Catholic clergy, why women of the inferior casts, who suffered themselves to be kept as concubines, by *Nayrs* of the higher casts, ought to be punished. By these means they supported a pagan custom, totally inconsistent with the spirit of true Christianity, which considers all mankind as children of the same father. This syncretism of the pagan and the Christian religion has at all times been allowed by the Church of Rome. In China, for example, the Jesuits declared the heavens to be a divinity, and permitted their adherents to worship it, as well as allowed different kinds of oblations. *F.*

"considerable damage, and that no compensation had "been made for it. CHAP. III.

"'In consequence of these complaints, His Majesty "has ordered, and commands by the present letter, "that all money borrowed from the church shall be "repaid as speedily as possible, with the usual legal "interest; and it is at the same time expressly forbidden "to borrow any thing from it in future. Those who "took possession of the boat shall be condemned to "pay a fine, and to give the proprietors of the boat a "proper compensation for the use of it. Those who "employed the kettle shall make good the damage, "and be over and above punished. The kettle shall "be immediately returned, and never again taken "from the church for any profane purpose.

"'That all these commands of His Majesty may be "strictly attended to, and immediately put in execu-"tion, His Majesty transmits to you, at *Ambalapushe*, "the present letter, by a *Velkaren* (one of his guards "of honor, armed with a pike and staff), who has "orders not to suffer you to quit your house till "every thing be punctually done as here desired. "Should you, however, be indisposed, His Majesty will "not enforce his orders with severity; but requests "that you immediately write to the *Cariacarer* (in-"ferior magistrate), and charge him with the execution "of these commands. The *Velkaren* will confine him "in his own house under a proper guard till every "thing is done to your satisfaction. His Majesty also "requests, that he may be informed by the *Velkaren*, "when this business is brought to the wished-for con-"clusion. This rescript shall be transmitted by the "clerk and secretary of the criminal court to the *Sar-"vadicariacàrer* at *Alampushe*, and be registered "among the royal rescripts. This was written, in "consequence of His Majesty's orders, by *Cumaren* "*Cembaga Ramàpulla Ramen*.'—On the back of it "were the following words: "*Ambalapusha Mughatta* "*Sarvàdicàriacarerka varuna Sadhànam*;' that is,

CHAP. III.

"letter to be transmitted to the chief magistrate at "Ambalapushe.

"This letter of a pagan minister may serve as a "proof how much power the light of sound reason has "among a people whom the Europeans call barbarous. "It affords a specimen also of the policy and attention "to the executive part of Government which prevail "at the court of this Malabar monarch. He has only "to command, and his orders are immediately executed "with the utmost punctuality. His ministers neither "can nor dare have recourse to such subterfuges as "those of the European courts. An oath from the "king, a small twig suspended at the door in his "name, or mere confinement at one's own house, is a "check upon the conduct of the minister, as well as "upon that of the other subjects. When such mild "measures, however, do not produce the intended "effect, the offenders are subjected to a fine, or to cor-"poral punishment; to imprisonment, banishment "from the country, or perpetual slavery in chains.

"As soon as I had received the two letters before "mentioned, I departed from *Padmanaburam*. The "minister paid me 100 *Kalis*, to defray the expenses "of my journey; and gave orders that the coolies "who carried my palanquin along the sea coast, from "one place to another, should be paid from the royal "treasury. When I arrived at *Parur*, the Mahometans "there protested against the king's order, and would "not carry me farther, under the pretence that, being "a *Tanguel* or Christian priest, I was an enemy to their "religion. I was obliged, therefore, to stop five whole "hours till the king's *Pravaticarer* appeared, who "caused the refractory coolies to be soundly beaten, "and commanded them again to take up my palan-"quin."* * * *

"In the month of April 1784, the overseers of the "temple of *Shiva* at *Mattincera* would not permit the "missionaries to sow the rice-fields which they had on "lease from them. As no other piece of land could be

CHAP. III.

"procured at that time, the missionaries complained to "M. VanAngelbec, Governor of Cochin. This gentle-"man, finding that the fields lay in the dominions of "the king of Travancor, and that he could do "nothing in the business, advised me to take a second "journey to *Padmanaburam*, in order to procure "another rescript from the king; and he at the same "time furnished me with some letters of recommend-"ation. On the 21st of April, I reached *Padmana-"buram* in safety. I carried along with me the Mala-"bar, English, and Portuguese grammar, which I had "composed at *Ciattiyàti*, and which the king had "required from me, that the ministers of his court "might learn English and Portuguese by the assistance "of the Malabar language. Scarcely had the king "heard of my arrival when he sent two young noble-"men, *Padmanàbhenpulla* and *Payampalli Curipu*, to "welcome me in his name, and to attend me to an "audience. I found the king in the *Varanda*, that is, "the portico of his palace, sitting on a Persian carpet, "and leaning with one arm on a large velvet cushion "ornamented with gold fringes. When I delivered to "him the grammar, his joy seemed to be beyond "all description. In my presence he sent for the two "lords of his bed chamber, before mentioned; shewed "them the grammar; advised them to study it dili-"gently; and represented to them how necessary it "was that Princes as well as Statesmen, on account of "their continual intercourse with the Europeans, "should make themselves acquainted with these lan-"guages. On this occasion, the king presented me "with a gold bracelet, a gold style for writing on "palm leaves, and a small knife for cutting these "leaves to the proper size. I received from him also "a letter to the civil officer at *Parur*, in consequence "of which he was to announce publicly that the king "had done me the honour to appoint me one of the "gentlemen of his court. The intrinsic value of the "above presents was indeed not very considerable, "for it was equal only to about twelve sequins; but

CHAP. III.

" in other respects, they were of the highest import- " ance, as the king gives such articles to those only " who have merited his favor. No person in Malabar " dare use any of them without the king's express " permission. They are marks of honor, which he " distributes in the same manner as our European " princes do ribbons of different orders. Those also " who receive them enjoy certain privileges and advan- " tages; such, for example, as that they cannot be " carried before any Magistrate till the king is pre- " viously informed; that they can travel every where " along the highways; that they are not obliged to " wait in the minister's anti-chamber, and that they " are not required to give place to any person what- " ever; with other things of the like kind.

" The king made no hesitation to cause a rescript " to be prepared, in virtue of which we were autho- " rized to sow our fields with rice. Having thus " accomplished the object of my journey, I set out to " return; and, proceeding along the sea coast, arrived " in five days at *Verapole*. Here I was obliged to " supply the place of vicar-general; for our Bishop, " Carolus à Sancto Conrado, had gone to Bombay, " where he fell ill, and died on the 6th of January 1785.

" On the 8th of September 1786 I again had an " audience of the king, *Rama Varmer* at *Parur*, where " I obtained another rescript, by which he granted to " the congregation at *Verapole* a small piece of land, " that had been gradually thrown up, and formed by " the river before our convent.

" In the year 1787 I remained at his court at " *Teruvandaram* during the whole month of April, " and defended there the privileges of the mission- " aries against the rebellious Christians, who refused " any longer obedience to the European Bishop of " that district.

" In the year 1788, I paid a visit to the king of " *Travancor*, near *Canigia*, at the country seat of the "before-mentioned Governor of Cochin, M. VanAngelbec, a man of great talents and integrity. Though "a Lutheran, he rendered us essential service upon "many important occasions, and particularly during "the disputes which the pagan governors began with "the missionaries and bishops. The prime minister "*Cumàren Cembaga Ràmapulla* had died, and was "succeeded by the king's secretary *Sampràdi Keshavapulla*. This ambitious young man assumed the "name of the Indian Bacchus, *Devanishi*, and exacted "from the subjects exorbitant taxes, in order to "increase the public revenue, and ingratiate himself "with the king. During the contest, in which we "were involved with the rebellious Christians of St. "Thomas, in the year 1787, he imposed on the missionary establishment at *Verapole* a tribute of 500 "crowns. The king, however, had long before "remitted this tax; but we had no written document "to adduce as a proof. *Devanishi*, just at this time, "took it into his head to send to *Verapole* six soldiers, "under a petty officer, with orders to confine the "apostolic vicar, Louis Maria à Jesu, to his apartment and to guard him there till the 500 crowns "were paid. The bishop having informed me, by a "note, of his arrest, I immediately repaired to the "king, who at that time was at *Perimannur*, not far "from *Angicaimal*. As *Devanishi* knew too well that "I was in great favor with the king, he refused me "the letter of introduction necessary to obtain an "audience, lest His Majesty should be made acquainted "with his bad conduct. The bishop had been already "two days in arrest, with two muskets placed across "each other before the door of his chamber. In this "state of distress I applied to M. VanAngelbec, and "informed him of every thing that had happened. He "sent for me to his house; and the king, as soon as "I appeared, saluted me with great civility, and we "immediately entered into conversation. All the "magistrates and members of the council at Cochin, "who were there assembled to pay their respects to

CHAP. III.

"the king, and to settle some business respecting the "Dutch East India Company, were struck with "astonishment. When I told him that our bishop "was in confiement, he seemed quite surprised; turned "instantly round to the minister, and asked who had "given such orders. The minister endeavoured to "exculpate himself; but M. VanAngelbec, interrupt-"ing him, said, that bishops ought not to be treated in "that manner. The king then caused a letter to be "written to the petty officer commanding the party by "whom the bishop was guarded, which contained an "order for him to withdraw his men; and the minister, "who heard all this, seemed greatly ashamed."

The above testimony, from a disinterested European missionary, is no ordinary compliment to Travancore, and is particularly valuable, especially at a time, when life and property in many other parts of India were in great jeopardy, and many territories were groaning under despotic rule, and most of them disturbed by gangs of robbers and plunderers.

The deep interest evinced by this Sovereign in the welfare of his subjects, fully justifies Fra. Bartolomeo's observations, and a review of some of the enactments enforced by the Maha Rajah would serve as additional corroborative testimony.

It has already been shown that judicial matters in Travancore were conducted on the principles of the Dharma Sastra or the laws of Manu and that the Sovereign acted as the head of the judicial department. The Sovereign of Travancore in the exercise of his legislative authority seems to have passed several special laws and rules under the designation of "Satta Wariola" for the administration of the affairs of the kingdom of which some only are preserved in the records and the last of them appears to be the one passed in the Malabar year 951 (1776 A.D).

As a specimen of this last mentioned enactment, we would here insert a few of its sections which will no doubt be interesting to the reader:

Translation of extract rules enacted by Vanji Pala Rama Vurmah Kulasekhara Perumal in the Malabar year 951 (1776 A.D.) for the guidance of the local officials and called "Satta Wariola."

"*Section* 14.—Provisions for the religious ceremonies and other wants of the Sircar shall be purchased from the inhabitants on payment of ready cash, and the established hire shall also be paid for carrying the provisions to the place where such are required; but in failure of immediate payment, the officer who conducts the transaction shall be made to pay the value with 50 per cent. interest and after paying the ryot, the surplus shall be credited to the Sircar as a fine for the neglect."

"*Sections* 17, 18 and 19.—Strict attention shall be paid to the charitable supply of water mixed with butter-milk to the weary travellers on the road, and the public inns, where this water is supplied, shall be thatched and kept always clean. Payment for butter-milk for this purpose shall be made daily and the pay of the person employed in giving water, shall be paid punctually in every month."

"*Section* 21.—The officials of every village shall inspect at every season all such lands as have suffered injury by the breaches of banks of tanks, canals, &c., and by any accumulation of sand and thus rendered unfit for immediate cultivation. The servants shall exert themselves in having such obstructions removed through the owners in all ordinary cases or cause the same to be removed by the owners of the adjacent lands conjointly; but if such works are found too expensive, the same shall be done at the Sircar expense and the land in question made cultivable at once without allowing the same to be laid waste for any time."

"*Section* 24.—Every village servant shall exert himself in exhorting the ryots to build fences round their gardens for protecting cultivation and have every garden planted with pepper, vines, cocoanut and plantain shoots. Measures shall also be adopted to prevent cattle trespass."

CHAP. III.

"*Sections* 31, 32, 33, 34 and 35.—Every dispute between ryots concerning landed property shall be settled by the decision of four men of the village, (in the form of Punchayat) through the Proverticar; if that officer does not settle the case immediately, he shall be summoned before the district cutcherry and an adequate fine imposed upon him and the case enquired into by thadasthers (jury) formed of the inhabitants of the village where the disputed property is situated and in the presence of the district officer. The parties shall be then made to pay each one fanam (one seventh of a Rupee) as a vow to Padmanabha Swamy, and when the case is so decided by the thadasthers (jurors), the party gaining the case shall be required to pay a fee at the rate of 10 per cent. on the amount of his suit, and the contra-party who looses the case shall be required to pay a fee of 5 per cent."

"*Section* 44.—The district officials shall not apply fetters, chains and manacles to those ryots who are found entangled in any criminal charge."

"*Section* 46.—The district officials shall hold no proceedings at their private residence and every transaction of public business shall be done at the public cutcherry."

"*Section* 47.—The district officials shall attend their office at 7 A.M. and commence business, adjourning at 12 for taking meals, and return at 2 P.M. and hold office till 9 P.M. That the account of collection and disbursement shall be read over and the cash chest examined by the Tahsildar every day before quitting the office; that on the 30th of every month the Mudelpedicaren or cash-keeper shall be made to pay any sum which he may have disbursed in excess over the sanctioned amounts."

"*Sections* 52, 53, 54 and 55.—When petitioners appear before the district cutcherry, with their complaints, their cases shall be decided reasonably so as to be concurred in by public opinion; but no petitioner shall be detained to his inconvenience and put to expense for feeding himself, pending the settlement of his case; that such cases as could be decided soon shall be settled then and there, and the parties dismissed. But such cases as would require time to settle shall be decided within eight days, and if any petitioner is detained before the district cutcherry beyond eight days, he shall be fed at the expense of the district officer."

CHAP. III.

"*Sections* 57 and 58.—When a female petitioner comes before the district cutcherry, her complaint shall be heard and settled at once and on no account shall a female be detained for a night."

"*Section* 59.—That not one of the subjects (ryots) shall be oppressed, by placing him in restraint, without allowing him even to attend to the calls of nature or making him stand within a given line in a stooping posture, or putting a stone on his back or keeping him in water or under the burning sun or confining him under starvation, neither shall he be subjected to any sort of disgrace.

"*Section* 70.—That no trees planted and reared by the inhabitants, such as mangoe and other fruit trees, which bear fruit for the use of the ryots shall be felled or cut for firewood on account of the Sircar. Firewood for Sircar purposes shall be invariably procured and cut from junglewood; that if any Sircar servant fells a jack tree or any other fruit tree on which pepper vine is grown, he shall be made to forfeit one-fourth of his pay as fine, and shall also be made to plant and rear ten such trees for the one that he has felled in the garden of a ryot, and he shall be held responsible for the care and protection of such plants for three years. No cocoanut trees or areca-nut trees shall be felled for Sircar purposes from the gardens of the ryots."

"*Sections* 72, 73, 74 and 75.—The attention of the district officer shall always be directed to the repairs of the public halting places called valiampalam (inns); that the repairs and newly erecting of bridges on

CHAP. III.

public roads, and repairing and levelling of public roads as well as placing good canoes at every ferry shall also engage the vigilant attention of the head of the district; the pay of the ferryman shall be paid monthly. That the care of the avenue trees, as well as planting the same, on sides of the roads where there are no trees, shall be observed and the district officer will employ special men for this purpose."

"*Section* 77.—For the transmission of the Sircar goods and provisions the required number of boats shall be provided by the Sircar at their own expense, by getting a number of logs and scooping them into boats for the purpose.

"*Section* 83.—The measures by which the ryots are required to give paddy to the Sircar in part-payment of the land tax, shall be annually examined by the district officer and the ryot himself will be allowed to put the paddy into the measures at a fixed height, and the measurement shall be made by clearing the bridge of the parah."

We will now conclude this chapter with a quotation from Rajah T. Madava Row's review of this Maha Rajah's career from his unpublished manuscript history of this reign, a Malayalim translation of which has already been given to the public, as has been said in the previous chapter by the Travancore Book Committee:

"It was during the reign we are bringing to a close "that the countries conquered by Travancore and "composing this State as it now is, were fully and "satisfactorily settled. Peace and order were com-"pletely established. The deposed Chiefs quietly "acquiesced in honorable retirement, and the new "subjects of the Maha Rajah found themselves in the "enjoyment of blessings to which they had long been "strangers. The wisdom, the moderation, the benevo-"lence of the ruler of Travancore were universally felt, "and acknowledged. Englishmen too proud to stoop "to adulation, called him the father of his people.

"The financial system of the country however cannot be said to have been improved during this reign. Liberal reforms were indeed not possible at a period when there were the most exacting demands upon the treasury. Monopolies were multiplied till almost every important article of trade was engrossed by the system. Pepper, cardamoms, ginger, cinnamon, areca-nuts, turmeric, salt, coppra, coir, tobacco, cotton, teak, blackwood and numerous other staples were brought and sold by the Sircar in view to benefit the public revenues. Of these pepper yielded considerable profits as it used to sell at 140 rupees per candy, and was much in demand for European markets. The cultivation of this spice was thereupon artificially stimulated beyond legitimate bounds, as proved by the circumstance that when the pressure of the monopoly was removed, the cultivation manifested a perceptible dimunition. The trammels placed on the trade of the country by means of monopolies and transit duties would have proved fatal to commercial prosperity, had it not been that this evil was considerably compensated by the extreme lightness of the land-tax which greatly favoured protection.

"Though the public revenues were thus augmented, they proved quite inadequate to meet the demands arising out of the war with Tippoo. The Maha Rajah was thus constrained to have recourse to a special war-tax. It was assessed exclusively on landed properties and limited to one year. The State imperatively required funds, and the Maha Rajah therefore imposed a heavy tax for a short period in preference to a light one for a long period. Indeed, the tax was one on capital and not on income. Though it might have been, in some cases, oppressive in its incidence, it had the advantage that it was demanded in the presence of the danger to which the country was exposed, and that its odium rapidly passed away. It had the further advantage that it could not be evaded, inasmuch as the general survey and assess-

CHAP. III.

"ment of landed properties, instituted in 948 by the "Maha Rajah's orders, had disclosed to the State the "individual possessions of all holders. It is also to "be noted that all descriptions of land, without "respect to tenure, came under this extraordinary "impost, which in the aggregate is said to have yielded "about one million and seven hundred thousand "rupees.

"But even extraordinary taxation failed to yield "adequate means to answer the incessant call for "funds. The Maha Rajah felt that he could not, "without exciting dangerous discontent among his "subjects, increase their burdens, and he saw no "alternative but that of raising loans. Funds were "indeed thus obtained to meet the pressing exigencies "of the State, but the obligations incurred inevitably "led to difficulties of the gravest character, difficulties "which embittered the closing years of the Maha Rajah "and culminated in a perilous crisis in the reign of "his successor.

"The Maha Rajah departed this life between 1 and "2 P. M. on Wednesday the 6th Kumbhum 973 (17th "February 1798), in the seventy-fourth year of his age "and the fortieth of his reign. Amid his sorrowing "subjects, with due pomp and circumstance, his remains "were, as usual, consigned to the funeral pile composed "of sandal-wood, camphor, and other rare and aromatic "combustibles.

"The deceased Maha Rajah may unhesitatingly be "pronounced a Prince who approached nearest to the "Hindu ideal of a good king." Menu the great law-"giver of the Hindus says :—

'Let the king prepare a just compensation for the good and a just punishment for the bad, the rule of strict justice let him never transgress.'

'A king was created as the protector of all those classes and orders, who from the first to the last discharge their several duties.'

'Let the king, having risen at early dawn, respectfully attend to Brahmans learned in the three Vedas and in the science of ethics, and by their decisions let him abide.'

'Constantly must he show respect to Brahmans who have grown old both in years and in piety, who know the scripture, who in body and mind are pure.'

'From them; though he may have acquired modest behaviour by his own good sense and by study, let him continually learn habits and modesty and composure, since a king whose demeanour is humble and composed, never perishes.'

'Through want of such humble virtue, many kings have perished with all their possessions, and through virtue, united with modesty, even hermits have obtained kingdoms.'

'Day and night must the king strenuously exert himself to gain complete victory over his own passions. Since that king alone, whose passions are completely subdued can keep his people firm to their duty.'

'He must appoint to public offices, men of integrity, well informed, steady, habituated to gain wealth by honorable means and tried by experience.'

'A king, even though dying with want must not receive any tax from a Brahman learned in the Vedas.'

'Of that king, in whose dominion a learned Brahman is afflicted with hunger, the whole kingdom will in a short time be afflicted with famine.'

'Let him not cut up his own root by taking no revenue, nor the root of other men by excess of covetousness: for by cutting up his own root and theirs he makes both himself and them wretched.'

'He must protect his people, discharging with great exertion and without langour all those duties, which the law requires him to perform.'

CHAP. III.

'As Indra sheds plentiful showers during the rainy months, thus let him, acting like the regent of clouds, rain just gratifications over his kingdom.'

"These and other cardinal precepts of the universal "legislator, the Maha Rajah kept constantly in view "and strove honestly to fulfil throughout his long "tenure of regal power."

"Judged even by the standard of modern times, the "Maha Rajah must be allowed a high place in the "catalogue of beneficent rulers. He was in every "sense the model of a mild Hindu, amiable, urbane, "just and generous. His humanity, compassion and "hospitality are the theme of traditionary praise to "this day. As a sovereign, he was remarkably truth-"ful, straightforward and faithful to engagements. "Blessed with a cool and calculating judgment, "wisdom and prudence characterized the tenor of "his long career, and as a consequence (to use the "words of a native courtier of the time), 'dangers "and difficulties which came like mountains, passed "away like mists.' Extravagance and wasteful dissipa-"tion, the curse of oriental monarchs, the Maha Rajah "can never be charged with. On the contrary he "carefully husbanded the public resources and pru-"dently restrained his personal expenditure. His con-"ciliatory disposition was conspicuous throughout his "blameless life. No one met him but carried away "the most favorable impressions of his virtues "and good nature. Fra. Paolino de San Bartolomeo "who sought and obtained the honor of an audience "says, 'For my part, I could not help admiring the "goodness of heart, affability and humanity of this "Prince, as well as the simplicity of his household "establishment and way of life.'

"The English Commissioners appointed to settle the "affairs of Malabar in 1792, and who also made the "personal acquaintance of the Maha Rajah add their "testimony by recording that, 'We own he left a "very favorable impression on our minds, both as to "his personal good qualities, and what we consider as "the unequivocal sincerity of his attachment to the "Honorable Company.' His memory is justly revered "for the rare solicitude he felt and manifested for the "welfare of his subjects. In his reign, to quote again "the words of Bartolomeo, 'Public security is restor-"ed throughout the whole country; robbery and "murder are no longer heard of; no one has occasion "to be afraid on the highways; religious worship "is never interrupted; the people may rest assured "that, on every occasion, justice will be speedily "administered. And Englishmen, seldom, prone to "indulge in the language of adulation, called the Maha "Rajah 'the father of his people.'

CHAP. III.

CHAPTER IV.

SREE PADMANABHA DASAVANJI PALA BALA RAMA VURMAH KULASEKHARA KIREETAPATHI MUNNAY SULTAN MAHA-RAJ RAJAH RAMARAJAH BAHADUR SHAMSHEER JUNG MAHA RAJAH.

CHAP. IV.

THIS young sovereign of sixteen years was installed on the musnud on the death of his uncle, on the 7th Kumbham 973 M.E. (18th February 1798 A.D). Though His Highness was of a good disposition, yet he appears to have been a singular exception to the many scions of this royal family, in regard to intellectual gifts and mental acquirements. He was completely in the hands of a set of favourites, among whom Oodiary Jayanthen Sankaren Numboory, a native Brahman from the Calicut Rajah's territories was the foremost and who seems to have been the moving spirit of the Government of the time. An uneducated man, Sankaren Numboory was devoid of all good principles, and possessed an ambitious and avaricious spirit.

This covetous Numboory aimed at the Dewan's post, and therefore the first step he took was to set the young Maha Rajah against the old and worthy minister, Rye Kasava Dass. The Numboory carried his intrigues to such an extent as to cause the Maha Rajah not to admit the minister to his presence whenever public business required that he should see the sovereign.

The national feelings in Travancore regarding loyalty are of a sacred nature under certain peculiar circumstances, a fact which has been already explained

BALA RAMA VURMAH MAHA RAJAH.

Published by Messrs. Higginbotham & Co.   C. Paczkery Lith. Madras

in the second chapter of this work, so that the position of the Travancore sovereign had become somewhat parallel to that of the Pope in Rome; and therefore neither the people nor the servants of the State would dare to disobey the king or act against the wishes of the sovereign, whether royalty was represented by an ignorant minor, or an educated sovereign in his dotage.

Under such circumstances the Dewan found himself in a position of some difficulty, as he could not carry on public business as freely and regularly as before or do anything without the sovereign's special commands.

In 974 M.E. (1799 A.D.), one Thottappaye Numboory of Cochin, a bosom friend of Jayanthen Sankaren Numboory, took advantage of this state of affairs and begged his friend to prevail upon the Maha Rajah to restore to Cochin the Karappuram territories which had been taken by Rama Iyen Dalawah, and ceded to Travancore by the Cochin Rajah by his last treaty. Jayanthen Sankaren Numboory succeeded in obtaining the young Maha Rajah's signature to a document drawn out by him, sanctioning the restoration of the Sharétalay district (Karappuram) to the Cochin Rajah, and handed the same clandestinely to the said Thottappaye.

This document which was called a Neet or royal writ, was taken with all possible secrecy by the Thottappaye Numboory, without the knowledge of the Dewan, or any of the ministerial officers.

The Dewan received private information about this treacherous transaction, a few hours after the departure of Thottappaye with the Neet, when the minister having posted horses by the sea-beach between Trevandrum and Quilon, proceeded northwards at once, in pursuit of the Numboory. On the Dewan's reaching Paroor Ootupurah, south of Quilon, he had the satisfaction to learn that Thottappaye Numboory had just halted there to take his meals at the Ootupurah. He was at once stopped, and the writ recovered from him.

CHAP. IV.

This faithful conduct of the Dewan irritated the young Maha Rajah, and offended the treacherous Oodiary Numboory to such an extent, that he began to devote all his attention towards compassing the ruin of the Dewan, and this being known to the minister, he began to feel very uneasy. The proceedings of the court itself at the time were anything but satisfactory, and matters began to go from bad to worse day by day.

A month or two after the anniversary of the late sovereign's death, 974 M.E. (1799 A.D.), the Dewan had one day the heart-rending mortification to see the Numboory sitting in the State palanquin that belonged to the late sovereign and being carried round the streets in procession in grand style as if it was a procession of the sovereign himself. This palanquin, the late Maha Rajah had always looked upon as a favourite piece of furniture, and therefore the Dewan had wished to preserve it in tact in memory of His Highness. A deep sense of regard and reverence for his departed sovereign, and a sense of his own duty impelled the Dewan to make some strong and severe remarks on the Numboory's improper conduct in thus taking advantage of the young Maha Rajah's kindness towards him. Soon after this event, the Dewan appears to have received what is generally called in Travancore a 'Velaku Neet,' (royal commission of dismissal) and he was confined in his house under a guard.

A few days after this, 8th Madom, the town of Trevandrum was shocked with the harrowing intelligence that Dewan Rye Kasava Dass was lying dead in his own bed in the chamber of his residence. It appears that there was not a soul in the Dewan's house except the guards.

The Dewan had no wife, or son or other relatives living with him at the time of his death. As he resided apart from them and close to his office, inside the Trevandrum fort and palace, nobody could explain the actual cause of the minister's death.

Some say that he was poisoned, at the instance of the Numboory, through the Dewan's cook, while others assert that the Dewan poisoned himself in consequence of the irregular, ill-advised and reprehensible proceedings of the young Maha Rajah who was now entirely under the influence of the Numboory, but the consensus of public opinion was in favor of the supposition that the lamented Dewan met with his death by foul play at the instigation of the Numboory. This opinion has been adopted as the only possibly correct solution of the question as to how he had met with his death by Lieut. Horsley who says in his work "Memoirs of Travancore" that, this Prince, from his weakness and other causes appears to have had great difficulty in contending with his ministers, who, devoid of all gratitude, alternately abused or usurped his power. The first person who seized on the administration in the character of Dewan, attained his success by the death of his predecessor and a long list of adherents who had supported his cause." That Dewan Rye Kasava Dass had been poisoned, was the view taken by the Court of Directors of the Honorable East India Company, who, in a general letter addressed to the Madras Government on the 29th September 1809 said: "The late Dewan (Kasava Dass) so much respected by the people was not suffered to live even in retirement. There is very strong reason to believe that he was taken off by poison."

Thus the old and faithful minister was cut off in the middle of his age, and almost within a year of the death of his sovereign master, of happy memory. It was very surprising, and is certainly matter for painful reflection that such a remarkable personage as Dewan Rye Kasava Dass, who had actually saved the country from the grasp of a powerful enemy, Tippoo Sultan, and ensured the permanent security of the country by strengthening the alliance with the Honorable East India Company, and who had improved it in every respect, was allowed to meet with such a

CHAP. IV.

shameful death, and that his remains should have been buried like those of an ordinary private individual without any public demonstration of regret or respect.

It is said that the Dewan's younger brother Cumaren Thamby, the then General and Commander-in-Chief of the Travancore army, and his nephew Erayimen Thamby, the Peishcar, with some other relatives alone formed the procession at the funeral of this truly great man.

This Dewan was not well known to the outside world, as in his days there were not many newspapers or periodicals criticising and eulogising men and measures as in modern times.

He seems to have had no other interest at heart save that of his sovereign and of his country, and he devoted his whole attention towards promoting the welfare of the people entrusted to his care. The office he considered as his house, and spent his time mostly in the discharge of his public duties. Owing to the weakness and minority of the Maha Rajah, and the animosity of the Numboory, this worthy Dewan's services were not recognised during this reign, but the popular indignation at his unexpected and mysterious end was so great that evil consequences were apprehended.

In the year 975 (1800 A.D.), when Colonel Macauly arrived in Travancore after his appointment as Resident, he instituted some enquiry into the Dewan's untimely death, when Samprathy Kunjuneelam Pillay and others were arrested, but in the absence of evidence to warrant their conviction, they were discharged.

The field being now clear Jayanthen Sankaren Numboory, found no difficulty in attaining the object of his ambition. He prevailed upon the young and simple-minded Maha Rajah to sign a Neet (royal commission) appointing him to the high post of Valia Sarvadhikariakar (prime minister), on the 4th day, 11th Madom

974, after the death of the meritorious and the much lamented Dewan, Rye Kasava Dass. CHAP. IV.

The new Premier, untrained and unfitted as he was for the high and responsible office of prime minister, was bewildered and almost helpless on his sudden exaltation. He selected for his council Chetty Thackalay Sankaranarayanen Valia Melaluthu (finance minister), and Mathoo Tharaken, an influential Syrian Christian of the north, who held the salt, tobacco and other contracts during the last reign. These two men were as unprincipled as the Numboory himself.

"Thus this triumvirate of ignorance, profligacy and rapacity came to rule the destinies of this interesting principality, in spite of the earnest wish which the Governor-General, Lord Mornington expressed 'that a really efficient ministry should be formed.'"

But after due consultation with his friends and supporters, the Numboory came to the determination of remedying the financial embarrassments, and thus please his young employer and benefit himself at the same time. In order to effect this, the council resolved upon raising a general contribution.

Rules were framed for a systematic levying of the contribution, with a clause authorizing the infliction of such punishment on refusal of payment, as the ministry and Prince may deem proper. These rules obtained the royal assent at once.

In accordance with a list which had been prepared, the ministry began to summon people before them and demand immediate payment of the sums fixed in the list against their names or to be prepared to undergo the infamy of being subjected to corporal punishment.

This inhuman and barbarous system of extortion went on for a fortnight, and a large sum of money was realised. Several respectable persons were flogged and imprisoned. Merchants, landlords, retired public servants, all suffered alike; so much so, that no family, even of ordinary circumstances, was spared. Cries

CHAP. IV. against all this injustice and tyranny were heard throughout the length and breadth of the land.

In the course of these arbitrary and tyrannical proceedings, one Valu Thamby Kariakar an ex-Tahsildar, was summoned before this detestable Numboory ministry for payment. The amount fixed against his name was 20,000 caly fanams equal to about 3,000 rupees. He was required to pay down the money immediately, or to be exposed to the disgrace of being lashed like those who could not pay. Valu Thamby, being a bold young man, of a respectable family, blessed with a quick understanding, would not submit to the affront thus offered him. He informed the Numboory premier, that he did not come there provided with money; that he would not submit to the punishment proposed to him in lieu of money; and that he would go to Nanjenaud and raise the money within three days to meet the demand. He was made to sign a promissory note to this effect before he took his departure.

Valu Thamby proceeded to the south, and convened a meeting of all the heads of villagers about Nanjenaud. He sounded the brazen drum, the ancient signal summoning the inhabitants about Nanjenaud on all emergent occasions, to rise, and also sent emissaries as far as Alleppey for apprising the people. After forming a council the leaders issued notices to the elders and others of the villages all round to join the assembly in order to take measures to put a stop to these arbitrary proceedings of the Numboory ministry.

The populace, being in a state of great indignation at the illegal and disgraceful proceedings of the ministry, Valu Thamby and other leaders of the insurrection found no difficulty in inducing people from the south as well as about Trevandrum to flock to their standard. The military secretly joined the assembly, and Valu Thamby found himself at the head of a large number of men, ready for an insurrection.

As Valu Thamby did not present himself with the money promised by him, and hearing that he was organizing an insurrectionary force, the ministry issued a proclamation for his apprehension and delivery at Trevandrum.

The proclamation had simply the effect of causing Valu Thamby and others to hasten their approach to Trevandrum, with the assembled multitude. They soon reached it, and encamped outside of the Trevandrum fort in the north, where a large number had already assembled from the northern parts of the kingdom.

Their sacred regard for the king and the royal family prevented Valu Thamby and his followers from venturing on a forcible entrance into the fort to seize the Numboory Valia Sarvadhikariakar and his comrades. At the approach of Valu Thamby and his host, the Maha Rajah was quite alarmed and awakened to a a sense of his duty. He deputed some of the officials, together with the high priest and other Brahman servants attached to the pagoda, to meet the people, and to convey to them His Highness' perfect willingness to accede to all reasonable demands. Valu Thamby, as the chief of the leaders, stated the cause of the gathering of such a large number of His Highness' subjects and demanded in the name of the people; (1), that the Numboory Valia Sarvadhikariakar should be immediately dismissed and banished; (2), that the Maha Rajah should execute a Neet binding himself not to recall him; (3), that Sankara Narayanen and Mathoo Tharakon should be publicly flogged and have their ears cut off; and (4), that the salt tax as well as all other odious taxes should be remitted.

These requisitions were immediately complied with by His Highness and the Numboory minister and his colleagues were dismissed on the 6th Methunam 974 (1799 A.D.), as by such a measure alone His Highness thought he could appease his infuriated subjects, but Valu Thamby would not be satisfied with the simple dismissal of the Numboory Valia Sarvadhikariakar, &c. He requested His Highness to order all the

CHAP. IV. dismissed officers to be given up to the assembly, with permission to deal with them according to their deserts.

They were accordingly made over to the assembly. A select party of the leaders forming a court or Punchayet sentenced the ex-Valia Sarvadhikariakar to be disgraced and banished the country, and Sankara Narayanen and Mathoo Tharaken as already proposed to have their ears cut off and be imprisoned.

This sentence was carried out at once. Sankara Narayanen Pillay was sent to the Udayagherry fort to be confined there in irons, while Mathoo Tharaken was imprisoned at Trevandrum.

After accomplishing all the above, the crowd dispersed, and a select party, headed by one Iyappen Chempaka Ramen Pillay of Sheraingheel, who was also one of the principal leaders of the insurrection, accompanied by Valu Thamby, presented themselves before the young Maha Rajah and placed their services at His Highness' disposal. They proposed the formation of a new cabinet and His Highness accepted their offer with alacrity.

Sheraingheel Iyappen Chempaka Ramen Pillay was appointed Valia Sarvadhikariakar, prime minister, and several others were selected for subordinate offices. Valu Thamby received the appointment of Mulakumadeseela Sarvadhikariakar (commercial minister).

Thus was a new administration brought into existence. The Valia Sarvadhikariakar, an able and experienced man, lost no time in correcting all the evils introduced by the infamous Numboory Valia Sarvadhikariakar, and in re-establishing the confidence of the people in the administration.

This wise minister adopted also the most important and essential measure of selecting and appointing as personal attendants on the young Maha Rajah, a few wise and disinterested men, of the Brahman, Kshatria and Sudra castes, and His Highness, though weak and simple-minded, was found to be docile, especially after these troubles. CHAP. IV.

This minister's tenure of office was not very long, for he died fourteen months after his appointment. Nevertheless, within this short interval, he proved himself to be equal to some of his predecessors. He was succeeded by Parechalay Padmanabhen Chempaka Ramen Pillay.

The new minister, partly from his unfitness for the high post, and partly from some underhand pressure soon met with his downfall, and was sent home relieved from the cares of office after a career of about eight months.

Now, Valu Thamby, Mulakumadeseela Sarvadhikariakar, who had all along been watching with an eagle-eye for the first favorable opportunity to obtain the high office of prime minister began to adopt measures for accomplishing his long cherished design. This ambitious officer gained over almost all the favorites of the Maha Rajah.

At this time 976 M.E (1801 A.D.), the principal favorite officials in the palace were Samprathy Kunjuneelam Pillay, Valia Meleluthu, Muthu Pillay and Shanapathy Suba Iyen. Besides these, there was a host of unprincipled men as favorites of the young Maha Rajah and all these favored the designs of Valu Thamby. But there were two able officers in the service, whose claims to promotion had been overlooked more than once. They were Thamby Chempaka Ramen Cumaren, the younger brother, and Erayimen, the nephew of the late lamented Dewan, Rye Kasava Dass. Both of these men had several English friends in Madras and Bombay owing to the influence of their relative the late Dewan. The two officers were in close correspondence with their friends which fact was well known to Valu Thamby and Kunjuneelam Pillay.

With the express view of disqualifying these two officials for the high office of prime minister, Kunju-

CHAP. IV.

neelam Pillay and his colleagues began to plot against them. Kunjuneelam Pillay fabricated false accounts at the palace showing a claim of several lacs of rupees against the late Dewan as having been appropriated by him, from the treasury, without the permission of the late Maha Rajah. These relatives of the late Dewan were called upon to liquidate the debt. They objected, and the matter created a good deal of unpleasantness in the palace. With the view of shielding themselves from the attacks of their enemies, they had been communicating with their English friends. This circumstance was misrepresented to the Maha Rajah by Kunjuneelam Pillay and others. They said that these officers, the general, and the peishcar, were engaged in a correspondence, involving a treacherous design against His Highness' kingdom, and that credible information had been received that they had been communicating with the English both at Madras, and at Bombay for this purpose and that their intention would be shortly carried into effect. To prove this assertion, they fabricated some letters in the name of those officers as if written by them to the Governor of Madras, and to the Nabob of the Carnatic, and produced the same before the Maha Rajah.

The Maha Rajah being naturally of a timid disposition and credulous in such matters, was quite alarmed and perplexed, and consulted Valu Thamby, who had now become Sarvadhikariakar, and who confirmed the report.

The general and the peishcar, together with a linguist named Padmanabha Pillay, and one Walikalampaut Neelam Pillay, were arrested on a charge of treason. Immediately after this, Valu Thamby was appointed Valia Sarvadhikariakar, (prime minister) and he proceeded to Alleppey to hold his office there, like Dewan Rye Kasava Dass.

Subsequent to the Sarvadhikariakar's departure from Trevandrum, the death-warrant of the two officers was signed by the Maha Rajah.

They were on a certain night, taken by the palace guards and dragged quietly to the sea-beach, where they were butchered in cold blood. A detailed account of this bloody act was obtained from an old horse-keeper, who had accompanied the party on that night to the scene of massacre. This event took place in the month of Vycasy 976 (1801 A.D.).

Intelligence of this sad and diabolical act was spread in Trevandrum only on the next day, when the military, as well as the ministerial servants, became enraged, and a rising was almost apprehended, but the Samprathy and his colleagues found means to quiet and pacify the enraged party, by making a free use of His Highness' name, and giving them to understand that the general and the peishcar were actually guilty of organizing a conspiracy to give up the country to the English and even to attempt His Highness'life.

The interpreter Padmanabha Pillay and his comrade Neelam Pillay, who were in confinement were sent to Mavalikaray, but on their way, the latter (Neelam Pillay), jumped over board at the Anjengo bar, and saved himself from the disgraceful death that awaited him. Padmanabha Pillay on reaching Mavalikaray, was executed at the eastern fort gate.

Samprathy Kunjuneelam Pillay engaged himself heart and soul in effecting the atrocious and disgraceful murder of the general and the peishcar, as this unworthy minion had considerable influence over the Maha Rajah. It is not improbable that the young sovereign who was immersed in pleasures and devoted his time to his seraglio, was ignorant of his having signed the death-warrant of two of His Highness' most meritorious officers. Rajah Madava Row says thus on this point: "It is certain, however, that one Kunjuneelam Pillay who filled the office of palace Samprathy (a secretary) was the head of the cabal. Crafty, unprincipled and ambitious, he had acquired a dangerous ascendency at the Durbar. Practically, the reins of Government were in the hands of this

CHAP. IV. low and depraved individual and the Maha Rajah occupied himself alternately with the pleasures of the seraglio and the ceremonies of superstition."

Valu Thamby was now appointed (977) as Dalawah, and he began a career, unprecedented in many respects.

He was a man of extraordinary ability and talents; of strong passions and quick sensibility and was amazingly bold and daring.

Though the career of this Dalawah had every appearance of despotism and cruelty, yet his intention throughout all his proceedings was honest, fair, and good, his attention being always directed to promote the public interests.

The most remarkable quality in this officer was his purity of character; his moral principles were so refined, that his equal was scarcely to be found in Travancore in those days.

The first step Valu Thamby took after his appointment was, to establish order among the people, and ensure the honest performance of their duties by Sircar servants throughout the kingdom. To effect this, he adopted punishments far exceeding in severity those prescribed by the law of the country, and the nature of the crimes called for.

The whole administration, revenue, civil, judicial and military, was assumed by him, and his orders were supreme in the country, which was altogether in a disorganised state since the dismissal of the renowned Dewan Rye Kasava Dass. The public services were thoroughly demoralised. There was no such thing as discipline. Heads of departments were independent and masters of their respective offices. Intrigues and cheating were the order of the day, and life and property were in serious jeopardy.

The above state of affairs was corrected and perfect security and safety established by the strong hand of Valu Thamby Dalawah, in the course of a few months.

VALU THAMBY DALAWAH.

PUBLISHED BY MESSRS. HIGGINBOTHAM & CO. C. PADEZENSKY LITH MADRAS.

The whole service was at once cleansed and corruption eradicated. The measures used for this purpose were such, that the very hearing of the particulars would startle and create emotion in the stoutest and boldest heart.

It would be tiresome, to enumerate in detail all the kinds of punishments inflicted by the stone-hearted minister, especially when public servants were convicted of any fault or misdemeanour. We shall only state just a few. Fraudulent appropriation of Sircar money was punished with incarceration in the jail for lengthened periods, and even with death in addition to forfeiture of the whole property belonging to the family of the delinquent, without regard to the amount of the fraud or embezzlement. Tampering with the Sircar records was punished with amputation of the palms or fingers of the right hand of the criminal. Bribery was punished with the infliction of corporal punishment on the back of the delinquent in the public bazaars and thoroughfares. Perjury was punished by cutting off the lips and nose of the criminal, and oppression of ryots was visited with corporal punishments and forfeiture of property; this latter punishment was resorted to, in almost every case, wherein a Sircar servant was convicted. The Dalawah being well versed in the laws of Manu and also in the prescriptions of the Mahomedan law, adhered strictly to the punishments therein prescribed. Robbers and thieves were alike visited with the extreme penalty of the law. Pocket-picking and breaking of locks entailed on the criminals the loss of their palms or the fingers of their hands. The violation of females and the offence of rape were often punished by the offenders being beheaded. Stealing fruits from gardens was generally visited with corporal punishment, and in special cases with amputation, impalement or nailing on the trees in the avenues and other public places.

By such extraordinary and fearful acts, a reign of terror was established in the country and crimes and

CHAP. IV.

misdemeanours, both among the Sircar servants and the people, became almost unknown. The very figure of the Dalawah, who was tall and proportionately stout with an imposing appearance, seemed ever present in the minds of all the Sircar servants, as well as rogues and criminals.

The Dalawah was always moving from one district to another on circuit, taking along with him a select party of his subordinate officials from the revenue, judicial and military departments.

The mode of transacting business was similar to that of a field officer in a country where martial law had been proclaimed; for the Dalawah used to hold his judicial and military courts even under trees and on the plains, when he received any serious complaint during his circuit. The whole time occupied by him in hearing and deciding cases, seldom exceeded four or five hours; within that interval, he would himself examine the complainant's witnesses, defendants or prisoners in the presence of his Sastri and Muffthee, and then pronounce judgment. If the case was one of murder, the convicted criminals would be hanged on the very tree under which he sat, before he started from the place.

The Dalawah was as severe as he was strict and impartial. Like Rama Iyen Dalawah and Rye Kasava Dass Dewan, he had also removed himself from his family influences in a great measure. His impartiality and strictness are strikingly exhibited in the following incident: There lived a Chanar near the Dalawah's house, who had a cocoanut garden, which he gave to a relative of Valu Thamby under the tenure of mortgage. He enjoyed it for a considerable time, paying the assessment tax to the Sircar in the Chanar's name, but when Valu Thamby came into power, the mortgagee succeeded in obtaining a registry of the garden, in his own name, without the knowledge and consent of the Chanar, through the influence of Valu Thamby, the Dalawah's mother. During a tour in the Southern districts, the Chanar made a complaint on the subject to the Dalawah, who, as usual, immediately called the Proverthy accountant and questioned him on the subject, when, to his surprise, he learnt that such a registry was made by the very accountant at the request of the Dalawah's mother, who, on being asked by the Dalawah, confirmed the statements of the accountant. The Dalawah looked at his mother with an indignant smile, observing that he little expected that *she* would cause such an odium to be cast on his name. Saying this, he sent for a carpenter, and a broad chisel, and in the presence of his mother, the Pillay's fingers were chopped off with the chisel, and he was dismissed from the service. He next caused the re-entry of the name of the Chanar into the Proverthy accounts as the owner of the garden alluded to.

As Valu Thamby was thus carrying every thing with a high hand, in 978 M.E. (1803 A.D), he began to experience strong opposition from the military, as well as from the ministerial servants and palace officials, who were all offended with him on account of the severity of his proceedings. And while the Dalawah was at Alleppey Kunjuneelam Pillay Samprathy and Muthu Pillay, Valia Meleluthu Pillay and a few of the most influential officers of the military, conspired against the Dalawah and prevailed upon His Highness to issue a royal warrant for his apprehension and immediate execution, appointing, at the same time, one Neelakunden Chempaka Ramen as Valia Sarvadhikariakar of the State.

Fortunately for the Dalawah, Major Macauly who had been appointed in 1800 as Resident of Travancore, arrived from Palamcottah and Valu Thamby's wisdom suggested to him, his taking Major Macauly's advice in all important matters. Ramalingum Moodeliar, the grandfather of Vedadrissadasa Moodeliar, the present third Judge of the Travancore Sudr Court, was appointed Sthanapathy or the Resident's Agent

CHAP. IV. at the Maha Rajah's Court, and the friendship and good-will of that person also the Dalawah managed to secure.

The Dalawah saw Colonel Macauly who was then at Cochin, and acquainted him with the particulars of the conspiracy against his life, and acting upon the Resident's advice, Valu Thamby went to Trevandrum for the purpose of paying his respects to His Highness and explaining matters, but through the intrigues of the palace officials, an audience was refused to him by the Maha Rajah. Valu Thamby communicated this to the Resident, informing him at the same time that Samprathy Kunjuneelam Pillay, Valia Meleluthu Muthu Pillay, Major Padmanabhen Chempaka Ramen Pillay, Vanchiyoor Papu Pillay, Pooliel Cochu Narayana Pillay Sarvadhikariakar and Vanchiyoor Padmanabhen Thamby were the principal persons who instigated the Rajah to sanction the unjust execution of the late general and peishcar. Colonel Macauly thereupon came to Trevandrum, along with Ramalingum Moodeliar, escorted by a few companies of the subsidiary force, stationed at Quilon, and held an immediate inquiry regarding the conspiracy and the cause of the execution of the general and peishcar. The charges of conspiracy and the innocence of the general and peishcar were established, and Samprathy Kunjuneelam Pillay, Valia Meleluthu Muthu Pillay and some others were suspected. Some of them were confined in the Udagherry fort, while others were sent to Alleppey and Mavalikaray to be confined there, pending a formal trial by a Court. But Valu Thamby Dalawah found an easy way of disposing them before a trial, for with the exception of Major Chempaka Ramen, Padmanabhen Pillay and Sarvadhi Neelakunden Chempaka Ramen Pillay, all the prisoners died before they could be put on their trial.

Though matters were thus arranged to the satisfaction of Valu Thamby, the Maha Rajah's advisers felt extreme displeasure, and they managed to embitter the mind of the Maha Rajah against Major Macauly, by whose influence they said the best men of His Highness' council had been taken away and destroyed. They said that the next step the Major would adopt would be to curtail His Highness' power and make him a puppet in the hands of the Resident. The Maha Rajah represented the matter to the Governor-General in strong terms and requested Major Macauly's recall and supercession. Major Macauly was called to Calcutta by Marquis Wellesley to offer a personal explanation, and after detaining that officer there for some time, he was sent back, when the Governor-General wrote to the Maha Rajah to the effect that "the Major being an able and energetic officer was sent to Travancore in the hope that he should conduct all affairs to your satisfaction. I am sorry to hear so from you. Major Macauly by our order came to Calcutta and fully related matters. He says that there are no differences between you and him, and I am very glad to hear this. Valu Thamby's appointment as Dewan was a source of great pleasure to the Government, because he is able and energetic."

During Major Macauly's stay at Calcutta he wrote to his agent at the Travancore Durbar the following letter:—

"CALCUTTA, *20th April*, 1802."

"I am happy to hear that the Travancore minister is going on so well. I have most particularly mentioned him to Marquis Wellesley, who has been gratified by hearing of the judicious choice made by the Rajah."

Marquis Wellesley, the Governor-General of India, sent to Valu Thamby through Colonel Macauly, a present of a pair of valuable shawls, gold dresses and kincob, according to the formality observed at the installation of Chiefs in India.*

* "You can present the minister with the shawls, and gold dresses and kincob from yourself when you go to Travancore.

Major Macauly to Ramalingum Moodeliar.

CHAP. IV.

During the able, though arbitrary administration of Valu Thamby Dalawah, soukars and bankers in the town, and bazaarmen as well as the peasantry in the country, could sleep with open and unbolted doors in perfect safety at night. Merchants and people of all descriptions could travel through any part of the country without fear of molestation.

Valu Thamby Dalawah caused a survey of all the lands and gardens throughout the kingdom to be made and new pattas or pathivus were issued to all the proprietors and other landholders. New auyacattoo or assessment account was completed and a regularity in the system of keeping and conducting accounts introduced and enforced. By this measure, an increase in the land revenue was effected, and the financial position of the country considerably improved.

Commercial speculations and pursuits specially engaged the Dalawah's attention, and therefore the traffic department of the Sircar was brought to perfection; and all the cash, which any source of revenue yielded to the Government, found its way into the Sircar treasury, instead of into the private purse of the servants as heretofore. Never had the conservation of public funds been more successfully accomplished since the demise of Rye Kasava Dass Dewan.

The finances of the Sircar having, as above stated, been brought into such a flourishing condition, the Dalawah was now able to pay off all the arrears of the salaries due to the Sircar establishments as well as to the various institutions, and also to clear off the State debts, which were very heavy at the time.

The Dalawah took great interest in improving Quilon, where new bazaars were built; several Tinnevelly and Madura merchants were invited to settle there, and with the view of making the place one of some importance, a large and spacious building for the cutcherries was constructed, as also a Hindu pagoda, a royal residence, and other requisite buildings. Quilon thus became a town of note like Alleppey.

During the whole of his administration the Dalawah was very careful in preserving the amity and friendship existing between the Honorable East India Company and the Travancore Sircar. This able minister, having been an admirer of Dewan Rye Kasava Dass, saw that the safest plan was to follow the system of Government adopted by that illustrious Statesman.

CHAP. IV.

The Dalawah devoted a great deal of his attention to the improvement of the town and port of Alleppey, for which purpose he often resided there.* He commenced opening up various roads for traffic to that important commercial town from various directions and established a market at Chunganacherry fifteen miles south-east, and another thoroughfare at Thalayolanparampu near Vycome, twenty-nine miles north of Alleppey. In these two thoroughfares, weekly and bi-weekly markets are still held, when all the articles produced in the interior of the country are brought and disposed of by the ryots, and whence they find their way to the ports of Alleppey and Cochin.

It was this Dalawah who cleared the bushy island in the middle of the backwater, north of Alleppey, and planted the same with cocoanut trees and converted a portion of it into paddy fields. A bungalow was also built there afterwards. This island is now known by the name of Patheramanapuram, and was in the possession of Mr. J. Munro, the present superintendent and magistrate of the Travancore Sircar's cardamon hills. It was lately transferred to a native at Thunneermukum. The Manjali market, in the district of Alangaud, was also established by this Dalawah.

The road from Quilon to Shencottah was opened, and in order to induce Brahmans and other travellers to pass by that road, and for their comfort an Ootu-

* "The minister is at Alleppey living in the Dewan's house; he has now been absent from the Rajah six weeks and seems to follow the example, in every thing, of the old Dewan."

Major Macauly to Ramalingum Moodeliar.

CHAP. IV. purah was established at Mampalathuray, and some other works for convenience of the public were constructed. The present hall of audience attached to the palace at Trevandrum, in the southern street of the fort, was built under the superintendence of the Dalawah. This was originally a part of the palace built by Rye Kasava Dass Dewan at Alleppey, and removed from thence to Trevandrum by the Dalawah.

While Valu Thamby was thus going on successfully, he thought it expedient to effect a retrenchment in the expenditure especially as there were arrears of subsidy to be paid to the British Government. The first item that engaged the attention of the Dalawah was the allowance of the Nair troops, whose maintenance, he thought, was, at that time, an unnecessary drain upon the exchequer. In this view the Resident fully concurred. This measure created a general disaffection in the military and kindled the fire of a rebellion, which being fanned by the enemies of the Dalawah, some of whom were then in custody in the Udagherry fort, as well as at Mavalikaray, extended throughout the country. The State prisoners were released and every military station was abandoned. The concentrated force proceeded to Trevandrum, with the object of insisting on the dismissal and execution of the obnoxious minister and all his associates, and the appointment of a minister to be nominated by the military. When the mutineers came *en masse* to Trevandrum, they found nobody to resist them, but on the other hand supporters in the persons of the enemies of the Dalawah. The Dewan was absent at Alleppey. The young Maha Rajah was perplexed at his singular situation, for there was not a single man of ability and firmness at the capital to cope with the difficulty. By this time, the news reached Alleppey, and the Dewan seeing that the Nair battalions there had also mutinied, fled to Cochin, where the British Resident then was, and after mutual consultation, the Resident ordered a body of troops from Tinnevelly to march to Trevandrum, and the

Dewan collected the Carnatic brigade who were faithful. He made arrangements for the marching of the subsidiary force at Quilon to Trevandrum. Having made these arrangements, he, with the Resident, came to Alleppey, and measures were adopted for the purpose of bringing to punishment the chief instigators and leaders of the revolt. Several of them were apprehended and hanged, beheaded, shot and blown from the mouths of guns. One of them suffered a most cruel and shocking death, for, his legs were tied to those of two elephants, and the animals made to run and tear the unfortunate man in two!! It has been said that when this mutineer was thus tied, and lying on his back, Valu Thamby Dalawah, who was just at the spot, approached him and asked him:—"Krishna Pillay (such was his name) how do you feel now?" The mutineer lifted up his head and said, "I feel as comfortable now, as if I was lying on the rascal Valu Thamby's velvet bed, on his family cot." This bears testimony to the courage and daring of the Travancore Nairs of the period.

By such cruel measures, and by disarming the best portion of the military, and disbanding several corps in the force by a royal proclamation, Valu Thamby was enabled to put down the mutiny effectually, though the general feeling against the Dalawah became stronger, and his opponents were only waiting for an opportunity to break out against him.

Valu Thamby Dalawah believed that with this fearful vindication of his power and authority he had brought the military as well as those against him, under subjection, and that he had nothing to apprehend from them, and so resumed his despotic administration.

When the news of the meeting of the Nair troops reached Calcutta, the following letter was addressed to the Madras Government by Lord Wellesley, the then Governor-General, under date the 17th December 1804:

CHAP. IV.

"MY LORD,

"The British Resident at the Court of the Rajah of Travancore has communicated to your Lordship the circumstances of an insurrection among the Nair battalions in the service of the Rajah of Travancore, and of the danger to which the authority of the Rajah, and the influence of the British Government in Travancore are exposed by the extent of that insurrection and the violence and activity of the insurgents.

"The treaty concluded between the British Government and the Rajah of Travancore in the year 1797 does not contain any express stipulation for the aid of the British power in quelling internal commotions within the territories of that Prince; but the spirit of the treaty certainly imposes upon us that obligation. The expediency, however, of affording such aid in the present crisis is obvious, especially under this consideration, that the avowed object of the insurrection is the subversion of the British influence in the councils of the Rajah.

"If, therefore, your Lordship should not have adopted measures for the relief of the Rajah of Travancore, I request that on receipt of this despatch your Lordship will issue orders directing the immediate despatch of a British force from the most convenient quarter, for the purpose of quelling the insurrection in the vicinity of Travancore, and of restoring the authority of the Rajah and the Dewan.

"I consider this occurrence to afford a favorable opportunity for the modification of our subsidiary engagements with the Rajah of Travancore. The modification which I propose is, that the British force at present subsidized by the Rajah be permanently stationed within his dominions, and that the British Government possess authority to regulate the dispositions of that force within the territories of the Rajah in such a manner as may appear best calculated to secure the object of its appointment.

"I have accordingly directed the Resident at Travancore to propose that modification to the Rajah of Travancore at the earliest opportunity. CHAP. IV.

"It may be proper on this occasion to state to your Lordship that the preservation and improvement of our influence in that country has been uniformly considered by me to be an object of the greatest importance to the interests and security of the British Government in India; and in my judgment the present exigency of the Rajah of Travancore's affairs justifies and requires a vigorous exertion of our force for the restoration of his authority, and for the preservation of the British interests in that quarter.

"Your Lordship will also observe from the tenor of this despatch, that my opinion of the necessity of supporting the cause of the Rajah of Travancore with the aid of our troops is founded on the obligations of treaty, combined with the importance of maintaining and improving our political connection with the State."

A copy of this letter was transmitted to the Resident by Lord William Bentinck and the Resident, after consulting Valu Thamby, submitted the correspondence to the Maha Rajah.

The Dewan's opinion was in favour of a revision of the existing treaty introducing special terms for the internal defence of Travancore. But he was not at all inclined to support any proposal for the augmentation of the subsidy. The Maha Rajah and his advisers were opposed to any new arrangements being introduced, and thus the consideration of the question of making a new treaty was postponed.

The Dewan and the Resident's agent had to wait upon the Maha Rajah and discuss the question often, and, at last, a draft treaty was framed by the Resident, in conjunction with the Dewan. A storm of opposition was raised in the palace when this draft was submitted by the Dewan to the Maha Rajah.

Valu Thamby Dalawah, however spared no pains in

CHAP. IV. persuading His Highness, in spite of all the evil counsels of the palace officials, &c., to ratify the new treaty, and Colonel Macauly also strongly remonstrated with the Maha Rajah by letters, as well as by messages through the Resident's agent Ramalingum Moodeliar, but being opposed by the intriguing characters already referred to, His Highness hesitated a good deal to give his assent to the treaty. The controversy regarding this important matter lasted some days, and at last through the unceasing exertions of Valu Thamby Dalawah, and with the judicious counsel and advice of the Resident's agent Ramalingum Moodeliar, the proposed treaty was signed by His Highness the Maha Rajah on the 12th January 1805.

The following was the new treaty which is still in force:

" Treaty of perpetual friendship and alliance between " the Honorable English East India Company Bahau- " der and the Maha Rajah Bahauder of Travancore."

" Whereas the treaty concluded in the year 1795 " between the Honorable Company of Merchants of " England trading with the East Indies, and His " late Highness the Rajah of Travancore was " intended to defend and protect the Travancore " country against the foreign enemies and to strengthen " and to fix the terms of the ancient friendship " and alliance subsisting between the Company " and the Rajah of Travancore, and whereas it is " evident that the intentions of the contracting parties " have not been duly fulfilled and whereas the said " Company and His Highness the Rajah of Travancore " have judged it expedient that additional provision " should at this time be made for the purpose of sup- " plying the defects in the said treaty and of " establishing the connection between the said con- " tracting parties on permanent bases of security in " all times to come, therefore, in order to carry into " effect the said intentions, the present treaty is " concluded by Lieut.-Colonel Colin Macauly, Resident "at Travancore on the part and in the name of His "Excellency the Most Noble Marquis Wellesley, K.P. "and K.C., Governor-General in Council of all the "British possessions in the East Indies, and by His "Highness the Rajah of Travancore for himself, "agreeably to the following Articles which shall be "binding on the contracting parties as long as the sun "and moon shall endure.

"*Article I.*—The friends and enemies of either "of the contracting parties shall be considered as the "friends and enemies of both, the Honorable the East "India Company Bahauder especially engaging to "defend and protect the territories of the Maha Rajah "Rama Rajah Bahauder of Travancore against all "enemies whatever."

"*Article II.*—Whereas by the seventh Article of "the treaty concluded in the year 1795 between the "Maha Rajah Rama Rajah Bahauder and the English "East India Company Bahauder, it was stipulated that "when the Company shall require any aid of his troops "to assist them in war it shall be incumbent on the "said reigning Rajah for the time being to furnish such "aid to such extent and in such numbers as may be "in his power from his regular infantry and cavalry, "exclusive of the native Nairs of his country, and the "Company now being willing to release the Rajah "from the obligation, it is hereby concluded and agreed "that the Rama Rajah Bahauder is for ever discharged "from aforesaid burthensome obligations.

"*Article III.*—In consideration of the stipula-"tions and release concluded in the first and second "Articles whereby the Company became liable to heavy "and constant expenses while great relief is afforded "to the revenues of the Rajah, His Highness engages "to pay annually to the said Company, a sum equiva-"lent to the expense of one regiment of the Honorable "Company's native infantry, in addition to the sum "now payable by the said Rajah for the force subsided "by His Highness by the third Article of the subsidiary

CHAP. IV.

"treaty of 1795, the said amount to be paid in six "equal instalments commencing from the first day of "January 1805 and His Highness further agrees, that "the disposal of the said sum together with the "arrangement and employment of the troops to be "maintained by it whether stationed within the Tra-"vancore country, or within the Company's districts "shall be left entirely to the Company.

"*Article IV.*—Should it become necessary for the "Company to employ a larger force than that which is "stipulated for in the preceding Article to protect the "territories of the said Maha Rajah against attack or "invasion, His Highness agrees to contribute jointly "with the Company towards the discharge of the "increased expense thereby occasioned, such a sum as "shall appear on an attentive consideration of the "means of His said Highness to bear a just and rea-"sonable proportion to the actual net revenue of His "said Highness.

"*Article V.*—Whereas it is indispensably necessary "that effectual and lasting security should be provided "against any failure in the funds destined to defray, "either the expenses of the permanent military force "in time of peace the extraordinary expenses described "in the preceding article of the present treaty, it is "hereby stipulated and agreed between the contracting "parties that whenever the Governor-General in Coun-"cil of Fort William in Bengal shall have reason to "apprehend such failure in the funds so destined, the "Governor-General in Council shall be at liberty, and "shall have full power and right either to introduce "such regulations and ordinances as he shall deem "expedient for the mutual management and collections "of revenues, or for the better ordering of any other "branch and department of the Government of Tra-"vancore or to assume and bring under the direct "management of the servants of the said Company "Bahauder, such part or parts of the territorial posses-"sions of His Highness the Maha Rajah Ram Rajah

" Bahauder as shall appear to him (the Governor-General " in Council) necessary to reduce the said fund efficient " and available either in time of peace or war.

" *Article VI.*—And it is hereby further agreed that " whenever the said Governor-General in Council " shall signify to the Maha Rajah Ram Bahauder that " it is become necessary to carry into effect the provi- " sions of the fifth Article, His said Highness Maha " Rajah Rama Rajah Bahauder shall immediately issue " orders to his amils or other officers, either for carry- " ing into effect the said regulations or ordinances " according to the terms of the fifth Article, or for " placing the territories required under the exclusive " authority and control of the English Company " Bahauder, and in case His Highness shall not issue " orders within ten days from the time when the appli- " cation shall have been formally made to him, then " the said Governor-General shall be at liberty to issue " orders by his own authority either for carrying into " effect the said regulations and ordinances, or for " assuming the management and collection of the " revenues of the said territories as he shall judge " expedient for the purpose of securing the efficiency " of the said military funds and of providing for the " effectual protection of the country and welfare of " the people, provided always that whenever and so " long as any part or parts of His said Highness' " territories shall be placed and shall remain under " the exclusive authority and control of the said East " India Company. The Governor-General in Council " shall render to His Excellency a true and faithful " account of the revenue and produce of the territories " so assumed, provided also that in case whenever " His Highness' actual receipt or annual income " arising out of his territorial revenues be less than " the sum of two lacs of rupees, together with the one- " fifth of the net revenue, of the whole of his territories " which sum of two lacs of rupees together with the " amount of one-fifth of the said revenue, the East " India Company engages at all times and in every

CHAP. IV. "possible case to secure and cause to be paid for His "Highness' use.

"*Article VII.*—His Highness the Maha Rajah "Rama Rajah Bahauder engages that he will be guided "by a sincere and cordial attention to the relations of "peace and amity established between the English "Company and their allies and that he will carefully "abstain from any interference in the affairs of any "State in alliance with the said English Company "Bahauder or of any State whatever, and for securing "the object of this stipulation it is further stipulated and "agreed that no communication or correspondence with "any foreign State whatever should be holden by His "said Highness without the previous knowledge and "sanction of the said English Company Bahauder.

"*Article VIII.*—His Highness stipulates and "agrees that he will not admit any European "foreigners into his service without the concurrence "of the English Company Bahauder and that he will "apprehend and deliver to the Company's Govern-"ment all Europeans of whatever description who "shall be found within the territories of His said "Highness without regular passport from the British "Government, it being His Highness' determined "resolution not to suffer even for a day any Europeans "to remain within his territories unless by the con-"sent of the said Company.

"*Article IX.*—Such parts of the treaty (A.D. 1795), "one thousand seven hundred and ninety-five between "the English East India Company and the late Rajah "of Travancore as are calculated to strengthen the "alliance, to cement the friendship and to identify "the interest of the contracting parties, are hereby "received and confirmed, and accordingly His High-"ness hereby promises to pay at all times the utmost "attention to such advice as the English Government "shall occasionally judge it necessary to offer him with "a view to the recovering of his finances, the better "collection of his revenues the administration of jus-

" tice, the extension of commerce, the encouragement " of trade, agriculture and industry, or any other " objects connected with the advancement of His " Highness' interests, the happiness of his people, and " the mutual welfare of both the States.

" *Article X.*—This treaty consisting of ten Articles " being this day, the 12th day of January 1805, settled " and concluded at the fortress of Theeroovanantha- " poorum in Travancore by Lieut.-Colonel Colin " Macauly in behalf and in the name of His Excellency " the Most Noble Marquis Wellesley, Governor-General " in Council, with the Maha Rajah Rama Rajah Bahau- " der, he has delivered to the said Maha Rajah Rama " Rajah Bahauder, one copy of the same English and " Persian, signed and sealed by him, and His Highness " the Maha Rajah has delivered to the Lieut-Colonel " aforesaid another copy also in Persian and English, " bearing the seal and signature, and signed and sealed " by Valu Thamby, Dewan to the Maha Rajah afore- " said, and the Lieut.-Colonel aforesaid has engaged " to procure and deliver to the said Maha Rajah with- " out delay a copy of the same under the seal and " signature of His Excellency the Most Noble Marquis " Wellesley, Governor-General in Council, on the receipt " of which by the said Maha Rajah the present treaty " shall be deemed complete and binding on the " Honorable Company and on the Maha Rajah Rama " Rajah Bahauder and the copy of it now delivered to " the said Maha Rajah shall be returned."

(Signed) C. MACAULY,

Resident at Travancore.

To the facts connected with this important subject, the following correspondence will bear testimony.

" I cannot finish my letter to Lord Wellesley until I first receive an answer to the following question :

" Wait upon the minister this evening, and let him " come to me with the Rajah's answer to the question

CHAP. IV.

"which His Highness' conduct this day makes it "necessary to ask before I see Mr. D'Veigas.

"Is it the determination of the Rama Rajah to "refuse entering into a new treaty with the East "India Company? Yes or no?"

Major Macauly to Ramalingum Moodeliar.

"Wait upon the Rajah with the letter I send, and "explain it to him distinctly. They are positively "mad; tell the Rajah that in case he thinks proper to "continue to avert his engagements and to oppose "himself to the wish of the Government it may "become my duty to publish a proclamation; my wish "has been and still is to preserve His Highness' "house in honor and dignity and it is to be ardently "hoped that for the sake of half-a-dozen of * * * * * * "His Highness may not reduce the Government to "the necessity of considering His Highness in any "other light than that of a friend and an ally."

Major Macauly to Ramalingum Moodeliar.

"The Dewan and myself waited upon His Highness "not sooner than three o'clock this morning, (it was "the lucky hour fixed by His Highness to receive his "Dewan) and returned just this moment. I have "delivered your message to him, and he fixed the "hour for you to see him at two o'clock this afternoon. "In the course of conversation, I seized opportunity "and used my utmost endeavours to explain him for "his own good and his country, the ready compliance "of the orders of the Government through you. I "gave several instances and opened his eyes stating "the bad consequence he had to expect on the con-"trary; he appeared as really convinced of it, pro-"mised in presence of his Dewan to place a faithful "confidence in all my advice (as he always heretofore "has done in many critical times) and pay a due "attention to your recommendation, and obedience to "the orders of the Government. For my part I

" assured that my advice always will be good for the " safety of him and his country, and your recom- " mendation will always be to promote his interest as " well as the country; then the Dewan, (Valu " Thamby) confirmed my advice and expressed his " opinion that it is proper he should not hesitate to " sign any agreement that you may think proper to " present him as any delay makes more confusion in " the country; he answered anything offered by you " shall be duly attended to, by all this I have every " reason to believe that His Highness, (if he possess " the same heart) will not hesitate to sign the treaty " when presented, but I think the delay will be only " for obtaining a lucky hour."

Ramalingum Moodeliar to Colonel Macauly.

7th January 1805.

That the delay in signing the treaty irritated Lieut.-Colonel Macauly may be inferred from the fact of a British force under Major-General MacDowel having been ordered to march from Tinnevelly to Travancore. As the following extract from the despatch of the 8th January 1805 of the Resident to the Governor-General in Council will show:—

" The Dewan having expressed an earnest hope that " the army under Major-General MacDowel should " not enter the lines pending the discussions I have " acquainted, in consequence of his promise and of my " confident hope that all the points enjoined by His " Excellency's instructions will be amicably adjusted, " General MacDowel has been therefore requested to " suspend his movements agreeably to the enclosed copy " of my letter to that officer under date the 4th instant.

" His Excellency has been already informed of the " objections urged by the Dewan to my considerable " increase to the subsidy.

" In the conference of yesterday with His Highness " these objections were again offered by His Highness.

CHAP. IV.

"The Dewan had strongly pressed upon my attention the difficulty of making good with their alleged deficient means of the payment of four additional lacs per annum. He would, he said, in proof of this deliver to me an authenticated statement of the receipts and disbursements of this country. I expressed much satisfaction at the disposition now manifested for the first time since my residence at this court, of fairly laying open the situation of their affairs. When this statement was received and examined, the whole subject would most undoubtedly meet with a deliberate and indulgent consideration from the Government.

"In the meantime until such statement should be prepared and received, it seemed advisable that a sum equal to the expense of one regiment of native infantry be inserted in the treaty.

"Under these circumstances it will be for His Excellency's considerations whether it might not appear to His Excellency to be advisable to authorise a remission of the payment of one-half of the amount of the additional subsidy for the period of one year from the conclusion of the treaty."

The pressure brought to bear upon the Maha Rajah may be inferred from the above letters. It requires no comment from us as some of the best English historians* of eminence and authority have thus recorded their views on this transaction with Travancore:—"The proceedings in Travancore were, in truth, among the least justifiable of the many questionable transactions by which the British power in India has been acquired or preserved. The protection of the Rajah was, in the first instance, generous and politic; the military command of his country, subsequently was necessary for objects of British policy, and was not incompatible with the pacific interests of the Rajah and prosperity of his limited dominion. To impose upon

* Mill and Wilson.

him the maintenance of a force infinitely more numerous than was necessary for the defence of the country, and the cost of which heavily taxed its resources, to urge the exaction with unrelenting vigour, and to resent with unpitying vengeance, the passions excited by a deep sense of national wrong among a semi-barbarous and demoralized race, were unworthy of the character of the British nation for justice and generosity, of the civilization it had attained, and the religion it professed."

The subsequent ceremonies connected with the accession of the Maha Rajah to the musnud and the difficulty of collecting revenues, in consequence of the continued disturbances above described, caused heavy financial embarrassments, and therefore the State was unable even to pay off the subsidy, in accordance with the treaty of 1795. But now the doubling of the subsidy made the burden simply intolerable. The Dewan found it necessary to seek even a temporary relief. With this view, a proposal was made to the Resident to allow the enhanced subsidy of four lacs a year to be paid in four instalments, as such a large sum of money could not be raised in one year by any measure of retrenchment. The chief retrenchment the Dewan thought fit to make was the disbanding of the Carnatic brigade. Colonel Macauly, who was closely acquainted with the state of the finances, considered the Dewan's proposal reasonable, and recommended it to the Supreme Government.

Extract from a Despatch, dated 13*th January* 1805.

" *Fifth.*—The provisions of the treaty now concluded will I trust be found to correspond with the whole tenor of His Excellency's commands, and particularly to the 19th paragraph of your despatch of the 17th ultimo, the stipulations seem essential to the interests of the British Government and the Rajah of Travancore, and they are entirely consistent with the obligations of justice and propriety.

" *Sixth.*—My sentiments respecting the increase to " the subsidy have been already in general submitted, " but as the retrenchments, reforms, and improvements " proposed to be gradually introduced here, cannot be " expected to produce their full effect for nearly two " years; it might be expedient to extend the remission " of the payment of one-half of the additional subsidy " for two complete years.

" *Seventh.*—One of the chief retrenchments in the " expenditure of this country is proposed to be imme- " diately made by reducing the brigade of Carnatic " sepoys, commanded by Colonel Daly, this reduction " may relieve the finances of His Highness to the amount " of nearly one-and-a-half lacs of Rupees per annum, in " the event of His Highness accomplishing this measure, " the future situation of the European officers attached " to the brigade will be for consideration."

The above proposal was, in a measure, acceded to by the Supreme Government.

The disbandment of the Carnatic brigade, the Maha Rajah considered derogatory to His Highness' position, and so he allowed the force to continue; but the Madras Government would not permit this. Their opinion was that " the Maha Rajah's observation that the discharge of the brigade would now be derogatory to his dignity and indicative of the diminished confidence on the part of the British Government in his attachment and fidelity appears to us to be devoid of solid foundation; but even admitting the contrary, justice surely requires that the Maha Rajah should submit to the inconvenience rather than expect from the British Government a sacrifice, the claim to which originates exclusively, in a concession previously made in his favour at a considerable loss to the Company, and which is supported by arguments deduced from His Highness' wilful disregard of a corresponding obligation."

On the 2nd May, the treaty was ratified by the Governor-General and was returned to the Resident for delivery to the Maha Rajah, and the Resident adopted measures in communication with the Dewan to make grand preparations for the occasion. Anjengo was nominated as the place for the ceremony.

Agreeably to the wishes of the Resident, the Dalawah made grand preparations for the Maha Rajah's procession to Anjengo. All the officers of the State escorted the Maha Rajah to the place and the delivery of the treaty was marked as a State ceremony. The Dewan acting as master of the ceremonies and moving about in his gorgeous State dress presented by the Governor-General, was particularly observed by his enemies, on this occasion.

After the return of the Maha Rajah to Trevandrum, the news of the signing of the treaty soon spread throughout the country, and the disaffection increased and the indignation of the people was rekindled.

Valu Thamby Dalawah proceeded to Alleppey; but before his departure he noticed strong symptoms of dissatisfaction and displeasure generally among the officers, and the sovereign himself was no exception; many remarked without any ceremony, "that they were now convinced of the object the Dalawah had in view and of his reason for joining the Resident, and that they little expected that any of the Travancore Rajah's faithful subjects would have ever made such an attempt."

The Dalawah felt considerably hurt on hearing such unjust remarks so freely made in the palace, while he was all the time devoting his entire attention to adopt measures for strengthening the protection of the kingdom. The Dalawah lost all confidence in his subordinates, while almost all the influential officials turned against him.

He stayed a short time at Alleppey and then proceeded to Trevandrum, and he resolved upon proving to the Maha Rajah that he was no friend to the British cause, and that he suggested no measures in order to

CHAP. IV.

serve his private interests. To attain this end, he actually held a meeting of all the officers, and explained to them the necessity and advisability of the new treaty though he perfectly concurred with them in the injurious consequences of the augmentation of the subsidy. But nevertheless there was a fresh outburst of indignation.

While matters were thus going on in Travancore, Colonel Macauly observed in his report of the ceremony at Anjengo to the Governor-General that "to explain the degree of joy visible in the countenance and demeanour of His Highness and of his court upon this important event, so essential to the welfare of Travancore would be difficult; their gratification appeared complete;" and, at the same time, Colonel Macauly assured his Government that "the practical benefit resulting to the Rajah and to all classes of the subjects by the provisions of that treaty appeared to be duly appreciated by His Highness. He seems now perfectly sensible that so far from having any tendency to impair his confidence and authority, it is on the contrary calculated to raise the one and to strengthen the other, not only in the view of his subjects, but also in His Highness' own estimation" and it was added that "the Dewan continues to conduct the general administration of the concerns of the State with his usual ability and address, grounded on the firmest integrity and on a disposition ardently ambitious of advancing the joint interests of his master and that of the Honorable Company. The chief obstacle to the practical reform of some inveterate abuses in the financial administration results from that system of peculation and corruption so long and so generally prevalent on this coast. Ever since the period of his elevation to the post of prime minister, he appears to have invariably regulated his conduct by principles of rectitude and probity in every measure connected with finance. He forms a very singular and honorable exception to the general depravity."

Valu Thamby Dalawah returned to Alleppey and strove hard to persuade the Maha Rajah and the officers through Sthanapathy Suba Iyen and the English Interpreter, Mr. D'Veigas to reconcile themselves to the new treaty, which he assured them will do no harm to the interests of Travancore. As the Dalawah had already secured the Government's sanction for the remission of half of the increased subsidy for two years, he was sanguine that he would be able to obtain a permanent remission of half of the newly increased sum. At the same time, he employed all his energy towards collecting the arrears of revenue to pay off the arrears of subsidy.

Suba Iyen's and Mr. D'Veigas' mission entirely failed. The Maha Rajah not only remonstrated with them against the Dewan's proceedings but also intimated to them his intention of complaining against Colonel Macauly to the Government.

On the Dalawah's pressing in the name of the Maha Rajah, for the permanent remission of half of the increased subsidy the resident observed "clearly and finally, that it is wholly and absolutely out of my power to propose in any case a continuance of that remission which was granted for two years. I also further inform you that Government is resolved on compelling the Rajah to execute the stipulation of the treaty, if compulsion be rendered necessary, Government being entirely satisfied of the justice of such proceeding, if disturbances be excited on account of * * * * * *" The Dewan despairing of success dropped the subject altogether, without bringing his failure to the notice of the Maha Rajah.

Sthanapathy Suba Iyen and Mr. D'Veigas appear to have communicated to Colonel Macauly the observations of the Maha Rajah during their interview with him, and the Resident in a letter to the Dalawah, said: "I am surprised to hear for the first time, that the Maha Rajah had any grievances, while he stands in this happy and amiable situation."

CHAP. IV.

In this interval, the Resident pressed the Dewan for the payment of the arrears of subsidy, and the Sircar, embarrassed by pecuniary difficulties delayed payment. The Resident considered this delay unjustifiable, and believing that the Dewan did not intend paying the arrears, especially as he had been applying for the entire remission of a part of the enhanced subsidy, a misunderstanding arose between them.

In February 1807, Colonel Macauly wrote the following letter to Sthanapathy Suba Iyen, which reveals the fact of the breach between the minister and the British representative :—

"TRAVANCORE, 18*th February* 1807.

"SOOBIAH,

"Day after day such ludicrous things *are said* "that when I reflect seriously upon the future, I "almost despair. I do not however judge of people, "either when they say wrong or when they say right, "by their saying merely. I wait to see if they carry "the sayings into practice.

"If the minister ultimately injure himself he will "do so (after this explanation), with his eyes open.

"Very soon after the conclusion of the late treaty, "I assured the Rajah that notwithstanding the treaty, "no change would take place. In proof of the truth "of this assurance, I gave him a ring as a solemn "pledge to remain with him and to be handed down "to his successor, in order that each time they looked "at the ring, they might repose an implicit confidence "in the assurance given by the Resident who nego-"tiated the treaty. But what did this imply? The "explanation and the right understanding of that "point is important. I suspected that there might "lurk in the Rajah's mind much uneasiness respecting "that stipulation in the treaty which empowers the "Company to assume the country. I resolved there-"fore to remove all uneasiness upon that score, and "I assured him that there would be no such change, "that is, that the country never would be assumed by "the Company or at all taken out of the Rajah's "management, such was the object and the extent of "the pledge made to His Highness—how, it may be "asked, came I to be so positive in such an assur- "ance? for the following plain and simple reason: CHAP. IV.

"By the treaty *the Sircar is bound* to follow the "advice of the British Government in all cases whatso- "ever, for the benefit of the country and people, the "Resident under this comprehensive stipulation "possessing the right of interfering by advice, enjoys "the means of correcting errors, obviating failures, "regulating justice, &c., and thereby removing all "pretext for assuming the country or rather rendering "the consideration even of such an extreme measure "for ever and for ever unnecessary.

"But again, it may be asked, what security has the "Resident, that his advice will be followed? Why "simply this—should any minister of this country be "daring enough to resist his advice when sanctioned "by Government—the Rajah and the Resident will "lay hold of that minister and throw him into the "Valiatoray* surf and proceed in the same manner "towards every succeeding minister who should design "the ruin of his master.

"Should it again be supposed that there may come "a Rajah who, to save a minister, would risk his own "musnud, I have no observation to make upon such "a case—the consequences are obvious to every one.

"Finally, it might possibly be asked, if the Resident "possess such power, why has he not during the last "two years had recourse to the Valiatoray surf, "against those who not only slighted his advice, but "who everywhere openly and secretly set him at "defiance?

"The answer to this last question could be given in "a few clear and plain sentences, but I have said, that

* A port about Trevandrum.

"I overlook the past—and nothing but necessity, a "necessity originating with others shall ever bring me "to refer to those subjects.

"This letter contains matters of high importance, "it must be distinctly explained to the minister and "impressed upon his mind. I also keep a copy of it."

Your's very obedient servant,

(Signed) C. MACAULY.

Up to the 30th March not even a part of the arrears of subsidy having reached the Resident's treasury, notwithstanding all the Resident's remonstrances and his disagreeable correspondence with the Dewan, the Resident was enraged, and wrote on the 23rd April that he had long submitted to the Dewan's impositions, and that he would not now accept any reply from, or by the Dewan, directly or indirectly. In one of the Resident's letters, dated the 10th April, he said that the Dewan "is a temporizing, equivocating, prevaricating and marauding boy."

This highly objectionable language employed against a person like the Dewan, filled him with indignation, and he resolved not to hold office as long as Colonel Macauly represented the Honorable Company in Travancore, and he gave the Resident to understand that he would rather give up his appointment than be exposed to such vile and humiliating treatment.

Taking advantage of this threat of the Dewan, the Resident wrote to Government on the 28th April, "that the Dewan was afflicted with a complaint which sometimes laid him up; that the Dewan himself had informed him that he was unable to conduct the duties of his office, and requested to be relieved, and that unless he be relieved, it is certain that the poor Rajah will be likely to be injured."

At this critical time, Colonel Macauly espoused the cause of Mathoo Tharaken, the notorious Syrian Christian contractor, one of the intriguers alluded to in the commencement of this reign, who had both of his ears cut during the insurrection of 1799, and who was a merchant prince in Travancore, possessing large estates in almost all the northern districts of that country. He had been restored to his former state of influence, subsequent to his being relieved from his late troubles, and his lands were confiscated by the order of the Sircar for non-payment of taxes.

On account of the incessant pressure of the Resident for payment of arrears of subsidy, the Dalawah as has been already said, was necessitated to leave no stone unturned in his endeavours to recover oldstanding revenue arrears. This remarkable landlord, Mathoo Tharaken, had not paid his tax on the lands possessed by him for some years. When called upon to pay the arrears, the Tharaken possessing the influence of the Resident, thought of obtaining a remission, on the plea, that he was imprisoned by the Sircar for some time, and that some of his goods had been confiscated and its value misappropriated by Valu Thamby. The Dewan would not admit this plea, and regardless of the Tharaken's attachment to Colonel Macauly he issued orders for the confiscation of those lands belonging to the Tharaken, on which the tax had not been paid. The Tharaken complained to the Resident, and Colonel Macauly requested the Dewan to cancel his orders. The Dewan reasonably delayed to attend to this requisition, and submitted a full explanation to the Resident on the subject of the Tharaken's arrears fully justifying his proceedings in regard to the confiscation of the lands. A good deal of correspondence passed between the Resident and the Dewan on this subject.

The view taken by Colonel Macauly of this proceeding of the Dewan, will be apparent from the following correspondence.

In a letter to Mr. D'Veigas, the Colonel says that the Dewan's proceeding in regard to the confiscation of the Tharaken's lands for arrears of tax "was dictated by a spirit of the most base treachery and

CHAP. IV.

tyranny," and that, if arrears of tax arose from the negligence of the Sircar, it should not reap any advantage from its own wrong and wilful negligence. The resident also adds that in the event of the Dewan's orders not being recalled :—" I solemnly declare that I will interfere in a way that will make him surely repent his conduct."

In his official of the 12th May 1807, the Resident writes to the Dewan: " you have desired Suba Iyen to intimate to me, through Mr. D'Veigas that you had taken upon yourself to issue orders to insist on Tharaken's paying what it is alleged that he owes for hilly grounds, &c. This intimation coming from you in their naked shape without any the most trivial document to support the ground you have taken, is (under the peculiar circumstances of Mathoo Tharaken's situation), very highly improper, irregular, and contrary to your bounden duty. You must withdraw those orders and transmit to me the reports of the different Kariakars, who reported to you the failures of Mathoo Tharaken, in order that the business may be regularly investigated, and the Kariakars called here to give evidence of the truth of their statement. Any other line of proceeding must be * * * * I will not allow you, from motives of base enmity to crush any man (though your subject or dependant) if I can possibly and honourably prevent it. What need I say more ?"

The Dewan now found it impossible to rely on the Resident's support, and thought it politic to concert measures to side entirely with the popular party. He also conceived a mortal enmity and hatred against Colonel Macauly and not against the Company's Government as some historians would have us believe.

Matters now began to approach a crisis. Colonel Macauly was determined to oust the Dewan from office. Though he was prepared to retire, he persisted in holding the reins of Government, simply because he knew the Resident was trying to get him out.

He convinced the Maha Rajah that the Resident's motive in endeavouring to cause his removal, was to confirm the increased subsidy and trouble His Highness for the immediate payment of the arrears. The Maha Rajah and his councillors now found that it would be injudicious to dispense with the services of such a man as Valu Thamby, who would not only be of great service on such a trying occasion, but would also be useful as a scape-goat, under unfavorable circumstances.

Colonel Macauly seems to have adopted all possible and practicable measures to compel the Dewan to resign. The minister was addressed in the most offensive terms imputing to him the vilest motives even in the ordinary transaction of public business. The Resident interfered with even the most trivial details of internal administration, and almost every letter of Colonel Macauly, on such occasions, was couched in insufferably vituperative language, the whole culminating in an intimation from the Resident that "he had formed a positive and final determination concerning Valu Thamby." This determination was, that Valu Thamby should retire from public life, and take up his residence in Cherakel, on a pension of 500 rupees per mensem, which he was to receive from Mr. Baber, the Collector of Malabar.

All these particulars were communicated in detail to the Maha Rajah, and though of a quiet and placable disposition, and seldom prone to anger, His Highness was much offended at the conduct of the Resident. Valu Thamby had no inclination to disconnect himself from the Maha Rajah's service. Neither did His Highness wish him to do so. His Highness tried his best to bring about a reconciliation between the Dewan and the Resident, but without success, as Colonel Macauly was a man of a vindictive nature, fond of command, of an imperious temper, and one who could ill-brook contradiction. On the other hand, Valu Thamby was of a haughty and arrogant disposition, of great reso-

CHAP. IV. lution, and so sensitive that he would put up with insolence and affront from no man. His Highness was sadly disappointed, but it was not a matter for surprise that the attempt to reconcile two men who were so bitterly opposed to each other failed.

The Maha Rajah complained in strong language against the Resident to the Madras Government, and His Highness solicited the favor of their appointing another Resident in the room of Colonel Macauly. His Highness submitted that his Dewan Valu Thamby performed his duties with due diligence and with the utmost fidelity, and yet the Resident was pressing on His Highness to dismiss him, a step which he was quite unwilling to take; and that the delay in discharging the arrears of subsidy was on account of the unsatisfactory state of the finances but that, nevertheless, His Highness had adopted measures for the payment of a part of the arrears without delay.

The above letter was followed by the payment of a moiety of the promised subsidy which was obtained by mortgaging most of the Crown jewels. On this being reported, the Government directed some relaxation of the demands.

The payment of the residue of the arrears was again delayed, and the Resident came down upon the Dewan most severely, on that ground. The Maha Rajah again complained and urged that the new treaty which was forced upon him by the Resident was unbearable, and that though the Dewan was straining every nerve to meet the demand, he was considerably hampered in his efforts by the unwarrantable interference of the Resident. His Highness therefore again requested the recall of Colonel Macauly, and the appointment of a new Resident.

On hearing these repeated complaints of the Maha Rajah, the dismissal of the Dewan was again peremptorily urged by the Resident.

Seeing the unreasonableness of the Resident's requisition, while the Dewan was working hard to meet the

PUBLISHED BY MESS.RS HIGGINBOTHAM & CO. E. PASZENSKY LITH: MADRAS.

MAHÀ RAJAH & HIS ATTENDANTS.

demands of the British Government, thus manifesting a rare integrity to which the Resident himself had already borne distinguished testimony, the Maha Rajah was astonished in no small degree. But being of a weak disposition, he considered it advisable not to interfere in the affair and left the Dewan and the Resident to settle matters between themselves. CHAP. IV.

The spirit of the offended minister was now roused and he was resolved to wreak his vengeance upon the British Resident.

Sthanapathy Suba Iyen, the medium of personal communication between His Highness the Maha Rajah and the Resident, took a great interest in promoting the good understanding between the Maha Rajah and Colonel Macauly, as he well knew the state of affairs at that time, and there had been frequent messages between the palace and the residency at which the Dewan took umbrage.

Suba Iyen paid a visit to the Dewan at Alleppey, perhaps with a message from the Maha Rajah, and on a certain night while he was engaged in a private conference with the Dewan he, (Suba Iyen) retired to the garden at about midnight. But, alas! he never returned. He appears to have been seized by the Dewan's people and strangled to death, and a report was given out that Suba Iyen died by snake bite, while he was in the garden.

While matters were in such a state in Travancore, the then reigning sovereign of Cochin, an extremely quiet and easy going Prince, was over-ridden by his prime minister Paliathu Menon (commonly called Paliathu Atchen), who assumed the supreme rule, reduced the Rajah to a mere cypher, and compelled the Prince to reside in a small village called Vellarapilli, north-east of Alwaye.

The minister, Paliathu Menon, was a bitter enemy of the ex-minister of the deceased Rajah of that State and of his commander-in-chief. Both those officers were

CHAP. IV.

highly distinguished in Cochin, and were held in great estimation by the late Rajah, as well as the people in general.

Paliathu Menon, on assuming power, seized both those officers and drowned them in the middle of the river, near Chanamangalom, and after this inhuman act,. he attempted to destroy, in a similar way, a promising young man of great talent and intelligence, whom the reigning Rajah had trained up from his infancy and made a deserving candidate for the premiership. The name of this person was Nadavarampathu Cunju Krishna Menon, who was afterwards Sarvadhikariakar or prime minister of Cochin. It will be also of interest to know that he was the father of the lady of the present Maha Rajah of Travancore.

Paliathu Menon adopted every possible means for seizing Cunju Krishna Menon, and the Rajah was actually obliged to lock him up in his own bed chamber at Vellarapilli for some days, to save his life. The Rajah opportunely sent an express messenger to Colonel Macauly, requesting him to grant His Highness an immediate interview in private. At the meeting, the Rajah handed over Cunju Krishna Menon to Colonel Macauly, requesting him to protect the young man's life against the cruel machinations of his minister, Paliathu Menon. Colonel Macauly gave his assurance to the Rajah, and took the young Menon along with him to the town of Cochin and protected him in his own residence.

On hearing these particulars, Paliathu Menon was greatly exasperated and swore that he would destroy Colonel Macauly and Cunju Krishna Menon together, and in order to accomplish this design, Paliathu Menon plotted measures, and resolved to gain over the disaffected Travancore ministry, for, almost all the Travancore officials the Menon knew were ill-disposed towards Colonel Macauly, and that he could thus easily make the Travancoreans the cat's-paw for carrying out his evil designs.

Paliathu Menon deputed a private messenger to Quilon, with a secret despatch to Valu Thamby Dalawah and the leaders of the disaffected military, proposing to them the massacre of the British Resident and his small garrison in the fort at Cochin, and offering his co-operation in the affair. CHAP. IV.

These officials were delighted at such a desirable proposal from the Cochin minister, and Valu Thamby, from his own vanity, thoughtlessness and desire of revenge agreed to the proposal, and a programme was arranged between the two ministers. A short account of this, has been thus recorded by Lieutenant Horsley: "We are unable to trace the successive steps that led "to the war, or more properly the insurrection which "took place in 1808; but it is perhaps to be attributed "less to the people in general who had everything to "lose from any change which should extinguish "British influence, than to the Rajah and to his "principal native servants, provoked as they were at "a control that threatened to moderate their excesses. "The Cochin minister seems to have been implicated "in those transactions. The character of this "personage and the cautious manner in which he "conducted these measures, countenance suspicion, "that he was one of the most zealous and artful "promoters of the troubles that ensued."

The Dewan now determined to resort to hostilities though in a covert way. He issued secret orders for the recruiting of Nairs and people of other castes and the strengthening of fortifications and the storing of ammunition. He wrote to the Isle of France and the Zamorin of Calicut for aid, and warlike preparations were made by the Cochin minister Paliathu Menon.

The Resident little knew of these internal arrangements. He continued, as usual, to press the Dewan and the Maha Rajah for the payment of arrears. The Madras Government continued their demand upon the Maha Rajah for immediate payment.

The Dewan had by this time formed the resolution

CHAP. IV. of assassinating the Resident. But he still feigned that he was using all his endeavours to cause the early payment of arrears and on the Resident's demanding either the liquidation of the amount or a change in the ministry, the Dewan pretended that he was on the point of retiring, and wrote to Colonel Macauly that he would start for Calicut and take up his residence there on a pension, and asked him for a party of British troops to escort him thither, his object being to draw the best part of the Resident's escort from Cochin to Alleppey, where the Dewan was then located.

Valu Thamby issued orders to the garrison at Alleppey and Paravoor and sent a detachment from Quilon preparatory to making a sudden descent upon the fort at Cochin for the massacre of the Resident together with Cunju Krishna Menon, arranging at the same time for the attack on the British garrison at Quilon, which was stationed there under the command of Colonel Chalmers.

The detachment moved from Quilon and Alleppey in covered boats, accompanied by Vycome Padmanabha Pillay, an intimate friend of the Dewan, who acted as his chief secretary, and the troops collected in the northern districts under the command of Cunju Cuty Pillay Sarvadhikariakar, stationed at Alangaud, also moved in covered boats to Cochin and both the forces effected a junction at Calvathi, at about midnight on the 28th December. They surrounded Colonel Macauly's house and opened fire. The sudden report of musketry, at an unusual hour, surprised Colonel Macauly, and with the assistance of a confidential Portuguese clerk, he managed to conceal himself, and in the morning got on board a pattimar at first, and subsequently on board the British ship "Piedmontese" which had just reached the Cochin roads, Cunju Krishna Menon also effected his escape uninjured, and joined Colonel Macauly on board the ship.

The Travancore sepoys overpowered the few British sepoys who formed the Resident's escort, killing many who resisted, and afterwards entered Colonel Macauly's residence, ransacked the house, murdered the domestic servants and others whom they found in the house, and afterwards returned considerably chagrined at not finding the Resident and Cunju Krishna Menon.

The disappointment, consequent on this attempt to murder Colonel Macauly, had cast a great gloom and dread among all the Travancore officials. Nevertheless, they prepared themselves for a defence against the attack which they expected every moment. They committed depredations in the town of Cochin, and returned to Travancore the next day. Valu Thamby foresaw the result and quitted Alleppey at once and proceeded to Quilon.

During this interval, three European military officers, including Surgeon Hume, together with a lady in one party, and twelve European soldiers of His Majesty's 12th Regiment, and thirty-three sepoys forming another party, were proceeding from Quilon to Cochin, and on coming near Poracaud, they were taken up by the military who had been scattered over those parts in large bodies, and who now began to exhibit a declared enmity towards the Company's people. In consultation with the ministerial officials stationed at Alleppey, all these were confined, the first party in the Poracaud bankshall, and the second at Alleppey. Subsequently the matter was reported to Valu Thamby Dalawah, with an application for his sanction for the immediate execution of those unfortunate and innocent men. The hard-hearted minister, who was a perfect stranger to mercy, sanctioned the wholesale murder of the helpless party without the least hesitation, and the unfortunate and unoffending men were all cruelly murdered there.* The three officers were butchered in cold blood at the sea-beach at Poracaud, and the

* This information was given to us by one Ramalingum, Major Sobudar of M. N. I. Regiment VI, who accompanied these three unfortunate gentlemen, and the sickly lady, and was present when they were murdered. He was then a dressing boy under Colonel Chalmers.

CHAP. IV.

European soldiers and sepoys were consigned to the bottom of the Pallathurthee river, on the eastern side of Alleppey. The lady was allowed to proceed to Cochin unhurt, it being contrary to the laws of Travancore to kill women, and she was besides in bad health, and many of the local officials pitied her weak and helpless condition.

The Resident lost no time in despatching a report to the Madras Government on the subject, and the following is an abstract of the report with which we were kindly furnished, together with a copy of the proclamation, issued under date the 15th January 1809, by the Government, by Mr. Ballard, the late British Resident in Travancore :—

" For some days past, I had been engaged in nego-" tiation with the Dewan at his own earnest solicitation, " and had concluded everything to his own entire " satisfaction, and was waiting only his arrival from " Alleppey to carry into execution the measure upon " which he had resolved on removing to Calicut, and " had at his earnest request weakened the party with " me to provide for his security, and had at his sug-" gestion, placed my boats and palanquins in conve-" nient places to take him on with comfort and expe-" dition. When a little past midnight, a party of " Nayrs to the number of about one thousand, headed " by the Dewan's confidential friend Pulpnabha Pillay " and by the minister of the Rajah of Cochin, sur-" rounded my house to prevent all escape, and com-" menced a smart fire of musketry at every opening, " first disarming the guard and killing a few who " attempted resistance, and then broke into the place " to destroy me, their design was providentially and " somewhat miraculously defeated, and after having " broken open every place, and package, pillaging the " house of the whole of my effects they withdrew at " break of day, the chief inconvenience at present " attending this proceeds from the loss of books of " record and official papers, but as the Dewan has "now broken out into open rebellion, and will be likely to assemble his followers on every side in the hope of producing an impression on the subsidiary force, I have sent to Colonel Cuppage a request to embark without delay for Quilon all force that he can spare." There had been a simultaneous attack on the subsidiary force at Quilon on the morning of the 29th December 1808. The Dewan arrived at Quilon, and encouraged the Travancore force concentrated thereabouts, and then proceeded to Kundaray, east of Quilon, whence he issued the following proclamation:— CHAP. IV.

"Whereas it is highly desirable to impress in the minds of the nobles, brahmans, officers of the State, Sudras, and all other classes of the nation, a clear idea of the nature and probable results of the measure now resolved upon as necessitated by the present critical occasion in which it is inevitable that Travancore cannot maintain itself unless its utmost energies are put forth, it is hereby promulgated.

"That, never has this State been yet disturbed with any troubles nor subjected to question during the several thousand years comprising the period from the foundation of Malabar and Travancore by Parasu Ramen up to the close of Cheraman Perumal's reign, nor during the sovereignty of the succeeding Thripada Swaroopam Dynasty.

"That, the Maha Rajah who died in 933 M.E. foreseeing the evil days to come, and that his successor will not be able to keep the land, entrusted to their care safe from harm, made a gift of it, in due form (with flower and water) to Sree Padmanabha Swamy, and the country was to be governed by the succeeding Rajahs as the representatives of Padmanabha Swamy. In keeping within such a position, they preferred the practice of religious rites, austerities, to the personal enjoyment of worldly pleasure, and were always bent upon the welfare and happiness of the subjects; and in order that the virtues and benefits accruing from such observance may always continue unabated, they initiated several religious ceremonies and practices for securing divine favour, established bhadradeepam, murajapam, sathrams or feeding houses, &c. Every one knows that it is for these reasons that in the present Kaliyuga there is not a single country from the Himalayas down to Cape Comorin which can rival Travancore as a land of charity. When Mahomed Ali had subdued and established his power at Arcot, Trichinopoly and the Deccan, it was stipulated that Travancore should send him an annual Nuzzoor of (6,000) six thousand Rupees and an elephant to preserve friendly relations with him, and the country has not been interfered with by any other power. While the land was thus in peace and tranquillity, two great powers appeared. Tippoo Sultan and the English East India Company. It was believed that of the two, the English East India Company was more to be relied on, and that they would not betray their trust, and in view to secure their friendship and assistance a very long time ago, they were allowed to build a fort and to establish themselves at Anjengo, and this led to hostilities breaking out with Tippoo Sultan, but we have known to our cost how our trust was betrayed, and our friendliness taken advantage of to bring harm upon us by this very English nation, who, as is well known to the whole world is unequalled for base ingratitude and treachery. Now see, what they have done. They gradually curtailed the power of the Nabob who gave them shelter and helped so much towards attaining their present importance, till they had destroyed his dynasty entirely and taken away his territories; next they laid hold of the neighbouring countries which were enjoying peace and comfort until at last the lights of their dwellings were extinguished, and themselves plunged into misery, and following up their treacherous inclination the English came over to Travancore; first, by craft, and then forcibly, they have taken steps to exterminate us from our land. We shall briefly mention here a few of the steps pursued by them: When Tippoo Sultan made war upon us, we sought their aid against him; they treacherously got out of us, taking advantage of our exigency, ten lacs of pagodas in return for the promised help. After this, partly by craft and partly by threats, they stipulated that we should pay them an annual subsidy of six lacs of Rupees promising at the same time that so long as Travancore and the English nation existed they would not ask for a chuckrum over and above the said sum, nor interfere with any act, however unimportant of the Travancore Government, and these terms were solemnly ratified in writing by the treaty of the year 968. While Travancore had been faithfully adhering to fulfil in all integrity the terms of the treaty, the English in violation of it, sent a Resident to reside here, and stationed three of their Regiments at Quilon, and like giving milk to a serpent, this Government had to build at its own cost barracks and dwelling-houses for the men of the Regiments, and in addition to put up to this day with all the acts of violence practised by them. A little after, in Magaram 980, the English Government demanded that two lacs of Rupees should be annually paid, beyond the sum stipulated before, and threatened in failure of this extra requisition being paid, to make war upon us, and actually brought down several pieces of cannon into different parts of the country. Seeing no other means of getting over the difficult position, the Government of His Highness yielded to the impending calamitous fate and paid the extra two lacs also. But the English Government were not satisfied even with all these concessions, and the point they next assumed reached the unreasonable and unwarrantable climax, of requiring the abolition of all religious and charitable institutions, and the disbanding of the armies of the country and payment to themselves of the money that would be saved thereby; it was required further that the Resident, Colonel Macauly, should be consulted and communicated with in all

CHAP. IV.

matters connected with the Government of His Highness' territories. In reply, the English Government was respectfully informed that according to the constitution of this country these demands could not be complied with, and our humbling ourselves to the very ground was of no avail. The English Government was inexorable, as we have been always opposed to these measures, and had taken active steps against them; we got a letter in Dhannu last from the English East India Company requesting us to resign our post and to quit Travancore, along with the whole of our family and some of the officials who had joined us, and to reside in British territory, and we were promised in the event of our complying with the request that every mark of respect and honor would be paid to us. The Resident, Colonel Macauly, thereafter intending to introduce reforms, and practically administer the Government. We were at the same time informed that we should be the cause of war being declared, in case we delayed to agree to the conditions stated in the letter, the contents of which we were required to bring at once to the notice of His Highness the Maha Rajah. We did not hesitate to reply that we should not, even should our refusal cost our life, be guilty of such treason to our sovereign and country, and once for all spurn the proposals made to us. The Resident, Colonel Macauly, thereupon and without having the slightest consideration or respect for the sovereign of Travancore or giving the least intimation, brought by sea and landed a number of European soldiers to Quilon and shipped back all the European women and children that were there, with all their property, and unjustly commenced war with Travancore. It had never before been nor is it now our intention to break out into war with the English. But now that they have begun the war, if we do not adopt prompt measures in our defence or on gaining the first success, if we do not at once avail ourselves of them to follow up the victory, we would lose all advantages we had gained and the consequences would be that hardships would befall us such as not a single soul in this country would be able to bear and pass his days. We shall give a few instances of those hardships and miseries. CHAP. IV.

It is the nature of the English nation to get possession of countries by treacherous means, and should they obtain ascendancy in Travancore, they will put their own guards in the palaces, Sircar buildings, and the fort gates, destroy the royal seal, do away with honorific palanquins, and other distinguishing marks, suppress the Brahmanical communities and worship in pagodas, make monopolies of salt and every other thing, measure up and assert themselves absolute owners of waste lands, impose exorbitant taxes on paddy lands, cocoanut trees, &c., get low caste people to inflict heavy punishments for slight faults, put up crosses and Christian flags in pagodas, compel intermarriages with Brahman women without reference to caste or creed, and practice all the unjust and unlawful things which characterize Kaliyuga.

Let us therefore exert ourselves to keep off impending calamities such as those we have sketched above, and endeavour so far as lies in our power that no disparagement or discredit may be imputed to us in guarding our homes, the charitable institutions, and the manners and customs of our land. The rest, of course, we must leave to the divine will. These measures which we have enumerated are incumbent upon us to adopt to defend ourselves against the action taken by the English."

KOONDARA, 1st *Magaram* 984.

By the Dalawah's strongly worded and powerful proclamation, the whole populace of Travancore was incensed and disaffected, and a revolt against the British force stationed at Quilon took place at once. The cantonment was attacked by large bodies of militia, assisted by the Travancore regular troops, stationed about Quilon, but they were repulsed as

CHAP. IV. often as they attacked, by the able Commandant Colonel Chalmers. The failure of the attempt to murder Colonel Macauly had not totally disheartened the Sarvadhikariakar of Alangaud, as he appears to have entertained hopes of success again. About 2,000 men, consisting of regular infantry and militia and the rabble, were kept up in the vicinity of Cochin, and the town was visited by them, now and then. The Cochin minister, Paliathu Menon, had also collected a force of about 2,000 men and kept them also in the neighbourhood to attack the town. The Judges and other Company's officers closed their offices and many of the inhabitants and merchants left Cochin for Calicut, and the fear of a combined rebellion in Travancore and Cochin against the English East India Company now became general. But the arrival of Lieutenant-Colonel Cuppage on the northern frontier, and of Major Hewitt's detachment at Cochin, with whom the Travancoreans had fought and failed, discouraged the northern Travancore force entirely, and they retreated to the south, thus leaving Cochin safe and secure in the hands of the Company.

At Quilon, the action under Colonel Chalmers was decisive, for on the 18th January, the Dewan's force was completely defeated, during a contest which lasted six hours.

The Madras Government published the following proclamation in Tinnevelly and Malabar which completely quieted the population of those districts:—

"*Proclamation.*

"The Honorable the Governor in Council of Fort St. George having been informed that the Dewan of Travancore has been endeavouring by artful intrigues to excite the inhabitants of Tinnevelly to rise in arms against the British Government, the Governor in Council thinks it proper to caution the inhabitants of Tinnevelly against listening to the delusive insinuations which the Dewan of Travancore has endeavoured to disseminate. The Governor in Council has no doubt that the inhabitants of that province will be sensible of their own interests and will continue to enjoy in tranquillity the advantages which they possess under the protection of the British Government."

"Dated in Fort St. George, the 15th day of January 1809."

Published by order of the Honorable the Governor in Council.*

The Government published the following proclamation on the 17th January 1809, for the information of the people of Travancore:—

"*Proclamation.*

"It is known to the inhabitants of Travancore that during many years the closest alliance has subsisted between the British Government and the Government of the Travancore country; that the British troops have long been employed in defence of Travancore, and that it was by the exertion of the British armies, that Travancore was saved from subjection to the power of Tippoo Sultan.

Under these circumstances, the Honorable the Governor in Council of Fort St. George has heard with extreme surprise, that military preparations of great extent have lately taken place in Travancore for purposes hostile to the interests of the British Government. That the person of the British Resident has been attacked by the Travancoro troops and that an assault has been made on the subsidiary Force stationed at Quilon.

The Honorable the Governor in Council has reason to believe that these unprecedented outrages have proceeded from the desperate intrigues of the Dewan of Travancore, who has been also endeavouring by injurious insinuation to excite rebellion in the territories of the Honorable Company; in order that the

* The same to the Collector of Malabar.

CHAP. IV.

daring plans of the Dewan may be defeated, the Honorable the Governor in Council has directed a large body of troops to move into Travancore, who will, in a short time, put an end to the power of the Dewan, and to restore order and peace in the country of Travancore. The Honorable the Governor in Council thinks it proper at the same time to make known to the inhabitants of Travancore that the approach of the British troops need occasion no alarm in the minds of those inhabitants who conduct themselves peaceably. The British Government has no other view in directing the movements of troops than to rescue the Rajah of Travancore from the influence of the Dewan, to put an end to the power of that dangerous minister and to re-establish the connection of the two Governments on a secure and happy foundation.

The Honorable the Governor in Council calls on the inhabitants of Travancore to co-operate in accomplishing these objects, and such of the inhabitants as shall not oppose the advance of the British troops may be assured of the entire protection of their persons and property; particular orders will also be given to give no disturbance to the Brahmins and religious establishments throughout the Travancore country."

" Dated in Fort St. George, the 17th day of January 1809.

" Published by order of the Honorable the Governor in Council.

(Signed) C. BUCHAN,

Chief Secretary to Govt."

The Travancore minister and his colleagues, as well as the military officials, had not to wait long for their fate, for a British force, under the command of the Honorable Colonel St. Leger, arrived at the southern frontier of Travancore and commenced an attack on the Aramboly lines and forced an entrance into the forts on the 10th February 1809.

Valu Thamby Dalawah who was at the time near the Aramboly garrison to support the operations, found it impossible to resist the British soldiers, and therefore had escaped to Trevandrum hastily.

Being a patriotic minister and a faithful subject of Travancore, and conscious of his own guilt and wrong doings, he resolved honestly to take the blame upon himself and save his sovereign and the country, and requested that all the blame may be clearly and distinctly imputed to him, when the British Government would question His Highness. Valu Thamby then took final leave of his sovereign master, and leaving the palace, he stole away, through the jungles to the north.

Colonel St. Leger and his force marched towards Nagercoil, Udagherry, Padmanabhapuram taking possession of all the arms, ammunitions, &c., &c., from the magazine, as also all the pieces of ordnance found on the batteries and other places. On reaching the last mentioned place (Padmanabhapuram), the party entered the palace and took possession of all the arms stored there.

Colonel the Honorable St. Leger wrote on the 24th February to His Highness, enclosing a letter from Colonel Macauly to the Maha Rajah and calling upon His Highness to deliver up the person of the Dewan within 24 hours after the receipt of his letter.

On the 21st February, the Resident, Colonel Macauly, wrote to His Highness from Quilon, saying that if, after three days from the receipt by His Highness of his note, any opposition or interruption be made or attempted to the movements of the British troops in any quarter of Travancore, such an act of hostility will be considered as furnishing a clear and decided proof that the letter now received, though bearing the signature of His Highness, proceeds from the unworthy and injurious counsel and influence of the treacherous Dewan, with a view to procrastination and further mischief.

CHAP. IV.

The Honorable Colonel afterwards marched to Trevandrum, and on reaching the neighbourhood, encamped at a place called Pappenecode, when the Maha Rajah sent a deputation headed by His Highness' favourite Ummany Thamby *alias* Marthanden Eravy, who conveyed to the Colonel His Highness' extreme regret at the occurrence of the insurrection created by Dewan Valu Thamby, and of the adoption of measures for the Dewan's apprehension and delivery. Colonel Macauly arrived in the camp on the 3rd March. Arrangements were made for the apprehension of the minister. A party of Travancore and British officers was despatched in pursuit of the Dalawah, and a reward of (50,000) fifty thousand Rupees was offered for his apprehension.

Ummany Thamby, the head of the deputation, was appointed Dewan on the 18th March 1809 with the full concurrence of the British Government, and he at once sent persons in pursuit of the Dalawah. The runaway Dalawah wandered in the jungles about Vallicote in the Kunnathoor district. He was hotly pursued by the officers even here. From this place he came to Munnady, in the same district, and took refuge in a vacant house belonging to a potty. The servant of Valu Thamby who wandered in the streets there with his master's silver and gold utensils, was seen by the officers and apprehended, and he revealed to them the Thamby's hiding place. He then fled to the Bhagavathi pagoda at Munnady, with his brother Padmanabhen Thamby and determined to put an end to his existence. He asked his brother to stab him. This the brother refused to do at first, when the Dalawah plunged his own dagger in his bosom. But as the self-inflicted wound did not prove mortal, he cried out to his brother 'cut my neck,' which request, the brother complied with, and in one stroke severed the neck from the body. By that time, the pursuers reached the pagoda and forced open the door when they found the lifeless body of Valu Thamby and his brother standing close to it with a drawn

UMMINY THAMBY DEWAN.

PUBLISHED BY MESS.RS HIGGINBOTHAM & CO.

sword. The brother was seized and the body removed to Trevandrum, where it was exposed on a gibbet at Kunnammalay for public execration. Lord Minto, the then Governor-General, most strongly condemned this insult offered to the body of such a great man as Valu Thamby.

The deceased Dalawah's brother Padmanabhen Thamby was hanged on the 10th of April, in the presence of the 12th Regiment at Quilon, on the supposition that he took part in the assassination of Surgeon Hume, and also in the most cruel and inhuman act of the drowning at Pullathurthee of a detachment of the 12th Regiment.

Ummany Thamby Dewan was dreaded by the relatives of the late minister, and his house was razed to the ground and plantain and castor trees planted thereon.

Most of the relatives were transported to the Maldives, but after going a certain distance, stress of weather compelled them to touch at Tuticorin. Some appear to have committed suicide, some died in prison, while the rest were flogged and banished. All these were done by Valu Thamby's successor Ummany Thamby.

Several of the promoters of the insurrection, chief among whom was Vycome Padmanabha Pillay, the murderer of the Europeans at Poracaud, Alleppey, &c., were punished by being publicly hanged at Quilon, Poracaud and Pallathurthee, the spots where the Europeans were massacred.

A short narration of the British army's operations during this insurrection will be found in the following lines from Colonel Welsh's "Military Reminiscences, Vol. 1." This officer was one of the commandants of the force which entered through the Aramboly lines :—

"On the 19th of January, I set out from Madras and reached the Honorable Colonel St. Leger's camp near the Aramboly lines of Travancore on the 5th

CHAP. IV. February, being a distance of 420 miles. The force was composed as follows :—

His Majesty's 69th Regiment under Lieutenant Colonel W. M'Leod.

Five companies of the 1st Battalion of the 3rd Regiment under Captain Pepper.

2nd Battalion of the 3rd Regiment, 1st Battalion of the 13th Regiment, Major Lang.

Five companies of the 2nd Battalion of the 13th Regiment, Lieutenant Stewart.

6th Regiment of Native Cavalry, Major Nuthall.

Artillery and field pieces, Captain Frank.

And 400 Pioneers, Captain Smithwart."

* * * *

" Having no battering guns with the force, and the nearest depôt being Trichinopoly, 200 miles off, it appeared desirable to take these lines by a coup-de-main which I proposed to Colonel St. Leger on the 8th of February, and on the 9th having satisfied himself that it was feasible, he consented, though not without much reluctance and considerable reservation. On the morning of the 10th we succeeded, and having escaladed the southern fortified hill, during the night, though defended by 50 pieces of cannon and 10,000 men, the whole lines were in our possession by 8 o'clock A. M. Our loss on the occasion was small beyond calculation, Captain Cunningham of the 69th Regiment killed, one sepoy killed, one surgeon and three privates wounded, and one subadar and six sepoys wounded. Thus we obtained possession of all the enemy's guns, and immense quantities of arms and stores. The army encamped inside the walls that day, and the Pioneers, &c., were employed in destroying the works on both sides the gate which was, however, left entire as a post to secure our communications."

* * * *

" On the 17th of February, the army marched for the interior. The advance commanded by Lieutenant

Colonel M'Leod, consisting of the flanking companies of the 69th Regiment, 350 caffries under Colonel Mornus, and six native flank companies and the Cavalry under Major Nuthall with six guns worked by the Royal Artillery. This party moved off from the right of the line at 3 o'clock A. M., the line following at half past four, and thus leaving a distance of three miles between them. Having got on six miles by day break, they found the enemy strongly posted in a village across a river with high banks, commanding the approach, and several cannon pointed down the high road. Their force was supposed to amount to six hundred men, and they had every advantage in point of position that men could desire. Colonel M'Leod immediately formed his line for the attack, and drove the enemy from their guns after a very heavy fire of both cannon and musketry, which unfortunately did considerable execution from the exposed situation of our troops in advancing. The enemy were completely routed, and dispersed in all directions for some miles; the country was said to be too difficult for the Cavalry to follow them, which doubtless saved many, if not the whole, from total destruction. Lieutenant Charles Johnstone, however, with a small party of our horse contrived to get in amongst them, and did some execution. Nine capital guns and several dead bodies were the fruits of this victory in addition to which we gained possession of two very fine villages, called Kotaur and Nagercoil. Our loss was Captain Lemo of the caffries, and Lieutenant Swayne of the 13th Native Infantry wounded, and forty-nine rank and file killed and wounded. After this brilliant affair, which did infinite credit to Colonel M'Leod and the brave fellows under his command, the army encamped, four miles beyond the village of Nagercoil.

Although, generally speaking, the enemy had proved far below our expectation, yet there were some exceptions on the 10th. A native officer in the lines, after being fired at by a soldier of the 69th cut him down

CHAP. IV. and was killed by another soldier, a few others also stood on both sides and refusing to surrender, were put to death on the spot. These instances deserve to be recorded because they were rare; for taking them all in all, I never beheld so dastardly a crew, nor did they deserve the name of soldiers although neatly clothed in military uniforms, furnished with capital arms, and in a country every inch of which might have been defended."

* * * *

"On the 19th of February, I had the honor to lead the advance, consisting of the picquets and some flank companies with two six-pounders expecting hard work, though the line was not very distant in our rear. After proceeding three or four miles, we met some peaceable villagers, who informed us that the two forts of Oodagherry and Pulpanavarum in our front, had been abandoned by the enemy, which was the first time we had heard of such fortifications, though we had been expecting to find some field-works to be taken. The news soon spread and ere we had advanced much further we could distinguish white flags flying on trees and sticks, when the whole head quarters gentlemen passed us preceded by some troops to explore the way. Shortly afterwards the road led us, on a sudden within musket-shot of a stone bastion, and curtain, mounting several cannon pointed on the road, and we found this to be part of the fort of Oodagherry, with white flags flying and not a soul within. I was directed to take possession of both forts with my own corps; and Pulpanavarum being the largest, a mile further on, I left two companies in Oodagherry and proceeding thither, disposed of the corps in an open space in the centre, posting Hindu guards in all the pagodas, and the officers taking possession of a large and very well built palace belonging to the Rajah. Here we found many valuable swords, dirks, pistols, guns, spears, rich muslins, kincobs, &c., as well as thousands of jewel-boxes broken open and pillaged by the flying enemy, to give us some idea of what we had lost. Several of the swords proved to be gold hilted and the blades were of the first water. Of course, all we could lay hands on were secured as prize property, and afterwards sold by public outcry."

"Whilst we thus were advancing from the southward, the subsidiary force at Quilon was by no means idle. Shut up in the heart of a strong country with the inhabitants all in arms against them, they had several severe actions, but invariably came off conquerors. Nevertheless, their situation was daily becoming more critical, until the news of our entering the lines reached the masses by which they were surrounded; when giving up every hopes of further success, they dispersed and fled in all directions, for these lines, ill as they were, calculated to resist an English force, had been hitherto deemed impregnable, and Tippu, in the zenith of his power, had been repulsed from there with great loss."

"Remaining at Pulpanavarum to collect prize property, we succeeded at last in breaking open the treasury and found all the cash chests open with one solitary rupee on the floor, and two small jewels evidently left on purpose for our annoyance. We had already captured sixteen elephants, and about 50,000 stand of arms, with some hundred guns; but the greatest curiosities were a gun and mortar both of exquisite workmanship, mounted on the parade in Oodagherry, and cast in this place by some European artist. They were made of brass, the gun sixteen feet long and bored as a twenty-two pounder, was so extremely massive that 1,200 men assisted by sixteen elephants could not move it, even for a few yards, when we had an intention of selling it to Captain Foote of His Majesty's ship "Piedmontaise," who offered us two thousand pounds sterling for it. The mortar was equally heavy, and I think had an eighteen-inch bore. They have since been removed, for I lately found only the old gun carriage in that place."

* * * *

CHAP. IV.

"While we were in this neighbourhood, Colonel St. Leger received a letter from the Rama Rajah, by a hurrikara which he answered by the bearer, accompanied by four troopers, intimating that the first proofs of the Rajah's sincerity would be his allowing two of the troopers to pass on to Colonel Chalmer's camp at Quilon, and returning unmolested with an answer. This was actually permitted, and the Rajah received them very graciously at Trevandrum, his capital, and gave them a shawl and sixty rupees each. They came back to our camp with letters from the Rajah, Colonel Macauly the Resident and Colonel Chalmers, in consequence of which an armistice was proclaimed in our force on the 26th February."

* * * *

"Trevandrum the capital of Travancore and residence of the Rajah is a large irregular town without much internal show of riches. There are some good houses in it, and the country around is picturesque and beautiful. The Rajah's palace is situated near the centre, and surrounded by a miserable attempt at fortification, but the interior is roomy and contains not only the palace, but many public buildings belonging to the Prince, such as an armoury, stabling for a large stud, a menagerie, full of wild beasts, temples of worship, barracks, &c. His Highness being somewhat in the back ground, we did not visit him, but after we had been two days there, and his entire innocence of any participation with his rebellious minister and subjects proclaimed, he delivered a man of some consequence into our hands as a hostage for the prime minister. His troops and subjects were quietly disarmed, and parties were detached in pursuit of the rebel Dewan, the Dalawah and general of his cavalry."

* * *

"March the 15th, the new Dewan paid a formal visit to our camp, where he was received with military honors, and a salute of fifteen guns and publicly proclaimed the accredited minister. All the native officers of His Highness' late Carnatic brigade being brought into the camp prisoners, and disgraced by the drummers of the line, who cut their jackets off their backs, and then turned them out with the "rogues march." A few days afterwards, it was discovered that the quiet Rama Rajah had got an arsenal within his palace walls containing one hundred and forty pieces of serviceable cannon, fourteen thousand stand of muskets and bayonets, and ammunition of every description in the greatest abundance, all of which he was obliged to deliver up, and our force returned by corps to Oodagherry to be cantoned there the last arriving on the 8th of April."

Though the new Dewan Ummany Thamby was blessed with considerable ability and intelligence, and had a general knowledge of the affairs of the country, yet he was too ambitious for power, and wished to acquire a reputation superior to that of his predecessor. With this view, he commenced altogether a new mode of administration, and being a favourite of the Maha Rajah was allowed to proceed on unhindered in accordance with his own views and taste.

Among the various measures adopted by this minister, there were also several useful ones such as the establishment of tannah's (district jails) throughout the country; the restricting the right of the Nanjenaud people, to assemble in large bodies to remonstrate against measures introduced by the Sircar; the establishment of a system of Kavels or watchmen in Nanjenaud, the clearing of tracts of land covered with bushes and weeds and lying between Neyattinkaray and Trevandrum; the building of bazaars and Brahman villages, royal residencies, and store-houses at that place, and thither the Dewan invited a number of weavers, and established several looms and called the place by the name of Balaramapuram, in honour of the reigning Maha Rajah. His object was to open a port at Velingium and make it a great commercial town.

"Balaramapuram three and a half miles W. N. W. of

CHAP. IV.

Neyattinkaray, is comparatively of recent date, having been founded by the Dewan Ummany Thamby about the year 1808. It was his intention to have made it a principal commercial town and to cut a navigable canal to communicate with the sea at Velingium, the ground offering every facility for such an undertaking." The building of this town was commenced on a grand scale, artificers of every description and also merchants were invited to settle there, but ere it could be completed according to the original plan, the progress of the works was arrested by the reverse of fortune, that befel Ummany Thamby. Since that period it has remained in its unfinished state, and is chiefly occupied by oilmongers and weavers. It has a tolerable bazaar extending down the central street." *Memoir of Travancore*, p. 13.

However, during a career of above two years, Ummany Thamby Dewan was not able to keep his subordinates in check, in consequence of which abuses of authority and irregularities in every branch of the administration became the order of the day. The subsidy to the Honorable East India Company again fell in arrears; the salaries of the various establishments became due, and the administration itself was soon in a disorganized state.

This minister was as arrogant as he was ambitious, and taking advantage of the weakness of the Rajah and His Highness' very yielding disposition, took to himself the sole authority and power of Government, and made the Rajah a nonentity! The Rajah was really apprehensive of the minister, who His Highness thought, would usurp his kingdom should he happen to displease him.

This minister, was allowed to go on according to his own inclination and pleasure, and hence the affairs of the country became more and more disorganised.

Colonel Macauly remonstrated often against this state of affairs, and pointed out the necessity of his taking active measures to correct the prevailing evils;

but the minister made use of the Maha Rajah's name in bringing forward all sorts of excuses for the non-payment of the kist, and matters went so far, as to induce the Honorable East India Company to give a formal warning to the Rajah of the necessity of enforcing the conditions of the treaty. Still, His Highness does not appear to have rightly understood the import of such a serious intimation, but turned his attention towards the performance of the sexennial ceremony Murajapam, which was closely approaching.

Colonel Macauly reported to Government that the Dewan expressed himself alarmed at the spirit of intrigue and hostility which had begun to display itself in the palace at Trevandrum and that His Highness had assumed a line of conduct dangerous to the public tranquillity. The Resident added that the Maha Rajah had become refractory and that he was instigated by the vicious Elia Rajah.

When the Maha Rajah knew of these proceedings of the Dewan, he disowned him, and insisted on his dismissal. But the Resident sided with the Dewan, observing that the Dewan's conduct was praiseworthy and that he was acting up to the treaty. One cause of the difference between the sovereign and his minister was the latter's desire to do away with the expensive Murajapam ceremony as by the saving thus effected he would be able to pay off a part of the subsidy. The minister's view on the subject was strongly supported by the Resident, but it irritated the Maha Rajah the more. When the Resident saw that there would not be the least advantage in resisting His Highness' reasonable wish to observe a time-honored ceremony, he yielded and allowed it to be performed as usual. Colonel Macauly thought it proper to order a battalion and two field pieces to be cantoned at Trevandrum during the Murajapam, and these were subsequently permanently stationed at the capital at the suggestion of the Dewan and the Resident.

The staunch friend and warm supporter of Dewan

CHAP. IV. Valu Thamby in the palace was the young Rajah of Mavalikaray, who being a near relative of the adopted Princesses, took his residence from his boyhood in the palace, all the male members of the Travancore royal family having become extinct with the exception of the Maha Rajah. This young Prince was looked upon by the people as the Elia Rajah. The Maha Rajah too considered him in such a light. The young Rajah styling himself Elia Rajah of Travancore now became the chief intriguer at the palace; the Maha Rajah listened to his counsel and advice, and the Dewan therefore suggested that the Rajah's deportation either to his native place of Mavalikaray or to Alleppey, but the Maha Rajah strongly opposed this step.

Dewan Ummany Thamby's life was threatened, and he complained to the Madras Government.

The Government of India considered that the Dewan was entitled to their protection and gave the Maha Rajah to understand that the Dewan's assassination would be an act of hostility against themselves. The Dewan had been unceasing in his complaint against the young Rajah and also against the Durbar. The Governor-General resolved that the Resident should stay at Trevandrum, to control the hostility of the Durbar, and subsequently, the Resident was instructed to institute an inquiry into the claims of the young Rajah to style himself Elia Rajah or heir apparent of Travancore. During the inquiry, the young Rajah's claim was invalidated by the statements of the Ranee, State officers, &c.

Nevertheless the Maha Rajah insisted upon the young Rajah's continuance in the court.

Colonel Macauly retired from the office of Resident in 985 M.E. (1810 A.D.), and Colonel Munro was appointed to the vacant post in the same year. This officer did his best to mend matters, and to bring the Dewan to a sense of his duty, but without the desired effect.

COLONEL MUNRO.

While things were maturing for the direct interference of the Resident, His Highness the Maha Rajah died at 12 o'clock on the night of the 26th Thulam 986 (7th November 1810) in the twelfth year of his reign, and the twenty-ninth year of his age. This event fortunately prevented the adoption of any active and disagreeable measures by the British Government. CHAP. IV.

The recollection of this reign and of the despotic administration of Valu Thamby Dalawah are most deplorable. The horrible and wholesale executions, murders, and assassinations of the chief ministerial and military officers of the State, who had been judiciously selected and whose services were highly appreciated during the former reign were among the memorable events of this reign.

A full review of the above facts are recorded by the Honorable Court of Directors of the East India Company in a general letter, dated 29th September 1809, addressed to the Madras Government.

" *Extract from a general letter from the Honorable " Court of Directors to the Government of Fort St. " George, dated 29th September* 1809, *given by Lieute- " nant-Colonel Newall, Resident in Travancore, to " Comaran Thamby* alias *Thamby Chembaga Ramen " Coomaran, a nephew of the late Rajah Kashava Dass.*

" The old Rajah was succeeded by his nephew, a " young man, whose character seems ever since to " have been marked by imbecility, caprice, and other " qualities which show him to be wholly unequal to " the task of Government. The old and faithful " Dewan of his uncle was supplanted by low and " vicious persons, who soon gained an ascendancy " over the Rajah and influenced the conduct of affairs.

" In 1799 an insurrection broke out in the district. " In 1800 a cabal headed by a person named the " Sumprathy, seized the reins of Government, gross " abuses prevailed in many of the public departments;

CHAP. IV. "the revenues were decreasing, whilst the bulk of the "people were in the lowest state of depression; and "another insurrection took place on account of "oppression in some branches of the collections. "The time of the Rajah is described to have been "chiefly engrossed by his pleasures, and by super-"stitious ceremonies among the Brahmans, who, with "their dependants, were reckoned to be equal in "number to the working class. The late Dewan, so "much respected by the people, was not suffered to "live even in retirement. There is very strong reason "to believe that he was taken off by poison, and the "British Resident thought it his duty publicly to "accuse Sumprathy of this foul murder, but after a "short arrest and an appearance of inquiry, in which "more solicitude was shown to avoid than to effect "discovery he was restored to his liberty and influence "at the Durbar. This man is stated to have charged "the late Dewan with ruining the interest of Travan-"core by connexion with Europeans, particularly the "English, and from all the details contained in the "ample correspondence carried on by the British "Resident at that time, it is strongly to be inferred "that neither the Rajah nor those employed in the "transaction of his affairs, regarded British connexion "with the ancient cordiality.

"In 1801, the Rajah, after repeated representations "from the Resident of the disordered state of the "country and the necessity of rescuing the manage-"ment of affairs from those whom he had permitted "to possess themselves of it, appointed a new Dewan "named Valu Thamby. This person had been at the "head of the insurrection of 1799; but being reputed "a man of ability and firmness, the Resident, in the "great want of persons of that description, approved "of his appointment, and had reason to expect that "he would be friendly to the connexion with the "British Government. His subsequent conduct how-"ever did not justify this expectation. The Resident, "after some absence from his station, on returning to

" it in December 1801, found that all the relations of " the old and respectable Dewan, who himself had " suffered a violent death, had also been murdered, and " that Sumprathy, the former favourite, had been " disgraced and imprisoned by means of the new " Dewan Valu Thamby.

" But those hopes were of short duration; by the " month of November the payment of arrears amounted " only to Rupees 60,000 and the balance due was eight " lacs. Instead of a further liquidation of debt, that " month produces only succession of informations from " the Resident, evincing with increasing clearness the " certainty of what the officer at first calls " something " like a systematic plan of contumacious resistance on " the part of the Dewan," which he says rendered it " necessary to apprize the Rajah, that with a view to " the proper regulation of the affairs of Travancore, " another person should be chosen for the office of " Dewan in the room of Valu Thamby. This is the " man who first comes into notice as the leader of an " insurrection in 1799, who, with the assistance of the " British influence was advanced to be prime minister " in 1801, whose early administration is clouded with " suspicion arising from the atrocious murder of the " family of the deceased respectable Dewan; who, in " 1805, vowed unalterable attachment to British inter- " ests, and only two months before professed sincere " contrition for his failure in this respect. He now " begins to appear as the sole ruler of the Travancore " State. The Rajah, though his disposition was deemed " to be favourable, to the British Government, is stated " to have been incapable of following the course of his " own wishes; he henceforth ceases to be seen in " public transactions, and the Dewan exercises in his " own person all the powers of Government. We " hear of a faction formed under his protection, of an " augmentation of Travancore sepoys, the manufac- " tures of bows and arrows, his training the inha- " bitants to arms, his success in exciting a ferment, " his sending to the Isle of France for 500 artillery men,

CHAP. IV.

"and expectation of assistance from thence, his rooted "purpose of determined hostility, his being capable of "instigating his partisans to an attack, and the expe- "diency of placing him as the prime mover and "instigator of hostility under arrest. Early in Decem- "ber you were told by the Resident that the Dewan "still continued with unremitting activity his plans "of hostile preparations and that in conjunction with "the Rajah of Cochin's minister, a person who appears "to have been a suitable confederate to him, and "made a conspicuous figure in the subsequent trans- "actions, he was endeavouring to force that Prince "into measures of hostility against the British Gov- "ernment, urging him to unite with other chieftains "friendly to Travancore for the expulsion of the "English, requiring him with that view to train par- "ticular classes of his subjects in the same manner as "had been ordered in Travancore. You were at the "same time informed by the officer commanding in "Malabar that a report prevailed there of an intended "attack on the British subsidiary force, and that an "army of 22,000 Travancoreans was assembled at no "great distance from it."

The financial condition of Travancore was very satisfactory when this Maha Rajah assumed the sovereignty, and therefore His Highness did not experience much difficulty in having the coronation ceremonies performed. Both the ceremonies called Thulapurusha danum and Padmagarbha danum were performed in due course, and the Maha Rajah was crowned, and became Kulasekhara Perumal.

During a reign of twelve years and eight months it does not appear that this Maha Rajah passed any enactments, either for the improvement of the administration, or for the amelioration of the condition of the inhabitants, as was done by His Highness' predecessor.

PUBLISHED BY MESS.RS HIGGINBOTHAM & CO. C. FAGLENBRY LITH MADRAS

HER HIGHNESS LEKSHIMI BHYE.

CHAPTER V.

SREE PADMANABHA SAVINEE VANJI DHARMA WARDHINEE RAJAH RAJAISWARI RANEE GOUREE LEKSHMI BHYE.

THE direct and legitimate heir to the vacant musnud was this young Ranee of twenty years of age. Her right was disputed by a collateral uncle, who brought forward his claims, which, on an impartial and just investigation by Colonel Munro, were set aside as invalid, and the young Princess was at once crowned under the auspices of the Madras Government and the Honorable Court of Directors of the East India Company. CHAP. V.

Colonel Munro, observing symptoms of disaffection in the pretended claimant and his partisans, sent the Rajah as a State-prisoner first to Tellicherry and afterwards to Chingleput, where he remained till the latter part of his days.

Her Highness Lekshmi Bhye commenced her reign in a manner quite different from that of her predecessor, and which could scarcely have been expected from a person of her age and sex.

Though young, Her Highness was possessed of a cultivated mind, was gifted with a sound judgment, had sagacity to discern what was good for her kingdom, and to adopt such measures as were calculated for its improvement.

She possessed an additional advantage in being wedded to one Rajah Rajah Vurmah, Koil Thampuran of Chunganacherry (the grand-uncle of the present Valia Koil Thampuran), who was an accomplished Sanscrit scholar and well versed in the institutes of

CHAP. V. Manu, as well as in all the Puranas. Thampuran who was only one year older than his royal consort, was the best counsellor of Her Highness in all matters, both domestic as well as public.

Her Highness' good qualities are too numerous to be described here, and the writer thinks that he would not be able to do justice in the narration, were he to undertake such a task; for, his inquiries lead him to the conclusion that a full volume might be written regarding the life and career of this accomplished Ranee, though her reign lasted only for a short period.

The principal quality in Her Highness was her firmness of mind and capability of resisting all idle counsellors and keeping herself free from flatterers and sycophants.

Her Highness, young as she was, had observed the weak points of her deceased uncle's character, the self-interested proceedings of Dewan Ummany Thamby, the disorganized state of the Government resulting from the mismanagement of affairs, and therefore Her Highness was most anxious to correct these evils, by which alone she knew the credit of her Government could be regained and the welfare of her subjects promoted. With this view, Her Highness resolved to entrust the Government of her kingdom into the hands of Colonel Munro, the Resident of Travancore.

The first step Her Highness took after her installation, was to dispense with the services of Dewan Ummany Thamby. Her Highness, after dismissing the Dewan, requested Colonel Munro to assume charge of the administration, and conduct the duties of the Dewan, along with those of Resident.

Colonel Munro, equally desirous for the restoration of order in, and the improvement of the country, and anxious to assist such a good Ranee in her praiseworthy desire, accepted the offer without any hesitation.

Thus, this wise Princess managed to place her king-

RAJAH-RAJAH VURMAH KOIL THUMPURAN.

PUBLISHED BY MESS.RS HIGGINBOTHAM & CO.   C. PALLENBERG LITH. MADRAS.

dom which was verging on ruin and was nearly falling into the hands of the Honorable East India Company, in a position of stability, and she thus relieved herself, not only from the cumbersome burden of Government, but also from a world of personal inconvenience.

Colonel Munro in his joint office of Resident and Dewan had no ordinary task before him, for he had to surmount difficulties which we can scarcely imagine now, considering the present state of the country.

The first object of Colonel Munro in accepting the office of the premier was, to establish order and regularity in the administration, and to reorganize the confused state of affairs which the mismanagement of the late Dewan Ummany Thamby had caused. It was the want of proper control over the subordinates, which had upset and destroyed the regular system of administration introduced by the most distinguished and renowned sovereigns of former times, and subsequently maintained, though somewhat cruelly and arbitrarily, by the able Dalawah Valu Thamby.

The first step Colonel Munro adopted, like Valu Thamby Dalawah, was to correct abuses and weed out corruption from the service, and to this end he worked most successfully. It would be too numerous to detail here the particulars of all the measures taken by him to carry out his project of reformation.

The foremost measure adopted by the Resident was to introduce corporal punishment in every instance of corruption and other immoral conduct on the part of Sircar servants.

Every case of irregularity the Colonel investigated before him, and after ascertaining the facts *pro* and *con* passed his decision.

A set of drummers from the Resident's escort was always ready before Colonel Munro for the correct execution of the award of corporal punishment, and the cat-o'-nine tails was largely employed for the infliction of such punishments.

CHAP. V.

Colonel Munro, moved on circuit from Thovalay to Paravoor accompanied by his own establishment and had order, regularity, discipline, and strict obedience ensured in the course of a year.

During this praiseworthy and memorable circuit of Colonel Munro, many a Sircar servant had lessons in morality imprinted on his back with the cat-o'-nine tails.

Colonel Munro's award of punishment was something like that of a school master; for none of the chastised servants was dismissed from the service. Soon after the administration of punishment, the incumbents were invariably ordered to continue in their respective posts and discharge their duties satisfactorily. Many of Colonel Munro's scholars had indeed their backs scored; but rose subsequently to very conspicuous and prominent positions in the service.

During the interval, the ex-Dewan Ummany Thamby incurred lasting disgrace by plotting certain measures against the life of the Colonel. The treachery having been discovered, Ummany Thamby was banished the country and was taken to Chingleput and detained there as a State-prisoner.

After re-modelling the service, Colonel Munro directed his attention to the introduction of a thorough reform in the general administration, and in consultation with the able and experienced people of the country, both conservatives and liberals, and in accordance with the rules established under the old sovereigns, new rules were framed for the guidance of revenue, criminal and civil officers, founded partly on the Dharma Sastram, (Institutes of Manu) and partly on the regulations then in force under the Honorable East India Company's Government.

These rules were called in the whole style Satta Wariolas, and they were promulgated under the sanction of Her Highness under date the 30th Chingom 987 M.E. (1812 A.D.)

Regular Courts of Appeal and zillah were constituted and established and the jurisdiction and power of judges were determined. CHAP. V.

A Huzzoor Court for the trial and punishment of all the Sircar servants was also established. The names of the district officials were changed and the head of every district was styled a Thasildar, instead of a kariakar, and he was made exclusively a revenue officer, the criminal functions being entrusted to the hands of the several tannah Naiks, who were bound to take up every police case and hand it over to the Zillah Courts.

The next measure was to organize the financial affairs of the kingdom, the expenditure of the State having been found to exceed considerably the receipts of the revenue, and Colonel Munro adopted efficient methods to maintain an equilibrium between the two.

All the establishments were modified and re-organised, a distinct and clear scale of pension for the chiefs and other dependants of the State was introduced, and a new scale of expenditure for the palace establishment was framed, and various other measures adopted.

On Colonel Munro's assuming charge of the administration, the State debt amounted to nearly one whole year's revenue of the State of Travancore, of which, the most part was due to the Honorable East India Company as arrears of subsidy, and the rest to merchants of Tinnevelly, Kottar, Cochin, Bombay and other places, and Colonel Munro appears to have been able to clear off this heavy burden of the State during the time of his administration. In every measure adopted, he received cordial co-operation from Her Highness the Ranee, the particulars of which will be shown in due course.

Valu Thamby, observing the various Devaswams in Travancore, the large estate each possessed, and the remarkable influence of the Devaswams over the people,

CHAP. V. contemplated the assumption of the whole and the annexation of the estates to the Sircar, hoping by these means to neutralize, if not totally destroy the influence of the Devaswams over the people, and thus check any future commotions that might arise; but before this plan could be matured, the Dalawah had the misfortune to be in trouble, and ultimately to lose his life.

On Colonel Munro being informed of this idea of the Dalawah, he thought it important enough to be worthy of adoption, and consultation with the principal officers of the State, and he framed rules in furtherance of the measure, so that thereby the future management of Devaswam affairs was to a very great extent vested in the Sircar, and with the sanction of Her Highness the Ranee, rules were drawn up. This measure was also the means of causing a permanent additional revenue to the State, for, after meeting the expenses of the various Devaswams, it left a good margin in favor of the Sircar.

A couple of intelligent Mahratta Brahmans accompanied Colonel Munro on his first coming to Travancore, of whom one was a talented Mahratta scholar, with a tolerable knowledge of the English language. His name was Reddy Row *alias* Vencatta Row. He had been very useful to Colonel Munro in the carrying out of his views and measures. Reddy Row being a clever Mahratta accountant, he was ordered by Colonel Munro to organize a regular Mahratta account department in Travancore, and to have also all the accounts translated and arranged.

After Reddy Row had finished the above work, he was appointed to superintend certain departments in the Huzzoor cutcherry, which duty having been satisfactorily discharged, he received further promotion and eagerly hoped to be advanced still higher in the service.

Colonel Munro selected mostly natives, both Numboory Brahmans, Sudras and Syrian Christians, who were well educated in their own language and also in Sanscrit, and who were possessed of a thorough knowledge of the Institutes of Manu, for the office of judges, &c., and he used to consult with them invariably in all important affairs. Of these, one Daven Padmanabhen of Trevandrum, and one Ramen Menon, a native of Cochin Sircar territories, were particularly attached to him and they were both appointed judges. CHAP. V.

During Colonel Munro's administration, he effected the abolishment of several items of oppressive imposts such as poll-tax, tax on nets, and other *moothraphas*, and also conceded a remission of all the arrears of fines, taxes, and other demands of the Sircar which accumulated to a considerable amount during former years.

Manufacture of country-salt was carried on in an improved system and foreign salt was also purchased. Salt-stores and bankshalls were constructed on better principles, and the collection of customs duty regulated by the establishment of additional chowkeys or custom-houses throughout the country.

The residencies at Quilon and Trevandrum were constructed during Colonel Munro's administration.

After the disturbance in 985 M.E. (1810 A.D.), under Valu Thamby Dalawah, the Travancore army had become almost extinct, and Colonel Munro organized two Nair battalions and one company of cavalry as body guard and escort to royalty, and European officers were appointed to the command of them.

While the Travancore State was brought again to a flourishing condition by this most able and distinguished administrator, the happiness of the people and the prosperity of the kingdom were crowned by the birth of a Prince in 988 M.E. (1813 A.D.). This was the first son of Her Highness the Ranee Lekshmi Bhye, the reigning Princess.

In the same year, Mr. Blacker, brother-in-law of Colonel Munro, arrived having been appointed Assist-

CHAP. V. ant Resident, and was nominated by the Colonel to look after the financial affairs of the Cochin State.

In accordance with usage and Hindu law, the little Prince was proclaimed Maha Rajah of Travancore, and Her Highness, the Queen-mother, continued to hold the sceptre as regent on behalf of the infant Maha Rajah.

Her Highness' Government, assisted by Colonel Munro's able administration, continued to distinguish itself most admirably both to the highest satisfaction of the people as well as of the Government of the Honorable East India Company.

Colonel Munro selected a successor to himself in the person of the above-mentioned Daven Padmanabhen, the then judge of the Huzzoor court, and Her Highness the Ranee appointed him as Dewan in 989 M.E. (1814 A.D.), and thus afforded relief to Colonel Munro who had acted as Dewan for a period of about four years.

This Dewan conducted the administration entirely under the sole advice of Colonel Munro, and distinguished himself in the honest discharge of his duties, but unfortunately, he died of small-pox, five months after his appointment.

Her Highness gave birth to another Prince in the year 990 M.E. (1815 A D.), but two months after this event, Travancore had the misfortune to be deprived of the rule of such an accomplished Princess, by Her Highness' premature death after a few days illness.

The people were plunged in great sorrow at the sudden and unexpected death of the Ranee. They felt her loss the more keenly as Her Highness' reign had been for so short a period as four years, and as Her Highness was as, if not more popular than her grand-uncle, Rama Rajah, who died in 973 M.E. (1798 A.D.)

In the course of four years this Princess had done much more good to the people than several of Her

Highness' predecessors had achieved during a much longer period, not in the quantity, but in the quality, of Her Highness' work. Almost in each of the four years during her reign, Her Highness had passed some very necessary enactments for the welfare of the country and of its people, whose interest Her Highness had paid better attention to than her own. Various items of objectionable income, introduced and maintained during former reigns, had been abolished and the revenue willingly sacrificed, under the valuable advice of Colonel Munro as has been stated above. CHAP. V.

All the enactments were promulgated in the form of royal proclamations, and Her Highness also authorized Colonel Munro to issue such acts under his own hand and seal. Numerous enactments of the kind are still in force for the conduct of revenue affairs, for the regulation of which there are scarcely any other or better provisions. Many of these rules had emanated doubtless from Colonel Munro himself, but the ready sanction of Her Highness to all proposals of the Colonel must reflect great credit on the wisdom of the Princess. There were, however, several important measures which originated from Her Highness directly, and were highly applauded by Colonel Munro.

Of the numerous enactments passed during this reign that for the abolition of the slave trade was one of the most important. This was promulgated by a royal proclamation under date the 21st Vrischigom 987 M.E. (5th December 1812 A.D.) As was the case in Britain, traffic in human flesh and blood, was carried on in Travancore as well as throughout the whole of India, and though the practise had been a good deal restricted during the time of many of the wise sovereigns of Travancore, this objectionable trade had never been entirely prohibited by any royal edict till the period of this happy reign, and the consequence was that during the time of dearth or famine, people of all castes, except the Brahmans, were publicly sold to those who wanted them. Scarcely a

CHAP. V. year after the installation of this Princess, and even before Colonel Munro had assumed charge of the administration, Her Highness had the benevolence and humanity to introduce this desirable prohibition.

The Satta Wariola which established the courts for the first time in Travancore and to which we have already made reference, was an Act containing 34 sections. It ran as follows :—

"Whereas the vital part of Government in all countries is the administration of justice which has not been properly regulated in Travancore, owing to the difficulty which the public experiences in approaching the presence of the Maha Rajah and the Resident for obtaining redress for their grievances, the various kariakars already overburdened with business, being unable to dispose of the several matters that go before them; and whereas it has been found expedient to provide a method by which justice could be administered according to the Dharma Sastra and the customs of the country, the following enactment is introduced with the sanction of Her Highness the Maha Ranee:

1. One superior court and five courts subordinate thereto shall be established in Travancore for the enquiry and adjudication of all suits appertaining to land and monetary transactions as also for the trial of criminal cases.

2. The superior court shall consist of the Dewan and three judges, two of whom shall be Brahmans and one a Nair.

3. Each of the lower courts shall contain three judges, two of them being Brahmans and the third a Nair.

4. There shall be under each court one Darogah and a certain number of tannahs and peons.

5. The establishment of the lower court shall be within the limits of each of the courts; viz.: a court

shall be established at Padmanabhapuram having jurisdiction over Thovalay and Agusteeswaram; a second, at Trevandrum to try the cases of Trevandrum north and south; a third, at Mavalikaray to try the cases of Mavalikaray and Ambalapulay; a fourth, at Vycome to try the cases at Yetmanoor and Cottayam; and a fifth, at Alwaye to try the cases of Alangaud division. CHAP. V.

6. All disputes and all matters, except those hereafter to be provided for, shall be determined according to the Dharma Sastra and customs of the land.

7. According to Hindu law, a heinous offence becomes capital in the following instances only; (a), raising rebellion and attempting to create riot; (b), compassing the death of the sovereign and attempting to do the same; (c), committing wilful dacoity.

8. The following punishments are provided for murder, assault, criminal trespass, &c., &c., death, banishment from the country, forfeiture of property, imprisonment of two descriptions, simple and rigorous, whipping and fine.

9. In offences relating to caste, religion, property, monetary transactions, the courts can award punishments in accordance with the Dharma Sastra and the customs of the country, death and mutilation excepted.

10. Though the punishments prescribed in Section 8 for murder and other offences are according to the Dharma Sastra and the customs of the land, yet the courts are competent to commute these punishments.

11. All trials by ordeals shall be abolished. All sentences shall be passed according to documentary evidence.

12. Syrian, Mahomedan, Parsee and other residents of Travancore shall be liable to punishment for all crimes, except murder, according to Hindu law.

13. If the plaintiff and defendant in a suit relating to property or monetary transctions be one and the

CHAP. V. same caste, the case shall be decided according to the established custom of their caste. But if they be of different castes, the case will have to be decided according to the established custom of the defendant's caste and creed.

14. People under the jurisdiction of a court shall not file suits of any description whether civil or criminal in another court.

15. Government servants as well as the inhabitants of a place are authorised to apprehend and deliver over to the local tannah, all offenders who commit highway robbery and murder, assault, causing grievous hurt, simple robbery, house-breaking and theft, cheating, smuggling trade, disobedience to lawful authority and public nuisance.

16. The apprehension of any such offenders shall be at once reported to the Dewan by the tannah people. If the Dewan finds it necessary to commit the offenders to the criminal court, he shall order the tannah people to take the culprits to the court to whose jurisdiction the culprit belongs, with the records.

17. As soon as the Darogah takes charge of the offenders he shall report the matter to the court, and communicate to the court the name or names of the offender or offenders and the nature of the crime committed. After holding a preliminary investigation the court shall fix a day for the final hearing of the case and shall issue summons to the witnesses.

18. The investigation of the court shall be conducted publicly and not privately. In all cases the witnesses shall be examined on oath in the presence of the defendants.

19. All cases of murder, robbery, &c., shall be investigated and decision passed from the court, so also all civil cases shall be settled. In the latter, if either the defendant or the plaintiff require the case to be settled by a punchayat, the court shall take their application on oath, and then order the case to be

settled by the punchayat, in which one of the court servants shall form a member. CHAP. V.

20. In all criminal as well as civil cases the following particulars shall be recorded, viz.: 1st, the nature of the crime and the evidence, the names of the witnesses, the various documents produced, &c.; 2nd, the documents, &c., of the defendants; 3rd, the decision of the court or punchayat as the case may be.

21. Except the sentence for murder and other heinous crimes and forfeiture of all property, all punishments shall be executed at once under the order of the sub-courts. The copies of the judgments of all cases shall be given to the parties. Copies of judgment shall also be sent to the kariakar (tahsildar) and tannah Naik of the respective districts to which the parties belong, who shall as soon as they get the copies put the sentence into execution in all minor cases. Copies of sentence on murder and other grave crimes shall be given to the Darogah, who will put the judgment into execution immediately under the orders of the court, provided the punishment be a light one. In cases where the sentences are for confiscation, banishment or such others, the Darogah shall act according to the orders of the Dewan, to whom he will at once communicate the court's decision.

22. If anybody lodges a complaint before a civil court, notice shall be sent to the defendant to appear before the court on a fixed day. If the defendant fails to appear on that day, a notice shall be published to the effect that if the defendant does not appear before the court within ten days of the issue of the notice, the case shall be decided ex-parte. In the event of defendant's non-appearance again, the court shall examine the plaintiff and his witnesses and decide the case ex-parte.

23. It is the duty of the tannah people to serve the notice on the witnesses in all cases, when such are sent from the court.

CHAP. V.

24. The tannah people shall receive security from a witness, if they have reason to think that the witness will abscond from the place.

25. If a person who lives under the jurisdiction of another court is cited as a witness, the court under whose jurisdiction he lives, shall be written to, and that court shall order the tannah people of that locality to cause the attendance of the witness.

26. The cases that come before a court shall be properly filed in a book, and the cases taken and decided according to the number in which they are filed.

27. When a complaint is brought before a court against a Government servant for having abused authority or exceeded his powers, the court shall take the plaintiff's deposition as well as those of the witnesses on oath, and without questioning the defendant, send the records to the high court who shall forward the records to the Dewan, and the court will act according to the orders of that authority.

28. In cases of murder, the sub-courts shall send their sentence and the records to the high court, who, after examining the case, will send it to the Maha Rajah if they find the guilt established against the defendant, and the Maha Rajah will sentence the prisoner, which sentence shall be communicated to the lower court, and the Darogah shall execute the sentence under the orders of the lower court.

29. In civil cases should the defendant or plaintiff express a wish to appeal against the decision of the lower court, he shall state the fact to the lower court within fifteen days after the passing of the judgment. The lower court shall then stop executing their sentence, and send all records connected with the case to the high court.

30. After reading the records sent them by the lower court, the high court shall go into the case themselves and adjudge the matter according to its merits.

When a lower court forwards the records of any

case of their own or that of a punchayat, and should the high court find any illegal proceeding on the part of the lower court, they shall at once communicate the same to the lower court and order the case to be re-investigated and pass their decision.

32. On appeal being made before the high court against the decision of the lower court, the court shall send notice to the lower court as to the day of hearing, when the witnesses will be ordered by the lower court to present themselves before the high court.

33. Should the high court agree with the decision of the lower court, and find that the appeal was vexatious, they shall punish the appellant and shall also order the defendant's costs to be paid.

34. All cases criminal and civil, as has been already said, will be first tried in the lower courts. But if a party requests the Dewan, he shall order the case to be sent from the lower court to the high court which will investigate and pass decision on the same."

The uncommon humanity of Her Highness Lekshmi Ranee has been shown by many acts. The one establishing ample rewards for the destruction of tigers, cheetahs, and elephants, &c., for the protection of the inhabitants of the hilly districts, who were molested and often killed, was one instance. In the former reigns, there had been the militia and the regular armies equipped with fire arms throughout Travancore, to whom the duty of destroying wild animals had been assigned, but since the abolition of the militia and the disbanding of the Travancore army, the inhabitants of that part of Travancore infested with wild beasts, had been exposed to the attacks of tigers, elephants and other wild animals.

The nature of the correspondence which passed between this Ranee and Colonel Munro, and the tenor of Her Highness' speech on the day of her installation prove sufficiently Her Highness' sagacity and her great faith in the justice and support of the Honorable East India Company. Specimens of the former shall

CHAP. V. be annexed. The following is an abstract of the speech delivered by Her Highness :

After passing the ceremonial part of the Durbar, Her Highness Lekshmi Ranee descended suddenly from Her Guddee and addressing Colonel Munro, said in a very clear and unagitated voice, in Malayalam, "Eithrayum Bahumanappetta Sahabay." *i. e.*, Most Respected Sir, I had not expected even in my dreams that I would be called upon ever in my life to assume a musnud which had been most worthily and deservedly occupied by my ancestors from time immemorial, and latterly supported and protected under the auspices of the Honorable East India Company. My uncle, who has been just removed from this world to a better one by Divine will, was only twenty-nine years of age, and if such had not been the will of Sree Padmanabha Swamy (alluding to the household god) my uncle could have held the sceptre for a greater length of time like my grand-uncle, who departed to heaven in the year 973, but since it has been the will and command of my household deity, Sree Padmanabha Swamy, I am ready to obey, but being a young female, quite unprepared and unqualified for such a high and responsible position, I cannot do better than to place myself under the guidance and support of the Honorable East India Company, whose bosom had been an asylum for the protection of an infant like Travancore, since the time Sree Padmanabha Swamy had effected an alliance with such a respectable company of the European nation. To you, Colonel, I entrust everything connected with my country, and from this day I look upon you as my own elder brother and so I need say no more."

The assembly was struck with admiration at the intelligent and graceful delivery of the speech, and Colonel Munro was fully satisfied that the Princess had more talent and intelligence than he had expected, and that he should be able to carry on his functions successfully in Travancore.

Translation of a letter addressed to Colonel J. Munro, the Resident of Travancore, by Her Highness the Ranee Lekshmi Bhye, under date the 19*th Edavom* 986 (1811 *A.D.*) CHAP. V.

" MY DEAR AND BROTHERLY COLONEL SAHIB,

" Since the Colonel is aware of the honor and position of my country and its customs and manners, it would be unnecessary for me either to write at length or to speak at large concerning them. All the systems established by my ancestors for the maintenance of the various charitable institutions, as well as for the protection and advancement of the welfare of my subjects, I request the Colonel will see, conducted according to *mamool* and without the least difference.

" The subject of paying the Brahmans, who had been deputed for *Sethu Snanum* (pilgrimage to Ramaswaram), and who have been complaining of non-payment, had already been brought to your notice by me requsting early disbursement of the same. Maha Sing Killadar had also been instructed to settle the matter at once.

" Speedy and correct despatch of business will, I think, be the more facilitated by our mutual correspondence on matters concerning the administration, and I have no doubt the Colonel will concur with me this opinion of mine.

" As I am a female, and have entrusted my brotherly Colonel with all my affairs, I have full confidence that you will have me and my country, with my subjects and all the charities, conducted in accordance with *mamool* (usage)."

(Signed) LEKSHMI BHYE.

TREVANDRUM,
19*th Edavom*, 986.

CHAP. V.

Translation of the abstract of a speech delivered by Her Highness Lekshmi Ranee, the 25th Chingom 989 (1814 A.D.), when Her Highness' first born child Prince Rama Vurma, was introduced at a Durbar.

"As the Honorable East India Company has been acting with justice, it pleased Sree Padmanabha Swamy to accomplish everything agreeably to their desire.

"At the instance of my household deity Sree Padmanabha Swamy, I have placed this child of mine on the bosom of the Company, and the responsibility for the future support and respectable treatment of this royal scion shall now rest with the Honorable Company. What more need I say."

This letter and the speech, as well as the one above alluded to as having been delivered on the occasion of Her Highness' accession to the musnud, unquestionably prove the Ranee's sterling worth. Such rare instances of sagacity and intelligence in females in power deserve prominent notice.

Travancore was widely known from the earliest times as a stronghold of Hinduism, where superstition prevailed to the highest extremity. Every European nation was considered here as low-caste, and reckoned as mlacha or hoonah (outcastes) and the high caste Hindus, such as Brahmans and Kshatrias, would not approach a European too closely, for fear of being contaminated.

The sovereigns of Travancore used to receive visits from Europeans in the early part of the 18th century, in a building at the beach south-west of the town of Trevandrum, known by the name Poontoray, and a few years subsequently, a bungalow was constructed for the reception of the Resident outside the Trevandrum fort, in a garden called Sinkaratope, where till the installation of this remarkable Princess, Durbars had been held on all occasions. The prescribed rules of the Brahmans in those days were that the Maha Rajah should undergo certain ablutions, ceremonies, and change his sacred thread (poonunool) after the Durbar, as the Rajah would be contaminated by touching the Resident. The female members of the royal family, like all the Hindu females of power and note, were not in the habit of appearing in public, and used to observe the character of Ghosha women. But this wise young Princess, Lekshmi Ranee, had the boldness and determination to break through all the superstitions and brahmanical opposition and to adopt a new course for her own career. CHAP. V.

On the demise of her uncle, though there was a collateral brother of her's in the person of a grown up Rajah of the Mavalikaray family, then residing at Trevandrum with aspirations for the vacant musnud, Her Highness wrote to Colonel Munro for an interview and received the Resident in an open Durbar in Her own palace, and informed him that however reluctant she had been to hold the sceptre of Travancore, Her Highness would not permit the line of sovereignty to be passed over to another house, as long as there was in existence a living member in the legitimate house.

This noble behaviour of the Princess ensured Colonel Munro's hearty espousal of the cause of the Ranee, and promoted Her Highness' installation to the vacant musnud.

Her Highness Lekshmi Bhye was really the pioneer to clear off the wild superstition which prevailed in the royal house as has been mentioned above with regard to association with Europeans, and to open the way for freer intercourse, for, whereas the very approach of a European at a certain distance was considered as defiling and polluting even in the beginning of the present century, there are now European gentlemen moving freely among the high caste people and in the interior of the royal houses, and a European Doctor attends and feels the pulse of a female patient of the

CHAP. V. royal family. But how was such a happy and desirable change effected?

It must be asserted that time has done it. Indeed, that time has to a certain extent influenced this change, may be a fact, but that in Travancore it was effected through the agency of the most accomplished and highly remarkable Ranee Lekshmi Bhye is a fact, which those conversant with the country firmly believe.

When Her Highness the Ranee fell ill, and her case was considered hopeless, she called her husband, the worthy Rajah Rajah Vurmah Koil Thampuran, and committed to his care her only juvenile sister Parwathi Ranee, and her three children (one little Princess and two infant Princes) requesting him, to render his most valuable assistance to her sister, when she should be placed on the musnud as Regent, during the minority of Her Highness' son, and two days afterwards, Her Highness expired to the great grief of the whole family as well as the misfortune of the kingdom of Travancore.

PUBLISHED BY MESSRS HIGGINBOTHAM & CO. C. FOSTER? LITH. MADRAS

HER HIGHNESS COUREE PARWATHI BHYE.

CHAPTER VI.

SREE PADMANABHA SAVINEE VANJI DHARMA WARDHINEE RAJAH RAJAISWARI RANEE GOUREE PARWATHI BHYE.

CHAP. VI.

THE royal family, at the demise of Her Highness Lekshmi Ranee, consisted but of four members, her sister, daughter and two sons. This small group was unfortunately a juvenile one, for, the eldest member, Gouree Parwathi Bhye, was only thirteen, and Rugmini Bhye, seven years of age, while the two Princes, Rama Vurmah and Marthanda Vurmah were respectively eighteen and three months old. They were therefore at that time, under the care and guardianship of Rajah Rajah Vurmah the Valia Koil Thampuran, the late Ranee's husband.

The senior member of the family, Gouree Parwathi Ranee was selected in the Malabar year 990 (1815 A.D.) to act as regent during the minority of Prince Rama Vurmah.

The young Princess, though only thirteen years of age, was imbued with a deep sense of her duty, like Her Highness' deceased sister, and had received a good education in Sanscrit and Malayalam. She was of a mild, kind, and very affable disposition, and being placed under her able brother-in-law, the Valia Koil Thampuran, Her Highness was also advised, like her sister, to follow implicitly the judicious counsels of Colonel Munro, the Resident.

The Resident, observing the good qualities and highly tractable disposition of the young Princess, was delighted; and though he was relieved from the oner-

CHAP. VI. ous duties of the Travancore prime ministership, he did not relax his exertions for the improvement of the administration. But, as he had to deal with a Princess of very tender age, Colonel Munro's responsibility became two-fold.

Since the premature death of the Dewan, Daven Padmanabhen, no successor was appointed, and the affairs of the administration were conducted by Dewan Peishcar Bappoo Row (one of the two Rows who followed Colonel Munro on his coming to Travancore).

Suba Iyen Sankaranarayana Iyen, a native Brahman of south Travancore, who had been an attaché in the palace from a long time, and whose experience in Government affairs had been considered great and valuable, was now selected and appointed as Dewan in 990 M.E. (1815 A.D).

The administrative capacities of this Dewan, did not at all prove equal to the exigencies of the time, and Colonel Munro was under the necessity of advising Her Highness to dispense with his services after a trial of ten months.

In the early part of the year 991 M.E. (1816 A.D.) Ramen Menon, a native of Cochin, who had been employed as a vakeel or pleader in the Travancore courts soon after the organization of the judicial department, and who had been subsequently employed as a judge of the Huzzoor court, was selected by Colonel Munro for the office of Dewan, and he received his commission from Her Highness the Ranee.

This Dewan fully understood his duties, and he commenced his administration in such a manner as to afford general satisfaction. He was honest, intelligent and active, and discharged the functions of his high office impartially and fearlessly.

Ramen Menon's attention was first directed towards the giving of increased efficiency to the system of administration so ably introduced and maintained by

Colonel Munro, for there was a laxity in the carrying out the rules subsequent to the demise of Dewan Daven Padmanabhen. CHAP. VI.

About this time, the appointment of a European to the rising port of Alleppey, as the Sircar commercial agent, was considered by Colonel Munro as desirable, and Captain Gordon, of the Bombay Engineers, who had already acted as Superintendent of the Travancore Forests, was nominated to the new post with the sanction of Her Highness.

Captain Gordon showed excellent capabilities for his new office, and began to make arrangements for the re-organization of the commercial department, as well as for commencing some speculations in merchandise, but in doing so, he displayed a spirit of independence, which the Dewan considered objectionable, and consequently a misunderstanding between the Dewan and the commercial agent soon arose.

Ramen Menon saw that some measures adopted by Captain Gordon were contrary to the established rules, and therefore took the matter at once into his own hands and investigated it, but in doing so, he was very severe against the agent, who had thus reason to apprehend not very gentle treatment at the hands of the Dewan. Though the original procedure of Captain Gordon, on being reviewed by Colonel Munro, was found to be somewhat irregular, yet he deprecated the Dewan's excessive severity towards a European officer, and Dewan Ramen Menon had the mortification, for the first time, to be discountenanced by Colonel Munro.

Reddy Row *alias* Vencatta Row, one of the two Rows alluded to above, and who had already received the appointment of Dewan Peishcar (assistant Dewan), had been watching the movements of the Dewan with an eager eye, with the view of supplanting him; so this officer took advantage of this incident, and commenced working out his plans for obtaining the highest post in his adopted country.

CHAP. VI. Scarcely had a year passed, before a new measure was suggested by Colonel Munro to Her Highness the Ranee, by which the defunct office of Dalawah was revived, and Dewan Ramen Menon was appointed to the new place, with a curtailment of pay and power; for he was doomed to pass his days in a corner of the palace in idleness, and as a Malayalam proverb would express it, bury his fiery spirit and administrative energies under his "*Paya and Charupalaka*" (mattress and reclining plank); for the officials in those days used to sit on a mattress and recline on a plank. The office now assigned to Ramen Menon was once considered the highest in the State, for in those days the post of Dalawah was the combined office of the commander-in-chief and the prime minister, but now the duty of the Dalawah was simply to sign death-warrants when criminals were sentenced to suffer the extreme penalty of law. This measure was effected in the middle of the year 992 M.E. (1817 A.D.) But it does not appear that Ramen Menon ever entered upon his new duties; he seems to have retired and considered himself a pensioner.

Dewan Peishcar Reddy Row acted for the Dewan for sometime and in the next year 993 M. E. (1817 A.D.), he was appointed Dewan.

Reddy Row having obtained the prize he coveted, began to distinguish himself in his office of Dewan, and Colonel Munro rendered him every help with great pleasure.

Six months after the new Dewan's appointment, Colonel Munro retired from the office of Resident and proceeded to England in the middle of the year 994 M.E. (1819 A.D.), and was succeeded by Colonel McDowall, in the same year.

During the incumbency of Reddy Row, some good was done to the country as under his advice, Her Highness had issued several enactments in the form of proclamations relieving the people from certain imposts and restrictions, details of which shall be briefly mentioned hereafter. CHAP. VI.

Generally speaking, Reddy Row's administration does not appear to have been attended with the success which marked the career of his predecessor, Ramen Menon, and public opinion at the time, was that venality amongst the Sircar servants which had been put down and almost eradicated by the strong hand of Colonel Munro, had now begun to crop up and became generally observable throughont the service.

Her Highness the Ranee, who had by this time gained some experience in the affairs of Government, began to feel a little want of confidence in the administration, and the court began in consequence to look minutely into the proceedings of the minister.

The new Resident, Colonel McDowall, reached Trevandrum in the early part of the year 1819 A.D., and he was accompanied by a Mahratta Brahman, named Vencatta Row who was far superior in talent, intelligence, activity and knowledge to his name-sake Dewan Vencatta Row. The new Vencatta Row being a first-rate English scholar, Colonel McDowall made him his interpreter and agent, which office gave him opportunities of frequenting the palace and cultivating an acquaintance with the court.

In a short time, Vencatta Row gained golden opinions not only in the court, but also throughout the kingdom of Travancore, and this secured for him, without much delay, the high post of Dewan Peishcar, and he was employed as an immediate assistant to the Dewan.

Vencatta Row's position with the Resident, added to his own talents and qualifications, made him most influential in the court, in the service, as well as amongst the people, so much so, that Dewan Vencatta Row's influence and fame decreased day by day.

Dewan Peishcar Vencatta Row devoted his attention to all such works as were calculated to secure the

CHAP. VI. confidence of Her Highness the Ranee and the good-will of the people, with the express view, no doubt, of paving his way towards attaining a footing on the highest rung in the ladder. This Peishcar repaired some buildings connected with the pagoda at Trevandrum; made a golden ornament in the shape of a coat for the image of Sree Padmanabha Swamy; improved the Ootupurah Department at Trevandrum; added various ornamental accessories to the royal processions, such as silver howdah, plated sticks or chobdars; and improved the dress of the sepoys and troops, imitating the Mysore fashion.

Such proceedings on the part of the Dewan Peishcar, while it strengthened his own influence the more in the court, created no little alarm in the mind of Dewan Reddy Row, who now found the instability of his position, as he had himself seen in his own past experience in the instance of his predecessor, Dewan Ramen Menon.

The then Cochin Dewan Nunjeppiah, a Coimbatore Brahman, was considered to be a friend of Colonel Munro as well as of Colonel McDowall, and so Reddy Row Dewan thought of working through him to strengthen his own position. Nunjeppiah ("a cunning old fox" as Colonel Welsh calls him in his work) was invited to Trevandrum under some pretext or other, and he used his power, not only with Colonel McDowall, but also with the court, in Reddy Row's favour; and Her Highness the Ranee had besides reason to be satisfied with Nunjeppiah for his exertions with Colonel McDowall in certain affairs wherein the court itself was interested. (This state of things would show that the cordiality between the residency and the court had been somewhat affected by the change of Resident.)

Nunjeppiah's mission was attended with complete success; for Her Highness the Ranee was persuaded by the Dewan and others to remunerate the Cochin minister for his labours by bestowing upon him, as a

PUBLISHED BY MESS[RS] HIGGINBOTHAM & CO.

PRINCESS RUGMINI BHYE.

token of Her Highness' approbation and liberality, a tract of land in the Paravoor district to the extent of some six or seven hundred acres, roughly estimated in value at twenty thousand rupees. The royal deed of this grant was dated 17th Audy 995 M.E. CHAP. VI.

This may be termed the Row period for, from this time, commenced the administration of the country by a succession of Row ministers.

The worthy guardian of the royal children took great pains in the management and education of the Princess Rugmini Bhye, who now attained her tenth year, had become a tolerably good scholar in Sanscrit, had studied many works of ancient authors and composed slokams in Sanscrit; she was also well trained in native music, and could play on several kinds of musical instruments, such as the veenah, surunggee, (guitar), tamburine, &c.

The two Princes, aged respectively seven and five years, were taught Malayalam, Sanscrit and also English, of which they had learnt much more than from their age one would have thought them capable of.

The Princess Rugmini Bhye having become marriageable, for the tenth year is considered the proper age for performing the marriage ceremony in the royal family, preparations were made and the ceremony was most satisfactorily performed in 995 M.E. (1819 A.D.) with all becoming pomp and grandeur.

During the celebration of this marriage, Her Highness the regent not only entertained for several days, Brahmans, Sudras, and her courtiers with sumptuous feasting, but also entertained in her own palace the European officers of her service, in addition to many outsiders.

Colonel Welsh, alluded to in the 4th Chapter, was one of the party so invited, and wrote an account of the entertainment, portions of which are quoted here in corroboration of the above facts. He says:—"I was proceeding to meet Major Southerland

CHAP. VI.

"McDowall, just appointed to succeed Colonel Munro "as Resident, * * * * but my friend had not arrived, "and I put up with Major M'Leod who commanded "the Ranee's brigade; Captain Gordon of Alleppey "being Acting Resident and living in the cantonment. "On the 20th May 1819, still waiting for Major "McDowall, who had not arrived from Calcutta, we "received an invitation from the Ranee, * * * * When "alighting at the palace gate, we were ushered into a "temporary building, * * * where, upon a silver throne "sat the Ranee of Travancore, who was really a very "interesting young woman and received us with much "kindness, * *. After the etiquette of a regular intro- "duction by Captain Gordon, we all took our seats and "were regaled by dancing girls about two hours, * * *. "There are two young Rajahs at present in the palace, "one the rightful heir to the throne, is now seven years "old and a very fine boy * * * *. The other "* * is only three or four. The two young Rajahs "sat on my knee alternately during the whole evening "without any restraint * * * *. The fire-works from "the state of the weather, were very poor, but the "affability and the good sense of Her Highness made "up in my mind for all the disappointment.* * *.

"On taking our leave at 11 P.M., the Ranee "entreated us to return next day, but one of the "ladies being unwell, the party was put off till the "22nd, when we again assembled at 8 P.M., and saw "some excellent fire-works* * * *.

"On the 25th, my worthy friend Major McDowall, "arriving from Bengal viâ Madras, the next day "at noon I accompanied him to pay his first visit "to the Ranee, and was really gratified with the "whole scene, as every native of distinction in the "country had assembled to do honor to the represent- "ative of the British Government, and all the troops "were drawn up to receive him. Not a soul but the "Ranee, however, and the European gentlemen sat "down, not even the Thumpooratty newly married, "her bridegroom, the Ranee's father and husband, "the widower of a former Ranee nor the Dewan or "prime minister. The two young Rajahs made "speeches to the new Resident, and the younger on "this occasion seemed the most at home; amongst "other questions he asked "how all the gentlemen at "Madras?" and sat down very contentedly on the "Major's knee; the heir apparent not appearing "equally to relish his propinquity to a stranger * * * *, "and we took our leave promising to return in the "evening.

"Having dined at the residency at 4 o'clock, at "half-past 9, we received Her Highness' summons, "when we proceeded to the fort, and were immediately "ushered into her presence in the hall of audience "* * *. We saw the fire-works from the front "verandah, which were certainly very grand, parti- "cularly some rockets, which ran on a horizontal line "guided by ropes attached to strong poles and some "of them fastened to figures, which they impelled "with surprising velocity; and also some batteries, "which after imitating the roar of cannon and mus- "ketry, suddenly exploded like mines; throwing "up a profusion of fire-balls. After this exhibition, "we descended to a similar hall on the ground-floor "where a good supper was laid out for the European "visitors; after partaking of which we again descended "to witness another Malabar play * * *, at the same "time six nice little boys were performing feats of "activity, with large knives and swords, by far the "best part of the entertainment; and we got home "nearly exhausted at 2 o'clock in the morning.

"On the 27th, we again assembled at the palace at "half-past 3 P.M. to dinner, after which we were enter- "tained with wrestling and feats of agility in the "court-yard * * *, at 9, a lady arising, the Ranee "kindly sent word, that as it was raining hard, she would "come down and sit with us, which she accordingly "did for an hour, when, telling us we had better take

CHAP. VI. "our suppers, she wished us good night and retired; "we accordingly followed her advice and broke up at "midnight.

"On the 28th, we had a repetition of the same feast-"ing and exhibitions as the day before; and the fire-"works, notwithstanding the rain, were really capital "and afforded us much amusement.

"On the 29th, there was another repetition, with all "the elements against us; and at 1 A.M., we took our "leave of this affable and interesting Princess." (Military Reminiscences, Volume 2, page 144.)

As Her Highness Rugmini Bhye was the only Princess to be married in the royal family at that period, and as there would be no occasion for such an expenditure till the birth of a female member, and her becoming marriageable, Her Highness the Regent wished that the marriage ceremony of the Princess should stand first in the list of such ceremonies, especially at a time when the finances of Travancore were able to meet such a demand, and thus the festivities connected with the ceremony were allowed to be continued for a fortnight.

Colonel McDowall died in 995 M.E. (1820 A.D.), and Colonel Newall was appointed Resident in the middle of the same year 995 M.E. (1820 A.D.)

Dewan Reddy Row had not only re-established confidence in the palace, but also stood high in the estimation of Her Highness the Ranee. After the satisfactory conduct of the marriage affairs, the minister now, taking advantage of the time, claimed some special consideration from Her Highness in recognition of his labours. Reddy Row gained over some influential parties about Her Highness, and worked through them to accomplish his object; and in the year 996 M.E. (1821 A.D.), he received a jaggeer consisting of the two villages of Shamboor and Wadakaray in the Shencottah district.

COCHU KOIL THUMPURAN.

Dewan Peishcar Vencatta Row was still watching for an opportunity for the overthrow of the minister, and he availed himself of the above incident to carry out his plans; while Ramen Menon Dalawah was ready to assist the Peishcar to revenge himself on Reddy Row for all the mortifications he had endured. CHAP. VI.

The Dewan's improper acceptance of a grant was brought to the notice of the new Resident, and after a thorough investigation, the Dewan was made to return the document he received from Her Highness, and ultimately the transaction resulted in the resignation of Dewan Vencatta Row, commonly called Reddy Row.

Towards the end of 997 M.E. (1822 A.D.), Dewan Peishcar Vencatta Row was appointed Dewan, and he commenced his career in quite a different way from that of his predecessor. Being an educated man and blessed with sufficient wisdom and intelligence, he imitated the mode of administration adopted by Colonel Munro and his task was lightened by the experience he had acquired in the various departments as a Dewan Peishcar.

In order to obtain popular approbation, his first step was to obtain Her Highness the Ranee's sanction for granting a general remission of arrears of tax accumulated since the administration of Colonel Munro. This measure had the desired effect, for the people of Travancore at once began to look upon the Dewan as a great benefactor, and every measure he adopted afterwards was viewed by the people with approbation and satisfaction.

A few months prior to the departure of Colonel Munro in the Malabar year 994, (1819 A.D.), the guardian of the royal children, the Valia Koil Thampuran urged the necessity of placing the English education of the two Princes under a competent tutor, and Her Highness the Ranee requested Colonel Munro to get one for the Princes. After careful inquiry, T. Subba Row, of Tanjore, was recommended by the

CHAP. VI.

Resident for the important office of training the two Princes.

The proposed tutor, Subba Row, arrived in Trevandrum a couple of months after Colonel Munro's departure and commenced his onerous labours. In the course of a couple of years both the Princes made considerable progress in their English studies; Subba Row training the Princes in the Mahratta language also. There were other masters to teach them Sanscrit, Hindoostani, Persian, Telugu, Canarese, &c., &c., and in all these languages the Princes made great progress; their guardian, the Valia Koil Thampuran also devoted his unremitting care and attention to their education.

The following observation by Colonel Welsh on the studies of these two Princes towards the middle of May 1825, bears out the above statement:

"Being on a tour of inspection during the month of "May, and stopping to pass a few days at the residency "with Colonel Newall, I had the opportunity of wit-"nessing the studies of the young Rajahs in private, "and forming an estimate of their progressive acquire-"ments and abilities. On the morning of the 16th "at 10 o'clock, I accompanied the Colonel in his gig "without attendants, to the fort, where we were "immediately conducted to a room in the palace and "found them with their father, their sister, her husband "and their school-master ready to receive us. The "elder boy, now thirteen, seemed greatly improved "in mind, though rather diminutive in person. He "read a chapter of Malcolm's Central India; the "Governor-General's Persian letter on the capture of "Rangoon; a passage in Sanscrit; another in Malaya-"lam and seemed equally clever at each. He then "took up a book of mathematics, selecting the forty-"seventh proposition of Euclid, sketched the figure "on a country slate; but what astonished me most was "his telling us in English, that Geometry was derived "from the Sanscrit, which was "jaw metor" to

DEWAN VENCATTA ROW.

PUBLISHED BY MESS^RS HIGGINBOTHAM & CO. S. PACZENSKY LITH: MADRAS.

" measure the earth, and that many of our mathema- " tical terms were also derived from the same source " such as hexagon, heptagon, octagon, decagon, " duo-decagon, &c., &c. His remarks were generally " apposite, but their language inelegant and ungram- " matical. This is much to be lamented, because with " so many studies on hand, he can never read enough " of English to correct his idiom; and the master, a " very clever Tanjore Brahmin, could not speak it " much better than himself. His Persian was pure " and elegant, but of the other languages, I am too " ignorant to offer an opinion. This promising boy is " now, I conclude, sovereign of the finest country in " India; for he was to succeed to the musnud, the " moment he had attained his sixteenth year. The " younger brother gave us various specimens of his " acquirements, somewhat inferior of course to those " of the rising sun of the country, but still very fair.

CHAP. VI.

" The Princess at whose wedding I was present in " 1819, was grown both fat and coarse. Their father, " a very handsome man about the middle age is their " joint guardian with the Ranee and Resident; but has " no other power or authority whatever. The Princess' " husband looks very much like her younger brother; " indeed, apart, I should not know the one from the " other. At noon we took our leave much gratified " with this domestic scene.

" I have not made any mention of the present " Dewan, an uncommonly handsome, fair, and elegant " Carnatic Brahmin. His name is Vencatta Row, and " he is one of the most intelligent, well educated men " I have met with in India, and writes an excellent " English letter. As far as I could learn he was most " attentive and unremitting in his exertions for the im- " provement of the country and the good of the State. " Such a man to educate the young Princes would " have been worth his weight in gold." (Page 235).

Dewan Vencatta Row's administration afforded perfect satisfaction to Her Highness the Ranee, to the

CHAP. VI. Resident as well as to the people in general. He established his head-quarters (Huzzoor Cutcherry) at Quilon, the centre of Travancore, where the appeal and other courts were located.

The Dewan grew popular day by day, as he made it a point to give free access to him, to all classes of people, every day at an appointed time, when he personally enquired into every petitioner's grievance regarding revenue as well as other matters. He was a capital revenue officer, while in his knowledge of magisterial functions he was scarcely surpassed by any one at the time in Travancore. Many a reform and improvement has been introduced by this Dewan, and under his administration the country was soon again in a very flourishing condition.

Colonel Munro had it in contemplation to construct two canals; one from Trevandrum to the backwater of Kadinamcolum, and the other to connect the Quilon and Paroor backwaters together, and thus extend water communication from Trevandrum to the north.

This most useful work was sanctioned by Her Highness the Ranee in the year 999 M.E. (1824 A.D.), and operations were commenced in the next year. In the course of three years the work was completed at a comparatively small expenditure.

Several other useful works connected with irrigation were undertaken and completed during the reign of Her Highness the Ranee, and under the administration of Dewan Vencatta Row.

It was this large-hearted and enlightened Ranee who sanctioned English missionary labors in Travancore, and it was in her time that regularly established Protestant Missions were commenced, though perfect toleration of Christianity had been guaranteed by the Travancore sovereigns from the earliest period of the Christian era. This is proved by the copper plate documents in the possession of the Syrian Christians at Cottayam already alluded to, especially the one given by Perumal Sthanu Revi Guptha, the second document published in the Madras Journal of Literature and Science, page 126 to 130, showing that the Travancore sovereign had permitted the Perumal to give a perpetual grant of a tract of land for building a Christian church. Subsequent to this event, other grants of lands for the erection of Christian churches were made and are continued up to the present day, and the immense number of places of Christian worship now seen on the Travancore territory, between Thovalay and Paravoor, furnish evidence of the impartial countenance the Travancore sovereigns have always given to the Christian religion, which indeed the Hindus do not generally view in a friendly light.

Though Mr. Ringeltaube, a Danish missionary, had established the nucleus of what was afterwards the London Mission in the year 1806 A.D., and had made some attempts to establish his mission on a proper scale in Myladee, the southern frontier of Travancore, his labours were not attended with much success for a long time, yet, it was during this Ranee's reign in 1816 A.D. (991 M.E.) that the London Mission was permanently established at Nagercoil.

Her Highness the Ranee not only sanctioned the location of a few missionary gentlemen within her territories, but also made generous and liberal donations for their assistance, as for instance, a sum of five thousand rupees and a large bungalow at Nagercoil to enable them to carry on their Mission labors. But what was still more extraordinary was that Her Highness even admitted one of these gentlemen belonging to the London Mission, the Rev. C. Mead, in her service as a Judge of the Zillah Court at Nagercoil.

In this very year 1816 A.D, (991 M.E.) Her Highness had, under the advice of Colonel Munro, sanctioned the erection of a large Protestant church at Alleppey and gave the teak timber, required for the building, free of all charges, permitting, at the same-time, the residence of the Rev. T. Norton at Alleppey as a Chaplain there.

CHAP. VI.

During this year, the Church Mission Society was also permitted to commence its operations at Cottayam, for the improvement of the Syrians, the oldest Christian subjects of Her Highness' territories. To these people, the Resident, Colonel Munro, devoted great attention, and the Church Mission Society commenced working conjointly with the Syrian Metran. In order to facilitate their work in the education of the Christian, a College was opened, and towards its maintenance, this most generous Ranee granted a donation of twenty thousand Rupees, with which they purchased gardens and paddy-fields, the income derived from which paid for the maintenance of the College. Colonel Munro in his address to the Government of Fort St. George on the state of Christianity in Travancore, thus refers to this event:—

"The temporal situation of the Syrians has also been "materially improved. I have frequently taken "occasion to bring them to the notice of Her Highness "the Ranee of Travancore; and her intelligent, liberal "and ingenuous mind has always appeared to feel a "deep interest in their history, misfortunes and char- "acter. She is aware of the attention excited to their "situation in Europe, and her anxiety to manifest "the sincerity of her attachment to the British nation "has formed, I believe, an additional motive for the "kindness and generosity she has uniformly displayed "towards the Syrians. She has appointed a con- "siderable number of them to public offices; and "lately presented the sum of twenty thousand Rupees "to the College of Cottayam, as an endowment for its "support. The Syrians are most grateful for her "goodness; and cherish, in no ordinary degree, "the sentiments of affection and respect towards her "person that are entertained by every class of her "subjects."

Subsequent events however, disorganized and shattered this most useful institution, and the lands were sold, minus that portion of the gift which fell on division to the lot of the Church Mission Society and which is still in the enjoyment of the society. This is called Munro's Island and is in the Kallada Proverthy near Quilon, which yields an annual rent of about two thousand five hundred Rupees to the said Society.* CHAP. VI.

Thus it will be seen that this worthy Ranee of happy memory, was the founder and supporter of the English missions in Travancore, and a generous promoter of the cause of education and of Christian knowledge in this fortunate kingdom. The present Nair brigade was formally organized during this reign, though it was partly in existence during the reign of Her Highness the late Lekshmi Bhye, when 700 men and a few mounted troopers out of the remains of the Travancore military force, were re-admitted and retained as an attendant force on royalty. But now, by the special request of Her Highness, the Madras Government sanctioned the proposal to have a Brigade consisting of 2,100 men under the command of English officers, and also to increase the mounted troop to fifty men forming a cavalry squadron. This was early in the year 994 M.E. (1819 A.D.) Captain Macleod of the 9th Regiment M.N.I., was the first East India Company's officer who commanded Her Highness' military forces. Two six-pounders and two nine-pounders had also been attached for firing salutes, which honor had been dispensed with subsequent to the rebellion of 1809.

The introduction of vaccination, though proposed and arranged towards the close of the last reign, was formally effected and the entertainment of vaccinators

* (a) In order to prevent the Syrians dissipating the gift of this Princess when the College lands were sold, the proceeds were deposited in the Resident's treasury till the year 1872, when the old College being re-established by the Syrians, the money now nearly doubled was given on mortgages and the interest supports thirty of these candidates learning for the priesthood, besides providing for teachers.

(b) The Church Mission provide two European teachers and ten native assistants at their own expense and have built another College and provides boarding for seventy-five lads and an equal number of day boys are educated by the proceeds of Munro Island rents.

CHAP. VI.

and the enforcement of a regular system of vaccination, practically attended to in the commencement of the first year of this Ranee's reign.

Of the numerous enactments, promulgated during Her Highness' reign, the following are the most memorable, viz.; 1st, the prohibition of the exaction of ooliyum service, from Christian ryots, when such was connected with any of the Hindu religious ceremonies; 2nd, the employment of Christians for any public works on Sundays; 3rd, the introduction of stamped cadjans for documents; 4th, the removal of restrictions as regards the wearing of golden and silver ornaments by Sudras and others; 5th, the abolition of the poll-tax on people of the Chetty and other castes, when they were Devaswam ryots; 6th, the introduction of coffee cultivation in general and the prohibition against judicial officers holding private conferences with parties concerned in cases, either at the court or at their private residences or even giving them admission into their dwellings, &c., &c., &c.

Towards the close of this reign, the tutor Suba Row, became very influential in the court. His royal pupils had grown up and completed their studies, and as the eldest of them was soon to ascend the musnud, Suba Row was naturally looked upon as His Highness' principal adviser, and the leader of the court.

When Suba Row's influence increased, Dewan Vencatta Row's power began to decline; for, the Dewan was now apprehensive of being supplanted by Suba Row, but though all arrangements for the overthrow of the minister, Vencatta Row, were ripe, Her Highness the Ranee would not sanction the measure, and left the question to be decided after the formal installation of the elder Prince, which event was then very nigh at hand.

In the Malabar year 1004 (1829 A.D.) His Highness Rama Vurma closed his sixteenth year of age and thus attained his majority, when that most worthy and illustrious Princess the Ranee made over the kingdom, with pleasure and cordiality to her sister's son. The State under her regency was well governed, the people were contented; the finances were in a flourishing condition, and an able and meritorious administrator in the person of Dewan Vencatta Row was at the helm of Government. Her most gracious Highness retired to enjoy a peaceful life, though retaining all the honors appertaining to a reigning sovereign, with a consciousness that every endeavour had been made by her for the happiness of all, and proud to hear public opinion unanimous in declaring that success had attended Her Highness' administration.

CHAPTER VII.

SREE PADMANABHA DASA VANJI PALA RAMA VURMAH KULASEKHARA KIREETAPATHI SWATHI RAMA RAJAH MUNNAY SULTAN MAHARAJ RAJA RAMA RAJA BAHADUR SHAMSHEER JUNG MAHA RAJAH.

CHAP. VII.

THIS illustrious sovereign was really the King of Travancore from the very day of his birth, but His Highness having now attained his majority, was formally installed on the musnud in his sixteenth year, and assumed charge of affairs from the regent Ranee, on the 10th Madom 1004 M.E. (21st April 1829, A.D.)

Notwithstanding his youth, His Highness' aptness for the right discharge of the functions devolving on him was something wonderful. Besides, His Highness was fortunate in receiving the kingdom from the hands of the Ranee in a most flourishing condition, the result of the judicious administration of the last eighteen years by two of His Highness' predecessors, his mother Lekshmi Ranee and his aunt Parvathi Ranee. The financial state of the country was promising. The State contained a very contented population, and the machinery of the administration was worked by the best agencies.

The young Maha Rajah had also the advantage of the advice and counsel of his worthy father, the able tutor, the meritorious Dewan, as well as many old and experienced ministerial servants, both in the palace and in other departments. The Resident, Colonel Morrison, C.B., a very able officer, was also a warm supporter of the Maha Rajah.

PUBLISHED BY MESS[rs] HIGGINBOTHAM & CO. C. PAEZENERY LITH: MADRAS

RAMA VURMAH MAHA RAJAH.

These auspicious circumstances and advantages, and His Highness'.talents, education, and the requisite qualifications and trained habits, gave prospects of a happy and glorious reign to which the people in general looked forward with feelings of pleasure.

Though a short biographical account of this remarkable young sovereign has already been given in the last chapter, yet a few words on the Maha Rajah's scholastic attainments may not be out of place here. By the time His Highness attained his majority, he had completed his education and become a perfect master of Sanscrit, English, Persian, Hindustani, Maharatti, Telugu, Canarese, Tamil and Malayalim. The fact that His Highness was a good English scholar will have been seen from the passage quoted from Colonel Welsh's "Military Reminiscences," in the previous chapter. That account, however, was written some four years previous to His Highness completing his English education. The Maha Rajah was also a remarkable Sanscrit author. He composed numerous poetical works on Metaphysics, Religion, &c., &c. A Sanscrit poetical work called a "Prabandham" containing historical collections, was also composed by him in addition to numerous songs and hymns in praise of the Almighty and the creation of the universe. He also composed similar songs in Telugu, Hindustani, Mahratta, and other languages and these are even to the present day well known throughout India.

A specimen of the Maha Rajah's Sanscrit composition as translated by the Reverend Mr. Mateer and inserted in his "Land of Charity," page 146, may be reproduced here as a proof of the Maha Rajah's skill in Sanscrit composition:—

"More special interest naturally attaches to a poem "composed and published by His Highness the late "Rajah Vunchee Pala Rama Vurmah, elder uncle of "the present Maha Rajah, who died in 1846. It is "considered by native scholars to be a good specimen

CHAP. VII.

"of modern Sanscrit poetry, the compound poetical "terms being formed according to standard rules, the "sentences skilfully constructed and the whole adapted "to be sung to the most popular and melodious "Hindu tunes. This work contains hymns in praise of "Pultmanabhen, the tutelar deity of the "charitable "kingdom," but of course is thoroughly superstitious "and, after a fashion, devout in sentiment and tone.

"The first hymn commences thus :—

"O thou, lord of earth, husband of Sree (the "goddess of prosperity.) thou, O God, who hast "lotus-like-eyes save me: O holy Pultmanabhen, "whose chariot is drawn by birds, save me! O thou, "who art worshipped by the king of the Suras "(celestials), thou, who art full of goodness, subduer "of enemies, giver of blessings to thy servants, thou "who hast arms admirably powerful, thou who art "adored by the holy ones, save me; O thou upholder "of mountains, thou enemy of Mura (a demon) thou "seat of mercy, remover of the suffering arising from "births and deaths.

"Remove my manifold sins, O Souri, (a name of "Vishnu), who walked in the most holy gardens of "bliss and happiness. Remove my manifold sins, O "thou destroyer of Kashipu, who was a terror to the "three worlds, thou who shinest like gold, remove my "manifold sins, thou purifier from sins, thou joy of the "shepherdess, thou who art adorned with features, "thou who art devoid of passions, whose lotus-like-"foot measures the universe. Remove my manifold "sins, O my lord, who takest away sorrows, thou O "Souri who hast the sun and the moon for thine eyes.

"The last hymn is an address to the soul as follows:—

"O my mind, be thou always fixed upon God. Ah! "tell me, art thou not incessantly fixed on self. O my "mind, know that this thy body is fragile; be not over "anxious, do not covet earth, delight in the history "of Madhava (Vishnu) which is full of joy, holy and

" divine, oh my mind, cherish not rude ignorance; let " not dreadful sins have place in thy thought; avoid " evil communications. O my mind, be kind to every " one. Consider, all things as thou considerest thyself, " put away thy sorrows, and with all thy strength, " incessantly serve the azure tinted Padmanabhen. " O my mind be thou always fixed upon God."

" It should be borne in mind that this poem is the production of one well acquainted with many of the truths inculcated by the Christian religion."

Besides the above, this Maha Rajah had composed a most valuable set of hymns under the denomination of Navarathna Mala (garland of nine gems) the substance of which shall be added to the Revd. Mr. Mateer's versions.

The Hindu religion lays down and describes nine kinds of divine devotions, viz., hearing, uttering, thinking, serving, adoring, worshipping, depending, or enslaving, believing and committing, and the Maha Rajah had composed a hymn on each of these nine items:—

" *Hearing.*

" O Padmanabha! (such is the Sanscrit appellation of the creator of the universe) bless me that both of my ears may be filled with the heavenly nectar of thy prayers which is a safe vessel for the conveyance of life through the ocean of birth and death, which prayer is the continual utterance of even the heavenly bodies and which is the pioneer to break through the mountain of sin to approach thy presence.

" *Uttering.*

" O Padmanabha! bless me, that I may utter thy name always without interruption. Thy holy name is the sure way to salvation for human beings. Thy name, though uttered unintentionally, saves even sinners as in the case of Ajmilen. Thy name is the constant utterance of Siva, one of the three great deities of heaven.

CHAP. VII.

" *Thinking.*

O Padmanabha! bless my heart, that I may constantly think of thee alone during the tenure of my worldly life. Thy thought is the only light like the rays of the sun which drives away darkness from the world, and which thought alone is capable of affording eternal bliss, pleasure and comfort without regard of poor or rich, O God! lord of the universe.

" *Serving.*

" O God, Sree Padmanabha! bless me, that I may serve thee in many ways, that I may be the bearer of thy shoes, that I may serve thee with a fan in hand, that I may shampoo thy holy feet, that I may hold an umbrella over thy holy person, and that I may with pleasure employ myself in collecting offerings to thee.

" *Adoring.*

" O God of the universe! bless me, that I may adore thee with my mind, word and deeds. Thou art the only holy ghost who removes sins, and who alone is capable of purifying the whole universe; bless me, O God! that I may seat thee on a throne set with nine gems, and that I may wash thee with odoriferous water, clothe thee in the whitest garments, anoint thee with sandals and other scents, adorn thee with all kinds of fragrant flowers, and make thee my offerings, O Almighty God.

" *Worshipping.*

" O God, lord of lords! I worship thy feet which is washed in heavenly water, and which is the only source of protection and salvation to the helpless.

" Depending or enslaving.

" O Providence! Sree Padmanabha! I entirely depend upon thy holiness which is the object constantly adored even by all the heavenly bodies, and which alone extends salvation or eternal happiness to all beings.

"*Believing.*

"O God! bless me, that I may place my entire belief always in thee who art the destroyer of all sin, and suffering in the universe; numerous deities and gods are worshipped, but I may not be changeable or doubting in my mind in regard to such worship, and that thy mercy be upon me, that my mind may be steadily directed to thy true belief as thou art the only supreme being who is capable of affording salvation.

"*Committing.*

"O God, lord of lords! bless me, for I commit unto thee my body, my soul, my habitation, my property and all other things of mine to thee, so that, thy protection may be constantly over these, like the owner of a thing purchased by him, and that thy mercy may be upon me; forgive me for all my sins and also my faults in my utterance of these hymns which are offerings of thy true devotee, and which I have directed as an offering unto thy holy feet, and I pray thee to accept these my humble and devoted prayers, as committed by thy pious servant."

His Highness had equally qualified himself in political matters by his assiduous study of various English and Sanscrit works, and he acquired a thorough knowledge of the Institutes of Manu. His Highness made it a point to discuss important questions on Logic and Rhetoric, both in English and in Sanscrit, and thus became capable of entering into the discussion of any subject, without fear of being defeated by other learned men.

Soon after the installation, His Highness' attention was directed to the remodelling of the cabinet, and as His Highness had a very high opinion of his tutor, Suba Row, and of his ability and knowledge, he wanted to appoint him Dewan, but the idea of dispensing with the services of the able and popular Dewan Vencatta Row, was not approved of by His Highness' father, by Her Highness the Ranee, and by the Resi-

CHAP. VII. dent, Colonel Morrison. The controversy on this subject lasted about six months, and in the interval the able Resident, Colonel Morrison, was removed, and Dewan Vencatta Row tendered his resignation. Two months afterwards, *i.e.*, in the middle of the year 1005 M.E. (early part of 1830) Suba Row was appointed to the vacant office of Dewan, and Cochu Sankara Pillay, a native of Travancore who was then holding the appointment of a Judge in the Huzzoor Court, was made Dewan Peishcar. These two appointments were followed by several other changes among the ministers.

The Huzzoor Cutcherry and other public offices which had been held at Quilon for a long time were removed to Trevandrum, and located inside the fort, close to the Maha Rajah's palace.

As Suba Row wanted to surpass his predecessor, he spared no pains to distinguish himself in his new sphere. He displayed all his experience and tact and commenced a career which fully justified His Highness' selection of him for the high post of prime minister.

The Dewan's conduct was quite in accordance with His Highness' urgent desire of bringing Travancore to such a state as to entitle her to the appellation of "model State." Suba Row had, at the very outset, established a reputation far superior to that of his predecessor.

Every suggestion emanating from Dewan Suba Row received ready sanction from His Highness the Maha Rajah, and every subordinate, from the Dewan Peishcar downwards, looked upon the Dewan with the greatest regard and respect.

Reformation and the maintenance of a rigid moral discipline were the chief aim and ambition of this young sovereign, and so the petty abuses which were overlooked during the late administration were totally checked by special enactments. Bribery and corruption were pointed out as crimes severely punishable, and those servants who gave cause even for suspicion

DEWAN SUBBA ROW.

PUBLISHED BY MESS.RS HIGGINBOTHAM & CO.

were visited with the royal displeasure. The Maha Rajah was so minute in his inquiries, as his attention appears to have been directed even to the irregularity of attendance on the public servants, and such remissness they were informed would render them liable to dismissal from the service. Tahsildars and other local officials were warned against any oppressive treatment of the ryots. In short, several useful measures were introduced by royal proclamation in the course of a couple of years.

His Highness had set apart a few hours every day to attend to public business, and days were appointed for receiving the Dewan, the Judges of the appeal court, the palace officers, &c., with their respective reports.

This measure of hearing reports directly from each department, facilitated the speedy conduct of public business by the several department officials.

Thus, the Maha Rajah by evincing particular interest in the conduct of public affairs encouraged men of talent and intelligence, and in the course of a few years after His Highness' ascent to the musnud the Maha Rajah's court and cutcherries had the benefit of several men of talent, learning and experience.

The Governor of Madras, Mr. Lushington, paid a visit to Travancore, and had an interview with the young Prince at Quilon, in the early part of August 1830.

His Excellency the Governor was highly delighted with the affability, intelligence, wisdom and gentlemanly disposition of His Highness. The object of this visit of the Governor appears to have been to satisfy himself as to the qualifications of so young a Prince for ruling Travancore.

It is also said, that there had been a little misunderstanding between the Travancore court and the Resident, Colonel Morrison, concerning the then Dewan Vencatta Row's proposed disconnection with

CHAP. VII. Travancore, and that Colonel Morrison had made some reports unfavorable to the state of things in Travancore, which circumstance induced Mr. Lushington to visit the country and ascertain the exact state of affairs by a personal inspection, while he was on a tour to the Malabar coast.

Mr. Lushington was the first Governor of Madras who visited Travancore.

On this occasion the Maha Rajah had an opportunity of witnessing the whole of the subsidiary force in full parade, and after His Highness' return from Quilon the improvement of the Nair brigade engaged his attention. New accoutrements were ordered, and the officer commanding was particularly requested to drill and train the sepoys and make them equal to the Company's troops.

The clothing of the mounted troops had also been improved, and new horses were supplied to the troopers. Old stables were repaired and made into three divisions, one for the troopers, one for the royal stud, and another for the horses to be supplied to the palace officials and attendants, as well as to the public officials who accompany the Maha Rajah during State processions, and also on other movements on urgent public duty.

The horse breeding establishment introduced and maintained at Thovalay during the former reigns and which supplied good horses to the Trevandrum stables, was improved. Some fine mares were procured, and all old and defective horses of different breeds were removed from the establishment.

The best elephants from the forest department and other places were selected and cantoned at Trevandrum for carrying howdahs, flags and other royal emblems.

To the Trevandrum stables was attached a menagerie where royal tigers, panthers, cheetahs, deer, boars and all sorts of wild animals which abound in the Travancore forests were collected and caged. And latterly, a lioness which had been imported from Africa into the French settlement at Mahé, was purchased and added to the collection of animals. CHAP. VII.

A large and spacious cow-stall was constructed within the Trevandrum fort, near the palace, wherein the finest cows and bulls of the country were stalled in addition to a good number of Surat, Guzerat and Nellore cows and bulls, and to complete the collection and breed, a beautiful English cow, with two calves, was procured direct from England.

Birds of all kinds, indigenous and foreign, were collected, and they had a place both in the menagerie and the palace.

The wild and ferocious animals were not only kept for sight-seers, but for purposes of sham sport. For this purpose, strong nets of a circular form were hung on deeply driven stakes, within which, several sorts of wild and fierce animals were let in one by one, and the Maha Rajah and all the spectators were amused and interested by seeing the movements and the fighting of the animals, while a number of huntsmen and others, surrounded the circle, equipped with spears, lances, and fire arms, ready to fall upon any animal which might accidently escape out of the nets.

Three years after the Maha Rajah's accession to the musnud, Munsiff's courts were established for the first time in every district throughout Travancore, for the disposal of petty civil cases, and in the next year, the Huzzoor court was abolished, and a Zillah court established at Trevandrum in lieu of it. Appreciative of ability and talent, and desirous of improving the administration, this young Maha Rajah conceived the idea of inviting persons of acknowledged qualifications and probity from the British territories and even in the British Government's service, in order to assist Dewan Suba Row in his exertions to introduce reforms.

The then Resident, Mr. Casamaijor, brought to His Highness' notice, the ability and intelligence of a

CHAP. VII. tahsildar personally known to himself in one of the talooks under the Malabar collectorate, who accompanied the Commissariat during the Coorg campaign in the year 1834. The Maha Rajah, authorized the Resident to invite that officer to enter the service of the Travancore Government.

This tahsildar's name was Itterarichen Cundappen, generally known as Cunden Menon. This person accepted the offer of a Dewan Peishcar's post in the Huzzoor cutcherry, and was accordingly appointed in the middle of the year 1010 M.E. (early part of 1835 A.D.)

Dewan Peishcar Cunden Menon proved to be an excellent acquisition to the Travancore service, and he afforded such great satisfaction to His Highness, and merited ere long his perfect confidence, that the Maha Rajah placed the details of the administration in the Peishcar's hands, and directed Dewan Suba Row to place similar trust in the Peishcar, ordering further that if the Dewan should entertain doubts on any points of importance, he should report the same personally to His Highness.

Cunden Menon Peishcar began to manage business and to afford general satisfaction. In a short time, he merited the applause of the people who now began to talk of him as second only to ex-Dewan Vencatta Row.

The principal object of the Maha Rajah in inviting Cunden Menon, was to compile a code of laws for Travancore, founded upon the enactments then in force in the Honorable East India Company's territories.

Cunden Menon undertook this most important and onerous task, and having formed a committee of experienced officers in the Travancore service, he consulted with them and examined all the rules then in force in Travancore. They then commenced the drafting and arranging of the regulations, which they finished in the course of a few months.

As the Peishcar had no knowledge of English, all his writings were translated by competent English scholars. The Maha Rajah and the Resident highly approved of the code, and it was printed at the Cottayam Mission Press (the Sircar having no press of their own at that time), and the new code was promulgated as the law of Travancore, and brought into force from the year 1011 M.E. (1836 A.D.)

This was the first code of regulations ever adopted and promulgated in Travancore. It consisted of eight chapters. The first five chapters contain the civil code and procedure and the constitutions of Munsiffs, Zillah and appeal courts; the sixth regulation vests tahsildars with police authority, and Zillah courts with criminal powers; and the seventh and eighth authorise appeal court judges to perform the functions of session courts.

To carry out the provisions laid out by the new code, it was necessary to have a staff of competent agents, and to place a qualified person on the bench of the appeal court, Cunden Menon Peishcar recommended His Highness to invite one of the Munsiffs in the Malabar zillah. In accordance with this suggestion, the services of one Bagavuntha Row, a Munsiff, were availed of, he having been invited through the Resident. Bagavuntha Row was appointed first judge of the appeal court on his arrival in Trevandrum.

By Regulation VI, the power of supreme magistracy was vested in the Dewan, and by that measure Cunden Menon Peishcar became virtually the head magistrate, and he took in hand the organization of the police and magistracy, while Bagavuntha Row, Judge, arranged every point connected with the civil and criminal departments. In the course of a few months, the powers of the judicial departments in Travancore were clearly established, and placed on a permanent footing, and the people became generally acquainted with the newly introduced system.

A couple of years subsequent to Suba Row's appoint-

CHAP. VII. ment as Dewan, he began to arrange for the conduct of a general garden survey, which was then over due in accordance with established rule, as no such survey had been held since the year 993 M.E., when one was commenced by the Dewan Daven Padmanabhen and concluded in 993, during the administration of Reddy Row. Dewan Peishcar Cunden Menon got the credit of carrying the measure into execution, during that officer's time, and this survey was concluded in the year 1012 M.E. (1837 A.D.), subsequent to the said Peishcar's death.

Dewan Suba Row, whose powers had been virtually usurped by the intelligent and painstaking Dewan Peishcar, had nothing to do beyond affixing his signature to all the communications prepared under the directions of Cunden Menon. The Dewan now grew jealous, and in consultation with his first assistant Dewan Peishcar Cochu Sankara Pillay, who was also highly envious of his junior colleagues' success in office, began to thwart the Peishcar in many of his really praiseworthy undertakings. But Suba Row's ill-devised endeavours against Cunden Menon were not successful, as the Peishcar had the firm support of the Maha Rajah and the Resident in all really important measures. But the successful career of Cunden Menon was arrested by his sudden and serious illness.

After a distinguished service of two years, he died at Trevandrum. In him, Travancore lost a most able and promising officer, from whom the people expected still greater benefits if providence had spared him.

In the Malabar year 1011 (1836 A.D.), the Maha Rajah sanctioned the abolition of duty on one hundred and sixty-five articles of different descriptions on which inland, as well as export and import duty, had been levied. The advantages of English education being fully appreciated by the Maha Rajah from personal experience, His Highness now thought of placing the same within the reach of his subjects, by introducing an educational system in Travancore.

In 1009 M.E. (1834 A.D), His Highness in consultation with the Dewan, sanctioned the opening of an English school at Trevandrum, and Mr. J. Roberts, who was then keeping a private school at Nagercoil, was invited to take charge of this institution, on a monthly grant of 100 Rupees. Subsequently, in the Malabar year 1012 (1836 A.D.) this institution was converted into a Sircar free school, and Mr. Roberts was admitted into the Sircar service, on a salary of 300 Rupees per mensem. The then Resident Colonel and afterwards General J. S. Fraser, a gentleman who delighted in the patronage of sciences and learning, also took a great interest in the spread of English education in Travancore. The establishment of the free school was followed by the opening of a few branch schools in the districts. Thus was English education introduced in Travancore by this illustrious sovereign, and thus was Western knowledge offered to the Maha Rajah's subjects free of any charge.

The Maha Rajah, even when a student, used to compare the relative connection between Sanscrit and English sciences, a fact which is also mentioned by Colonel Welsh; and as His Highness had a good knowledge of the Hindu science of astronomy, he had often discussed the subject with the then commercial agent of Alleppey, Mr. Caldecott, who being well versed in that science, used to make astronomical observations with several portable instruments of his own. Mr. Caldecott's descriptions of his observations of the various movements of the heavenly bodies, closely corresponding with the calculations and observations of the Hindu Astronomers, the Maha Rajah was most anxious for a thorough investigation of this science.

At about this time, the Maha Rajah being on a tour to the northern districts, visited Alleppey, and had thus an opportunity of examining several interesting astronomical instruments, belonging to Mr. Caldecott, who suggested the construction of a small Observatory

CHAP. VII. at Alleppey; but the Maha Rajah wished to have a good building erected at Trevandrum. His Highness therefore desired Mr. Caldecott to make an official proposal, through the Resident, Colonel Fraser, for the construction of an Observatory at Trevandrum. The measure was duly proposed, and it having been readily sanctioned by the Maha Rajah, Mr. Caldecott was appointed His Highness' astronomer.

The Observatory was built under the superintendence of Lieutenant (now Colonel) Horsley, of the Madras Engineers, and Mr. Caldecott, having placed his private astronomical instruments at the disposal of the Sircar, and having also obtained a few more from England, commenced operations in 1837. Subsequently, many valuable and choice instruments were purchased and the Trevandrum Observatory being thus placed on a fair footing, became a most important institution of the kind in India.

The following abstracts of Mr. J. A. Brown's magnetical observations, while distinctly showing the origin and maintenance of the Trevandrum Observatory, bears strong and impartial testimony to His Highness' qualifications and character, as described above:—

"The Trevandrum Observatory owed its origin in "1836, to the enlightened views of His Highness "Rama Vurmah, then reigning Rajah of Travancore, "and to the encouragement given to them by the late "General Stuart Fraser then representing the British "Government at Trevandrum.

"The advantages which might accrue to science by "the establishment of an Observatory in the most "southern part of the Indian peninsula were first "brought to the Rajah's notice by Mr. J. Caldecott, "then the commercial agent of the Travancore "Government at the port of Alleppey. His Highness, "desirous that his country should partake with Euro-"pean nations in scientific investigations, sanctioned "the construction of an Observatory, named Mr.

" Caldecott its director, and gave him power to furnish " it with the best instruments to be obtained in " Europe. CHAP. VII.

* * * * * *

" His Highness was celebrated throughout India " for his love of learning, for a cultivated mind, great " poetical powers, and a thorough knowledge of many " languages. His Highness is well known also for his " decision of character, and took the whole subject at " once under his special protection."

* * * * * *

The virtues of European medicines and the benefits to be derived from European medical treatment having been thoroughly appreciated from experience, ever since the appointment of a Doctor, as medical attendant upon the royal family, this benevolent Maha Rajah wished that his subjects should also share in its advantages. He therefore sanctioned the establishment of a charity hospital at Trevandrum, under the superintendence of the palace physician.

The construction of the Sree Padam palace, during the former reign, on a plan drawn by a European Engineer, had impressed His Highness, even when quite young with a favourable opinion of European engineering skill. The recent construction of the Observatory simply confirmed this impression. The Maha Rajah, desirous of introducing a knowledge of European engineering art into Travancore, in consultation with the Resident Colonel Fraser, sanctioned the organisation of an experimental engineering department, and Lieutenant Horsley was offered, and accepted, the post of a Visiting Engineer and Superintendent of Irrigation and other important works at Nanjenaud and Trevandrum.

An irrigation maramuth department was established at Nanjenaud and a superintendent appointed. A few companies of pioneers were formed for irrigation works at Nanjenaud, under the general supervision of the visiting Engineer Lieutenant Horsley, who began to

CHAP. VII. devote his unremitting attention to the improvement of all the maramuth works in Travancore.

This very able Engineer's literary work "Memoirs of Travancore" written at the request of the Resident, Colonel Fraser, shows his knowledge of the country, and how he exerted himself to be closely acquainted with everything connected with Travancore.

The Maha Rajah commissioned His Highness' Astronomer, Mr. Caldecott, to procure a small printing press, and employ the same in connection with the Observatory; but this gentleman at first introduced lithography, and subsequently, in consultation with the Resident, printing presses were ordered from England and a printing department established. Mr. Sperschneider (the father of the present Dr. Sperschneider of the Nair brigade), was appointed superintendent of the printing department. In the year 1839 the first Anglo-Vernacular Calendar of Travancore (for the Malabar year 1015) was issued from this press.

The maramuth department, for repairing and constructing palaces, pagodas, and similar works, was now reorganised on a larger scale, and a person of experience was appointed, with an adequate salary, as superintendent.

The sudden death of Cunden Menon Peishcar was the subject of general remark. Though he died a natural death from a carbuncle on the back, and though he was attended by the palace physician and the residency doctor, yet the popular voice had it that the Peishcar had fallen a victim to the arts of witchcraft practised against him by some of the devil-worshippers of the south, under the support and instigation of the Peishcar's enemies.

His Highness the Maha Rajah had reasons to be dissatisfied with Dewan Suba Row, and his assistant Cochu Sankara Pillay Peishcar. About this time some serious charges were preferred against these high officials by a number of petitioners. In 1012 M.E.

(1837 A.D.), the Maha Rajah issued orders with the concurrence of the Resident, Colonel Fraser, for the suspension of the Dewan and the Peishcar. The first Judge of the appeal court, Narayanen Kasaven, was dismissed in 1010 M.E. (1835) on certain charges which were pending inquiry before the palace. A commission was now appointed, consisting of two European officers and as many natives, presided over by the then Conservator of Forests, Mr. Munro, a son of the late Resident, Colonel Munro, to inquire into the charges against the accused. After a prolonged inquiry of about two months, the impeachment was found to be unsustainable, and the commission closed their sitting, but the Maha Rajah being dissatisfied, thought it proper not to re-instate the Judge, the Dewan and the Peishcar in their respective offices. After the suspension of Dewan Suba Row and Peishcar Cochu Sankara Pillay, Mr. Runga Row, the then Dewan Peishcar, was authorised to assume the functions of Dewan. Runga Row was the younger brother of the former popular Dewan Vencatta Row, and the father of Rajah Sir T. Madava Row, and being a very active and honest officer of the Sircar, he conducted the administration most satisfactorily.

The Maha Rajah, remembering the good qualities and ability of the ex-Dewan, Vencatta Row, entertained the idea of re-appointing him to the office of Dewan, and in consultation with His Highness' brother, the Elia Rajah, this wise measure was resolved upon. His Highness the Elia Rajah then wrote to Vencatta Row, who expressed his willingness to accept the kind offer. The Maha Rajah then deputed His Highness' favourite attendant, one Cunjen Thampan of Vycome, to Combaconum, to arrange personally with Vencatta Row regarding his return.

In the next year 1013 (1838 A.D.), Vencatta Row arrived at Trevandrum, and was at once appointed Dewan.

He began to display his characteristic energy in the

CHAP. VII. administration, and his proceedings gave entire satisfaction to His Highness the Maha Rajah. As the new Dewan was progressing in his brilliant career, he had the misfortune to fall out with Captain Douglas, the then Acting Resident. Finding that they could not agree, Vencatta Row tendered his resignation, though much against His Highness' wish, in the month of Meenam 1014 (1839 A.D.), after a career of only twelve months.

Dewan Peishcar Runga Row, having resigned his office, when his brother Vencatta Row was appointed Dewan, there was no fit officer at the time in the Huzzoor establishment to conduct the administration, and consequently, the Maha Rajah, in consultation with the Resident, Captain Douglas, called in the other ex-Dewan Suba Row, in the year 1014 M.E. (1839 A.D.), to resume charge of the administration. His absence of a little more than two years from office, and even the inquiry beforementioned did not seem to weigh upon his mind in the least, and Dewan Suba Row resumed charge of the office in the gayest spirit as if he had been attending the cutcherry all the time.

Though the resignation of Vencatta Row was generally and deeply regretted by the people, yet Suba Row was also not wanting in popularity. Dewan Suba Row kept in his old groove. His administration was marked by great success, and the Maha Rajah considered the arrangements best suited to the times.

In the year 1015 M.E. (1840 A.D.), the Dewan's power was increased and his hands strengthened, for, the heads of the several departments of the Huzzoor cutcherry were now prevented by a royal writ, from corresponding directly with the palace, and the Dewan was made the only officer in the Huzzoor cutcherry competent to issue orders and instructions to the various subordinate officers.

By this time, the Maha Rajah's reputation and renown were spread throughout India, and His Highness' court became the cynosure of attraction.

It was always thronged by men of learning from all parts of India. Sastries from Bengal, Benares, Combaconum, and other places noted for learning, now resorted to the capital of Travancore, partly to take service under so renowned a Maha Rajah, and partly to display their knowledge. A distinguished scholar, by name Sankara Jossiyer, who was one of the principal pundits of the court of His Highness Runjeet Sing, Maha Rajah of Lahore, and who had highly distinguished himself in northern India, was now entertained in the Maha Rajah's service, as the first judge of the appeal court. Native astronomers and astrologers from all parts of India, were also in the Maha Rajah's employment. The Maha Rajah was also a patron of music, and several distinguished musicians from Tanjore, Tinnevelly, Palghaut, Mysore, and Malabar were now taken into the service. Mussulman singers of renown were invited to the court. An East Indian was employed to practise English music. Portable organs, musical boxes of various sizes, and several other musical instruments, were purchased.

Many native medical practitioners of note visited the Maha Rajah's court. A Huckeem of some note from Delhi had been in the court for some time, and the renowned Huckeem of Tinnevelly, Madar Hoossein, Tahsildar's son Hayathally Khan, was employed, and that old man is still in the service.

A number of native boxers from Travancore and other parts of Malabar skilled in the art of fencing, single combat, sword, stick, and other exercises, were entertained for the amusement of the court. To witness the mode of champion-fighting in other countries, the Maha Rajah got from the court of Mysore a few sets of trained athletēs called mullaga jetties, who fight in single combat, till the combatants' bodies are bathed in blood. The Maha Rajah's curiosity was very peculiar, as His Highness used to take a great interest in seeing all kinds of wonderful feats and rarities. His Highness, who had already seen specimens of nearly all the European nations, now wished to see a Chinese, of whose skill in arts and manufactures His Highness had heard a good deal. Two Chinese jugglers were brought and were for a long time attached to the palace. As they had a very funny way of taking their meals by means of two small sticks, the Maha Rajah used to see them fed at the palace in his presence. They remained in the palace for a long time, and afterwards were allowed to return to their native land loaded with presents.

Arabs, Negroes, Turks, Malays, Japanese, Nepaulese, and people of almost every nationality of India were brought to Trevandrum one by one at different times, to satisfy His Highness' curiosity. A set of pyalwans (Mussulman champions) from Hyderabad who perform wonderful feats and exhibit extraordinary powers of muscle, were entertained at the court for some time. The performances exhibited by these men would be considered exaggerated, even if correctly related. One of them, a young man of about thirty years of age, with a strong-built body, used to lie on his back and allow a thick granite stone slab to be placed on his breast, and have the same split into pieces by pounding it with a thick iron pestle. He used to throw large iron cannon balls into the air and receive them on his head, back and breast.

In short, there was no science in India which had not a representative of it in the Maha Rajah's court during this period. And this highly satisfactory state of affairs at the court and the proper administration of the country of Travancore excited the admiration of all the neighbouring countries, while the Madras Government expressed their unqualified satisfaction at the young Maha Rajah's conduct of the administration.

A very rich and influential native of Madras, Veeraswamy Naidoo, repaired to Trevandrum, and after having had an interview with the Maha Rajah, resolved

FOR HIGGINBOTHAM & Co.

GENERAL CULLEN.

to stay at His Highness' court. A short time afterwards, the Maha Rajah appointed him as the fourth judge of the appeal court. This man had a good knowledge of horses, and so he was allowed to have the supervision of the Maha Rajah's stables. A richly gilt and splendid car was constructed for the Maha Rajah's conveyance on State occasions under Veeraswamy Naidoo's superintendence, and on his own plan, and this beautiful carriage was admired by all who saw it, and even European Engineers have expressed their surprise at the native workmanship and the ingenuity displayed in its execution.

In the early part of the year 1016 M.E. (1840 A.D.), General (then Colonel) Cullen was appointed Resident of Travancore; and a young Telugu Brahman by name Krishna Iyen, afterwards known as Krishna Row followed the Resident to Travancore. This Brahman appears to have been under General Cullen while he was in the Commissariat at Madras. Although he had only a limited knowledge of English, he wrote a good hand, and was a very fast writer and intelligent and active in his habits.

General Cullen was struck with the eloquence, affability and knowledge of the Maha Rajah at their first interview, and as the General was a good scientific scholar, he applauded the Maha Rajah's learning, his poetical taste, as well as His Highness' patronage of the Western sciences and began to co-operate with His Highness in all his scientific improvements.

Krishna Row, was a great favourite of General Cullen, and he now began to be ambitious, and desirous of getting into the Travancore service. Though there was no opening at the time, the Maha Rajah thought it wise to do something for the young Brahman with the view of pleasing the Resident, and accordingly, a new office was created for him in the Huzzoor cutcherry under the denomination of deputy Peishcar on a monthly salary of 300 rupees. His duty was to manage the Devaswam, Ootupurah and

CHAP. VII. Sawyer departments. Matters went on satisfactorily and harmoniously for some time, but Krishna Row aspiring to a higher position began slowly to work with the view of overthrowing Dewan Suba Row.

The Maha Rajah was naturally very sensitive, and therefore would not submit to the least contradiction, or slight thrown on his authority, from any quarter whatever.

General Cullen, being a little defective in his sense of hearing, the Maha Rajah had to speak in a loud tone during his interview with him. This was not at all agreeable to His Highness. He was rather delicate in constitution, and the strain on His Highness' lungs seemed to injure his health. His interviews with the Resident therefore were not very frequent and when a private meeting was sought, the Maha Rajah often tried to avoid seeing him under some excuse or other.

The Deputy Peishcar, Krishna Row, was the principal person who used to furnish information to the Resident on all matters connected with the Government, and he took this opportunity of prejudicing General Cullen's mind against Dewan Suba Row, intimating that the excuses of the Maha Rajah and his unwillingness to receive visits from the Resident, proceeded from a personal disregard to the Resident; that the Dewan advised the Maha Rajah not to make himself too friendly with the Resident; and that His Highness was acting solely under the counsel of Suba Row. Thus the first seeds of misunderstanding were sown in General Cullen's mind, and he being a proud man, and of a somewhat resentful disposition, though kind and affable, as a rule, began to view things in Travancore with a prejudiced eye, and to weigh matters with a biased mind. Decisions on public questions of importance were altered, and objections to every measure proposed and suggested by the Dewan under the authority of the Maha Rajah, became the order of the day. The Resident commenced receiving petitions from parties concerned in police, revenue, and civil cases pending before the respective officers and tribunals, called for reports and records from the Dewan and the appeal court, and gave final opinions and decision on all questions brought to his notice. This as a matter of course, attracted the attention of grievance-mongers, who used to resort to the residency with their complaints, and thus the Resident's office became virtually a court for hearing, inquiring and settling all questions brought before it, questions affecting the general internal administration of Travancore. CHAP. VII.

The Resident assumed almost sovereign authority. Every appointment of importance, such as tahsildars, munsiffs, superintendents, &c., were ordered to be made after official communication with the Resident and after obtaining his special sanction. In short, the Dewan's hands were tied up, and he was rendered incompetent to give even an increase of salary to the writers and others in his own office without the special sanction of the Resident.

This extraordinary interference of the Resident irritated the Maha Rajah, and the misunderstanding between His Highness' court and the residency became stronger and stronger. Meanwhile, General Cullen continued representing matters to the Madras Government so as to place the Maha Rajah's administration of the country in an unfavorable light. The Government though reluctant to deal with such questions upon *ex-parte* statements, yet naturally placing confidence in the statement of their representative, viewed matters prejudicially to the Maha Rajah.

The Maha Rajah also represented the state of matters to the Madras Government. But it was too late, and the Government did not give to his representation that attention which it deserved.

The Madras Government passed several Minutes wherein unfavourable opinions were recorded regarding Travancore affairs at this period, and these

CHAP. VII. opinions were endorsed by even the Honorable Court of Directors.

The Deputy Peishcar, Krishna Row, who was anxiously waiting to obtain the coveted office of Dewan ever since he set foot in Travancore, now thought that the time for accomplishing his object had arrived, and he began to use his influence with re-doubled vigour.

The people of Travancore, both officials and non-officials, who were quick in foreseeing things, anticipated the ultimate fate of Dewan Suba Row, and the advancement of the Deputy Peishcar Krishna Row. Krishna Row became the head of a strong party, and thus arose two factions in Travancore. Suba Row's influence gradually weakened, and he became simply the nominal Dewan. Matters continued thus for some time. The Dewan now found the necessity of withdrawing from the conflict, and the Maha Rajah was constrained to accept his resignation. He was allowed to retire on a monthly pension of 500 rupees. After the retirement of Suba Row, Krishna Row was promoted to the post of Head Dewan Peishcar, and was put in charge of the administration in 1017 M.E. (1842 A.D.) Thus did this protege of the Resident attain the object of his desire.

The Maha Rajah had become disheartened ever since he felt his authority interfered with by the Resident, and the administration of the State unfavourably commented on by the Madras Government.

This state of things hurt the Maha Rajah's feelings considerably, and one day His Highness calling in his father and his brother the Elia Rajah (heir apparent), observed to them that the Madras Government appeared to be solely guided by the partial reports of General Cullen, and were thus doing great injustice to His Highness. He said that it was surprising that that Government should pretend to evince more interest in the welfare and prosperity of Travancore, than the Maha Rajah himself who was the owner and the sovereign of the country, while the Honorable

East India Company was only an ally of His Highness; that the present conduct of the Madras Government and of their representative towards His Highness and General Cullen's constant interference with the internal administration of the kingdom, would seem to imply just the contrary; that the Maha Rajah had at present, in his court, well informed persons from many parts of the Company's Indian territories, and also from the native kingdoms of Mysore, Tanjore, Hyderabad, Cochin, &c., from whom His Highness had learnt that those countries were not better ruled than Travancore; that the Maha Rajah's rule in the earlier part of his reign had been highly approved of, not only by the Madras Government but also by the Government of India; that it was highly mortifying to find that fault had been now found with His Highness' rule after a career of about twelve years, and after His Highness had become experienced in the art of Government, and that if the destinies of Travancore were to remain in the hands of a Telugu Brahman (referring to Krishna Row), the Maha Rajah would rather relinquish his connection with the kingdom, than be subjected to such humiliations. After these observations His Highness produced a long address which he had prepared to be forwarded to the Supreme Government, and handed it over to his brother. This letter was strongly worded, and His Highness the Elia Rajah as well as his father were quite alarmed at the Maha Rajah's determination. They prayed His Highness to postpone his proceedings for further consideration and soothed His Highness' troubled mind. Subsequently, Her Highness Parwathi Ranee, His Highness' aunt, the ex-Dewan Suba Row, and several trusted officials and courtiers, waited upon the Maha Rajah, and requested His Highness to refrain from writing either to the Government of Madras or to that of India, against General Cullen and his protege, Krishna Row. Though the Maha Rajah yielded to the earnest solicitations of His brother, father, tutor and officers, still he was so much offended, as to

CHAP. VII.

declare that His Highness would not retain Krishna Row in the service, but would send him away even at the expense of the country.

The Maha Rajah informed the Madras Government that His Highness had no confidence in the head Dewan Peishcar in charge, and that he would not be confirmed in the Dewan's office.

As there was no fit person in office whom the Maha Rajah could select for the office of prime minister, His Highness sent for the old ex-Dewan Vencatta Row, commonly known by the name of Reddy Row, who had come to Travancore along with Colonel Munro, and who was Dewan during the reign of Her Highness Parwathi Ranee. Reddy Row responded to the call and was appointed Dewan in the Malabar year 1018 (1843 A.D.). The head Dewan Peishcar was however allowed to remain in office, but was only in charge of certain departments of the Huzzoor. This was done at the earnest solicitation of the Maha Rajah's brother (the heir apparent), and His Highness' father, who feared an open rupture with General Cullen.

The Dewan Reddy Row, though nearly forgotten in the country from his long absence and from the material changes it had undergone during a period of above twenty years, began a career quite different from that of his predecessor Suba Row. No sooner had he once more come into office, than a host of relatives and followers surrounded him, and ere long two of his sons were employed in the Huzzoor cutcherry.

The head Dewan Peishcar, Krishna Row, and the Dewan Reddy Row could not agree, and the Huzzoor cutcherry became again the scene of divided partisanship. The Dewan had the support of the Maha Rajah, while Krishna Row was backed by General Cullen, who induced the Madras Government to believe that Krishna Row was the only honest and able officer in the Travancore service, and who had the welfare of the country at heart. A few months previous to the appointment of Dewan Reddy Row, the two ex-Dewan Peishcars (both native Nairs of Travancore) were taken back into the service. One of them Kasava Pillay, was employed in the Huzzoor and the other, Cochu Sankara Pillay was appointed palace Peishcar. These men had great experience in the service, both of them having risen gradually from the lowest grade to the high post of Dewan Peishcar. The appointment of a palace Peishcar was objected to by General Cullen, on the ground of its being a new office; but His Highness observed that the Resident need not extend his interference with the Maha Rajah's domestic affairs.

The proceedings of Krishna Row as head Dewan Peishcar were anything but satisfactory to His Highness. He always sought for an opportunity to make himself obnoxious to the Maha Rajah. Finding that the existence of Krishna Row in office was an obstacle to the Dewan in carrying on his business and that his party was growing powerful day by day, the Maha Rajah was determined to remove him from the service, and with all the support that General Cullen could give him, His Highness' resolution prevailed, the Madras Government agreed with His Highness and allowed him to act according to His Highness' own views in the matter.

In the commencement of the year 1019 M.E. (1843 A.D.), six months after the appointment of Dewan Reddy Row, head Dewan Peishcar Krishna Row was dismissed from the service, and as the Maha Rajah prohibited his remaining at Trevandrum, the fallen Statesman was obliged to take up his residence at Quilon.

General Cullen considered these proceedings of the Maha Rajah as a slight offered to him, and under this impression, began to work for tho expulsion of the Maha Rajah's tutor, the ex-Dewan Suba Row, from Travancore. A good deal of correspondence passed between the Maha Rajah and the Resident, as well as the Madras Government, and at last, Suba Row's

CHAP. VII. removal from Travancore was insisted upon by the Madras Government, and the Maha Rajah yielded to the decision of the paramount power.

After some time, the Maha Rajah succeeded in recalling Suba Row to his capital from Tanjore, where he had proceeded in obedience to the orders of the Madras Government. But the Maha Rajah was greatly affected by the decision of Government which he looked upon as unnecessarily severe. The Maha Rajah thought that His Highness' authority and power in his own country had been set at nought. From this time His Highness became indifferent regarding the administration of the country and was dejected in mind. His health began to fail and a complaint which added to the uneasiness of his mind, began to prey upon His Highness' delicate constitution.

Being a learned monarch, His Highness now began to devote his time more to religious devotions than to anything else, and spent his time mostly in prayer, ablutions, and in attending to the worship of the great pagoda at Trevandrum.

The Maha Rajah began to fulfil his vows by devoting large sums of money to His Highness' household deity Padmanabha Swamy, ever since the commencement of his ailments. On days when His Highness went to offer or fulfil the vows, he used to fast and abstain from taking his usual food and from receiving visits from any one; so much so, that His Highness even denied an audience to his nearest relatives. Hence, the Dewan could not find time for submitting his reports as usual, nay, he could hardly get admittance into the royal presence more than once in a month.

In every month, several days were devoted for the fulfilment of the vows at the pagoda, and on each occasion a large sum of money was given to the shrine. On one occasion, the amount was one lac of Surat rupees, which was heaped in front of the idol of Sree Padmanabha Swamy, and the Maha Rajah took the numerous bags containing the rupees and poured the contents into the silver vessels which were kept there for the purpose. This work engaged His Highness about an hour, and he had the determination of mind to go through the labour even in his delicate state of health.

During this period, money was apparently considered by the Maha Rajah as dust, and the palace expenditure became most extravagant and lavish. Purchases of sundry articles, such as silks, velvets, kincobs, neeralum (gold cloth) and other descriptions of cloth, alone absorbed an annual sum of about three lacs of rupees : all valuable jewels brought for sale were at once purchased, and made over to the pagoda as votive offerings to the deity.

Costly buildings were constructed, such as the Karamanay stone bridge attached to the old palace, &c.

There was a total discontinuance of interviews with the Resident, General Cullen, against whom the hatred of the Maha Rajah seemed to increase day by day, so much so, that his servants were afraid to utter the Resident's name in the Maha Rajah's presence. His Highness would, in conversation with his attendants, when alluding to the Resident, speak of him as "Shuvatha" in Sanscrit, "Panddarah" in Mahratta, and "Wallah" in Malayalim.

Latterly, the Maha Rajah would not see or receive visits from any European gentlemen, and even His Highness' physician could not pay his visits to the ailing Maha Rajah, who totally refused to attend to any advice from the doctor or to allow himself to be treated by him.

During this interval, Lord Hay, the son of the Marquis of Tweedale, the then Governor of Madras, came to Trevandrum, and it was with the greatest difficulty and in deference to the entreaties of the Elia Rajah and His Highness' father, that the Maha Rajah was persuaded to see that nobleman.

CHAP. VII.

In the middle of the Malabar year 1019 (1844 A.D.), the Maha Rajah proceeded to south Travancore, with the express purpose of performing certain religious ceremonies and to worship in the renowned pagodas of Sucheendram and Cape Comorin and other shrines of note. This trip was attended with a very large amount of expenditure for the whole Huzzoor and palace establishments had to follow the royal procession. Even on this occasion, the Maha Rajah abstained from showing himself to the people of Nanjenaud as is usual, for His Highness' time was always devoted to religious observances. Nanjenaud is considered from time immemorial as the country inhabited by the most loyal subjects of Travancore, and the people of the twelve villages forming Nanjenaud had precedence on all occasions over those of any other part of the country. Every new measure adopted during the former reigns connected with the administration of the kingdom, was first proposed to the people of Nanjenaud, and they had been invariably consulted as they had a voice and vote in the affairs of the kingdom. Consequently, whenever the sovereign visited Nanjenaud, the first thing he used to do was to give an audience to the chiefs of that district. On this occasion, however, the Maha Rajah did not do this, from an apprehension that some of the old loyal chiefs might moot the question of the present state of affairs in the country, and make some remarks regarding the unusual interference of the Resident with the Maha Rajah's sovereign authority, and of His Highness' implicit submission.

After an absence of more than a month, His Highness returned to Trevandrum and resumed his usual devotional exercises. About this time, the Maha Rajah thought it proper to invest an amount of four lacs of rupees in the Government loans; especially as the reserve fund in the palace treasury was being drained away day by day.

The numerous acts and proceedings of the Maha

Rajah, fully attested His Highness' refined moral principles, and had also shown that the Maha Rajah was a bitter enemy to corruption and immorality. About this time, the career of Dewan Reddy Row gave room to His Highness to suppose that he was too much given up to his dependants and relatives, and that it was through them that the affairs were managed in an unsatisfactory manner.

At this interval, the Resident, General Cullen, reported to the Madras Government concerning the objectionable measure of the Dewan, in entertaining two of his sons in responsible offices in the Huzzoor cutcherry which was immediately under his charge, and the Government recommended the removal of those officers from their respective posts. The Maha Rajah was only too glad to attend to this advice of the Government.

In the year 1020 M.E. (1845 A.D.), the Dewan proceeded on a circuit to the Northern districts while the Resident was at Balghauty. Reddy Row visited several of the districts north of Quilon, and remained at Paravoor for some time, inquiring into certain charges brought against the tahsildar of that district. While there, the Dewan with all the officers and servants of the Huzzoor cutcherry accepted an invitation from Anantha Rama Iyen, the son of Nunjappiah, the late Dewan of Cochin, who had done some good service to Reddy Row during his former incumbency in the reign of Her Highness Parwathi Ranee.

The Dewan, on this occasion, not only received presents himself from Anantha Rama Iyen, but also allowed his followers, the officers and servants of the Huzzoor cutcherry, do the same. In conducting the inquiry against the tahsildar of Paravoor, great irregularities had been practised by the subordinate officials as well as by the Dewan's private agents, who had followed him thither for the express purpose of enriching themselves. The Dewan's settlement of a

CHAP. VII. boundary dispute with a certain Devaswam in the north called Nayathottum, was also open to suspicion.

By the time of the Dewan's return to Trevandrum, every detail connected with his visit to Anantha Rama Iyen's house, and his inquiry into the charges against the tahsildar, reached the Maha Rajah's ears. The Resident, General Cullen, too, was in possession of similar facts.

The Maha Rajah refused to give audience to the Dewan after his return, and, a few days afterwards, made the premier to understand that the disagreeable necessity of a public inquiry into his conduct might be avoided by his immediate resignation. Reddy Row wisely accepted the proposal, and sent in his resignation the next day. Upon another occasion, a Dewan Peishcar, a very able and experienced officer, who was in great favour with the Maha Rajah, was dismissed the service on a charge of corruption. The following is an abstract translation of the short royal rescript issued to the Peishcar:—

"As we had reason to appreciate your ability and "long experience on public business during the time "you were holding minor appointments, we promoted "you to the office of Dewan Peishcar, but, in course "of time, you proved yourself to be extraordinarily "avaricious like other mean persons, and various evils "have resulted, in consequence, we therefore have dis- "missed you from your present office."

Soon after Reddy Row's retirement, Sreenevasa Row, the then first Judge of the appeal court, was appointed head Dewan Peishcar, in charge of the administration. This officer was a very honest and quiet man, but had not that administrative tact which characterised many of his predecessors. Being called upon to assume charge of the administration at a time when the ablest Dewan would have found it difficult to manage affairs satisfactorily, he experienced great trouble in coping with the emergency. Reddy Row had brought the administration into a state which

Sreenevasa Row's hand was too weak to rectify. The gradually growing illness of the Maha Rajah and his consequent indifference to the affairs of the State, the increasing misunderstanding between the court and the Resident; the general inactivity of the district officials, who had all a firm belief in the speedy return of Krishna Row to office, and above all the financial embarrassments of the country, were evils which Sreenevasa Row found too hard for him to surmount. People knew that his hands were tied, and that he had no power to act in any matter for himself. The Resident called for reports on every point connected with the administration, while he was utterly unable to get a reply from the palace to his references on important matters for months together. Revenue collections fell into arrears. The tabacco revenue, which was then the chief item among other branches, began to suffer owing to the prevalence of smuggling, while the daily expenses in the palace increased on account of ceremonies and other demands. The large sum of money amounting to upwards of thirty-four lacs of Rupees which was the surplus in the treasury during the prosperous administration of Dewan Suba Row, and which had been transferred to the palace treasury on his retirement was all spent in vows and religious ceremonies at the pagodas, and the palace treasury also soon became empty. Thus, the financial difficulty became greater than all the other difficulties with which the acting premier had to deal. The head Dewan Peishcar, Sreenevasa Row, was often found in a pitiful state, especially when the time for paying the monthly subsidy to the Resident's treasury approached.

The allowance to the various establishments had been in arrears, and every day the Huzzoor cutcherry was invaded by crowds of people expecting and requesting payment.

Sreenevasa Row had some good qualities. He was quite amenable to reason. He used to seek advice from able and honest officials of his cutcherry, without

CHAP. VII. regard to their rank and position. He never shrunk from retracing his steps when he found it was necessary to do so. By such a sensible line of conduct Sreenevasa Row was enabled to show improvement in the financial department and in the general administration.

In the next Malabar year 1021 (A.D. 1845), the Maha Rajah wishing a change of air visited Quilon, and this entailed an enormous additional expenditure. Towards the close of the year, to aggravate the already existing difficulties, a great misfortune befell Travancore. An unusually heavy storm burst over the country destroying both life and property to a considerable extent.

The storm and the consequent floods destroyed many of the irrigation works in the south. Numbers of trees, houses, &c., &c., in the north came down and many ryots had their houses washed away. By this event the improvement in the financial condition of the country was considerably retarded.

In this year, the Maha Rajah's father died. This was an irreparable and deeply felt loss to the State. From this date, the Maha Rajah's ailments began to increase. He loved seclusion and solitude, and as his malady increased, his habit became more sedentary. No person had access to His Highness, save his personal attendants, of whom one man waited at a suitable place to attend when summoned. Even the physician attached to the Maha Rajah could not get any correct information regarding the state of His Highness' health. His Highness' brother, the Elia Rajah, who had a good knowledge of the medical science was his only medical attendant. Even the Elia Rajah himself could not go to see his brother without special permission. There were several native practitioners of some note and ability at hand, but they were of no use, as His Highness refused to admit any of them to the royal presence. The Maha Rajah at this time was unable even to walk a few paces.

His Highness one day called his brother the Elia Rajah, and observed that Sreenevasa Row, being a quiet man, would not be able to cope with the opposition of the Resident, General Cullen, and do his duties satisfactorily, and as His Highness had already permitted Krishna Row to return to Trevandrum and reside there, His Highness intended giving him a fresh trial, as he wished to see what effect that measure would produce in General Cullen's mind. His Highness the Elia Rajah entirely agreed with the views of the Maha Rajah, and the next day, very early in the morning, when the Maha Rajah went to bathe in the tank, His Highness sitting there, called the palace Rayasom (writer), and dictated a Neet (commission) of appointment to Krishna Row as Dewan Peishcar. After this, Krishna Row was summoned to the royal presence. Not knowing for what purpose he was so suddenly called to the palace, Krishna Row was frightened, but no sooner was he ushered into the presence of the Maha Rajah, than His Highness in a very unusual way, smiled and said, "Here, Krishna Row accept your re-appointment into my service. I forgive and forget all what is past; from this day you are my man and not General Cullen's. Go, work honestly for the advancement of my country and render every possible assistance to Sreenevasa Row."

Krishna Row became speechless, shed tears copiously, and all that he could say in his own Telugu tongue was, "Maha Rajah! Maha Rajah! I am your Highness' slave and waiting boy, protect me, protect me." This was the last commission of appointment signed by the Maha Rajah, and it took place on the 26th Vrichigum 1022 M.E. (10th December 1846).

Though the Maha Rajah now began to sink day by day, he kept this fact concealed from the notice of every one of his attendants, nor did he confine himself to his bed-chamber for any number of days. On the morning of the 12th Dhanu 1022 M.E. (25th December 1846,) His Highness did not go to his bathroom as

CHAP. VII. usual, neither did he stir out of his bed till 9 P.M. This created some alarm, and the servants soon communicated the matter to His Highness the Elia Rajah, but His Highness would not venture to enter the chamber without being called in by his brother: such was the fear, even the heir apparent and immediate brother, had of the Maha Rajah. The alarm reached Her Highness Parwathi Ranee, the Maha Rajah's aunt, and Her Highness together with His Highness' brother-in-law hastened to the palace and all the three stood near the door. But none attempted either to enter or to rouse the slumbering Maha Rajah. At about 10 A.M., the Maha Rajah hearing a whisper at the door, and recognizing the voice of His Highness' aunt whom His Highness held in great regard, called out to the attendants, and inquired of them if Her Highness was there and what the time was. There were only two attendants privileged to enter into the bed-chamber, and one of whom informed the Maha Rajah that it was then 10 o'clock and that the Princess and the Elia Rajah were there, in consequence of the Maha Rajah's not stirring out of bed even at such a late hour. The Maha Rajah got up, but so weak had he become that his legs failed to support him and when about to fall back, the attendant approached to help him. His Highness turning, stared at his face, holding the wall by one of his hands, and said "what! are you trying to trifle with me? I am not going to fall, neither am I in such a state of health." So saying, the Maha Rajah boldly walked out and seeing his sorrow-stricken relatives, asked Her Highness the Ranee with a respectful smile :—"*Ammachee amertha kalinho ?*" i.e., "mother, have you taken your breakfast?" Turning to the Elia Rajah, His Highness observed that he had slept a little longer than usual, and then gave them leave to depart. Her Highness wished that they should stay there till His Highness took his breakfast. His Highness, though fast sinking, endeavoured to conceal his weakness, but being unable to reach the bathing place, he said that he would perform his ablutions in one of the adjoining rooms, and while seated there His Highness sent for the head cook and gave him instructions to prepare a very light meal which was served at about 11 o'clock, but His Highness partook of it very sparingly, and then again bidding the sad group of relations adieu, re-entered the chamber and laid himself on the bed.

His Highness the Elia Rajah returned to his palace, and sent for the palace doctor, and told him in what state his royal brother was. The doctor wished for an interview with the sovereign, but this was found impracticable. Dewan Peishcar Krishna Row was ordered by His Highness to intimate at once to General Cullen the state of His Highness' health. During the course of the day, the Elia Rajah went more then ten times to the palace, but did not venture to enter the room or enquire personally how his brother was, for fear of disturbing him. Towards evening, however, His Highness went again to the palace, when taking courage, he approached the door and found the Maha Rajah still lying on his bed, in the same state as in the morning. They exchanged a few words, after which the Maha Rajah permittod his brother to retire. His Highness left after ordering the attendants to inform him of any change in the state of the Maha Rajah.

At about 10 P.M., the Maha Rajah called out to his attendants and ordered a little liquid food, which, being brought, His Highness sipped a little of it and then told them to leave the room. He reclined as usual on his bed, and apparently went to sleep. Towards morning, at about 3 o'clock one of the attendants looking in observed that the Maha Rajah lay in his bed motionless and breathless. He called out to another attendant who was also watching there. They both attentively looked from the door, and then slowly entered and went close to the bed side, but alas! there were no symptoms of life descernible. One of them ran to His Highness the Elia Rajah's palace and

CHAP. VII. gave the alarm, when the heir apparent got up from his bed and ran to the palace, loudly lamenting the loss of his brother. But all had been over some few hours before. Even the attendants knew nothing as to the real state in which the sovereign was.

The scene at the palace on the occasion defies description. His Highness the Elia Rajah lamented and cried like a child, while Her Highness the Ranee, who had also hastened to the palace at once, tore her hair and wept most bitterly. Her Highness was followed by all the other members of the royal family. Before day-break, the palace was thronged and filled by people. Officials, as well as all the immediate attendants at the palace, the nobles and other principal men of the town of Trevandrum, crowded in. Nothing but cries and lamentations could be heard in the palace until 7 A. M., when the funeral procession started. The four main streets of the fort were crowded by the mourning population, who followed with heart-rending cries and sorrowful ejaculations. His Highness the Elia Rajah walked bare-headed and barefooted, close to the State conveyance wherein the deceased Maha Rajah's remains were placed. All the other male members of the royal family walked behind the heir apparent.

Deep mourning was observed voluntarily by every class of people. The bazaars were all shut, so were the gates of all the houses wherein weeping and cries could alone be heard. Groups of females, with dishevelled hair, were seen at different places in the streets and gardens, beating their bosoms and heads with loud cries of grief and lamentations.

His Highness the Elia Rajah, the chief mourner, performed all the ceremonies, and undertook to perform the daily ceremonies called "Deekshah" for one year; during which period, His Highness was to abstain from all luxurious living and lead the life of a hermit in grief and mourning in accordance with the customs of the Hindus.

Thus ended the worthy career of this Maha Rajah in the thirty-fourth year of his age and in the eighteenth year of his glorious reign. Compared with the majority of his predecessors His Highness had highly distinguished himself and eclipsed many of his contemporaries in India, and from whom his subjects and dependants had always reason to expect reforms and other benefits.

Besides the numerous rules and regulations introduced by this lamented sovereign for the proper government of the country, as described above, there were several useful enactments, amply illustrating the state of civilization to which Travancore had been brought under this reign.

It was during His Highness' reign that the long established custom of disgracing female criminals, by shaving their heads and afterwards banishing them from Travancore with ignominy, was abolished.

The ghee ordeal at the pagoda at Sucheendram, whereby Numboory Brahmans were required to immerse the fingers of their right hand in boiling ghee, to prove their innocence when charged with adultery, was prohibited.

A revenue law, for remitting one-fourth of the tax on cocoanut and other trees planted and reared by ryots, was introduced in order to encourage agricultural pursuits.

The Maha Rajah continued to encourage and patronize science and education even to his latter days. This will be evident from His Highness' handsome contribution to the Rev. Mr. Bailey's Malayalam and English Dictionary, for the publication of which the Maha Rajah had rendered considerable pecuniary assistance.

It may not be out of place to insert here a copy of Mr. Bailey's acknowledgment, prefixed to his work, as corroboration of this fact.

CHAP. VII.

"To

"HIS HIGHNESS

The Rajah of Travancore.

"SIR,

"I beg to acknowledge my grateful obligations to Your Highness, not only for permitting me to dedicate the following work to you, and thus to present it to the public under the auspices of so great a name, but also for the very liberal aid you have so kindly offered me and the deep interest you have taken in the work. It exhibits another instance of Your Highness' readiness to encourage and patronize general education and the promotion of literature among your subjects.

"The great difficulty and labour attending such an undertaking, and the attention which I have been necessarily obliged to pay to my other important duties, have contributed to retard the publication of the work much longer than I anticipated.

"That the life of Your Highness may be long spared, and that you may be permitted to witness the beneficial results of the efforts now made to promote good and sound education in this country, based on the best principles is the sincere wish of

Your Highness' most obliged,

Humble servant,

(Signed) B. BAILEY.

COTTAYAM,
July 1846.

Mr. Peet's Malayalam Grammar was also published under the auspices of His Highness. Many of the works composed by this royal author are now forgotten, though there are numerous hymns and songs at present well known all over India.

LITHOG.D BY ROSE BROTHERS. FOR MESSRS HIGGINBOTHAM & CO

MARTHANDA VURMAH MAHA RAJAH

1022-1036 M.E. (1847-1861 A.D.)

CHAPTER VIII.

SREE PADMANABHA DASA VANJI PALA MARTHANDA VURMAH KULASKHARA KEREETAPATHI BHAGHEODAYA RAMA RAJAH MUNNAY SULTAN MAHARAJ RAJAH BAHADUR SHAMSHEER JUNG MAHA RAJAH OF TRAVANCORE.

THIS sovereign was born in the month of Chingam 990 M.E. (August 1814 A.D.) and was thirty-two years of age when he was destined to assume his ancestral musnud. The formal installation of the Maha Rajah took place on the 16th Koombhan 1022 (26th February 1847). CHAP. VIII.

Having been educated along with his late brother, His Highness Marthanda Vurmah Maha Rajah, was as a good a scholar in the English, Sanscrit, Hindustani, Mahratta, Malayalum and Tamil languages as the demised sovereign.

The only difference between the two was in poetical talents, and musical accomplishments, in which His Highness Marthanda Vurmah Maha Rajah was inferior to his lamented brother. But in politics he excelled, and he had a peculiar tact, whereby he used to accomplish what he had in view.

It appears from Colonel Welsh's testimony, that this Maha Rajah, when a youth, was very lively and sociable in European company. These genial qualities seemed to be developed as he advanced in age. The Europeans, resident in Travancore were more intimate and friendly with this Prince, than with his brother the reigning Maha Rajah. Both brothers lived together up to the time of the formal installation of the

CHAP. VIII. elder Prince in 1829, and then they occupied separate residences.

In his daily intercourse with the European gentry in Trevandrum, His Highness' defective pronunciation of English, which was a great drawback in those brought up under Dewan Suba Row's system of tuition, was often the subject of remark, as observed by Colonel Welsh; and consequently this Prince resolved upon improving himself in this respect. Being very friendly with the Resident and also with the residency Surgeon, Dr. Brown, His Highness prevailed upon the latter to aid him in acquiring a correct accent and to direct his English studies generally. Dr. Brown, who was of a very obliging disposition, gladly acceded to the wishes of His Highness, and contributed much to the Prince's proficiency in the English language. A few months later, His Highness felt an inclination to study the Doctor's own profession, and seeing the intelligence and aptitude of the Prince, that gentleman most willingly undertook to teach the science of medicine to this knowledge-seeking scion of royalty; and in the course of this study, the cognate branches of Chemistry and Anatomy were also taught.

Though Dr. Brown was obliged to leave India before completing his praiseworthy labours to make this Prince master of the sciences which he was so anxious to learn, still His Highness persevered in a course of self-study by procuring and reading the works of eminent authors.

As His Highness had not the least expectation of being ever called to reign over Travancore in succession to his brother, who was his senior only by one year and a half, his object was to make himself useful to his countrymen by popular undertakings and at the same time to devote his leisure hours to the pursuit of science and literature. Mr. Caldecott, the Sircar Astronomer, also rendered some assistance to His Highness in acquiring a tolerably correct knowledge of Chemistry, and that gentleman furnished him with the necessary apparatus and chemicals. CHAP. VIII.

At first, His Highness procured from the Durbar physician's dispensary a small supply of medicines, with which he commenced treating ordinary cases within the circle of his own attendants and their families; and subsequently supplies of almost all description of medicines were procured from Messrs. Bruce and Co., (now Barrie and Co.,) of Madras and also from druggists at Bombay. At this time, His Highness opened a correspondence with Madras and Bombay and became a constituent of almost all the principal business-houses in those presidencies. Messrs. Arbuthnot and Co. were appointed His Highness' Agents at Madras, and at a later period, when His Highness began to order articles direct from England, Messrs. J. Cockburn and Co. were selected in London for the agency, in private transactions. Every new medicine discovered and advertised in the newspapers was procured, and in the course of a few years a large room, which had been converted into a private dispensary, being found insufficient, a separate building was constructed on an enlarged scale to provide the necessary accommodation. Persons were selected from among His Highness' own attendants and trained by him to perform the duties of dressers. The arrangements of the dispensary were so complete, that the Durbar physician himself was struck with the taste, method, and neatness displayed, and the dispensary was the admiration of all the Europeans who visited it.

His Highness used to spend the greatest part of his leisure hours there, in treating cases himself, and latterly, this private dispensary became a regular hospital. The Hindu portion of the patients preferred this institution to the Sircar's charity hospital, for in it the patients were not only treated, fed and clothed, but were invariably favoured with presents of some sort when they were discharged. The Numboory Brahmans, who would not even touch English medi-

CHAP. VIII. cines, under the idea that most of the liquid substances contained spirits, began to take them freely from His Highness' dispensary. His Highness would explain to them the good effects of European medicines and how speedily diseases could be cured by their means. Several of the Hindu gentry came from great distances, not only for the cure of ailments, but also for the purpose of having an opportunity of seeing His Highness while they are under treatment. Trevandrum is seldom without a religious ceremony of some kind being performed there, and the noted men among Numboory Brahmans who constantly resorted to the place, had spread throughout Malabar, among their community, reports regarding His Highness' medical knowledge and the virtues and efficacy of European medicines. During the Murajapom, and other remarkable ceremonial occasions, His Highness' dispensary was the principal, nay, the only resort of Numboory Brahmans for medical aid. A learned Gouda Brahman Sastri, who came from Benares, and who was suffering from chronic dyspepsia and its attendant colic pains, which had proved obstinate against all kinds of treatment, the poor patient being scarcely able to retain a mouthful of food even for a few minutes, was successfully treated and restored to health by His Highness in the course of three months. On this occasion, His Highness' brother, the then Maha Rajah, was highly pleased and expressed his great surprise at the ability his brother displayed in the cure of diseases. On another occasion, the Maha Rajah himself was cured of an attack of diarrhœa, which baffled the doctors as well as the native Vydhians of the time.

His Highness also performed minor surgical operations, such as opening boils and tumours, cutting away proud flesh, &c., with considerable dexterity. His Highness was well up in vaccinating, and most of the palace attendants were vaccinated with his own hands.

Besides the dispensary, His Highness had a laboratory wherein all the various apparatus and chemicals which were purchased through Mr. Caldecott were preserved, together with stills of various sizes, glass retorts, boilers, evaporating dishes, crucibles of different kinds, and many other things necessary for conducting chemical experiments. There were a powerful electric machine, a galvanic battery, an air-pump, an ice-making machine, Daguerreotyping apparatus and several smaller machines for purposes of amusements, as well as experiments. Several kinds of optical instruments, such as stereoscopes of various sorts, telescopes of sizes, opera glasses, were also in the laboratory. All these were admired by the Numboories and other people who had not only never before seen them, but had not an idea of the existence or uses of such wonderful instruments.

His Highness enjoyed a vigorous constitution and his active habits would not permit him to keep himself within doors. He used to drive out almost every evening, and visited his European friends. Frequently, His Highness was found in the evening in some European house, forming the principal figure in a circle of ladies and gentlemen, talking merrily and exchanging jokes and playing familiarly with the children, so that one cannot but call His Highness the merriest and happiest royal personage, socially speaking, amongst his contemporaries.

From infancy, His Highness took a fancy to European styles and fashions, and gradually in all his mode of living he became almost Europeanized. His dress, occupations, furniture, amusements, &c., were all after the European style. A vest, trowsers and coat, with slight changes in the cut, formed his ordinary attire, and rich and profusely laced coats made to order at Calcutta, were His Highness' favourite costumes on grand occasions.

His Highness being very fond of riding, kept many good horses for his personal use, as well as for his numerous favourite attendants, who were privileged to have horses assigned to them from the stables to

CHAP. VIII. follow His Highness in his daily rides and on State occasions.

In the out-door exercises he regularly took, His Highness was attended by no less than a dozen attendants on horse back, and it was a grand sight to see him daily riding or driving, accompanied by such a number of horsemen and mounted troops. In such movements, the party often halted here and there to join in a picnic entertainment or some other amusements.

One morning, during His Highness' drive to the sea-beach at Sankhu Mukham (Trevandrum), about the year 1013 M.E. (1838 A.D.), he observed a vessel riding at anchor near Valiathoray, about a couple of miles south of the Trevandrum beach bungalow. Looking through a telescope, His Highness described a signal of distress flying from her top-mast. His Highness at once sent on board one of his attendants, who was accompanied by a trooper to ascertain her requirements. The ship was found to be Her Majesty's frigate "Jupiter," bound for Ceylon commanded by Captain Fullerton, and she was conveying Her Majesty's 97th European Regiment under the command of Colonel Campbell from England. The vessel had encountered bad weather after rounding the Cape of Good Hope, and had been detained unusually long on her voyage. The supply of water had run out, and there was not a drop on board since the previous day. His Highness lost no time in ordering a supply for present use at his own expense, and then procured orders from his brother, the then reigning sovereign, to the Dewan, to ship a good supply of water, free of all charges. His Highness accompanied by his father and several others from the palace, went on board the frigate the same day, and met with a hearty reception. The Commander, Captain Fullerton, was about to fire a salute, when the regimental surgeon informed His Highness that the report from the heavy guns would prove injurious to the health of two of the ladies on board, one being in delicate health, and the other (Major Walter's daughter) suffering from pulmonary disease in an advanced stage. His Highness, very promptly and earnestly requested the Commander to dispense with the honor intended, and it was with difficulty that Captain Fullerton was prevailed upon to accede to the request.

His Highness remained about four hours on board, inspecting every part of the frigate and the heavy pieces of ordnance and their arrangement, as it was the first time he saw a vessel of the kind; and being a great admirer of the British troops, observed with much interest the arms and accoutrements of the men on board. His Highness, at the same time, kindly procured from shore, fruits, &c., for the soldiers and seamen.

The Commander went on shore to arrange for the shipment of water, and after an interview with the Dewan, it was agreed to commence work from an early hour the next morning, as the surf was very high in the afternoon every day. This arrangement afforded His Highness an opportunity to visit the vessel again the next day, accompanied by Captain Daly, one of the Commandants of the Nair brigade, and the Durbar Physician Dr. Allardice. A few Nair sepoys were also taken for Colonel Campbell's inspection.

After the usual compliments, His Highness expressed a wish to see the British soldiers at drill, and Colonel Campbell was only too glad to gratify His Highness' curiosity. Forty men were paraded on deck, and His Highness was highly pleased to see them go through their exercises. His Highness then desired Captain Daly to parade his men for the amusement of the officers and others of the frigate, which he did. The officers expressed astonishment at the activity of the movements and the manœuvres of the sepoys, but the pity was that some of the sepoys were soon seized with the usual symptoms of sea-sickness. His Highness was greatly touched at the sympathy shown by the

CHAP. VIII. English soldiers, who, at once, came to the assistance of the sepoys, and raised those who had fallen on deck, and helped them with soda water and other remedies, while the sailors promptly cleaned the decks.

His Highness gave a treat to the soldiers and sailors on this occasion in the shape of fruits, sweets and other refreshments, and wished very much to give them a formal entertainment the next day, but Captain Fullerton could not delay, and His Highness took leave and left the vessel at about dusk, amidst loud cheers from the officers and men.

Colonel Campbell seemed willing to accede to His Highness' request, and would have postponed his departure for a day, but it was said there was some difference between the Colonel and the Commander of the vessel on the question of further delay.

From his youth His Highness took a great delight in native dramatic performances. A group of actors was entertained at his private expense, and the most renowned of the profession in Malabar were invited and enlisted in his private service, so that latterly many of His Highness' servants were theatrical performers.

His Highness' affability and sociableness, benevolence and kindness, as well as his unfailing good temper, were qualities that were the marvel of the people. An instance of his temper and good nature may be mentioned here: His Highness was one day trying a new glass retort made to order in England, to distil essence of rose, and as the process was going on, an attendant (the writer himself), who had the honor of being admitted as a companion and classed among the favoured ones, and who used to superintend the medical stores, was told to raise the retort a little to regulate the spirit lamp; when he took it up with the aid of a towel, he found it so very hot that he let go his hold, dropping the heated retort, which was shattered to pieces. He was naturally in great terror, but His Highness, instead of displaying the least sign of anger or displeasure, quietly asked him if he had hurt himself. As regards the retort, His Highness said, he could get hundreds of the kind, but he would feel sorry if his attendant had burnt his fingers, or in any way injured himself. CHAP. VIII.

This period of His Highness' life as Elia Rajah seems to have been the happiest, the merriest and the most pleasurable in his whole career, and consequently, he never wished for a change in his position.

A strong affection for his family was a very peculiar trait in His Highness' character. He looked upon his brother with even filial regard and always wished he would live longer than himself.

On one occasion, three boys attached to the palace, while amusing themselves in one of the out-houses by burning blue lights, accidently ignited a quantity of gunpowder kept in the room and burnt themselves very severely. Hearing of this, His Highness had the unfortunate lads brought before him immediately and treated them under his own directions. At the same time, an express messenger was sent for the Durbar physician, who, on his arrival, simply approved of the remedies which had been employed by His Highness. On the doctor observing that he had thought, from the nature of the message, that some member of the royal family was in danger, His Highness replied that as regards human suffering, there was no difference, whether the sufferer was a king or a slave.

From His Highness' European style of living and his predilections for everything European, also from his moving in European society, without the least show of superstition, especially with regard to pollution, such as is displayed by Hindus in general, and his approaching tables where fish and animal food were served, many a European supposed that His Highness would shake off caste restraints altogether, and even a great English Statesman was led to form the idea, that it was not quite improbable that His Highness

CHAP. VIII. would visit England some day. A little incident which occurred during the time this royal personage was Elia Rajah, serves to illustrate this notion. A Prussian Prince, who came to Trevandrum about this time, paid a visit to His Highness, and on the return visit of His Highness', the Prince being absent from his residence, His Highness left his card there. The Prince appears to have kept that card in his pocket for a long time. After his return to his native land, he went over to England, and when he called on Lord Elphinstone, the late Governor of Bombay, that nobleman being absent from home, the Prince left his card and returned to Prussia, without having an interview with Lord Elphinstone. The card which the Prince left appeared to be that of His Highness the Elia Rajah, and Lord Elphinstone wrote at once a letter of apology to His Highness, saying that he felt really sorry that he was out at the time His Highness kindly called at his residence. This letter, which arrived by the Overland Mail, caused His Highness at first some astonishment; the mystery was however cleared afterwards. This incident gave His Highness an opportunity to commence and maintain a correspondence with Lord Elphinstone. His Highness moreover kept up a friendly intercourse in writing with several gentlemen in England and Scotland, and was enjoying a pleasant and easy life, free from care and turmoil, when he was suddenly called upon to assume the responsibility of governing the kingdom, the aspect of whose affairs afforded the new sovereign afar from cheering prospect.

This Maha Rajah possessed none of the advantages which his deceased brother had at the time of his assumption of sovereign authority. On the contrary, he was destined to face difficulties and disadvantages at the very commencement of his reign. Besides, His Highness was without the assistance of good and experienced counsellors like his late father and other old and able men of the court. The kingdom was then something like a ship without ballast or a compass in the midst of a storm, and without having on board an experienced pilot or helmsman. The treasuries, both of the palace as well as of the State, were almost empty, and the financial condition of the kingdom was in utter confusion. Sreenevasa Row, the head Dewan Peishcar in charge of the administration, was of too mild a temperament, and without abilities above mediocrity and with an inability to cope with extraordinary contingencies. He was, in addition to this, in disfavour with General Cullen, the Resident. The salaries of most of the public establishments were considerably in arrears. The revenue was falling off from various causes, the principal of which was that the tobacco revenue was very greatly reduced in consequence of the prevalence of smuggling, and, to crown all, the additional expenditure attendant on the ceremonies connected with the late Maha Rajah's demise was urgently pressing on the Government. The only favourable circumstance was that His Highness had the good fortune to be on friendly terms with General Cullen, from the time of his arrival in Travancore as Resident, and those relations had continued undisturbed. His Highness resolved to inaugurate his reign by giving effect to the principle adopted by his mother Lekshmi Ranee and followed by his aunt Parwathi Ranee, which was, to be guided by the advice and counsel of the British Resident; indeed a better course could not have been adopted at this critical time.

After his formal installation and the performance of all the consequent ceremonies, the Maha Rajah voluntarily suggested to General Cullen the desirableness of making a change in the administration, and proposed to relegate the head Dewan Peishcar Sreenevasa Row to his former post of first Judge of the Appeal Court, and to appoint Dewan Peishcar Krishna Row to act as Dewan, a measure which met with no objection on the part of General Cullen and was carried into effect, with the full approbation of the Madras Government.

CHAP. VIII. Krishna Row entered upon his new office of acting Dewan by concentrating his energies to improve the unhappy condition of affairs, and to do justice to the Maha Rajah's selection of him to that most important post in which he was no mere tyro, as he had once before discharged the duties of Dewan.

Though a protege of General Cullen, Krishna Row acquired in a short time, by his good behaviour, the full confidence of the Maha Rajah, who now determined to render him every support to enable him to repair and restore the shattered condition of the Government; but without replenishing the treasury and meeting emergent demands in the way of arrears of salary, &c. Krishna Row, could not retrieve the fortunes of the fallen State with all his extraordinary activity and exertions.

Soon after his appointment, Dewan Krishna Row submitted to His Highness a full and detailed report on the financial position of the State, with exhaustive statements showing that there was only a sum of eighty thousand Rupees in cash in the treasury; that the pay of every establishment was due from the commencement of the year, *i.e.*, for the previous eight months; that the contractors of Jaffna and Tinnevelly tobacco, as well as the other merchants who supplied various articles to the Sircar had not been paid for months together; that similarly, all the Devaswams and other charitable institutions had been left unpaid, and that these dues amounted to nearly six lacs of Rupees, while the collection of revenue had fallen in arrears to the extent of a like sum or even more.

On receipt of this report, the Maha Rajah was not a little perplexed and devoted himself to the hard task of setting right the prevailing disorganisation, and the Dewan soothed His Highness' troubled mind with assurances that he would use all his exertions in collecting the arrears of revenue and paying the State dues.

Officers of ability and experience were promoted

DEWAN KRISHNA ROW

LITHOGD BY ROSS BROTHERS FOR MESSRS HIGGINBOTHAM & CO

and placed at the head of the several departments, and one of these, Dewan Peishcar Kasava Pillay, an official of long service and tried ability, was appointed head Dewan Peishcar, and was made the immediate assistant to the Acting Dewan, who had now an efficient staff to assist him in the work of administration.

During this reign, Lord Gifford, a son of the then Madras Governor, the Marquis of Tweedale, paid a visit to Travancore and the Maha Rajah received him with due honors. This young nobleman, accompanied by Major Shirreff, the commandant of the Nair brigade, and a select party of gentlemen, for some time enjoyed the sport of elephant shooting on the Neduvangaud Hills.

In the first year of Dewan Krishna Row's accession to office, he attended to the due performance of all the ceremonies connected with the demise of the late Maha Rajah, to the satisfaction of the royal family and of the people of Travancore generally, and this secured him a good name and earned for him the additional satisfaction of the Maha Rajah's good will.

In 1023 M.E. (1847 A.D.), the deceased Maha Rajah's anniversary ceremonies had to be performed, and the reigning Prince was pleased with the manner in which this obligation was fulfilled.

It was after this ceremony that the Maha Rajah had sufficient time at his command, to engage himself actively in administrative affairs.

Meanwhile, Krishna Row had the misfortune to incur an amount of odium among many of the European residents of Travancore. As he had the warm support of General Cullen, he paid little or no attention to the European gentlemen in the Travancore service or to other Europeans, resident in the country.

One of his weaknesses was a slight tendency towards arbitrary proceedings, which he found at times unable to repress in the discharge of his functions. He had heard a good deal about the Dalawah Valu Thamby

CHAP. VIII. and Colonel Munro, who had introduced reforms in old times by the use of the rattan and whip, but he does not seem to have thought that times and circumstances were altered. Unmindful of this, he kept a pair of half-hunters in his office and used them freely in correcting irregularities and abuses, without any formal process, so that while he was engaged in checking abuses, his own acts acquired a name which gave his enemies a handle to hold him up to public reproach.

The then editor of the *Madras Athenæum*, Mr. Meade, the famous writer of the "Centenary of Plassey" in the *Friend of India*, was furnished with particulars of these summary proceedings by certain gentlemen in Travancore, and his mind was prejudiced against Krishna Row's administration.

At this juncture, a correspondent under the designation of "Not the last" began to publish in the *Athenæum* unfavourable accounts of the Dewan, depicting him in the worst colours possible, and dragging General Cullen also into unpleasant notoriety.

Torture, in its vilest forms, was stated to have been practised immediately under the Dewan's eye and by the police, throughout the country. Every little irregularity was magnified and presented in a highly exaggerated form.

General Cullen, though he keenly felt these attacks, was too proud to descend to any refutation, and was content to treat them invariably with silent contempt.

These publications continued thus unnoticed for a year or more, and the result was, that, the general impression became unfavourable towards the Travancore administration, and people believed that there was not a worse ruled kingdom in India than Travancore. General Cullen did all in his power to keep the Madras Government acquainted with the facts, but, nevertheless, that Government was not quite free from an uneasy feeling as to the real state of things. This bad impression was shared by the Government of India, as will be shown hereafter. CHAP. VIII.

The Maha Rajah foresaw the evil which would result from such unchallenged statements, which he perused with the greatest concern, and the Dewan was often summoned to the royal presence, and warned to take every precaution not to give just cause for complaint, and at the same time to use every exertion to remove any evil which might be in existence. The Maha Rajah used to read every paper and make notes of whatever concerned Travancore. One of the palace writers was ordered to have all the articles bearing on the affairs of the country copied in a book in their entirety, after their perusal by the Maha Rajah.

His Highness also deputed private emissaries to the local districts to see if torture or other acts of oppression were practised by the police, and Dewan Krishna Row on the other hand was not idle. He instituted thorough enquiries and made examples of a few whose misconduct was discovered, but this course, instead of being viewed favourably, was taken as corroborative of the existence of oppression and arbitrary practices as urged by "Not the last," and the articles in the *Athenæum* began to appear with redoubled force and vehemence.

The Maha Rajah used to take a great interest in the English education of His Highness' nephews, of whom there were four Princes, the eldest of whom laboring under unsoundness of mind, and the third not having a sharp understanding, the training of His Highness' second nephew, the present Maha Rajah, and that of his younger brother, His Highness the present First Prince, was conducted with great attention and care.

The late Dewan Suba Row, as a privileged instructor of the royal family, commenced teaching the Princes English, and his sons afterwards undertook this duty. But subsequently, one Sankara Menon, a scholar of the Cottayam College was appointed as tutor. The

CHAP. VIII. present Maha Rajah, the then first Prince, made very satisfactory progress during the five years he was under the tuition of Sankara Menon, and wrote excellent letters and began to distinguish himself in conversation with Englishmen. His Highness' brother too made considerable progress under the same tutor and began to write short essays.

A few months after the Maha Rajah's installation, His Highness began to comtemplate the placing of the education of His Highness' nephews upon a better footing, getting some Europeans from Madras when Vasudeva Row, the eldest son of the ex-acting Dewan Runga Row, wrote to His Highness requesting him to take under His Highness' patronage his brother T. Madava Row, and the Maha Rajah, in consultation with General Cullen, resolved to appoint the young man as tutor to the Princes.

In the month of Makaram 1024 M.E. (January 1839 A.D.), the Maha Rajah proceeded to Attingal, near Anjengo, for the annual worship in the pagoda there, and agreeably to previous arrangements the Peninsular and Oriental Steam Navigation Company's Steamer "Achilles" anchored off the Anjengo roads, on a certain morning during the Maha Rajah's stay at Attingal. This was done simply to gratify His Highness' curiosity as he was most anxious to see a steam vessel. On the anchoring of the steamer, the beach at Anjengo was crowded with people, as they had never before seen a steamer so close to the land, nor had they a correct idea of the agency by which such vessels were moved without sails. Tents were pitched for His Highness and the Dewan, and at about noon, on the said day, the Maha Rajah proceeded to Anjengo, accompanied by the Dewan and all the principal officers of the State. A military detachment, under command of Captain Daly, also lined the beach to receive His Highness.

Several large and good sea-boats were prepared for conveying the royal procession on board. The Maha

Rajah embarked in a very commodious boat expressly prepared by the British authorities at Anjengo, and his followers were all conveyed comfortably in the others. The boat prepared for the Dewan Krishna Row, though a good and long one, was not flat bottomed, and when he was just getting into it, Captain Daly came up accompanied by his attendant bugler, and they were also accommodated in the same boat, but to make them comfortably seated, the Dewan ordered two chairs to be placed in the boat, to which the steersman objected, urging that the boat was not suited for chairs; but the dignity of the Dewan, and the impracticability of the Captain's squatting in the boat with his splendid and tight uniform would not permit his listening to the boatman's protest. The writer of this was one of the persons nominated to accompany the Maha Rajah on board, and for want of room in the boat in which His Highness embarked, he had kept himself back, and now, seeing the Dewan launching his boat, he also got into it. He had with him the Maha Rajah's valuable gold watch and guard, pencil and pocket book, together with his purse. The boat was launched, and it scarcely passed the first surf when it lurched on one side. Captain Daly's bugler who was standing behind him as his orderly, inclined to that side, and held fast the Captain's chair. This sudden movement capsized the boat.

The Dewan, in his patriarchal attire, consisting of a broad gown of blue satin and broad trowsers, made of kincob, and Captain Daly, in his new uniform, began to struggle in the surf. The bugler was very faithful to his Commander; he would not allow the Captain to be drowned alone. He held him by his neck and hung himself about him, and both were rolling together in the sea. The Dewan's bearers, who were then standing on the beach, were fishermen from Masulipatam and were splendid swimmers. On seeing their master's perilous condition, they jumped into the sea, one by one, and dragged the Dewan ashore, before

CHAP. VIII. he sustained any serious injury. Captain Daly was picked up with his bugler by a boatman. In the meantime, the writer crossed the surf and swam in the direction of the steamer and getting on board a boat which then passed by him, he reached the steamer in safety, without losing any of the articles he had in his hand, belonging to the Maha Rajah.

After looking into every part of the vessel and examining all her engines, the Maha Rajah wished to see the steamer in full steam, which request was complied with at once. The Maha Rajah looked very attentively at the dexterous motion of the paddles, and after proceeding about a couple of miles, the vessel returned to her former anchorage. His Highness was highly pleased, and Captain Evan, the Commander of the vessel was presented with a costly diamond ring, and a sum of money was given to be distributed among the crew of the vessel.

His Highness remained on board the steamer for about four hours and then returned.

About this time, His Highness thought of inviting an able and experienced native officer from the British service, in the Malabar collectorate, to co-operate with the Dewan in the improvement of the administration, expecting satisfactory results, as was the case when the late Dewan Peishcar Cunden Menon was appointed. One P. Ramen Menon, the Naib Sheristadar of the Calicut Huzzoor Cutcherry, expressed a desire to join the Travancore service, and he was appointed at first as a Deputy Peishcar on a monthly salary of three hundred Rupees and placed in charge of the magisterial and maramuth departments, both of which His Highness considered, demanded immediate and more careful attention.

All the departments of the Huzzoor began to work well when they saw the face of a stranger among them, and the affairs of the Government, showed generally an appearance of improvement.

The first munificent act of this Maha Rajah after his installation was to remit all the accumulated arrears and other dues to the Government by the ryots, during a series of years and amounting to upwards of a lac of Rupees. If the realization of these dues was insisted upon, many families would have been ruined, and for this reason alone these items of arrears were allowed to remain uncollected; but the Maha Rajah had the courage and humanity to issue a proclamation authorizing the remission of all the arrears.

Like His Highness' late brother, the Maha Rajah was a warm patron of literature, science and education, and took much interest in the improvement of all the institutions, wisely introduced during the late reign.

The Observatory, Free School, Charity Hospital and Printing office were often visited by His Highness, and he used to stay at those places a few hours whenever he visited them. Mr. Caldecott, the Astronomer, having been a great friend of His Highness (to whom His Highness owed, in some measure, his knowledge in Chemistry), took always an interest in showing His Highness the use of the various valuable instruments lately procured and adjusted in the Observatory, and in order to observe some of the early rising stars and planets, His Highness used to remain in the Observatory sometimes very late after sun-set.

About the end of this year 1024 M.E. (1849 A.D.) Mr. Caldecott died in his house at Trevandrum, and His Highness felt the loss very deeply.

Before his death, Mr. Caldecott had impressed upon His Highness the necessity of procuring the services of a first rate Astronomer from England, as his successor. He had also suggested to His Highness the establishment of a Museum at Trevandrum.

At the request of His Highness, the Resident, General Cullen, who was a scientific scholar himself, and

CHAP. VIII. who took a deep interest in the affairs of the Observatory, wrote to England and engaged the services of Mr. J. A. Brown, who soon arrived in Trevandrum and took charge of the Observatory as its director.

The preface to Mr. Brown's magnetic observations testifies to the Maha Rajah's encouragement of science, and the following is an abstract of the same :—

"His Highness Marthanda Vurmah, to whom I owed my appointment, died in 1860. His Highness was a warm-hearted gentleman, whose death was regretted by all who knew him. His knowledge of science, though greatest in Chemistry, gave him a personal interest in the Observatory, and he was ever prepared to accept any proposition likely to aid the work done in it. I shall never cease to entertain with the liveliest feelings His Highness' memory.

"His Highness Marthanda Vurmah the Rajah of Travancore having named me for the direction of his Observatory, I left Europe on the 11th November 1851, and arrived at Trevandrum on the 11th January 1852, when I took charge of the Observatory."

The Printing department was a favourite establishment of the Maha Rajah, for, from its very establishment, His Highness was in the habit of getting several little things printed for himself. His Highness, while Elia Rajah, had a portable hand-press, expressly made to order in England, which was capable of printing a page about 6 inches long and 3½ inches broad.

The Travancore Calendar, which was half English and half Malayalam, was altered at His Highness' suggestion, and two separate Calendars were printed, one in English and the other in Malayalam. Both of these were improved every year, the Maha Rajah himself correcting the proof sheets, especially the Malayalam Calendar, and so in time the Travancore Calendars, particularly the Malayalam one, became a repository of various information concerning science, literature and politics. CHAP. VIII.

As regards His Highness' encouragement of literature, the Reverend Mr. Bailey's letter published in his English and Malayalam Dictionary would be the best evidence, and the same is hereunder annexed:—

"To

"HIS HIGHNESS

The Rajah of Travancore.

"SIR,

"The very obliging manner in which Your Highness has been pleased to permit me to dedicate the following work to you, the favourable sentiments which Your Highness has graciously expressed regarding it and my former work, together with the liberality and patronage you have so condescendingly afforded me, demand my most grateful acknowledgments.

"My sole object in publishing this and my former Dictionary dedicated by permission to Your Highness' late brother and predecessor, together with other important works which I have been permitted to carry through the press, has been a sincere desire to diffuse real useful knowledge and learning among Your Highness' subjects.

"The works just referred to have required great labor and attention on my part, and I trust my labors will, through the blessing of Divine Providence, be eventually attended by beneficial results.

"Your Highness has always patronized the dissemination of literature and education, and when these are grounded on the best principles, the results will most assuredly prove highly advantageous.

"Such results I shall not be permitted to see, but that the life of Your Highness may be long spared, and that you may be permitted to witness great and

CHAP. VIII. essential benefits issuing from the various plans now in operation for promoting real good education among Your Highness' subjects, is the heartfelt wish of

Your Highness' most obliged,
Humble servant,
(Signed) B. BAILEY.

COTTAYAM,
November 1849.

In the promotion of education the Maha Rajah was not behind-hand. He was, when Elia Rajah, a great friend of Mr. J. Roberts, Master of the Free School, and took a deep interest in that institution, giving Mr. Roberts every reasonable assistance for the improvement of the school. The Maha Rajah invariably attended the examination of the boys, and prizes were distributed by himself, with promises of future advancement to those who took high places in the various classes.

Some of the students of the first class were especially patronized by His Highness when he was Elia Rajah, and they were permitted to pay their respects to His Highness in the palace on appointed days, and to follow His Highness during his evening drives. Most of the boys advanced in knowledge and attached to the first class, were young men of respectable families, and His Highness was very kind to them.

By the time His Highness assumed the sovereignty, nearly all the students of the first class had left the school and were capable of being employed, and in fact, a few had already entered Government service.

Foremost among those students was a young man named Vadadrisadasa Moodeliar, the only son of T. Soolochenum Moodeliar, the Naib Sheristadar of the Tinnevelly Collectorate and the grandson of Ramalingum Moodeliar, Colonel Macauly's dubash in the Travancore Court to whom allusions have been made in Chapter IV.

The young Moodeliar, after leaving the Trevandrum school, was taken by his father to Bombay to complete his education in the Elphinstone College, where he studied for three years as an honorary scholar, and after obtaining the highest prizes of the day, left the College and returned to his native place Tinnevelly, where he was employed in the Tinnevelly Session Court.

During this period, the Maha Rajah resolved to give a stimulus to the education imparted at His Highness' Free School by bestowing respectable employments on all the successful scholars of Mr. Roberts.

One Ananthu Pillay, a record-keeper in the Huzzoor English office, was promoted to the high post of Melaluthu or Accountant-General, Mr. White, a volunteer of the office and the son of the then Dewan's Secretary was appointed Assistant Secretary; P. Shungoonny Menon (the writer) then an English clerk, was promoted as manager of the English office; Valu Pillay, the nephew of the then head Dewan Peishcar and now the pensioned Peishcar Kasava Pillay was appointed Cundu Crishi Sarvadhi, superintendent of the Agricultural department; and several others were promoted and appointed to various departments. At this time, the Maha Rajah, who had not forgotten his favourite, Vadadrisadasa Moodeliar, wished that he should also share His Highness' patronage. He was therefore asked to come to Trevandrum and take up an appointment. The Moodeliar was at this time promoted to the head writership of the Session Court. However willing the young Moodeliar was, his father, the influential and celebrated Soolochenum Moodeliar of Tinnevelly, would not permit him to resign his post, but after his death Vadadrisadasa Moodeliar gave up his appointment, although promoted at the time to the post of Sheristadar in the Session Court and responded very loyally to the Maha Rajah's call. On his arrival at Trevandrum, he was favoured with the

CHAP. VIII. coveted appointment of the first Judgeship of the Quilon Zillah Court.

Agreeably to arrangement, T. Madava Row arrived in Trevandrum towards the close of the Malabar year 1024 (1849 A.D.), and was appointed tutor to the Princes on a monthly salary of Rupees two hundred.

In consequence of the depressed condition of the finances, no purchase of pepper had been made from the ryots for the previous four years, and the Madras Government had made some unfavourable observations on the subject even during the former reign. Besides, the ryots themselves had complained to the Maha Rajah, representing the difficulty and inconvenience they were undergoing to get possession of large quantities of pepper grown in their grounds since the last four years.

In 1025 M.E. (1849 A.D.) a consultation was held by a committee of officers, presided over by the Dewan Krishna Row, by the express command of the Maha Rajah to devise the most effective measures for purchasing pepper from the ryots. The opinion of the majority of the officers was in favour of raising a loan of a lac of Rupees from merchants and others. But P. Shungoonny Menon, manager of the English office (the writer), suggested that instead of raising a loan of a lac of Rupees among the merchants, the ryots themselves may be made the lenders, and the collection of pepper from the ryots be made on receipts granted to them for the value of the article, which, being immediately sold by the Government through the commercial agent, payment could be made to the ryots on the producing of such receipts. This suggestion was generally approved of, and when communicated to His Highness and the Resident, they concurred in this opinion, and the Maha Rajah said that Shungoonny Menon himself might be deputed to the duty of taking charge of the pepper and granting receipts for the same. In the course of four months, a large quantity of pepper was received from the ryots and despatched to the Commercial Depôt at Alleppey, where that energetic and painstaking Sircar Agent, Mr. H. Crawford, effected a speedy and profitable sale of the stock, and with the proceeds of the sale the ryots were paid, and with the surplus the costly ceremony, Thulapurusha danam, was performed in the year 1025 M.E. (1849 A.D.) CHAP. VIII.

In this year, the Madras Government intimated to the Maha Rajah regarding the intended holding of the London Exhibition of 1851, and requested the aid of His Highness' Government in making contributions to the great show. The Maha Rajah ordered the Dewan to nominate a committee of officers for collecting articles for the Exhibition, and in communication with the Resident, Dr. Paterson, the Durbar Physician, Mr. Kohlhoff, a Judge of the Appeal Court, and Ramen Menon, Dewan Peishcar, were desired to form a committee, with manager Shungoonny Menon as Secretary. A very satisfactory collection consisting of all the raw products and manufactures of Travancore was made. On this occasion, an ivory State chair, in the shape of a throne, which was under construction some time previous for the use of His Highness the Maha Rajah, was considered to be a fit specimen of Travancore workmanship to be exhibited in London, and so His Highness issued instructions to hasten the completion of the work. When it was finished, the Maha Rajah forwarded it along with the other articles for the Exhibition, with a wish that Her Majesty the Queen of England would accept the throne after the Exhibition, as a token of His Highness' regard and esteem. This idea was highly approved of by Gėneral Cullen, the Resident, as well as the Madras Government, and the State chair and the other articles were despatched to England *viâ* Madras, with a letter from the Maha Rajah to Her Majesty.

CHAP. VIII.

The following is a copy of the Maha Rajah's address to Her Most Gracious Majesty the Queen :—

"To

Her Most Excellent Majesty Alexandrina Victoria, By the Grace of God, Queen of the United Kingdom of Great Britain and Ireland.

&c. &c. &c. &c. &c.

"From

His Highness Sree Padmanabha Dasa Vanji Pala Marthanda Vurmah Kulaskhara Kereetapathi Bhagheodaya Rama Rajah Munnay Sultan Maharaj Rajah Bahadur Shamsheer Jung, Maha Rajah of Travancore.

"May it please Your Majesty.

"Major General W. Cullen, the British Resident at my court, and my valued friend and adviser, having conveyed to me a communication from the Court of Directors of the East India Company through the Government of Madras, intimating that Your Majesty had been pleased to appoint certain learned and eminent gentlemen as Commissioners for carrying out a project formed at the instance and under the distinguished patronage of Your Majesty's Royal Consort His Royal Highness the Prince Albert, for the collection and exposition in Your Majesty's city of London in the ensuing year 1851 of the specimens of produce, manufactures, and arts of all countries and nations, and awarding prizes to the most approved productions, and requesting the co-operation and aid of my Government in the promotion of this most laudable and important object by collecting and forwarding to the said Exhibition specimens of articles from my country, I have given the most particular instructions to my Dewan for the furnishing of the choicest and most useful and interesting of the productions, which instructions are now being executed with all care and expedition under the immediate direction of my friend Major-General W. Cullen. CHAP. VIII.

"The transmission of articles from this country for the Exhibition has afforded me an opportunity of which I am anxious to avail myself of forwarding also to London a chair of State, made of ivory, carved and ornamented, the production wholly of the native artists of my country, and which I request permission to offer for Your Majesty's acceptance as a curiosity, and at the same time as a slight token of my profound respect for Your Majesty's exalted person and for the numerous and great virtues for which Your Majesty is so eminently distinguished.

"I beg Your Majesty will graciously condescend to receive this friendly, but humble tribute, from the Native Prince of a country situated at the very southern extremity of Your Majesty's vast Indian empire, who is, as every one of his predecessors has always been, a faithful ally and dependent of the British Government, which, on its part, has ever extended to us its protection and favor, a relation which I humbly trust will continue to the end of time. And wishing Your Majesty a long happy reign and Your Majesty's Royal Consort, and all the members of Your Majesty's illustrious family long life and happiness.

I beg to subscribe myself Your Majesty's most devoted faithful friend and servant."

TREVANDRUM PALACE,
11*th October* 1850.

A regulation for admitting pauper suits was passed and the number of Munsiffs was reduced from 25 to 16, and the jurisdiction of both the Munsiffs and Judges extended in this year 1025 M.E. (1850 A.D.)

In the next year there were several fires in the town of Trevandrum, and many poor families became houseless. The Maha Rajah, with his usual generosity, made gifts to the various families who suffered from

CHAP. VIII. the conflagrations and were reduced to poverty. His Highness took this as a fitting opportunity to insist upon the people who lived in the town and its suburbs, to have their dwellings tiled. In former times, there was some restriction regarding the use of tiles, as certain classes of people could not avail themselves of the privilege of tiling their houses, without royal permission; but this restriction was entirely removed by a royal proclamation during the former reign, when a very serious and destructive fire broke out in the town and bazaars of Alleppey. In the course of about a year the town of Trevandrum and the Challay bazaar could boast of many new tiled buildings.

At the close of the year 1851 A.D., a reply from Her Majesty the Queen of England reached General Cullen's hands, through the Madras Government, and when the happy news was communicated to the Maha Rajah, His Highness' joy and delight were almost inexpressible.

As this was the first event of the kind in Travancore, nay, in any native court of India, a letter under the Sign Manual of Her Majesty never having been known before, His Highness considered it no ordinary honor to be thus favoured, and he therefore determined to mark this occasion with all possible grandeur and pomp.

A special temporary portico was added to the Durbar hall and was adorned with all kinds of choice decorations. The whole building (Durbar hall) was richly furnished and tastefully arranged. This being the time of the sexennial ceremony called "Murajapam," every part of the town was crowded with Numboory Brahmans from all parts of Malabar and Travancore.

A day was fixed for the reception of Her Majesty's letter and a general order was published by beat of tom-tom requiring every family residing in the town and its suburbs to have their gates decorated with flowers, plantain trees, &c., and their walls adjoining the streets white-washed. Sircar servants were ordered to see the decorating of all the principal streets and other places in the town.

In the evening of the previous day, a few companies of the Madras Native Infantry stationed at Quilon arrived at Trevandrum by appointment, under the command of Colonel Hutton.

The next day was fixed for the grand Durbar. At noon, the troops consisting of all the available sepoys of the Nair brigade and the few companies of the British troops, together with the mounted Body Guard of the Maha Rajah and several huge elephants fully caparisoned and decked with silver howdahs, flags and other emblems of the State were paraded on the plain facing the hall of audience, in the southern street where the Durbar was to be held.

A little before the appointed time which was 1 P.M., the European ladies and gentlemen of Trevandrum, Quilon, Nagercoil and other places, who were specially invited for the occasion, arrived one by one, and the hall below and the newly erected pavilion began to be filled with European gentlemen, some in their military uniforms and others in their morning dress, and ladies in the fashionable costumes of the period. All were waiting for the arrival of the Maha Rajah and the Resident, and were moving about in the Durbar hall by twos and threes, admiring the tasteful arrangements of the rooms and pavilion, and minutely examining the various splendid and excellent mirrors, pictures and the magnificent portraits of the royal family, executed by European and native artists with which the walls were adorned.

Mr. Lewis, the celebrated European artist, who came to India at this time, was invited by the Maha Rajah to Trevandrum, and this gentleman was now engaged in taking a sketch of the Durbar.

CHAP. VIII.

All the State officers, with the exception of the Dewan and the first Judge of the Appeal Court, were ordered to proceed to the residency to accompany the procession of the Resident, with the Queen's letter, to the Durbar hall.

The largest elephant in the State was richly caparisoned and a silver howdah was placed on it, for conveying the letter. Major Drury, the Assistant Resident, mounted on the elephant in his uniform and sat in the howdah, having the royal letter covered in gold cloth in his hand, and the procession moved slowly from the residency to the Fort, a distance of above a mile, accompanied by the State officers in their carriages, a battalion of the Nair brigade, a few troopers with a portion of the brigade band, and a number of native musicians, and a large concourse of people merrily cheering, shouting and showing demonstrations of joy. The road leading from the gate of the residency to the front of the Durbar room was filled with people of all descriptions, and as the procession approached places where females were gathered, these set up their usual shouting "Kurawah" (hurrah), which they generally do, in token of their regard for the sovereign of the country, as well as on all joyous occasions such as marriage, child-birth, &c.

The Resident, General Cullen, reached the gate a few minutes before the procession arrived, so as to receive the letter from his assistant in time, and as Major Drury dismounted from the howdah, General Cullen advanced and took charge of the letter and with it he entered the Durbar hall. The Maha Rajah, His Highness' nephew and relations, and all the officers of the State and many nobles and chiefs of the country, were present in the hall, where two rows of ladies and gentlemen had already taken their seats. The assembly in the hall was so large that it was considered to be the first gathering of the kind in that room since its construction. All the noted Namboory Brahmans were also present, regardless of their superstitious notions of pollution, and defilement at the approach of Europeans, Sudras and others. CHAP. VIII.

The Maha Rajah stood in the centre of the assembly and the Resident, General Cullen, approached His Highness with Her Majesty's letter in his hand. The Maha Rajah advanced a few paces, and with a graceful air received the valued packet with a low bow, and raised the same thrice to his head to show His Highness' profound respect for the Queen, and then opened the seal and perused the letter himself with a smile, while his eyes were filled with tears of joy. His Highness then again raising the letter to his forehead and applying Her Majesty's Sign Manual, which was just on the top of the letter, to His Highness' head, handed it over to the Dewan, Krishna Row, to be read out to the assembly. The place then resounded with the roar of a royal salute in honor of Her Majesty, and three volleys of musketry both from the British troops, as well as from the Nair brigade. Salutes were also fired as usual on the arrival and return of the Resident, and the band struck up the national anthem. Native music of various descriptions almost deafened the ears of the multitude from the commencement of the ceremony to its conclusion.

By the time the Durbar was concluded, Mr. Lewis finished a correct sketch of his view of the spectacle, and the same was subsequently enlarged and painted. When finished, it was taken to England by him and he had it engraved and printed there.

The following is a copy of Her Majesty's letter above alluded to :—

Sign Manual (VICTORIA.)

" *Victoria, by the Grace of God of the United Kingdom of Great Britain and Ireland, Queen, Defender of the Christian Faith,*

&c. &c. &c. &c.

" To

His Highness Sree Padmanabha Dasa Vanji Pala

CHAP. VIII.

Marthanda Vurmah Kulasekhara Kireetapathi Bhagheodaya Rama Rajah Bahadur Shamsheer Jung, Rajah of Travancore.

"We have received safely the splendid chair of State which Your Highness has transmitted to England for our acceptance.

"It was a source of much gratification to us that Your Highness' attention enabled us to exhibit in the great exposition of the industry of all nations, so beautiful a specimen of the ability acquired by the natives of Your Highness' country in the carving of ivory.

"Your Highness' chair has occupied a prominent position amongst the wonderful works of art which have been collected in our metropolis, and Your Highness' liberality and the workmanship of the natives of Travancore have there received due admiration from a vast multitude of spectators.

"We shall find a suitable opportunity of conveying to Your Highness some token of our esteem, and we hope that it may please the Almighty to vouchsafe to Your Highness the enjoyment of many years of health and prosperity.

"Given at our Court at Osborne, this 21st day of August in the year of Our Lord 1851, and in the fifteenth year of Our reign."

"By Her Majesty's command.

(*Countersigned.*) BROUGHTON."

The affairs of His Highness' Government were progressing satisfactorily, when several unforeseen events and certain misfortunes befell the Maha Rajah and the country, which threw the whole administration into confusion, affecting the financial condition of the State most seriously.

In the following year 1028 M.E. (1852 A.D.), the excessive rainfall caused inundations and destroyed all the crops which were then being harvested in the northern districts of Travancore, while the cultivation for the next year 1029 M.E. (1853 A.D.) was ruined throughout the kingdom. The land revenue, the source of the prosperity of the people and of commerce, suffered severely. Paddy and provisions were sold at famine prices and even at those high rates the necessaries of life were not procurable in the country. It was in this year for the first time, that Bengal paddy and rice were imported into Travancore, through the Sircar's Commercial Agent, Mr. Crawford, who displayed his usual energy in procuring large quantities of grain to save the lives of the famine-stricken.

Simultaneously with this dire calamity to the finances, the Honorable East India Company abolished their tobacco monopoly, which circumstance paved the way for the smuggling of tobacco into Travancore from British territories, and the measure proved highly detrimental to this source of revenue in Travancore. The revenue from the commercial department of the State was the chief item wherewith the monthly disbursements were met, and a failure of the usual profits of this department caused great embarrassment and added to the already existing financial difficulties. Dewan Krishna Row now found that it was merely a transition from the frying pan into the fire.

While the Dewan was strenuously exerting to meet these difficulties, Her Higness Gouree Parwathi Ranee, the Maha Rajah's aunt, who had been once the Regent in the kingdom fell ill and died after a short illness. This unexpected and melancholy event threw the Maha Rajah and the whole royal family into the greatest grief, especially as His Highness had regarded his aunt as his own mother, whom His Highness had not the fortune to see, as she died when he was but three months old.

As Her Highness was the senior Ranee and once regent, the funeral ceremonies and other observances on the demise of a sovereign were to be performed without any omission. The whole kingdom was in

CHAP. VIII.

mourning for about a week, and the bazaars and public offices were closed for three days as usual.

This event caused an additional expenditure, which admitted of no delay; for the expenses attending the performance of the various ceremonies connected with the demise of Her Highness were to be continued for a year and concluded at the anniversary, and so it was no ordinary trial to the Dewan at this critical time.

However, the Dewan surmounted all difficulties and managed affairs to His Highness' entire satisfaction.

The head Dewan Peishcar, Kasava Pillay, died in the previous year, but the Maha Rajah having in contemplation certain arrangements in connection with that vacancy, it was not filled up immediately.

For three years Madava Row labored hard and completed the education of His Highness the third Prince (His Highness the present first Prince). Special pains were also taken to perfect His Highness the first Prince's (the present Maha Rajah) knowledge of English, and the Maha Rajah noticing his abilities wanted to transfer the young man, Madava Row, into the public service, feeling sure that he would be of great use to the country in time.

In the early part of this year 1028 M.E. (1853 A.D.), deputy Peishcars Ramen Menon and Veeraswamy Naidoo were promoted as Dewan Peishcars, and two vacancies were thus created. T. Madava Row was selected to fill one of these vacancies, and was put in charge of two departments of the Huzoor, viz. the Chowkey and Devaswam (customs and religious institutions). The newly appointed officer began to distinguish himself in his new sphere.

About this period, a question was raised by the late Reverend Mr. Hawksworth of Thiruvellah concerning the right of men of lower castes on embracing Christianity, to move among the higher castes of people. The Madras Government called upon General Cullen, the Resident, to institute an inquiry and

H.H. THE THIRD PRINCE.

bring the matter to a satisfactory conclusion. The Maha Rajah appointed the Deputy Police Sheristadar, P. Shungoonny Menon, Commissioner, and he proceeded to the north and took down the evidence of the Vicar Apostolic of Quilon, the Vicar-General of the Bishopric of Cochin, stationed at Quilon, the Bishop and Vicar Apostolic of Malabar stationed at Verapolay, the Syrian Metropolitan of Malabar residing at Cottayam, and the Mahomedan Thankel and Cazi of Calliquilon, and also of some of the Heads of the Hindoo community, concerning the custom prevailing among people professing each of those religions in regard to Christian converts from the lower castes. After concluding the inquiry, the matter was finally decided according to the Commissioner's report.

The Madras Government about this time moved the question of the abolition of slavery in Travancore; but the subject had already engaged the Maha Rajah's attention for the last two years, and great difficulty having been experienced in convincing the various jemmies and landed proprietors (to whom the slaves belonged, and who urged that the abolition of slavery would tend to the ruin of agriculture), His Highness left the matter in abeyance.

In the Malabar year 1029, (1853 A.D.), His Highness, by a proclamation, declared that all future children of Government slaves are free from bondage, and also made provisions for the improved condition of the other slaves and a couple of years subsequently, the Maha Rajah abolished slavery in His Highness' dominions by a royal proclamation. This was towards the middle of the year 1855 A.D.

In the year 1028 M.E. (1853 A.D.), the first Judge of the Appeal Court, the late head Dewan Peishcar Sreenevasa Row, died from apoplexy, and that post became vacant. The Maha Rajah wished to give a trial to the third Judge of the same Court, one Paramasuren Numboory, a native of the Malabar collectorate, who had taken service under the late Maha Rajah as a Munsiff,

CHAP. VIII.

and was since promoted to the Alleppey Zillah Court and thence to the Appeal Court.

He was considered a man possessing great knowledge of the land tenures of Malabar and the rights of castes among the Hindus, and also as having a slight knowledge of the civil regulations of the British Courts.

This Numboory Judge was now promoted to the first Judgeship of the Appeal Court, and early in this year 1029 M.E. (1854 A.D.), by his activity and zeal in the discharge of public business, he justified the choice of the Maha Rajah.

It was already mentioned that a stone bridge was being built under the supervision of Lieutenant Horsley across the Karamanay river, during the late reign. This work was now completed and the Maha Rajah proposed to open the bridge personally with due ceremony.

A certain evening about the middle of December 1853, was appointed for the ceremony, and on that day, the bridge, a very magnificent building, constructed at a cost of above a lac of Rupees, was tastefully decorated with banners of different descriptions, flowers, banana and plantain fruits with stocks, lines of festoons, made with flowers and tender leaves of the cocoanut and palm. Two fine tents were pitched on either side of the bridge, and they were also adorned with flowers and splendid fruits, &c. The roads between the bridge and the fort gate were decorated with festoons and flowers, as is generally done on all occasions of State processions.

Early on the morning of the appointed day, invitations were issued by the Dewan to all the ladies and gentlemen of Trevandrum, and the Commandant of the Nair brigade was desired to parade all the available sepoys at the northern side of the bridge, leaving a couple of companies to escort His Highness to the bridge.

At about 4 P.M., a large assembly consisting of European ladies and gentlemen, as well as native officials and men of rank, crowded on the northern side of the bridge, while multitudes of people, men, women and children, gathered on either side of the river. The brigade sepoys formed a line, with a full complement of European and native officers, who stood in front of them.

At about 5 o'clock, His Highness the Maha Rajah arrived in procession in the State car, accompanied by their Highnesses the first and third Princes, and by all the other members of the royal family. A royal salute announced the arrival of the Maha Rajah, and the further reverberation of 17 guns informed the people of the Resident's joining the party. General Cullen was received by His Highness in the tent, where all the ladies and gentlemen were assembled, and after a few minutes conversation, His Highness, set out on foot with General Cullen, followed by their Highnesses the first and third Princes, and all the ladies and gentlemen, for the ceremony of opening the bridge. The brigade sepoys with the officers and the brigade band, together with the mounted troops and the several huge elephants with howdahs and the royal ensigns, preceded His Highness and party to the bridge. The roar of the artillery and the sounds of the native drums and music deafened the ears of the crowd.

On the procession reaching the southern side of the bridge, it halted for a few minutes and turned back in the same style as before, and the Maha Rajah and party re-entered the large State tent, where luncheon for the ladies and gentlemen was ready, and the party remained there for about an hour to refresh themselves. The Maha Rajah, together with his nephews, also stayed there till the luncheon was over, and then the party broke up, delighted and satisfied with the proceedings of the evening. Thus successfully concluded the ceremony of opening a bridge, the

CHAP. VIII. foundation of which was laid personally by His Highness the late Maha Rajah.

Though one of the two ceremonies appertaining to the coronation was performed in the year 1025, M.E. (1850 A.D.), the other one, Hirannya Garbha danam, was still delayed owing to financial difficulties, and as a formal coronation of the Maha Rajah was indispensably necessary in a religious point of view, the Maha Rajah was obliged to undergo the expense connected with that grand ceremony, and in consultation with His Highness' friend, General Cullen, it was resolved to perform it in this year 1029 M.E. (1854 A.D.) Dewan Krishna Row undertook to make all the necessary preparations for it. The ceremony was conducted with all due pomp and grandeur and concluded most satisfactorily to His Highness, as well as to all others concerned. A detailed account of this ceremony having appeared from the able pen of "a Travancorean," and the same having been quoted in the first chapter of this work, it would be unnecessary to repeat it here.

The population of Travancore had not been ascertained since the year 1836, and it was now considered necessary to take the census, for which the Dewan was ordered by His Highness to adopt measures. The mode of reckoning the populace adopted in the last census was now followed without any improvement, and consequently the result recorded was the same as that obtained by the last census, with a slight decrease. The system observed on these two occasions was to commission the local proverthecars to count the houses and their inhabitants in the classification of the various castes, and forward the accounts which are generally written on olas (palmyra leaves) to the respective tahsildars and through them to the Huzzoor, where it was finally computed and adjusted. The results of the census of this year, 1854, showed a total of 1,262,647 inhabitants while that of the year 1836 was 1,280,668 showing a decrease of 18,021 souls.

The above figures were not at all correct as was proved by the subsequent systematic reckoning. CHAP. VIII.

Having been requested by the Madras Government to collect and forward articles for the Paris Exhibition in 1855, the Maha Rajah ordered a Committee, presided over by Major Grant, the then Commanding officer, Dr. Reid, and the Deputy Peishcar Madava Row to be the members thereof. A very satisfactory and handsome contribution was forwarded for the show and it afforded general satisfaction in Paris and elicited the approbation of the spectators.

The constant appearance in the *Athenæum* of various unfavourable accounts of Travancore; the depressed condition of the finances, and the excess in the expenditure had attracted the notice of the Governor-General, Lord Dalhousie, and when information regarding the great expenditure incurred in performing the Hirannya Garbha danam at such a time, reached him, the annexation fever broke out afresh, and His Excellency considered that it was a favorable opportunity for the Government of India to interfere with the affairs of Travancore.

Lord Dalhousie, while at tho Noilgherry Hills, wrote a minute containing instructions to the Madras Government, to impress upon the Travancore Maha Rajah, the necessity of immediate reformation, and correction of the disorganized state of affairs, and accordingly, the Madras Governor, Lord Harris, sent a strongly worded communication to the Maha Rajah. General Cullen also did not escape unscathed.

The Maha Rajah felt this remonstrance very deeply, especially as the Governor-General had founded his minute upon conjectures and misrepresentations, and had no opportunity of knowing the real worth of His Highness, as well as the true state of affairs in Travancore.

His Highness the First Prince (the present Maha Rajah) who was about 24 years of age, was treated

CHAP. VIII. as a companion by the Maha Rajah, without whom His Highness seldom moved beyond the palace doors and without whose counsel the Maha Rajah seldom transacted any important business, was the first confidential personage consulted on the subject of the Government communications, and His Highness the first Prince, who was even then blessed with a sound judgment and a calm reasoning power, suggested to his royal uncle the mode of responding to the call of the Government.

A meeting of the public officers, consisting of the Dewan, the first Judges of the Appeal and Zillah Courts, and the palace Sarvadhikariakar, was ordered under the Presidentship of His Highness the first Prince, T. Madava Row, acting as Secretary. The subject was warmly discussed, and the draft of a reply prepared; which after being carefully read by the Maha Rajah, was adopted, and forwarded to Government through the Resident, General Cullen.

The Madras Government was satisfied : so also was the Government of India, and the fear of annexation entertained by the ignorant portion of the people and talked about throughout Malabar, was removed.

In this year 1030 M.E. (1855 A.D.), the Maha Rajah issued a proclamation abolishing the monopoly of pepper, and making that article a dutiable one like other staples of the country.

About this time, the Commander-in-Chief of the Madras Presidency, General Anson, paid a visit to Travancore. When the Maha Rajah received positive information as to the date of his arrival at Balghauty in Cochin, His Highness deputed Police Sheristadar P. Shungoonny Menon and deputy Peishcar Valu Pillay, the former to proceed to Balghauty to meet His Excellency and offer the Maha Rajah's compliments to His Excellency, and the latter to wait at Arookutty, the northern frontier of Travancore, to welcome His Excellency on his arrival there. From thence these officers were to escort General Anson to

H. H. THE FIRST PRINCE.

Trevandrum. The Dewan was directed to proceed to Quilon and receive His Excellency on his arrival at that place. CHAP. VIII.

The Commander-in-Chief and suite consisting of Colonel the Honorable Curzon, His Excellency's Military Secretary, Major Denison, Aide-de-Camp, and Colonel Reid, Quarter Master General, arrived at Balghauty towards the end of August 1855, when the Sheristadar met His Excellency there and conveyed His Highness' message to the Chief and then accompanied the party to the frontier Arookutty, there the Deputy Peishcar waited to receive him with all pomp and ceremony. As His Excellency and party neared the frontier (Arookutty) in cabin boats, the blowing of trumpets and the noise of drums and other musical instruments, as well as the shoutings of the crowd collected there, surprised the party. Bouquets of fragrant flowers, fine ripe limes and beautiful bunches of ripe plantains were taken to the boat by the Peishcar, and His Excellency and party were highly delighted at this, the first manifestation of the Travancore Maha Rajah's regard and attention towards the Chief Military Officer of the Madras Presidency.

General Anson and party reached Alleppey, and the Commercial Agent, Mr. Crawford, gave them a hearty reception, and they were entertained at a grand dinner that day. As it was very late when the party broke up they had to postpone their departure to Quilon to the next day. After dinner at 5 P.M., His Excellency and party set out from Alleppey, the Peishcar and Sheristadar keeping pace with the boats of the party.

Before day-break, they reached Quilon and was received by the Dewan and the Officer Commanding at Quilon (Colonel Pinson), with all the other Officers attached to the Madras Native Infantry Regiment stationed there.

On His Excellency's way from Alleppey to Quilon, at Ambalapulay (Karumady), Thrikunnapulay, and

CHAP. VIII. other stages where there was a relay of rowers, there were grand pyrotechnical displays, got up by the local officers.

There was a grand party at the residency on that and the following day given by the Military Officers.

Leaving Quilon, the Commander-in-Chief and suite reached Trevandrum and stayed at the residency. As the Resident, General Cullen, was absent at Courtallum, the Maha Rajah arranged everything for His Excellency's comfort during his stay at the residency.

In the afternoon of the Chief's arrival at Trevandrum, the Maha Rajah received His Excellency in Durbar, and General Anson was exceedingly pleased with the affability and gentlemanly disposition of the Maha Rajah.

After the Durbar, the Maha Rajah drove General Anson in his own carriage to the palace, where His Highness' niece (the only Princess) was residing, and had an interview with the Ranee and her first son, the infant Prince. His Excellency and party left Trevandrum, highly satisfied and carrying with them a very favorable impression regarding His Highness and his beautiful country. The Sheristadar followed the party up to the southern frontiers of Travancore.

The following official report from Dewan Krishna Row to General Cullen, concerning the Commander-in-Chief's visit will not be uninteresting :—

"No 1588. "HUZZOOR CUTCHERRY,

Trevandrum.

"LIEUTENANT GENERAL W. CULLEN,"

"*British Resident of Travancore*

&c. &c. &c.

"SIR,

"I have the honor to report for your information that His Excellency the Commander-in-Chief together with his Staff arrived at Quilon on the morning of the

H. H. PRINCE ATTHUM THIRUNAL.

25th instant, and at Trevandrum last evening at 7 o'clock." CHAP. VIII.

"The Deputy Peishcar, Valu Pillay and the Police Sheristadar Shungoonny Menon, met His Excellency at Arookutty, the northern frontier of Travancore, and have accompanied him down to this place, and I am glad to state that he has expressed that every attention was paid and assistance offered to His Excellency and suite all along the way.

"I myself proceeded to Quilon and met His Excellency there, by the desire of His Highness and immediately returned to this place.

"This evening at 4 o'clock, His Highness the Maha Rajah received His Excellency the Commander-in-Chief at the hall of audience at a public Durbar, and all military honors were paid to His Excellency on that occasion. His Excellency, in company with His Highness, visited Her Highness the Ranee and the infant Prince. His Excellency intends leaving Trevandrum to-morrow afternoon for Cape Comorin, whither the police Sheristadar will also accompany His Excellency, and I have sent orders to all the local officers in the south to afford every assistance and attention to His Excellency on his way throughout their respective districts.

I have, &c., &c.,

(Signed) V. KRISHNA ROW,"

Dewan.

The sudden death, from apoplexy, of Dewan Peishcar Veeraswamy Naidoo, towards the close of the last Malabar year, left his place vacant and the Maha Rajah promoted to that post deputy Peishcar Madava Row in the Malabar year 1030 (1855 A.D.)

Dewan Peishcar Ramen Menon drafted various rules with the view of introducing reforms, and he submitted them to the Maha Rajah and the Resident. But changes in the existing system were not favorably viewed at the time by General Cullen and the Dewan

CHAP. VIII. Krishna Row. One of the proposals of Ramen Menon was the establishment of separate divisions in the kingdom, each under a Dewan Peishcar.

Scarcely a year had elapsed after Madava Row's promotion, when he made a similar movement regarding the introduction of a system of division of labor among the highest revenue officials. He supported his proposals with powerful reasons, and his arguments for promoting the interests of the Maha Rajah's Government and the welfare of the people were found to be very cogent and irresistible both by Dewan Krishna Row and General Culien while the Maha Rajah had already taken the side of the Dewan Peishcar Madava Row.

In the early part of the year 1856 (middle of the Malabar year 1031), a rule was passed under the Maha Rajah's sanction establishing two divisions, one in the south, comprising the districts of Thovalay, Augusteeswarom, Kalculam, Eraneel, and Velavencode; and the other in the north, consisting of the districts of Sharetalay, Vycome, Yetmanoor, Cottayam, Chunganacherry, Meenachil, Thodupolay, Moovatupolay, Cunnathnaud, Alangaud and Paravoor.

Madava Row was appointed Dewan Peishcar of the southern division, and Ramen Menon of the northern division, the management of the intermediate districts resting with the Dewan as before.

Towards the close of this year, Dewan Krishna Row found great difficulty in adjusting the annual accounts, owing to the non-payment of the arrears of the various establishments, and the dues to the several contractors who supplied tobacco, salt and other articles to the Sircar, and the Maha Rajah considered it imperatively necessary to assist the Dewan in paying off the arrears.

A loan of five lacs of Rupees was received from the Trevandrum pagoda (Devaswam fund), at 5 per cent. per annum, with a promise to clear the debt by monthly

HER HICHNESS LEKSHIMI RANEE

LITHOG^D BY ROSS BROTHERS. FOR MESS^RS HIGGINBOTHAM & CO

instalments of Rupees (7,500) seven thousand five hundred. CHAP. VIII.

With the above amount, payments of all the arrears were made, and the Dewan continued his administration with fresh vigour.

In 1856, Lord Harris, Governor of Madras, proposed to hold an Exhibition in Madras, of the various minerals, manufactures and raw materials of the Presidency. Intimation of the same having been received in the early part of 1855, a Committee consisting of Major Grant, the Commanding Officer, Madava Row, the Southern Peishcar and Shungoonny Menon, Police Sheristadar, was formed by order of the Maha Rajah, the last named officer acting as Secretary to the Committee. A very fair collection of articles was made and forwarded to the Exhibition, together with some valuable old jewels, and a collection of rare coins, belonging to the Maha Rajah's palace. The Secretary prepared a clear and copious report on the resources of the Maha Rajah's kingdom, and forwarded the same along with the articles to Madras. A first class Medal was awarded to the Maha Rajah and a second class one to the writer of the report which was published by the Madras Government along with the results of the Exhibition. Travancore held a high place in the Madras Exhibition and competed well with many of the Collectorates under the Presidency.

The regulation introduced in the Malabar year 1010 for holding circuit sessions for criminal trials was rescinded in this year 1032 M.E. (1857 A.D.) and a new enactment was introduced by the Maha Rajah establishing Session Judges in each of the Zillahs in Travancore, on the same system as that then in vogue in the British territories.

Towards the beginning of the ensuing year, a great calamity plunged the whole kingdom of Travancore in sorrow. This was caused by the sudden and unexpected death of Her Highness the Ranee (Attingal Mootha Thampuran), the only niece and surviving

CHAP. VIII. female member of the royal family, and the only hope of the Maha Rajah for continuing the ancient royal line. Her Highness the Ranee gave birth to her second son on the (25th September 1857) 11th Canny 1033, and died on the 22nd of the same month, after a very slight illness, at the age of twenty-eight years.

It is impossible to describe the grief of the Maha Rajah and the rest of the royal family on this sorrowful day.

Though this irreparable loss could not be easily forgotten by the Maha Rajah, yet it felt that immediate measures should be taken for the adoption of some female members into the royal family.

It will be seen from the foregoing chapters, that whenever the female line of this royal house become extinct, one or two members used to be adopted from the family of the Kolathnaud Rajah, and now as the near relatives of the last adopted Princess were residing at Mavalikaray, the adoption of two young Ranees from that family was decided upon by the Maha Rajah.

This proposal was strongly seconded by General Cullen, and the Madras Government acceded to the measure at once. The adoption ceremony was performed in the same year.

The Maha Rajah's feelings of gratification on this occasion are fully evinced in one of His Highness' letters to General Cullen, a quotation from which is inserted here:

"Your name is associated in our memory with many "important and interesting events, the most conspicu-"ous of which is the permission made through your "powerful intercession for the continuation of the line "of succession to the musnud of Travancore, an event "which nothing can erase from the memory of myself, "family, and the whole country, and for which we "cannot adequately feel grateful."

PRINCE MOOLUM THIRUNAL

LITHOGD BY ROSS BROTHERS FOR MESSRS HIGGINBOTHAM & CO

The adopted Ranees were their Highnesses the senior Ranee Lekshmi Bhye, and junior Ranee Parwathi Bhye. They were eight and six years of age respectively at the time of their adoption.

In this year the tariff value of articles fixed in 1011 M.E. (1836 A.D.), was revised and a new scale introduced throughout Travancore for affording further facility for the increase of trade. By this arrangement several articles were exempted from the payment of duty.

The sepoy mutiny of 1857, caused the Maha Rajah great consternation and regret, and the Cawnpore tragedy, pierced his heart deeply as if the dire calamity had befallen his own country. Dewan Krishna Row received immediate instructions from His Highness to attend to every requisition of General Cullen and render all possible assistance to the British Government.

Every seaport, every town, and every place of note, was ordered to be carefully guarded. Every pilgrim from the north, going to Ramaswaram, was thoroughly searched before he passed His Highness' dominions, in order that all secret communications and all people travelling under disguise, might be detected.

The Maha Rajah with his usual liberality took a share in contributing to the aid of the families who suffered from the mutiny.

In the course of a year and a half, the Dewan was able to pay off not only the dues of the Sircar, but also a part of the loan received from the pagoda. In addition to these, he managed to have a large sum of money in the treasury for the performance of the Murajapam, which was to be commenced at the first quarter of this year 1033 M.E. (end of 1857 A.D.)

At the commencement of this grand ceremony (Murajapam), Dewan Krishna Row fell ill, and in the course of a week he died.

CHAP. VIII.

On the day of his death, Krishna Row expressed a wish to see the Maha Rajah, who very kindly called on him, accompanied by His Highness' nephew, the present Maha Rajah. The dying Dewan had thus the happiness of seeing and conversing with his gracious master just before his death.

This loyal and faithful Dewan begged His Highness' pardon for all the faults and errors he might have committed during his tenure of office, and informed the Maha Rajah that he was the most fortunate among all His Highness' servants, for Providence destined him to die in the service of the Maha Rajah. The Maha Rajah acted the part of a spiritual minister to his dying Dewan, recommending his soul to the mercy of the Almighty, and advising him to think of nothing but of his merciful Creator.

Dewan Krishna Row breathed his last a few minutes after the Maha Rajah's departure. General Cullen, the Resident, the Dewan's patron, also paid him his last visit an hour before the Maha Rajah's arrival. All the State officials were present at his death-bed, and Krishna Row spoke to every one of them in his last moments, retaining full consciousness to the very last. He died at about 11 P.M.

The Maha Rajah felt very deeply the loss of Krishna Row, and his funeral ceremony was ordered to be performed with all the marks of respect due to his rank and position as prime minister. Almost all the State officers followed on foot the funeral procession, and his remains were cremated in one of his own gardens.

The unexpected death of Dewan Krishna Row at such a critical time placed His Highness in a great dilemma with regard to the filling up of the vacancy.

There was Ramen Menon, the senior Dewan Peishcar, and a candidate by right, to the post of the deceased Dewan. This Peishcar was a capital revenue officer, and had experience in the magisterial line, having been employed from his boyhood in the British service, and gradually rising to the highest office to which a native could aspire at that time under the Malabar Collector. His experience was very great in the British and Travancore territories. This was the tenth year of his service under the Travancore Government, and he was now holding a position next to the Dewan.

Every one in the country, including the State officials, both ministerial and judicial, was in favor of Ramen Menon's appointment as Dewan, and General Cullen, the Resident, was also in a measure inclined to view Ramen Menon's claims favorably. But the Maha Rajah who always adopted important measures after due consideration, and never committed himself to a policy without due deliberation and foresight, did not quite concur in their view. His Highness was principally guided by a great anxiety to further the interests of his country and the welfare of his people.

While admitting Dewan Peishcar Ramen Menon's claims to the vacant office, His Highness considered that the Dewan Peishcar was not exactly the kind of person suited for the times. As usual, His Highness, consulted his nephew, the present Maha Rajah, on this important question, and asked His Highness' opinion as to the propriety of appointing T. Madava Row, Dewan Peishcar, as the successor of the deceased Dewan. His Highness the Prince approved of that measure as the best to be adopted under the circumstances, and he was of opinion that the Maha Rajah's views should be carried into execution without any further delay.

The Maha Rajah, acting upon his own resolution and the advice of his nephew, sent an express communication directing Dewan Peishcar Madava Row to repair to Trevandrum post haste, the matter having been personally arranged already with General Cullen, who also approved of the Maha Rajah's choice.

Dewan Peishcar Madava Row reached the capital on the third day after Dewan Krishna Row's death, and

CHAP. VIII. the young officer was at once placed in charge of the Dewan's duties and he continued discharging them for a month and a half when he received his appointment as acting Dewan. This was in the middle of January 1858 (2nd Makaram 1033 M.E.)

The disappointment thus made caused the Dewan Peishcar Ramen Menon to resign his appointment, though the Maha Rajah offered him the post of head Dewan Peishcar on a salary of 800 Rupees per mensem, and promised to increase the salary to 1,000 Rupees; but he would not be satisfied with a subordinate post under Madava Row, and so he was allowed to retire on a pension of 175 Rupees, equal to the salary which he was receiving in the Calicut Huzzoor Cutcherry as Naib Sheristadar, when he was invited to Travancore.

As regards the fitness and qualifications of the acting Dewan Madava Row for the important office of prime minister, proofs were not wanting. Madava Row commenced a career almost unprecedented in Travancore in modern times, and the Maha Rajah began to forget the loss of Krishna Row as an efficient premier.

Simultaneously with the appointment of the acting Dewan, several changes were made by the Maha Rajah. Shungoonny Menon, Police Sheristadar, was promoted to the office of Deputy Peishcar, and put in charge of the southern (Padmanabhapuram) division, vacated by Dewan Peishcar, Madava Row.

With the Maha Rajah's sanction, acting Dewan Madava Row introduced several changes for the efficient carrying on of business. He was very earnest in introducing reforms and manifested a great desire to adopt various new measures, but the Maha Rajah's prudent and calm discrimination prevented in a measure the rapidity of the acting Dewan's progress in this direction. Besides a great many of the prerogatives of Government were reserved to the palace the head officials of which seldom yielded to any new proposal emanating from the Dewan, without a discussion.

DEWAN MADAVA ROW.

LITHOGR BY ROSS BROTHERS. FOR MESSRS HIGGINBOTHAM & CO

Acting Dewan Madava Row was bent not only upon the improvement of the internal affairs of the country but also upon the maintenance of the best relations with the Madras Government. He did great service with his pen by giving a true account of the state of affairs in Travancore, and thus disabusing the minds of several great officers and the conductors of the leading papers in India as well as in England.

On receipt of the Maha Rajah's explanatory answer, the Government of Madras had changed their opinion about Travancore, but subsequent to Madava Row's appointment, they evinced entire satisfaction with the mode in which the administration was conducted.

Lord Harris, the Governor of Madras, visited the Neilgherry hills about this time, and while there, the Maha Rajah addressed His Lordship early in September 1858, requesting him to honor Travancore with a visit. Many of His Highness' friends including General Cullen, the Resident, expressed their doubts as to whether the Governor would accept His Highness' invitation, but fortunately the result was quite different; for the Maha Rajah received an immediate reply from the Governor accepting His Highness' invitation, and promising a visit to Travancore towards the close of the year.

On receipt of this favourable reply, preparations were at once commenced to give His Lordship a suitable reception.

The re-building of the eastern fort gate which had been commenced a couple of years before, was now expedited and completed. Fort walls, on either sides of this gate, were newly built. The southern side of the hall of audience, where stood a line of buildings for the maramuth department, was converted into a spacious parade ground; the streets were all improved; in short, the whole town of Trevandrum looked as if it had been renovated. Similiar arrangements were ordered to be made both at Quilon and Alleppey, as well as at the northern frontier.

CHAP. VIII. Towards the middle of November, the Maha Rajah and the Resident received official imformation of His Lordship's probable arrival at Cochin on the 24th of that month, and the former lost no time in summoning deputy Peishcar Shungoonny Menon from his station at Padmanabhapuram, and ordering him to proceed to Balghauty for the purpose of meeting His Lordship and conveying to him the Maha Rajah's respectful compliments. He was further ordered to accompany His Lordship from thence to Trevandrum. Shungoonny Menon waited at Balghauty where General Cullen, the Resident, was getting everything ready for the reception of Lord Harris. Preparations on a great scale were at the same time being made by the Cochin Sircar to give His Lordship a fitting reception.

The Governor and suite arrived at Balghauty on the morning of the 24th idem, and was received at the landing place by General Cullen, the Cochin Dewan, Vencatta Row, the Maha Rajah's messenger Shungoonny Menon and several European and native gentlemen of rank and position.

The Governor's suite consisted of the Chief Secretary, Mr. Pycroft; the Private Secretary, Mr. Murray, Military Secretary, Captain Roberston; Aide-de-Camp; the Honorable Captain Harris and Doctor Sanderson.

After breakfast, Shungoonny Menon was introduced to the Governor and he discharged his mission by conveying to His Lordship the Maha Rajah's greetings.

The Governor and party stayed two days at Balghauty and left that place on the evening of the 26th November in Her Majesty's Steamer "Feroze," which brought His Lordship from Calicut to Cochin. General Cullen preceding the party by backwater to Quilon.

The acting Dewan Madava Row was now confirmed in his office, and the Maha Rajah ordered him to go to Quilon, to receive the Governor on his landing there.

A large temporary shed was erected on the Quilon beach, with profuse decorations, and it was neatly furnished. All the available officers and men of the 2nd Regiment, M. N. I., stationed at Quilon, lined the beach to salute the Governor on arrival.

Lord Harris and party landed at Quilon on the morning of the 27th, and was received by the Resident, the Dewan, and by all the officers, Civil and Military, assembled there. The party proceeded to the Residency and remained there till the evening of the 29th when they proceeded by backwater to Trevandrum, where Lord Harris reached early on the morning of the 30th, and as may be imagined, had a warmer and grander reception than at Quilon.

The landing place was covered with a number of splendid temporary buildings. A large State tent was pitched there. The steps leading to the buildings and the tent were decorated with roses and other fragrant flowers, and the road was lined on both sides by the brigade sepoys and mounted troopers. A salute of 19 guns was fired as soon as Lord Harris set his foot on the landing place. The party, after staying a few minutes in the tent, proceeded to the Residency, the Governor and General Cullen getting into the Maha Rajah's magnificent carriage drawn by four horses, and the others following in other equipages.

The gubernatorial party were lodged in the Residency, which building had been previously prepared for the grand occasion. State tents were also pitched in the Residency premises for their accommodation.

His Highness the third Prince (the present first Prince) paid a visit to Lord Harris after breakfast and had a few minutes conversation with him.

The next day, His Lordship the Governor required a little rest after his fatiguing journey from the blue hills to Trevandrum, and consequently, the Maha Rajah postponed his visit to the next day.

At noon on the 1st December, the Maha Rajah set

CHAP. VIII. out in His Highness' splendid State car, accompanied by His Highness the first Prince (the present Maha Rajah), and his brother (the present first Prince), and followed by the Dewan and the rest of the officials of the State. A crowd of spectators mingled with various servants of the Government, the military, mounted troops, howdahs, State, horses, &c., lined the two sides of the road, from the fort gate up to the door of the Residency.

The Maha Rajah alighted at the steps, which were beautifully lined with crimson cloth where General Cullen received His Highness and led him to the drawing-room, where Lord Harris received His Highness with great cordiality and kindness, and both His Highness and the Governor took their seats on a sofa, which was purposely placed just in the centre of the northern end of the room. The Maha Rajah's nephews, their Highnesses the first and the third Princes, took their seats on either side, and the line was continued by the Resident, the Governor's staff, the European and Civil and Military officers of Travancore, and the ladies and gentlemen specially invited for the occasion. After a few minutes conversation, the usual formalities of distributing flowers and attar were gone through. The Maha Rajah took leave and returned to the palace. On arrival at, and returned from, the Residency, royal salutes were fired by the brigade artillery.

After the Durbar, Lord Harris and party, accompanied by General Cullen, visited the Observatory and some other places and returned to the Residency where there was to be a grand dinner in the evening.

The Maha Rajah paid a visit to Lord Harris that evening during dinner, and, without any ceremony or scruple, sat near the Governor and commenced a conversation with great familiarity. His Highness with his suavity of temper, winning manners and affability, found no difficulty in gaining the friendship of such an accomplished nobleman as Lord Harris.

The dinner was over at 11 P.M., and the Maha Rajah took leave of the Governor like an old friend. CHAP. VIII.

On the next day, Lord Harris paid a formal visit to His Highness at a Durbar which was held in the hall of audience. A little after 12 A.M., a royal salute from the brigade artillery, at the eastern fort gate, announced the Governor's entering the fort. The Nair brigade, under the command of Lieutenant Colonel Faunce, paraded in the large square, in front of the hall, together with the brigade band and troopers of the Maha Rajah. Huge tuskers, richly caparisoned, stood in a row behind the line, with silver and gold howdahs on their backs.

Lord Harris, on alighting at the steps of the hall, was received by His Highness the First Prince (the present Maha Rajah), and led to the stair-case, where the Maha Rajah was ready to conduct His Lordship to the seat in the hall. The arrangement of seats and all the ceremonies were precisely the same as those observed on the previous day at the Residency. A sofa, richly lined, was placed in front of His Highness' throne, at the western end of the hall on which the Maha Rajah and the Governor were seated. His Highness the First Prince, the Resident, the Chief Secretary and others taking their seats on either side as was pre-arranged, and after the usual formalities of distributing flowers and attar, the Durbar broke up, and the Governor returned to the Residency amid the cheerful greetings and applause of the people assembled in the plain.

In the afternoon, the Governor visited His Highness' Free School and held an examination of the boys, and here the Maha Rajah also joined His Lordship. The examination was conducted for about an hour, and Lord Harris was quite delighted at the success that attended that useful Institution as evidenced by the progress made by the pupils. After the examination, the Maha Rajah drove His Lordship in his carriage, with General Cullen, to the Karamanay bridge, the

CHAP. VIII. architecture of which was much admired by His Lordship. His attention was particularly attracted by the material (a peculiar kind of hard laterite stone called *Narikallu*) with which the bridge was constructed. His Highness the First Prince also followed his uncle and party in another carriage, with the Chief Secretary, Mr. Pycroft.

In the afternoon of the 3rd December, Lord Harris paid a private visit to the Maha Rajah and had more than half an hour's conversation with His Highness at the palace; after which His Highness introduced to His Lordship his nieces (the adopted Ranees), and his grand nephew. The Maha Rajah then conducted His Lordship to the adjoining buildings which were His Highness' private Dispensary, Laboratory, Library, and Menagerie, all well supplied and neatly arranged. The Governor and suite were much pleased with what they saw and were astonished at the attainments of the Maha Rajah, and the very intelligent interest he took in the pursuits of science. In the Menagerie there were several rare animals belonging to Travancore. A large rhinoceros and a couple of camel leopards attracted the attention of the party, and His Highness' taste in this branch of natural history was warmly applauded by Lord Harris and his followers, who then took leave of the Maha Rajah quite pleased and delighted with what they saw. In fact, they considered the day's interview to have been the most interesting.

On their way back to the Residency, His Lordship and party visited the Sircar printing office, and inspected the several presses of the establishment and its branches, the book-binding, type-founding and paper-making departments, every one of which received Lord Harris' commendation.

The next day having been fixed for His Lordship's return, the Maha Rajah wished to give a grand dinner at the Residency, and all preparations were commenced early on that day. General Cullen's butler, an able and experienced man, and the Quilon Residency butler, an equally clever servant, combined their experience and skill and prepared the bill of fare for the occasion. In addition to the Residency cooks, some experienced hands were also entertained, and a dinner was prepared, on a scale which surpassed anything of the kind ever done before in Travancore on similar occasions. Game of all kinds was ordered from Neduvangaud and other hilly districts and partridges, quails, snipe and other savoury birds were procured and added to the other delicacies. While the dinner was being cooked and prepared at the Residency, the Maha Rajah ordered his own cooks to prepare some fifty different sorts of sweetmeats such as are peculiar to Malayalam, Tamil, Mahratta and Hindustanee countries. These were forwarded to the Residency in beautiful dishes and silver plates. The table was laid at about 7 P.M., and the dinner lasted till 10 o'clock, after which the Maha Rajah invited the Governor and party to the Durbar hall to see a display of pyrotechnics.

The party adjourned to the hall which was most tastefully decorated, furnished and brilliantly lit. A grand illumination, commencing from the Residency gate in an unbroken line to the gate of the audience hall, with farewell mottoes to His Lordship, in large characters at intervals, were arranged. The front of the hall, a broad square, seemed to be in a blaze of light. In the hall upstairs the numerous lustres whose brilliance was reflected by the large mirrors on the walls, filled the place with uncommon refulgence. Roses and jessamine wreaths hanging down from the canopy above diffused the sweetest odours, and the atmosphere of the whole room seemed to be loaded with the perfume of Persian attar. The seats were arranged just as on the previous occasion. His Lordship was seated with the Maha Rajah in the sofa, and they were engaged in pleasant and friendly conversation for a few minutes. There was an attempt at a nautch, but the Maha Rajah's prudence suggested the discontinuance of it at once. When the fireworks were ready, the Maha Rajah led Lord Harris by the arm to the southern verandah, where rows of seats had been arranged. The display lasted about half an hour, and it was considered to have been a complete success. At the southern end of this square, and in the midst of the pyrotechnical show, a particular work was ingeniously contrived by a skilful artist exhibiting in large blazing characters, exquisitely designed the words "Welcome to Lord Harris." After the fireworks, and the distribution of flowers and attar the party broke up. Salutes were fired on the arrival and departure of the Governor, but they could hardy be heard from the deafening reports of the numerous little cannons called *Kathenas* which continued without intermission, from the commencement of the Durbar up to the departure of the Governor.

The Maha Rajah did not bid adieu to Lord Harris then, as His Highness wished to do so on board the steamer.

Early in the morning on the 4th December, the booming of guns announced the Governor's departure to the steamer and the Maha Rajah resolved to follow Lord Harris thither, partly to show His Highness' extreme consideration for the noble Lord, and partly to satisfy his Highness' desire to see beautiful steamer "Feroze."

Before Lord Harris' departure to the steamer, the Maha Rajah thought it was proper to forward a valedictory letter to His Lordship, and accordingly addressed the following communication, in His Highness' own style and handwriting, and forwarded the same through General Cullen before daybreak.

"PALACE,

"TREVANDRUM, *4th December* 1858.

"MY LORD,

Please allow me, my Lord, before personally taking leave of your Lordship to do myself the pleasure of reiterating my most sincere thanks for the honor conferred on me by your truly kind visit to my capital, and the invariable kindness evinced by your Lordship during the few, but most agreeable days, I had the pleasure of spending in your Lordship's noble society. I beg to assure your Lordship that I shall always look back with unfeigned pleasure and gratification to this most happy event which will ever be fresh in my memory. CHAP. VIII.

"I shall always feel myself proud to have the honor of corresponding with your Lordship either in India or in your native land.

"Wishing your Lordship a safe and pleasant voyage to your residency, and a long life, attended with uninterrupted health, and all manner of the choicest blessings.

I remain, My Lord,

Your most sincere friend,

(Signed) MARTHANDA VURMAH,

H. S. Rajah."

"*The Right Honorable G. F. R. Lord Harris,*

Governor of Fort St. George.

&c. &c. &c."

At about 12 M., the Maha Rajah proceeded to the beach, and alighted at the palace there, when His Highness had the pleasure of receiving the following reply from Lord Harris:—

"H. M. STEAMER "FEROZE."

"OFF TREVANDRUM, *December 4th*, 1858."

"YOUR HIGHNESS,

"I have had the honor and pleasure to receive your very kind letter of this date transmitted through General Cullen.

"It gives me infinite satisfaction to find that my visit has afforded your Highness so much gratification and to have been received with so much kindness and distinction.

CHAP. VIII.

"It is the wish of myself, and of the Madras Government, to support your Highness' position, and I feel we can best do so by endeavouring to the best of our power to assist your Highness in improving the fine country and the interesting people over whom it has pleased the Almighty to entrust to you the rule.

"I can assure your Highness, that I reciprocate most heartily and sincerely your kind wishes of health and prosperity, and I trust you may be spared to enjoy a long and happy life in the midst of your family.

"It will always give me sincere pleasure to hear of your Highness' well being, and to be of any use to you should occasion offer when I return to England.

"I have been taught from my earliest years to take an interest in and to benefit the people of India. I had endeavoured to do so to the best of my abilities, and I shall continue to do so till my life's end.

I have the honor to be,

Your Highness' very obedient servant,

(Signed) HARRIS."

"His Highness,

The Maha Rajah of Travancore."

At about 1 P.M., the Maha Rajah accompanied by their Highnesses the first and third Princes, Colonel Faunce, the Commanding Officer, and Doctor Waring, the Durbar physician, embarked in a large boat and were soon on board the steamer, where Lord Harris received His Highness most cordially, and a salute was fired from the largest of the guns on board, sixty-eight pounders, which were highly admired by the Maha Rajah, who expressed a wish to see ball and bombshell firing which was done at once. His Highness' astonishment was very great, especially at the dexterity and ease with which the men performed the work. After this, every part of the vessel and its machinery were minutely and attentively inspected by His Highness, who intimated to Lord Harris a desire to see the working of the engines, which were then placed at full speed, the vessel making an excursion to the north to a distance of about five or six miles and returning to her former position, in the course of half an hour. CHAP. VIII.

At the time of parting, the Maha Rajah having obtained His Lordship's permission to present a sum of money to the sailors, handed a purse to the Captain of the "Feroze" for distribution among them. Afterwards, the Maha Rajah took leave of Lord Harris and descended into his boat. Immediately after the boat had left the ship's side, Lord Harris and party standing on the deck waved their hats, and at the same time, the air resounded with the booming of the guns on board the steamer. The "Feroze" weighed anchor after the safe landing of the Maha Rajah and party.

This was the Governor who sent the despatch of 1855, by the order of the Governor-General Lord Dalhousie, as has been already stated. His Lordship must have now felt the tone and tenor of his late Minute to have been unnecessarily severe, as his personal acquaintance with His Highness and with the affairs of his Government could not but have satisfied him that matters had been misrepresented to him.

The reasonableness of the above conjecture must be apparent from the spirit of His Lordship's reply to the Maha Rajah.

Soon after the Governor's departure, the deputy Peishcar Shungoonny Menon rejoined his division in the south, but he had the mortification to find, that, during his absence fresh misunderstanding had arisen between the Hindus and the Shanar converts. The spirit of hostility between these two sections of the inhabitants had lain dormant for some time chiefly through the interference of the Sircar authorities, but it seemed to have been again roused up, and the disputes this time were of a more serious nature. The Peishcar's efforts to throw oil on the troubled waters and bring matters to a satisfactory conclusion proved in the long run abortive; although he succeeded in restoring harmony between the parties temporarily.

CHAP. VIII. The misunderstanding had originated entirely from the Shanar Christian females assuming the costume of high caste Hindu females. They had been doing this from the early days of their conversion, and instead of endeavouring to suppress what might eventually cause serious complications, the Missionaries encouraged them and fostered among them a spirit of hostility against the high caste Hindus. The Sircar had been necessitated, in 1814, to interfere and legislate for the future guidance of the Shanars, but notwithstanding this during a period of fifteen years there were quarrels on various occasions between the parties. Matters now looked serious and the interference of the Government seemed to be again called for. There had been a legislative enactment in 1829, at the very commencement of the reign of the greatly renowned Maha Rajah who died in 1022 M.E. (1847 A.D.) In this enactment, it was clearly laid down that the female Shanar converts were at liberty to cover their bosoms with a jacket, and a strict prohibition was laid down against their adopting high caste Hindu costumes; but the aim of the converts had been persistently to defy the higher class Hindus and to despise their brother Shanars, who professed Hinduism (certainly with a hidden motive), and the converts were supported all along by the Missionaries whose intention apparently was to introduce English customs as if they were in civilized England instead of Travancore. They also claimed perfect toleration and liberty for their converts, without taking into consideration the time, the country, the nature of the Government, and their own position in foreign land and the consequence was that it was difficult to settle the dispute at once, while on the part of the Shanars there was an open defiance of the laws of the land, which, on account of the encouragement they received from the Missionaries, it was difficult to curb. And the Travancore Government, being reluctant to come in contact with the Missionaries, owing to its regard for the paramount power, desisted from taking active measures, and the result was that the Hindus and the Shanar converts and their respective supporters openly assumed hostile positions against each other. CHAP. VIII.

Such a feeling existed between the parties from the earliest period of the Mission works in south Travancore, but by the strong protection and toleration afforded to the promotion of the Christian Missions by the Travancore Government, the work of the Missionaries progressed most rapidly, and in the course of the next thirty years conversions to Christianity increased, and in the villages in Nanjenaud and the adjacent districts numerous Chapels, Churches and Schools were built. These places were crowded with large numbers of Shanar converts, and Catechists commenced to itenerate through all Hindu villages with their tracts and books and began preaching to the Hindus. This circumstance must naturally have roused the jealousy of the Hindus, while the converts instead of keeping themselves within bounds, took advantage of their support by the Missionaries and began to prove themselves a source of annoyance to the Hindu portion of the people, by openly defying them whenever there was an opportunity and the result was the complication above alluded to.

It is a matter worthy of particular remark, that the Mission work of conversion in south Travancore was mostly, if not exclusively, confined to the Shanars, Parayars, and other low caste people, who form but a minor portion of the population of the districts, while conversions among the higher orders were seldom effected. At the same time, while the Church Mission Society in the north did its work quietly and without endeavouring to introduce reforms violently, the London Mission in the south seemed to pursue quite a different policy for nearly half a century.

The system adopted by the London Mission savoured more of the undue and illegitimate exercise of power than persuasion and well meant endeavours to impress

CHAP. VIII. upon people the truth of the principles of religion, and hence, the chief cause for the Hindus to be dissatisfied with them and to consider their proceedings offensive.

This fact can be seen from a fact connected with the founder of the London Mission in Travancore, the Reverend Mr. Ringeltaube, who, on paying a visit to the then Dewan Valu Thamby, for the express purpose of endeavouring to obtain a footing for the London Mission in Travancore, in 1806, being asked by the minister what religion he professed, the Reverend gentleman answered "Colonel Macaulay's Religion,"* instead of saying the Christian religion or the religion established by Christ, who He was, when and how Jesus Christ was born, what wonders and miracles Christ had performed in the world, how He became the Saviour of mankind, how He suffered, and how His resurrection took place after His crucifixion and burial and so on. Let the reader note the severe rebuke implied in the following remark which that great Hindu Statesman made on hearing what Mr. Ringeltaube said about his professing "Colonel Macaulay's religion," "I never knew that there was such a religion" said the Dewan, meaning of course, a religion invented or professed by a private individual, for Christianity was in existence in Travancore for more than a thousand years before that period.

Acting under such selfish principles, it is no wonder that the Missionaries considered themselves to be entitled to respect from the Hindus. Why the Society did not think of proceeding in a more conciliatory manner with the Hindu portion of the population, and why they endeavoured to create in the Hindus a spirit antagonistic to the Christian religion are points for inquiry.

The very illustration in Mr. Mateer's work, page 277, will show plainly how the females of the Shanar converts were taught to imitate the costume of the higher

* See Reverend Mateer's Land of Charity, page 262.

class Hindus, while there are numerous modes of costumes adapted for Christians which would be more desirable from a European point of view. It is clear that this style of costume adopted by the Shanar converts was with the express object of annoying the Hindu section of the population of the districts. CHAP. VIII.

The costume in question was not the only cause for offence which the Shanar converts gave to the higher classes, but in various other ways they rendered themselves obnoxious to the Sudra community.

For instance, one Shanar Puthathan Cutty and his wife, Eshakee, were the cultivators of Mādom Pillay, a Sudra landed proprietor. These became converts and left Mādom Pillay's service, and Puthathan Cutty subsequently became a Catechist under a Missionary, and his wife assumed a costume similar to that of Mādom Pillay's wife. Now, both the Catechist and his wife came to Mādom Pillay's house and began to converse with him, on terms of equality, commencing a discussion with Mādom Pillay on the subject of religion and calling him "an ignorant man" and a sinner (as all the heathens are put down by the Mission people in the vernacular, in the category of "*Agnanikul,*" ignorant men). Was it possible for Mādom Pillay not to resent the impertinence of those who were but lately his dependents; and their sole object in coming to his house—the wife dressed in a costume similar to that of Mādom Pillay's wife—must have been to cause him annoyance? It is also worthy of note that on a quarrel ensuing between the Shanar converts and Mādom Pillay, the Missionary who used to support him, espoused the cause of the Catechist and appeared himself before the authorities and adopted measures for the punishment of Mādom Pillay in which favored by the advantages of his color and position he succeeded. Here is a solution of the question why the Missionaries are considered by the Hindus as acting partially towards the converts and prosecuting the Hindus. Besides if even a reasonable

CHAP. VIII.

complaint were made by Sircar official, he would be represented by the Missionaries as partial and in a communication to the Resident denounced as *corrupt, unprincipled*, and so forth. The Missionaries at the same time did not hesitate to drag the *Government* into the discussion. The Missionaries by their writings can make the world believe that terrible persecutions against Christianity are carried on in Travancore, and the British Government invariably gives credence to statements thus disseminated, and being the paramount power, they can come down upon the Travancore Sircar with rebuke and strong disapproval,* ignoring the fact that Christianity as professed by the Syrians and Roman Catholics existed in Travancore from time immemorial. A convincing instance in support of this statement shall be given presently.

Though the matters connected with the upper cloth dispute between the Shanar converts and the Hindus were temporarily adjusted by the exertions of the deputy Peishcar, yet the disputes broke out again in a short time and several quarrels and disturbances took place between the parties in the markets and thoroughfares where the females of Shanar converts appeared in Hindu costumes. Just at this time, the Dewan Madava Row paid a visit to the south and finding the serious nature of the rupture between the parties, he issued a proclamation on the 27th December 1868, as a precautionary measure and with the view of preventing further disturbances. The tenor of the proclamation was that, it was clearly wrong to violate ancient usages; that the law laid down for the observance of the parties

* Mr. Whitehouse reported the case of Aroomanayagum, a converted slave, who was beaten by his master Mādom Pillay, and another Sudra for attending Christian worship. Although the serious injuries inflicted on the poor man were certified in detail by the Court physician, Dr. Reed, a mere nominal fine of only 5 Rupees each, was inflicted by the Magistrate on his assailants. But an appeal being made to the Madras Government, the fines were increased to seventy Rupees and the Travancore authorities were reproved for their unjust lenity.—Mateer's "Land of Charity," page 296.

concerned, by a royal proclamation in the year 1829, should be respected; that whoever infringed the law would be liable to severe punishment, that Shanars were to bear the same in mind and act accordingly; that Sudras and people of the higher caste were not to do anything themselves against the Shanars and cause a breach of the peace, and that should they commit anything contrary to the law, due notice would be taken of their conduct.

This proclamation had nothing new in it. It was entirely founded upon the enactment passed under the judicious advice and counsel of Colonel Munro in 1814, and in 1829, with the full concurrence of the able Resident, Colonel Morrison, C.B.

The rules prescribed by the Circular Order of 1814, and the proclamation of 1829, were precisely the same, and were calculated to prevent collisions and preserve peace between the contending parties. The sum and substance of those rules were that Shanar females, converted to Christianity should wear the costume worn by other Christian females, *i.e.*, jackets similar to those used by the lace-making Shanar females, as represented in the "Land of Charity," page 272, but no prohibition whatever had been issued against the convert females covering their bodies. Those rules were observed and matters went on smoothly for about thirty years. The Missionaries, for the time being, were contented with these rules, and preferred to wait for an opportunity to get them amended in a manner favoring the aims and fancies of the Shanar and Parayar converts.

Under these circumstances, Dewan Madava Row's judicious proclamation was considered by the Missionaries as a proof of his "gross and unconcealed partiality," and they therefore at first petitioned the Maha Rajah and then the Madras Government praying for the cancelling of the Dewan's proclamation, the Circular Order of May 1814, and the proclamation of February 1829.

CHAP. VIII. By this time, Lord Harris, the Governor of Madras retired, and was succeeded by Sir Charles Trevelyan, before whom the question was laid for decision. His Excellency seemed to have taken a one-sided view of the question, and without giving the matter calm and deliberate consideration, and reflecting on the real meaning of the Circular Order and proclamation alluded to, came to the conclusion that the privilege of covering their bosoms had been denied to the females of the Shanar converts by the Travancore Government, and under this impression wrote in the following decisive terms to General Cullen :—

"I have seldom met with a case in which not only truth and justice, but every feeling of our common humanity are so entirely on one side. The whole civilized world would cry shame upon us if we did not make a firm stand on such an occasion. If anything could make this line of conduct more incumbent on us, it would be the extraordinary fact that persecution of a singularly personal and delicate kind is attempted to be justified by a royal proclamation, the special object of which was to assure to Her Majesty's Indian subjects, liberty of thought and action so long as they did not interfere with the just rights of others. I should fail in respect to Her Majesty, if I attempted to describe the feelings with which she must regard the use made against her own sex of the promises of protection so graciously accorded by her.

"It will be your duty to impress these views on His Highness the Rajah, and to point out to him that such prohibition as those conveyed in the Circular Order of May 1814, or in the proclamation of the 3rd of February 1829, are unsuited to the present age, and unworthy of an enlightened Prince."

This communication from the new Governor startled the old General, and he pressed upon the Maha Rajah to pass an act in accordance with the views of His Excellency but by adopting such a sweeping measure, the Maha Rajah apprehended still greater evils, and, consequently, after due and long deliberation and consultation with the able Dewan, a new royal proclamation was prepared and published in July of the same year 1859, making further concessions to the Shanar females in the matter of their dress. But this concession did not imply any permission to the convert females to assume the costume of Brahman women. The Missionaries were not quite satisfied with this proclamation, but it sufficed to check further disturbances on the score of dress. CHAP. VIII.

The spirit of the Missionaries in this matter is evident from the Rev. S. Mateer's work entitled "Land of Charity;" Chapter XII, pages 295-306. In his quasi-sensational writings, the Reverend gentleman animadverts rather strongly, and it must be said, with a good deal of unfairness, on the proceedings of a Government which had tolerated Christianity hundreds of years before protestantism came into existence and which had protected the very London Mission itself from its cradle, so to speak, and this in a country whose people and sovereign profess orthodox Hinduism.

The unfair animadversions of the Missionaries cast a reflection on the reputation of the Maha Rajah and of his Government and created an unfriendly feeling between them and the Hindus, who charge them with want of gratitude, after they had been allowed to work freely and open Missions in their land.

The senior Ranee, one of the two adopted Princesses, having become marriageable, according to the usage of the royal house, Her Highness' wedding was resolved on by the Maha Rajah, and in the month of Mādom 1034 (April 1859), the royal marriage was performed with great pomp and grandeur. Her Highness was wedded to a young Koil Thampuran of Chunganacherry, a grand nephew of the Maha Rajah's father.

In the commencement of the next year 1035 M.E. (1859 A.D.), the Maha Rajah contemplated the establishment of two more divisions, one at Quilon and the

CHAP. VIII. other at Trevandrum, and the placing of the whole administration under four divisions, viz., Padmanabhapuram, Trevandrum, Quilon, and Sharetalay, thus affording relief to the Dewan in the arduous work of conducting the administration. Accordingly the measure was adopted in the first quarter of the Malabar year. By this arrangement Shungoonny Menon, deputy Peishcar at Padmanabhapuram, was transferred to the Quilon division, which was larger and more important than the southern division. Now, the affairs of the country began to be more satisfactorily managed than before.

General Cullen, the Resident, who had been appointed twenty years ago when the country was in a highly flourishing state, and witnessed many a change during his long tenure of office, had now the pleasure of seeing the country in a better condition, and so he resolved to bid farewell to Travancore. The Veteran General retired in the early part of January 1860, to the very great regret of the Maha Rajah and every one of the State officers, as well as of the whole population of Travancore. To His Highness, General Cullen was the kindest of friends; to the officials, he was a benevolent patron, and to the inhabitants, he was an affectionate and judicious protector. Under such circumstances, the old General made up his mind to reside in Travancore and finish his worldly career in this country and his wish was accordingly gratified, by divine will, in 1862.

In appreciation of the interest General Cullen always evinced in the welfare of Travancore, His Highness instituted a scholarship in the General's name at the the Madras High School, under the designation of "Cullen's Scholarship."

Mr. Maltby succeeded General Cullen as the Resident, and in him the Maha Rajah found a friend not less valuable than General Cullen.

After Lord Harris' return to England, His Lordship apparently mooted the subject of forwarding the present, graciously promised by Her Majesty Queen Victoria to His Highness the Maha Rajah. It was accordingly despatched, and reached Madras, and ultimately Travancore, towards the end of April 1860, and on an intimation being given by the Resident to the Maha Rajah, His Highness' joy and delight knew no bounds. Arrangements for a grand Durbar for the reception of the present were at once ordered, and preparations, set on foot for the occasion in the same style, as on the occasion of the receipt of Her Majesty's letter in 1851.

In consultation with Mr. Maltby, the Resident, the 2nd of May was fixed for the reception of the present, and the Dewan issued the usual invitations to all the ladies and gentlemen, and instructions to the officers commanding the Nair brigade.

The hall of audience was properly and magnificently decorated and furnished, and the houses in the town and their gates and the streets were also neatly decorated with flowers, plantains, and fruits, and festoons of flowers and the green leaves of palm trees plaited into ornamental shapes, hung across from house to house. The Nair brigade sepoys and mounted troops paraded in front of the hall of audience, where State elephants, richly caparisoned with howdahs and trappings of silver, velvet, &c., with the State horses, formed a line.

The Durbar was to take place at about 4 P.M.; but soon after 3 o'clock, a large number of ladies and gentlemen were seated in the lower room of the Durbar hall, as customary, for the assembly were not supposed to go upstairs until the Resident's arrival.

At about 4 o'clock the British Resident, Mr. Maltby, arrived in grand procession accompanied by Colonel Stevenson, the Commanding Officer at Quilon, who was in charge of the Queen's present. The Resident was saluted by the troops and the band struck up the national anthem. The Resident was met at the steps

CHAP. VIII. by His Highness the first Prince (the present Maha Rajah), and a little further on by the Maha Rajah himself. Mr. Maltby then delivered a letter from the Right Honorable Sir Charles Wood, now Viscount Halifax, the Secretary of State for India, and the beautiful case containing the Queen's present into the Maha Rajah's hands. His Highness receiving them with a joyful countenance and a low bow, raised the case to his head to show his great respect for Her Majesty and then raised the lid. It contained a handsome ornamental belt, with rich gold embroidery, and a buckle set with precious stones, the centre of the belt containing a gold watch with the monogram of the Queen on one side, and that of the Maha Rajah on the other. The initials were beautifully set with brilliants in blue enamel. The belt was put on the Maha Rajah's girdle by the Resident, and His Highness bowing again to show his respect for Her Majesty delivered a short speech expressive of His Highness' great gratification at the gracious consideration of Her Majesty, and declared at the same time that His Highness considered himself the most fortunate among all the Princes in India in being thus highly favoured.

On delivering the Queen's present, a royal salute from the brigade artillery and three volleys of musketry were fired, and after spending a short time in agreeable conversation, the Durbar was concluded by the usual distribution of garlands of jessamine and attar of roses.

The general joy caused by this incident was however marred by the terrible bereavement which the Maha Rajah sustained by the death on the very night of the Durbar of His Highness' lady, who had been laid up for the last two months.

Soon after this event, the Maha Rajah wished to commemorate this manifestation of Her Majesty's kindness and good-will towards His Highness, and in consultation with His Highness' friend Mr. Maltby, and his able Dewan Madava Row, it was resolved to organize a Public Works Department, and to construct certain works in Her Majesty's name.

Mr. Collins, a Civil Engineer, was entertained in the service of the Sircar in the same month (May), and the Maha Rajah subsequently proceeded to the fertile parts of His Highness' dominions (Nanjenaud). The excavation of a new canal from the south to Trevandrum which, it would appear, had been contemplated once in former times, was now resolved upon by the Resident and the Dewan, and the proposal being communicated to His Highness, sanction was at once accorded and the work was commenced in the same month. After the ceremony, usual on such occasions, His Highness removed the first turf with his own hand, with a silver spade expressly made for the purpose, and the canal was designated by the Maha Rajah "Victoria Anantha Marthanden Canal," a combination of Her Majesty's and His Highness' names, and connecting the two was the appellation of the Maha Rajah's household deity's vehicle, *Ananthen* (the endless).

While in the south, the Maha Rajah was unfortunately taken ill by a slight attack of fever, which he got over soon, under the able treatment of the Durbar Physician. But the germs of the disease, seemed still to lurk in his system.

His Highness returned to the capital without further delay. After reaching Trevandrum he had a slight relapse, followed by an attack of bowel complaint. But without paying much heed to his ailments, His Highness managed to perform his daily ablutions and attend to his other avocations. This distemper continued preying on the Maha Rajah's constitution which was very strong and powerful, but in a short time he was reduced to a very deplorable state. His Highness nevertheless bore up boldly and did not confine himself to his bed for any length of time. A couple of months passed thus and none apprehended any serious results from His Highness' illness, neither did

CHAP. VIII. the Maha Rajah himself seem to be much concerned about his health. But towards the middle of July, *i.e.*, about two months after His Highness' return from the south he grew worse and the physician, Dr. Waring, did all that he could to arrest the course of the disease, which for a fortnight did not make further progress. All of a sudden, however, dangerous symptoms were observed, and the physician considered recovery hopeless, but still the Maha Rajah did not seem to be of the same opinion.

On the night of the 17th of August (2nd Chingam), the Maha Rajah was quite restless and had not a wink of sleep, and the next morning the 18th, His Highness himself was convinced of his approaching end, but without losing his usual presence of mind, he endured all his sufferings with becoming fortitude.

The next day, was the Maha Rajah's birth-day and the usual festivities being then celebrated, His Highness called in all of a sudden his affectionate and favourite nephew (the present Maha Rajah), who was always the companion of His Highness and who had been constantly with His Highness ever since he became indisposed, and spoke to him calmly and in a low tone that His Highness the Prince and the rest of the royal family need entertain no hope of the Maha Rajah's recovery, and that the Prince should not grieve but bear up with the calamity and manage matters without creating any confusion. His Highness desired the Prince to call in the Dewan and the other State officers who were waiting outside, to obtain the Maha Rajah's sanction for commencing the birth-day ceremonies which the Maha Rajah said he was doubtful if he would live to see. His Highness the Prince was much touched by such an announcement from his uncle, nay the Prince became almost senseless, but taking courage from the repeated advice of his dying uncle, the Prince managed business as became his high position.

The Dewan and other officials were ushered in by

the order of the Prince and when they appeared in the Maha Rajah's presence, the Dewan was spoken to very kindly, and all the others had also a word or two from their amiable sovereign. Though the Maha Rajah began to breathe pretty hard, yet His Highness retained perfect consciousness and power of speech. All the members of the royal family now stood around the dying Maha Rajah. To each of them the Maha Rajah gave his blessing especially to His Highness' favourite nephew and his brother (His Highness the present first Prince of Travancore), and from the eyes of both of them tears were flowing; in short, there was not a single individual in and about the room whose eyes were dry. The Maha Rajah then turned towards his nephew and desired him to give a general order to keep the doors of the palace opened and to admit all the attendants, officers, palace servants, and such others into the hall where His Highness was lying, so that they may have a last look at the Maha Rajah. All the ceremonies and donations according to the prescriptions of the Vedas were performed by His Highness in full consciousness, and then His Highness desired his nephew to see everything conducted according to usage. The Maha Rajah subsequently ordered to be brought to him the sacred offering of the household deity from the pagoda, but by the time it was brought, the Maha Rajah was fast sinking. Nevertheless, at the very sight of the sacred thing, His Highness stretched his hands to receive it and applied the same to his eyes, and forehead and folding his hands, closed his eyes and reciting prayers in the name of the Almighty, the pious Maha Rajah slept his last sleep, without a struggle or the least sign of his being in agony, while the whole of the royal family who surrounded the dying Maha Rajah, and the State officials, and the royal attendants present there were one and all plunged in the greatest sorrow.

The palace and the adjoining buildings, as well as the premises, were filled with cries and lamentations

CHAP. VIII. and when the intelligence of the Maha Rajah's demise went beyond the palace walls, the scene outside was heart-rending. It is enough to say that a more melancholy spectacle was not seen in Trevandrum for many a long day.

His Highness the first Prince (the present Maha Rajah) although he deeply felt the loss of his uncle bore up with becoming fortitude and consoled his brothers and others, and began to follow the last advice of the deceased Maha Rajah by looking after affairs connected with the State.

His Highness the present first Prince was the chief mourner and undertook to perform and observe all the obsequies which lasted for a year. His Highness' brother joined in the ceremonies up to the twelfth day only, and then the affairs of the State demanded his attention.

The numerous virtues and good qualities of this Maha Rajah, of happy memory, would fill volumes were one to write a full account of them, and the writer thinks that he has scarcely done justice to all the events which he has described and narrated as having occurred in this memorable reign.

Various items of importance have been omitted for want of authority to particularize them in their chronological order, and so a few of them shall be stated here, though at random.

The Maha Rajah's partiality for European sciences and arts, as well as amusements, was widely known and European exhibitors began to visit Travancore soon after His Highness' accession to the musnud.

An Italian juggler first came to Trevandrum and entertained His Highness with his feats of legerdemain. The Maha Rajah being greatly delighted with his performances, the juggler was detained at Trevandrum for some time and he was handsomely remunerated on his departure.

A couple of years later a party of equestrians arrived at Trevandrum and astonished the Maha Rajah by their extraordinary performances. This party also received a handsome remuneration besides presents from the Maha Rajah, and left Trevandrum highly satisfied with the liberality of His Highness.

After some years, another party of equestrians, consisting of both sexes, paid a visit to Trevandrum and they were also treated with becoming hospitality and liberality.

A Doctor Kight, an Aeronaut, came to Trevandrum with his balloon and the Maha Rajah agreed to witness his ascent. Preparations were made, and on a certain morning, after filling his balloon with gas, the Aeronaut made the ascent to the great wonder and the astonishment of the Maha Rajah and the multitude of the spectators. In about half an hour the balloon ascended so high as to be scarcely discernible to the naked eye. The Maha Rajah became very anxious about the safety of Mr. Kight, and though previous arrangements had been made to watch the balloon and numerous boats had been provided to render assistance in case it fell into the sea, yet the Maha Rajah instructed those around him to despatch a number of His Highness' mounted troops to the different parts of the town and its suburbs to see if any intelligence could be obtained regarding the balloon.

The Aeronaut, Mr. Kight, made his descent at Neyattunkaray, about 12 miles east of Trevandrum at about 12 M., where he found one of His Highness' horsemen. Mounting the horse, Mr. Kight rode up to Trevandrum in full speed, leaving his balloon in charge of the local officials, and came before His Highness at 2 P.M. The Maha Rajah was delighted at the safe return of Mr. Kight, his mind being relieved of a good deal of anxiety as regards his safety. The rewards and remuneration Mr. Kight received from His Highness were far beyond his expectations.

Subsequent to the above event, an Italian repaired

CHAP. VIII. to Trevandrum bringing with him a number of figures of wax representing some of the crowned heads of Europe, as well as several eminent men of the Continent, and he requested the Maha Rajah's permission for an exhibition of these wax statues. The Maha Rajah acceded at once to the request with his usual affability and the Italian made a great show of them in the palace and received a good round sum in return. The figures were all in the form of dolls neatly clad, and closely resembled the personages whose effigies they were represented to be. Though the Maha Rajah was not quite satisfied with the show, still His Highness gave him money simply because the man had taken a great deal of trouble and had undergone some expense in bringing those figures from a distant place for the express purpose of exhibiting them to such personages as the Maha Rajah with a view of benefitting himself.

In generosity and liberality, the Maha Rajah's equal it would be difficult to find. His Highness was very particular in recognising merit during his reign. There were scarcely any meritorious servants of the State, high or low, who escaped His Highness' notice and recognition.

In Travancore, the manner in which merit is recognised and rewarded by royalty is by the bestowal of bangles or bracelets. There are several description of such. The first class is called *Veerachangala*, the presentation of a pair of which is considered to be the greatest mark of distinction. In this reign it was particularly observed that none of the really meritorious was seen unornamented by these decorations. Besides bangles various other rewards were also given by the Maha Rajah to his servants as well as to strangers.

Once when the writer of this history, distinguished himself in the detection of a very serious dacoity, the Maha Rajah showed his satisfaction and approbation by forwarding to him a purse containing a sum of money, with an autograph letter expressing his appreciation of his services though the Maha Rajah had already bestowed on him Veerachangalas and bangles. CHAP. VIII.

For business-like habits, the Maha Rajah was unequalled. There was not a branch in the whole administration, from which His Highness did not receive a report. Even the petty departments in the palace had to submit a direct report to His Highness, and it was a matter of great surprise amongst every one that the Maha Rajah found time to attend to all these details.

His Highness used to keep a diary regarding all matters, public as well as private, which came to His Highness' notice. The Maha Rajah never omitted writing his diary even for a day, and would not take his supper before the day's diary was written up. The entries were mostly made by himself and several volumes of these diaries are bound and preserved, and any particular transaction or event which took place during the reign of His Highness for a period of fourteen years will be found clearly recorded in these volumes. This is a fact which will excite surprise not only in Travancore, but in many other parts of India.

The Maha Rajah's diary forms a sufficient guide in all State ceremonies connected with public, as well as domestic affairs, and it prescribes even the etiquette to be observed in Durbars and other public occasions and at meetings with persons of note among Europeans as well as natives.

The kindness, benevolence, generosity and philanthropy of His Highness, his piety and devotion were unrivalled, and such a combination of good qualities are rarely found in men of such high position. His Highness was really a godly man and somewhat like a minister of God. Many of the Hindu spiritual preceptors would not bear comparison with His Highness in his devotional observances.

Every day the Maha Rajah spent no less than three hours in the morning and evening in prayers and

CHAP. VIII. devotions which often interfered with His Highness' taking his meals at the proper time. There was scarcely a day on which the Maha Rajah took his breakfast before one P.M., and supped earlier than twelve in the night, and on certain particular days of fasting or on the occasion of any other ceremonies, His Highness would not swallow even a drop of water during the day and would take his meals only at night after all the ceremonies were over.

His Highness Marthanda Vurmah Maha Rajah composed a Drama when he was living a merry life as Elia Rajah, under the title of *Simhadhwaja Charithum* (a chronicle of the life of a supposed king under the denomination of Simhadhwaja.)

This dramatic work is most instructive in regard to divine faith, and it was highly applauded by all Hindu learned men who had an opportunity of perusing it.

The ground-work of this poem is something similar to the account given of Job in the Bible. The most interesting part of this valued work shall be briefly described here :

The supposed King, Simhadhwaja, was childless, and he apprehended the extinction of his house; consequently he convened a meeting of all the learned men, and they unanimously recommended a pilgrimage to Benares and his supplication to the Almighty as the only means of realizing his wishes. The king commenced his journey on the very day, leaving the country in charge of his minister. In the course of his journey, he did not see any favorable signs; on the contrary he met with many misfortunes and trials, but he nevertheless did not despair and grew more firm and determined in his resolve, and continued his journey. Soon after, the sovereign lost every thing and there did not seem to be any prospect of his reaching Benares. In despair, the king resolved upon abandoning his throne, and turning a sannyasi and wandering about on a devotional pilgrimage. In company with his wife, he travelled in the direction of some holy place where he determined to undergo his penance together with her. CHAP. VIII.

As the king was travelling with his wife through the hills and jungles, a *Rakshasen*, giant, suddenly obstructed their path in the wilderness and attempted to take away his wife, but the king being a strong man and a warrior, fought boldly and desperately with the giant, who overcoming the king, snatched at first his weapons and arms and destroyed them in his presence making him completely powerless and after beating him soundly, the giant walked away with the king's wife.

Notwithstanding this great calamity which had overtaken him, the king would not discontinue his prayers and devotions to the Almighty and began to submit all his grievances to Providence alone, with unshaken faith in God's mercy and providence. Now God Almighty was pleased with the piety and fidelity of the king, and the Lord of Heaven appeared in the form of a human being in a vision to the king, and blessed him, saying that the Almighty was quite satisfied with the true faith of the king, and that he should have all his desires gratified. So saying, God Almighty ordered the angel, (for it was an angel in the shape of a giant, who carried away the king's wife), to restore the monarch's spouse at once and it was accordingly done.

Having received the divine blessing, the king returned to his country with his wife and lived several hundred years with his sons, grandsons, daughters and grand-daughters, in the enjoyment of sound health and prosperity.

From the plot and tenor of the above composition, we can see clearly what a pious man His Highness Marthanda Vurmah Maha Rajah must have been.